kare kano

his and her circumstances

volume four

by Masami Tsuda

TOKYOPOP®

LOS ANGELES • TOKYO • LONDON

Translator - Amy Forsyth
English Adaption - Darcy Lockman
Editor - Jodi Bryson
Retouch and Lettering - Judi Csotsists
Cover Artist - Gary Shum
Graphic Designer - Monalisa de Asis

Senior Editor - Julie Taylor
Production Managers - Jennifer Miller and Jennifer Wagner
Art Director - Matthew Alford
VP of Production & Manufacturing - Ron Klamert
President & C.O.O. - John Parker
Publisher - Stuart Levy

Email: editor@TOKYOPOP.com
Come visit us online at www.TOKYOPOP.com

A ⚙ TOKYOPOP® Manga
TOKYOPOP® is an imprint of Mixx Entertainment, Inc.
5900 Wilshire Blvd. Suite 2000, Los Angeles, CA 90036

KARE KANO 4
KARESHI KANOJO NO JIJYO by Masami Tsuda © 1993 Masami Tsuda
All Rights Reserved. First published in Japan in 1997 by HAKUSENSHA, INC., Tokyo
English language translation rights in the United States of America
and Canada arranged with HAKUSENSHA, INC.,Tokyo
through Tuttle-Mori Agency Inc., Tokyo

English Edition
English text © 2003 by Mixx Entertainment, Inc.
TOKYOPOP is a registered trademark of Mixx Entertainment, Inc.

ISBN: 1-59182-059-6

First TOKYOPOP® printing: July 2003

10 9 8 7 6 5 4 3 2 1
Printed in U.S.A.

kare kano
volume four

TABLE OF CONTENTS

KARE KANO: THE STORY SO FAR

Yukino Miyazawa is the perfect model student: kind, athletic, smart. But she's not all she seems. She is really the self-confessed "queen of vanity," and her only goal in life is winning the praise and admiration of everyone around her. Therefore, she makes it her business to always look and act perfect during school hours. At home, however, she let her guard down and let her true self show.

When Yukino enters high school, she finally meets her match: Soichiro Arima, a handsome, popular, and ultra-intelligent guy. Once he steals the top seat in class away from her, Yukino sees him as a bitter rival. Over time, her anger turns to amazement when she discovers she and Soichiro have more in common than she ever imagined. As their love blossoms, they promise to stop pretending to be perfect and just be true to themselves.

When the school's token pretty boy, Hideaki, tries to come between them, things are rocky for awhile...but soon, Yukino and Soichiro's relationship is better than ever. They have accepted each other for who they are, and have truly become boyfriend and girlfriend. But they've been concentrating more on each other than on their schoolwork, and it shows. When the two best students in school suddenly let their grades drop, it draws the attention and concern of one of the teachers. He wants Yukino and Soichiro to break up so they can concentrate on their grades again. And he even calls a dreaded parent-teacher conference to tell their parents his concerns. No one knows if they'll split up for good... Once that is resolved, however, there's another obstacle to hurdle: Maho, a jealous classmate, is convinced that Yukino is deceiving everyone and vows to turn everyone against her. Will Yukino be able to deal with the mounting pressure, and will her relationship with Soichiro suffer as a result?!

DAFFODIL = UNREQUITED LOVE

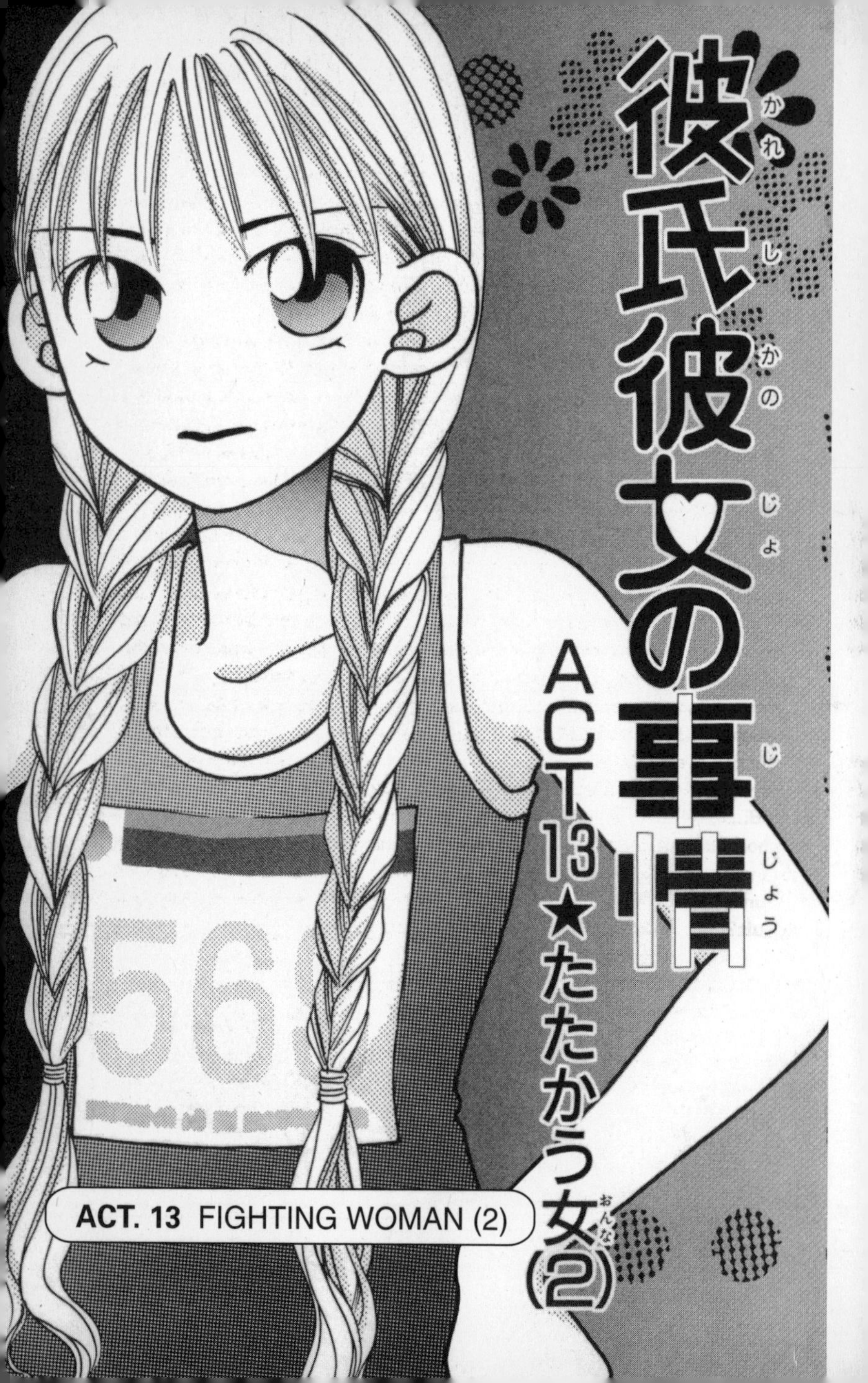
彼氏彼女の事情
ACT13★たたかう女(2)
ACT. 13 FIGHTING WOMAN (2)

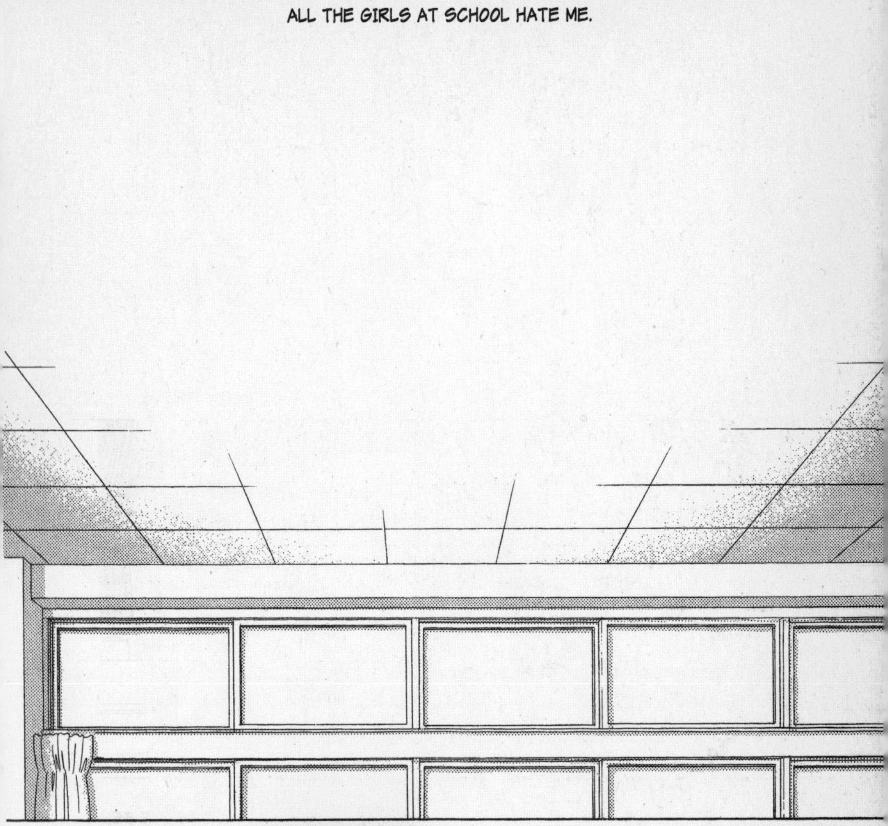
ALL THE GIRLS AT SCHOOL HATE ME.

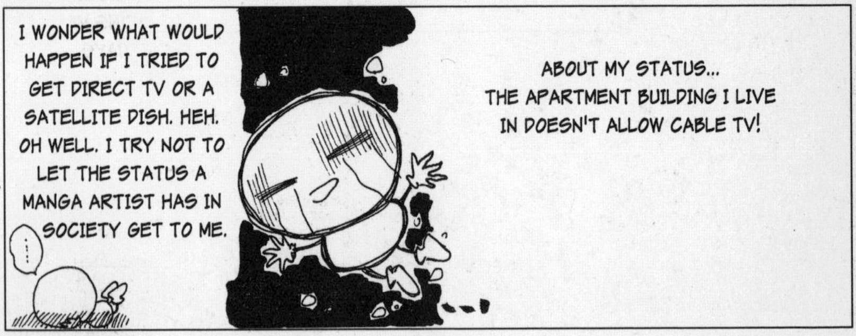
ABOUT MY STATUS... THE APARTMENT BUILDING I LIVE IN DOESN'T ALLOW CABLE TV!
I WONDER WHAT WOULD HAPPEN IF I TRIED TO GET DIRECT TV OR A SATELLITE DISH. HEH. OH WELL. I TRY NOT TO LET THE STATUS A MANGA ARTIST HAS IN SOCIETY GET TO ME.
...

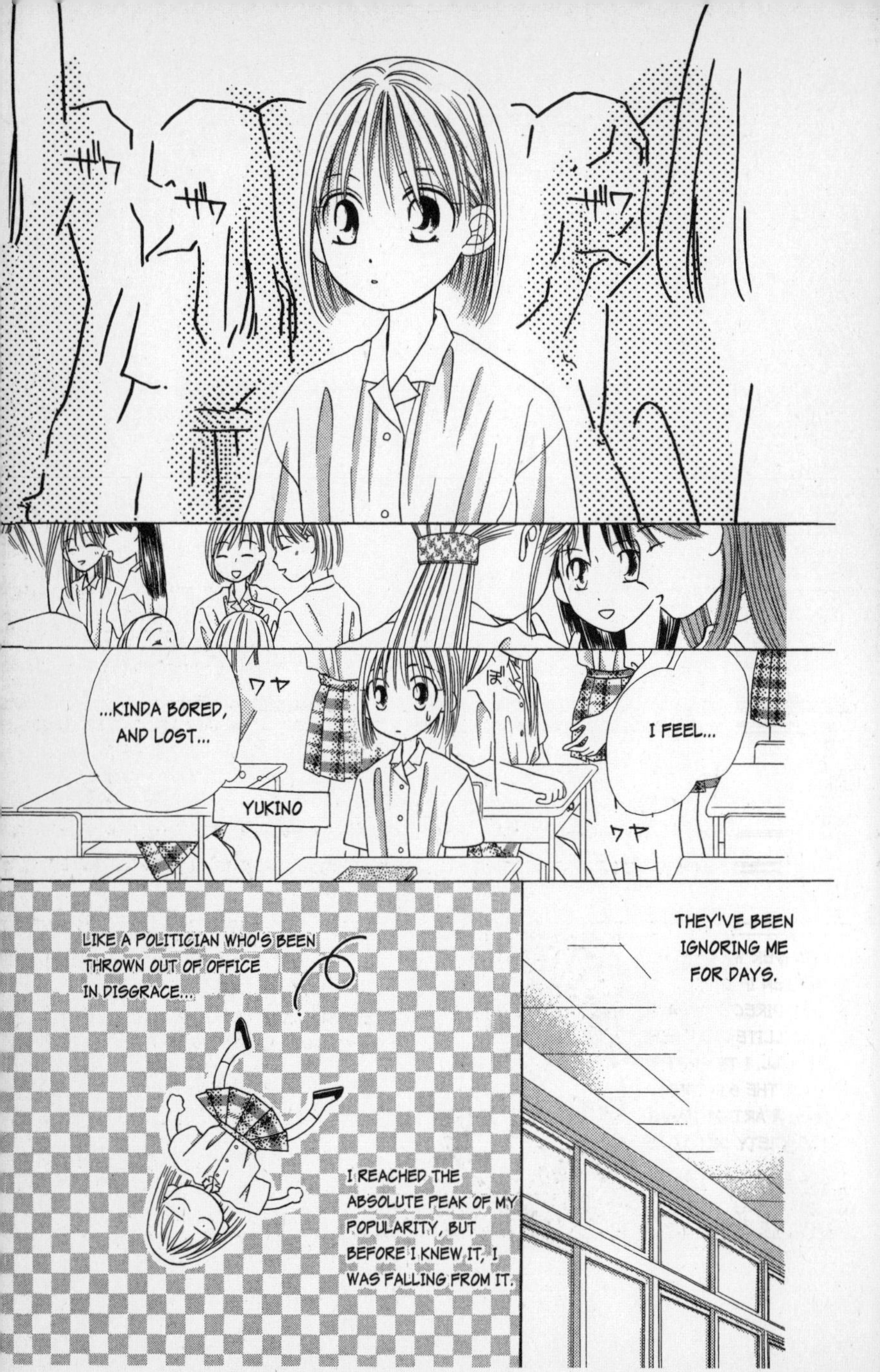
ザワ
ザワ
ザワ
I FEEL...
...KINDA BORED, AND LOST...
ワヤ
YUKINO
ワヤ
THEY'VE BEEN IGNORING ME FOR DAYS.
LIKE A POLITICIAN WHO'S BEEN THROWN OUT OF OFFICE IN DISGRACE...
I REACHED THE ABSOLUTE PEAK OF MY POPULARITY, BUT BEFORE I KNEW IT, I WAS FALLING FROM IT.

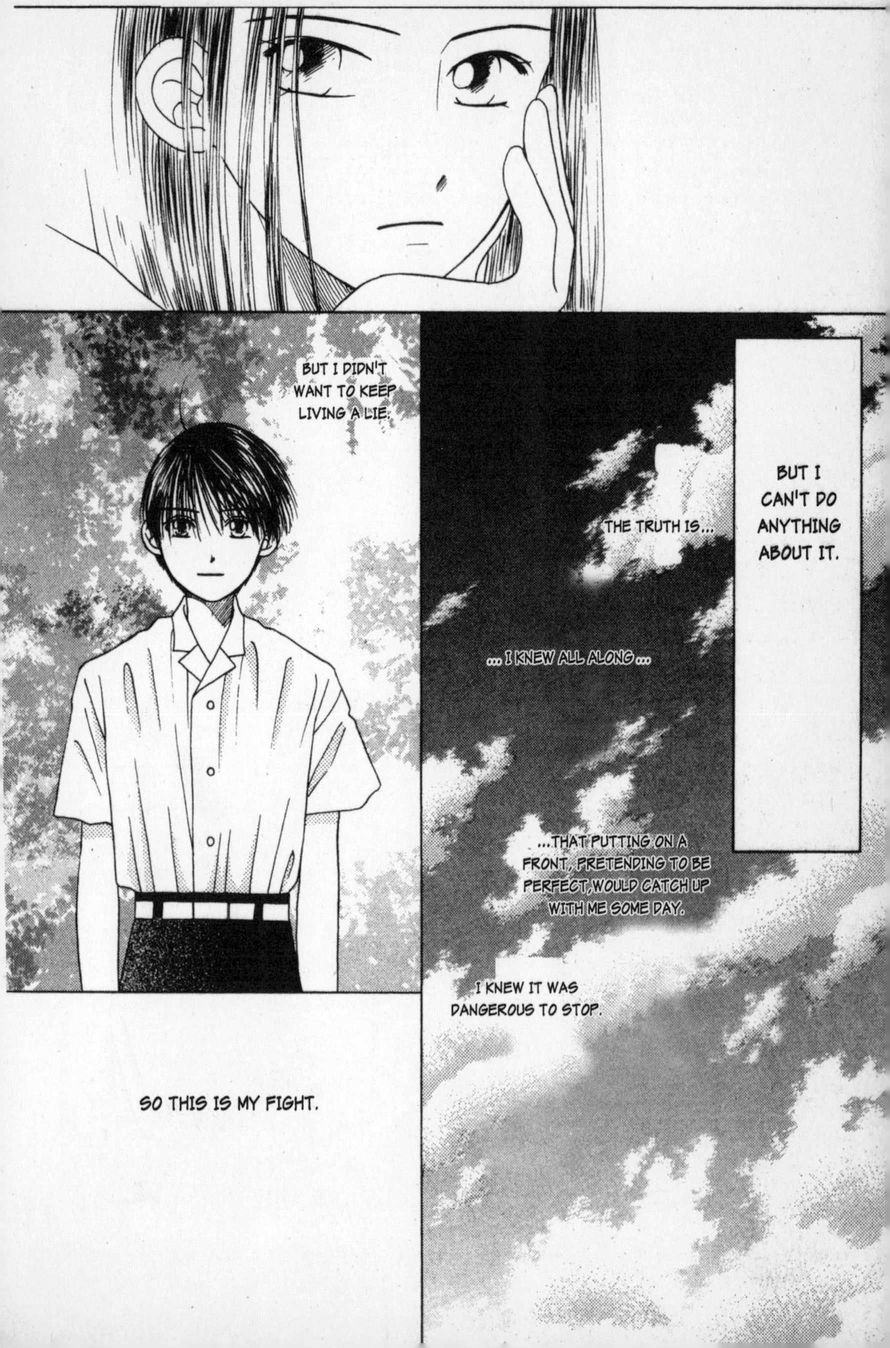
BUT I CAN'T DO ANYTHING ABOUT IT.
THE TRUTH IS...
...I KNEW ALL ALONG...
...THAT PUTTING ON A FRONT, PRETENDING TO BE PERFECT, WOULD CATCH UP WITH ME SOME DAY.
I KNEW IT WAS DANGEROUS TO STOP.
BUT I DIDN'T WANT TO KEEP LIVING A LIE.
SO THIS IS MY FIGHT.

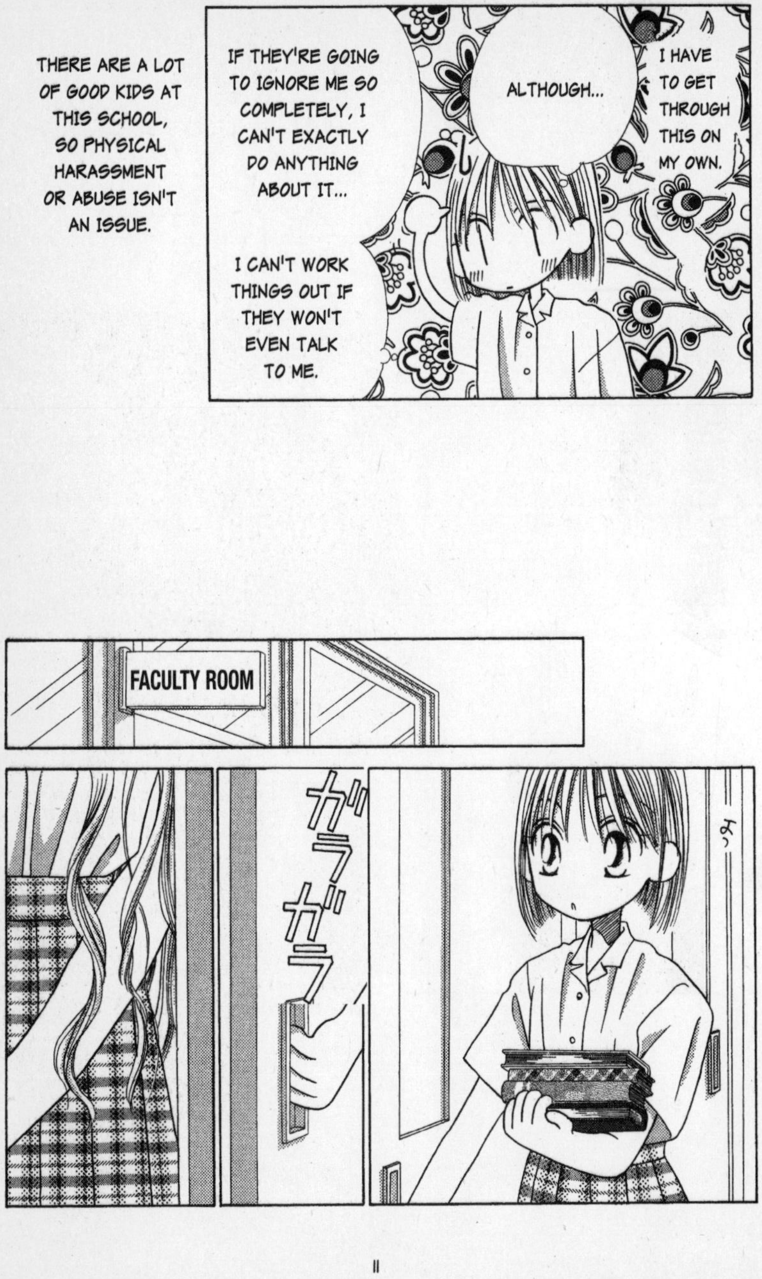
I HAVE TO GET THROUGH THIS ON MY OWN.
ALTHOUGH...
IF THEY'RE GOING TO IGNORE ME SO COMPLETELY, I CAN'T EXACTLY DO ANYTHING ABOUT IT...
I CAN'T WORK THINGS OUT IF THEY WON'T EVEN TALK TO ME.
THERE ARE A LOT OF GOOD KIDS AT THIS SCHOOL, SO PHYSICAL HARASSMENT OR ABUSE ISN'T AN ISSUE.
FACULTY ROOM
ガラガラ

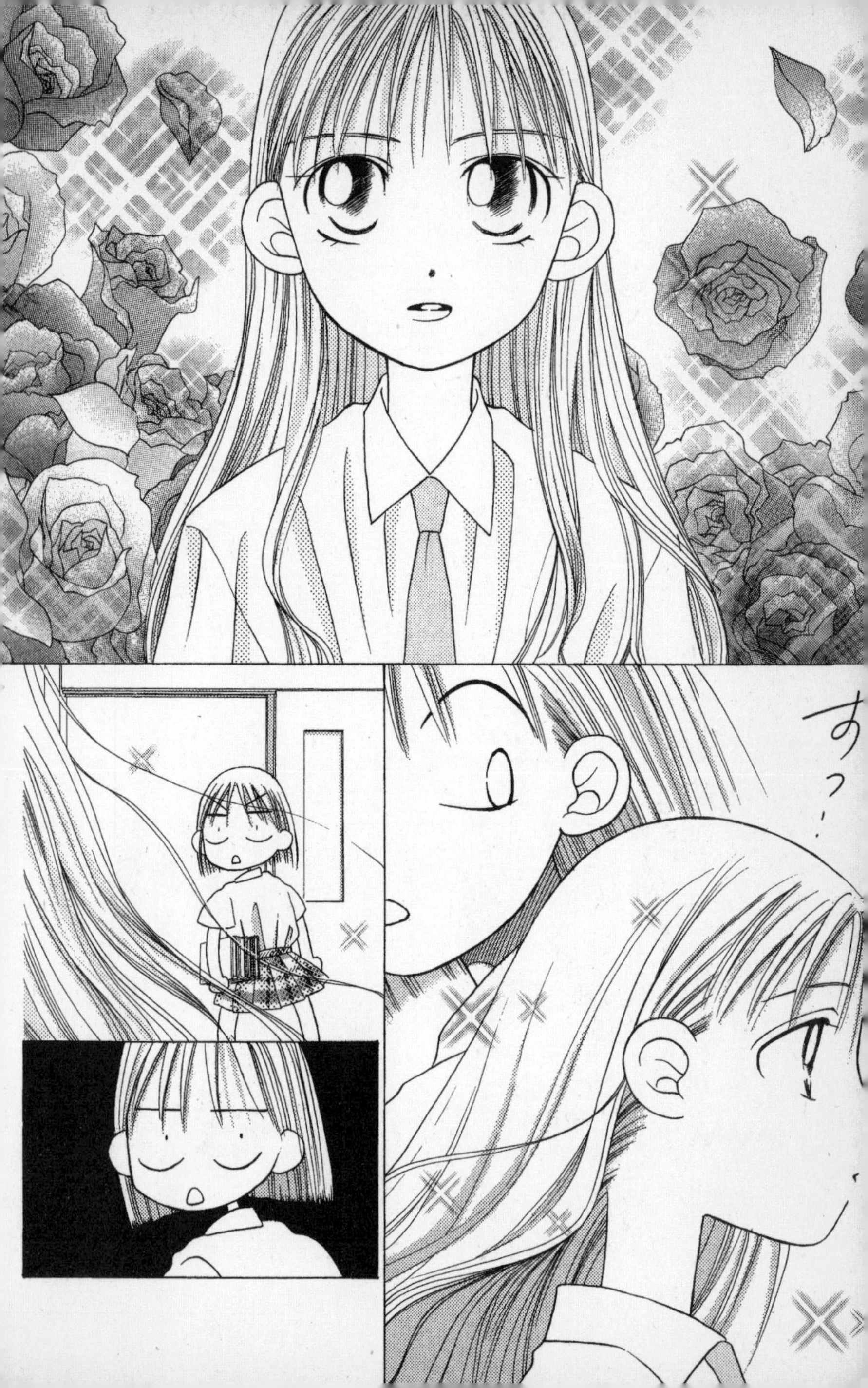
すっ…!

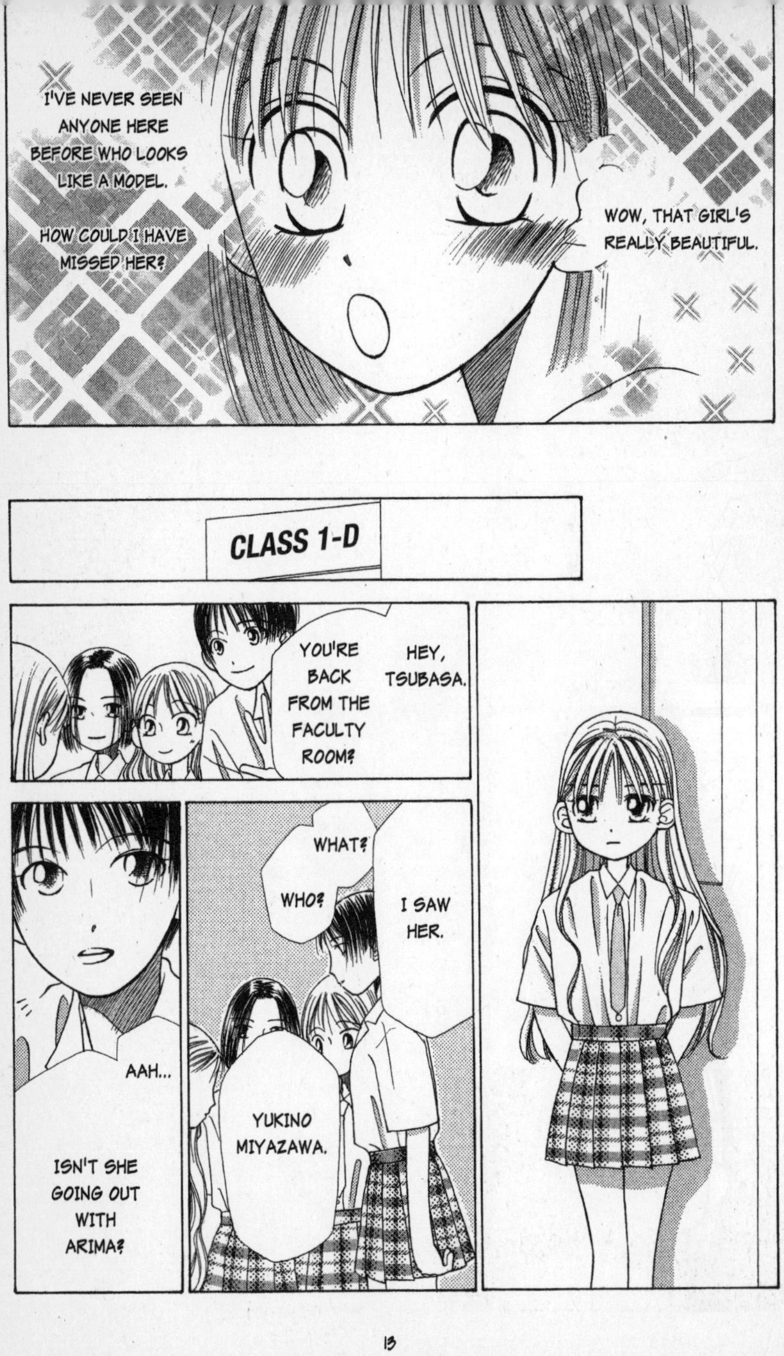
WOW, THAT GIRL'S REALLY BEAUTIFUL.
I'VE NEVER SEEN ANYONE HERE BEFORE WHO LOOKS LIKE A MODEL.
HOW COULD I HAVE MISSED HER?
CLASS 1-D
HEY, TSUBASA.
YOU'RE BACK FROM THE FACULTY ROOM?
I SAW HER.
WHAT?
WHO?
YUKINO MIYAZAWA.
AAH...
ISN'T SHE GOING OUT WITH ARIMA?

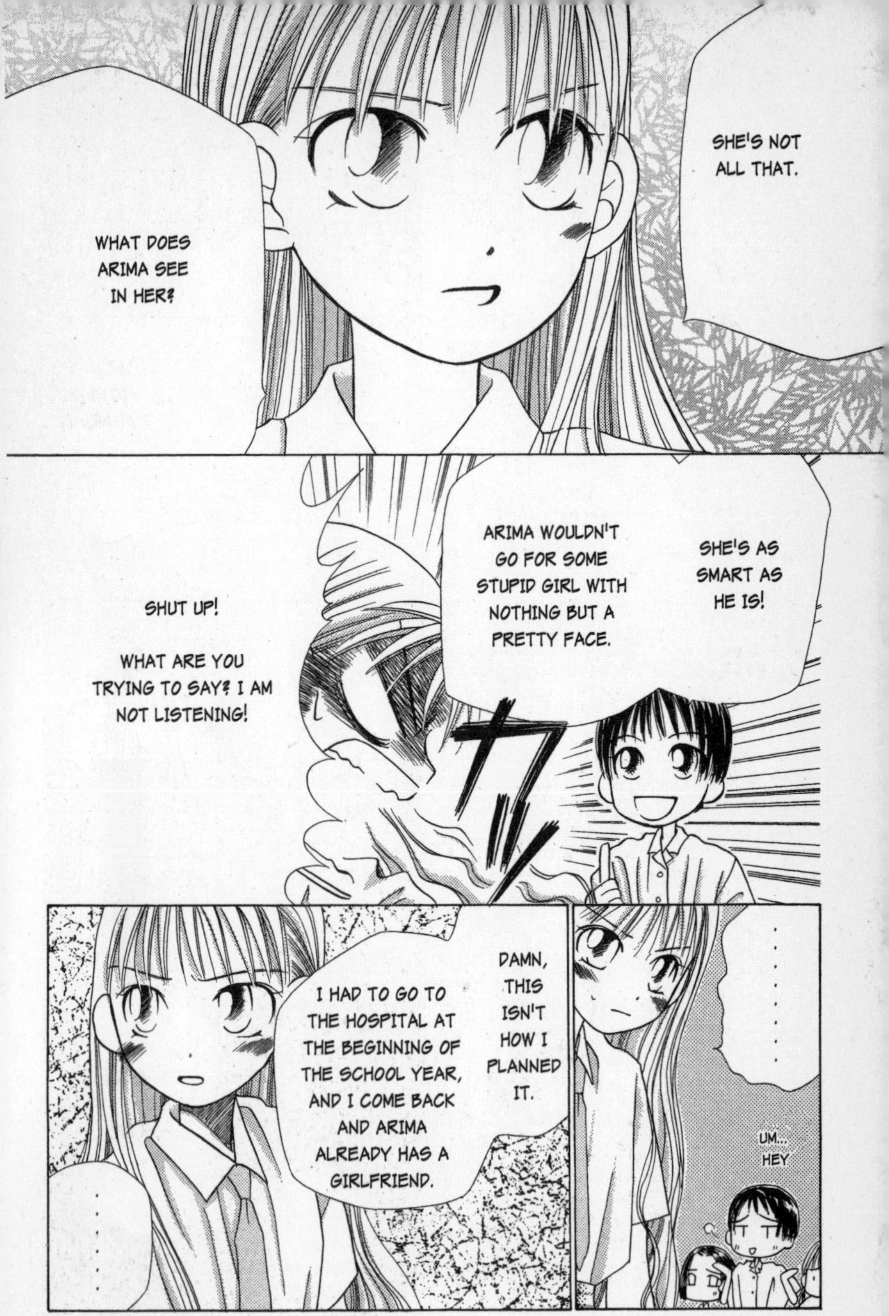
SHE'S NOT ALL THAT.
WHAT DOES ARIMA SEE IN HER?
ARIMA WOULDN'T GO FOR SOME STUPID GIRL WITH NOTHING BUT A PRETTY FACE.
SHE'S AS SMART AS HE IS!
SHUT UP!
WHAT ARE YOU TRYING TO SAY? I AM NOT LISTENING!
......
UM... HEY
DAMN, THIS ISN'T HOW I PLANNED IT.
I HAD TO GO TO THE HOSPITAL AT THE BEGINNING OF THE SCHOOL YEAR, AND I COME BACK AND ARIMA ALREADY HAS A GIRLFRIEND.
......

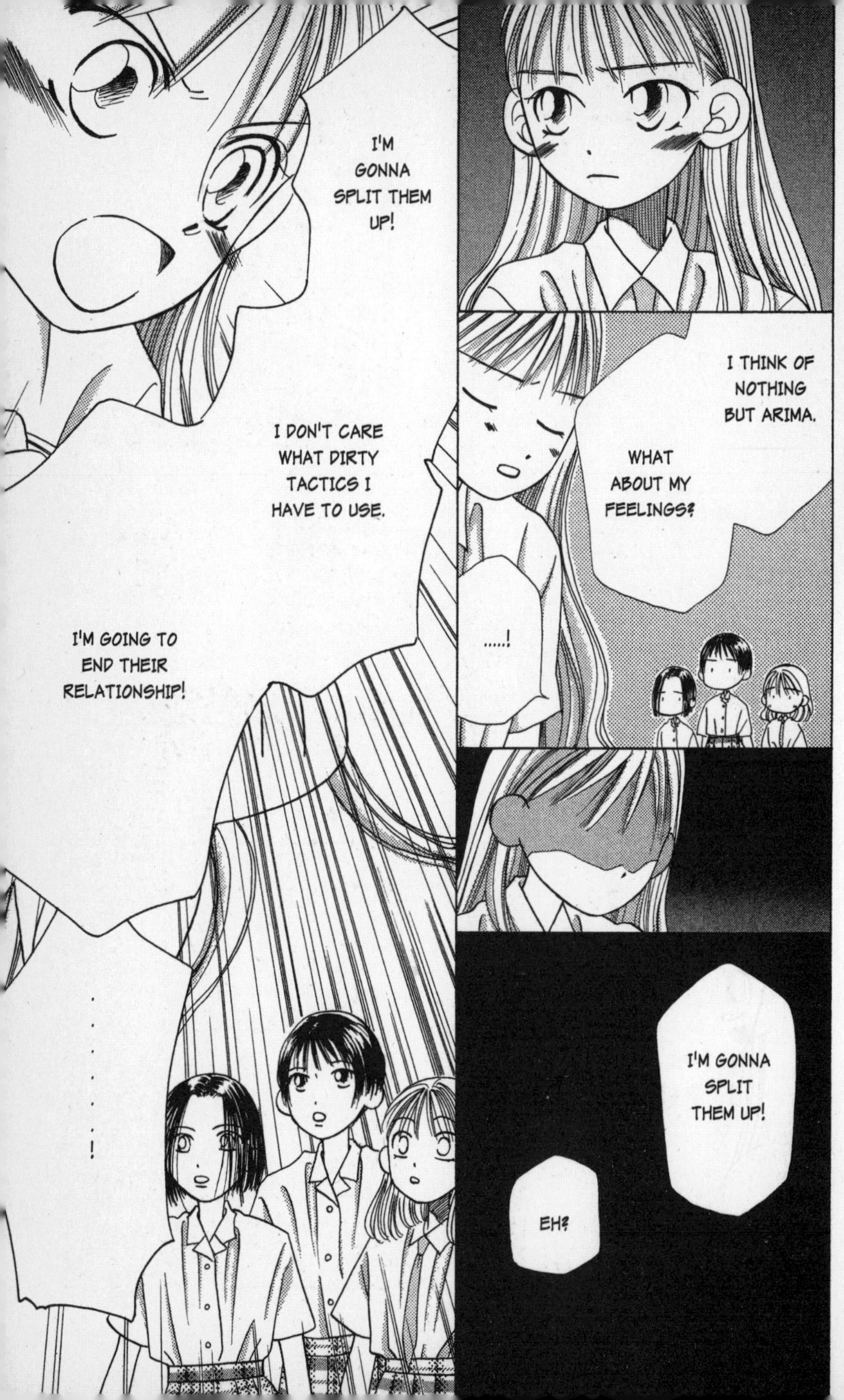
I THINK OF NOTHING BUT ARIMA.
WHAT ABOUT MY FEELINGS?
.....!
I'M GONNA SPLIT THEM UP!
EH?
I'M GONNA SPLIT THEM UP!
I DON'T CARE WHAT DIRTY TACTICS I HAVE TO USE.
I'M GOING TO END THEIR RELATIONSHIP!
. . . . . !

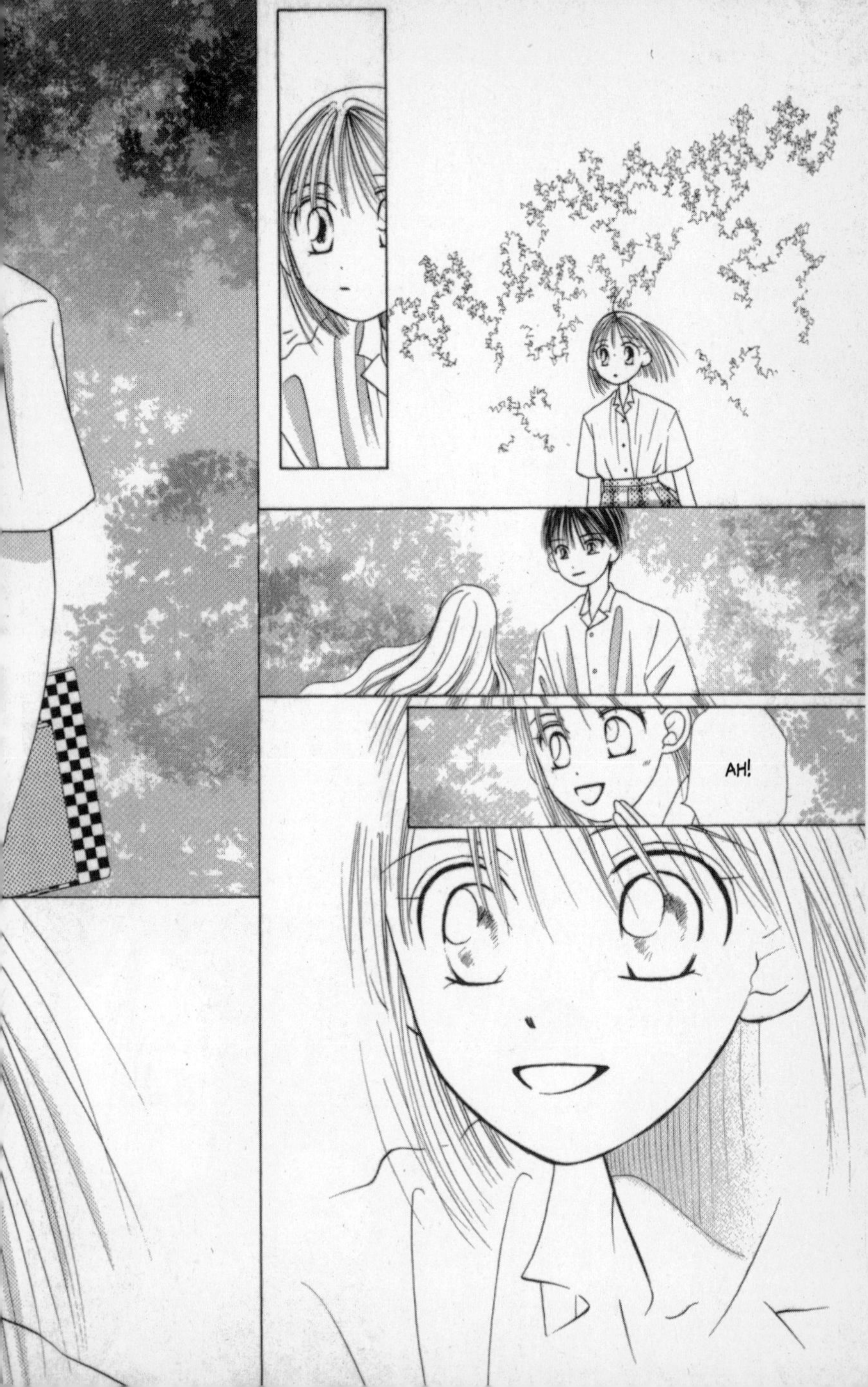
AH!

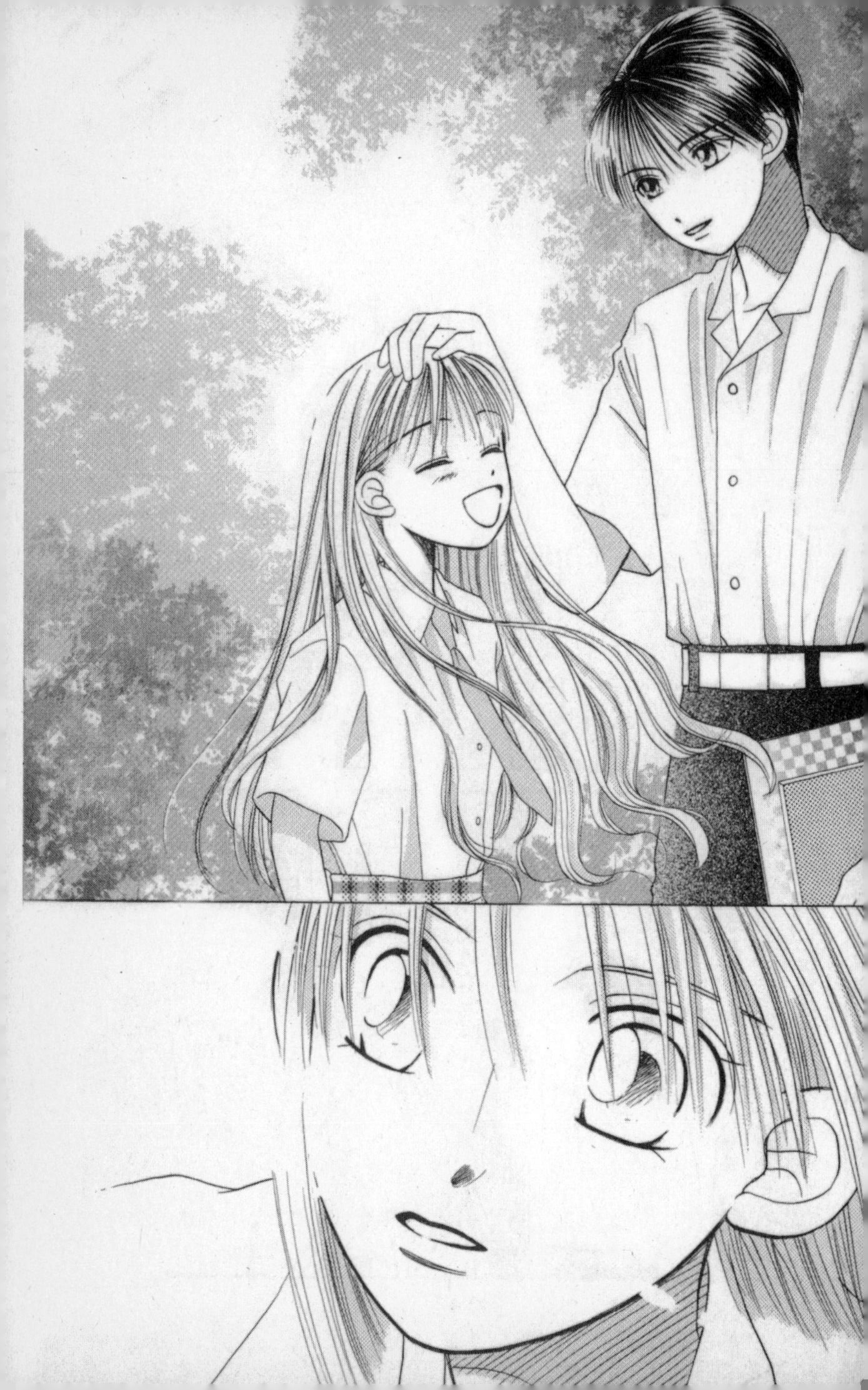

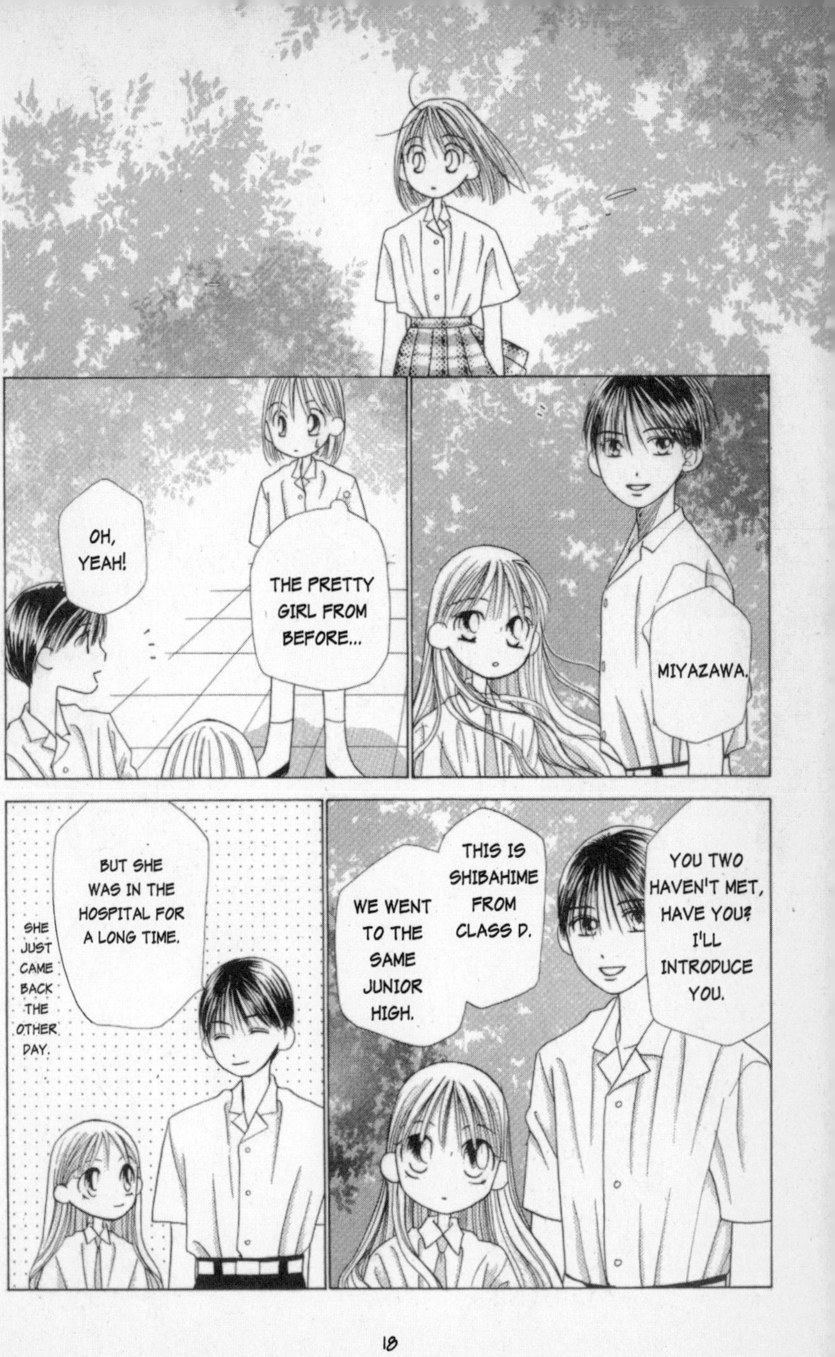
MIYAZAWA.
OH, YEAH!
THE PRETTY GIRL FROM BEFORE...
YOU TWO HAVEN'T MET, HAVE YOU? I'LL INTRODUCE YOU.
THIS IS SHIBAHIME FROM CLASS D.
WE WENT TO THE SAME JUNIOR HIGH.
BUT SHE WAS IN THE HOSPITAL FOR A LONG TIME.
SHE JUST CAME BACK THE OTHER DAY.

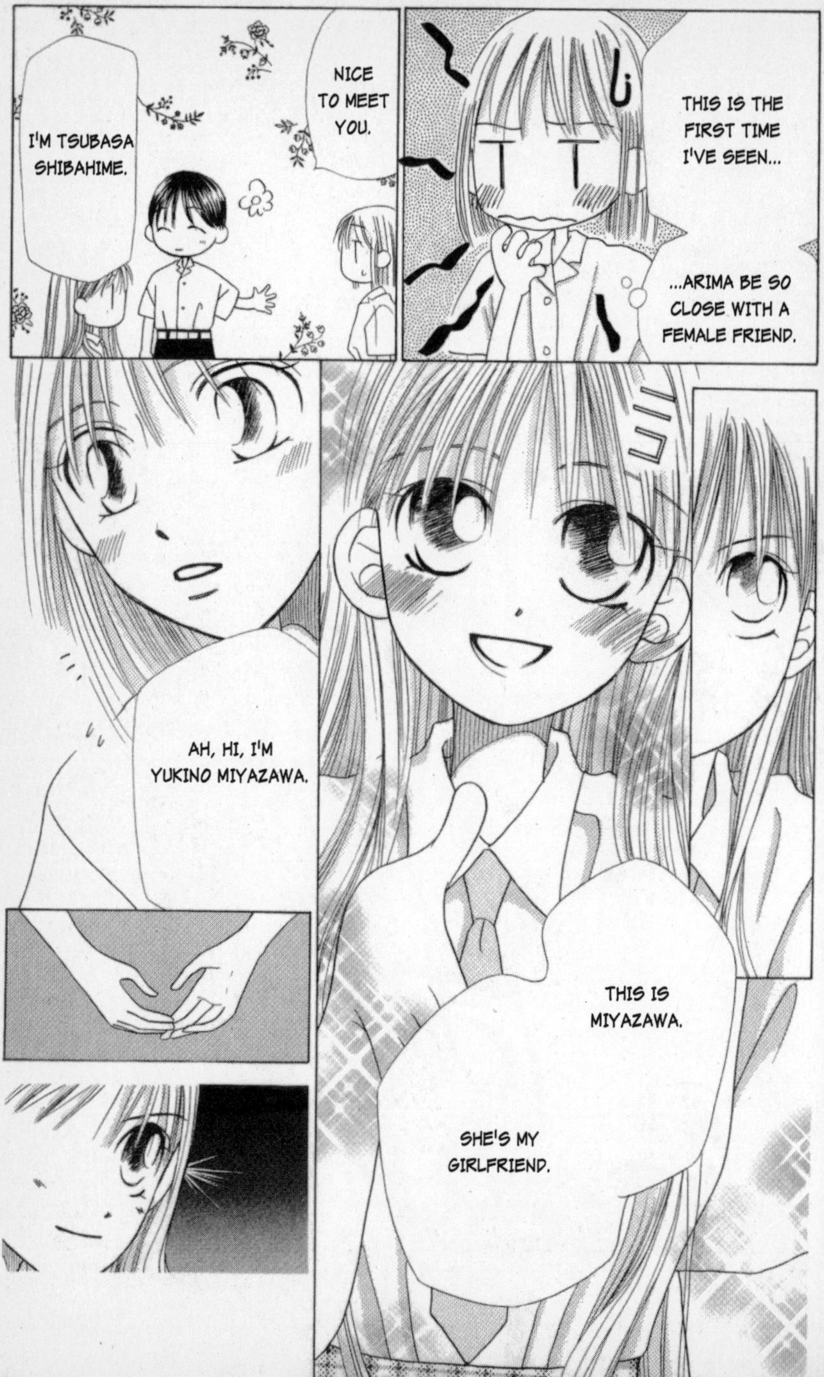
THIS IS THE FIRST TIME I'VE SEEN...
...ARIMA BE SO CLOSE WITH A FEMALE FRIEND.
NICE TO MEET YOU.
I'M TSUBASA SHIBAHIME.
THIS IS MIYAZAWA.
SHE'S MY GIRLFRIEND.
AH, HI, I'M YUKINO MIYAZAWA.

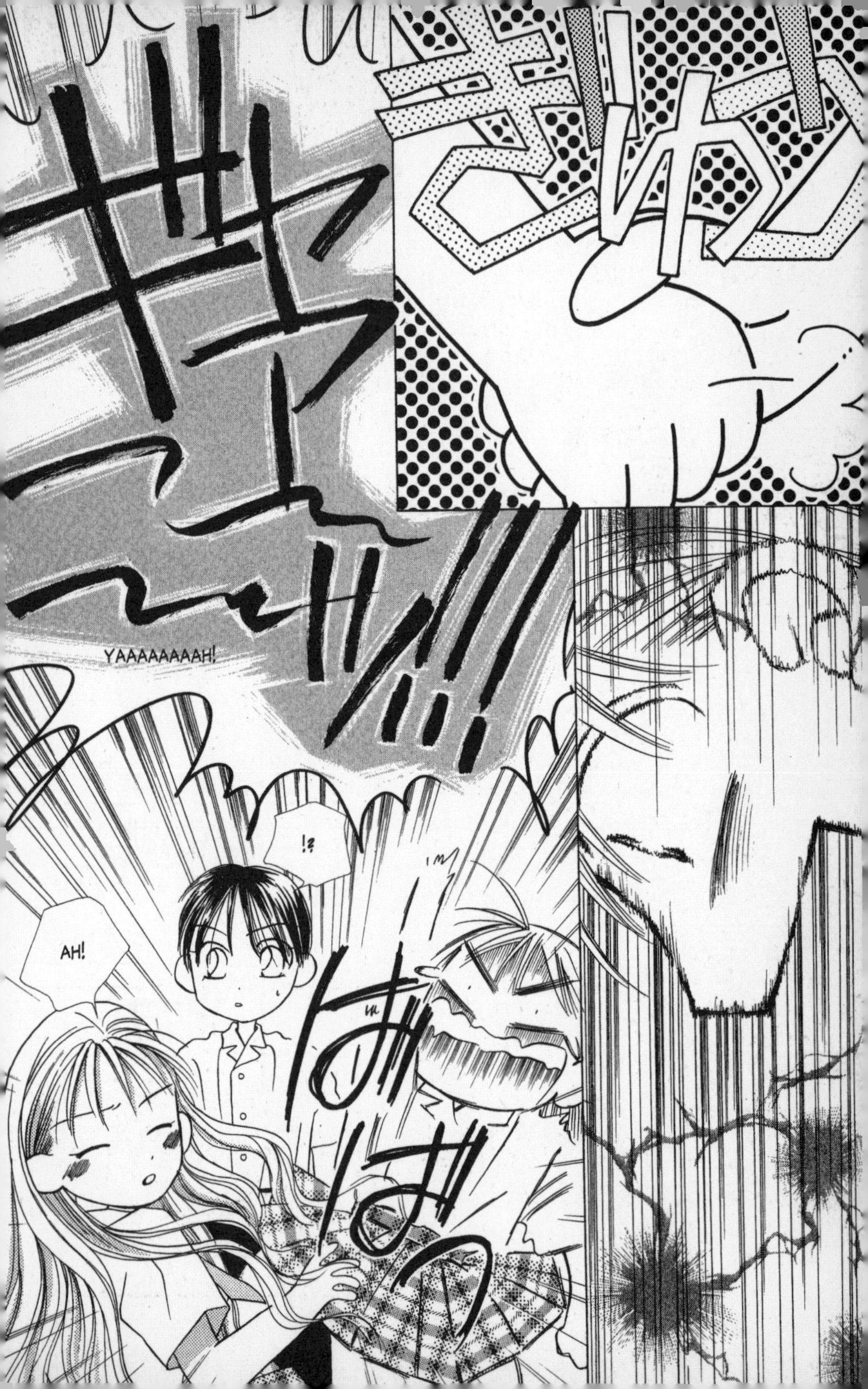
YAAAAAAAAH!
!?
AH!

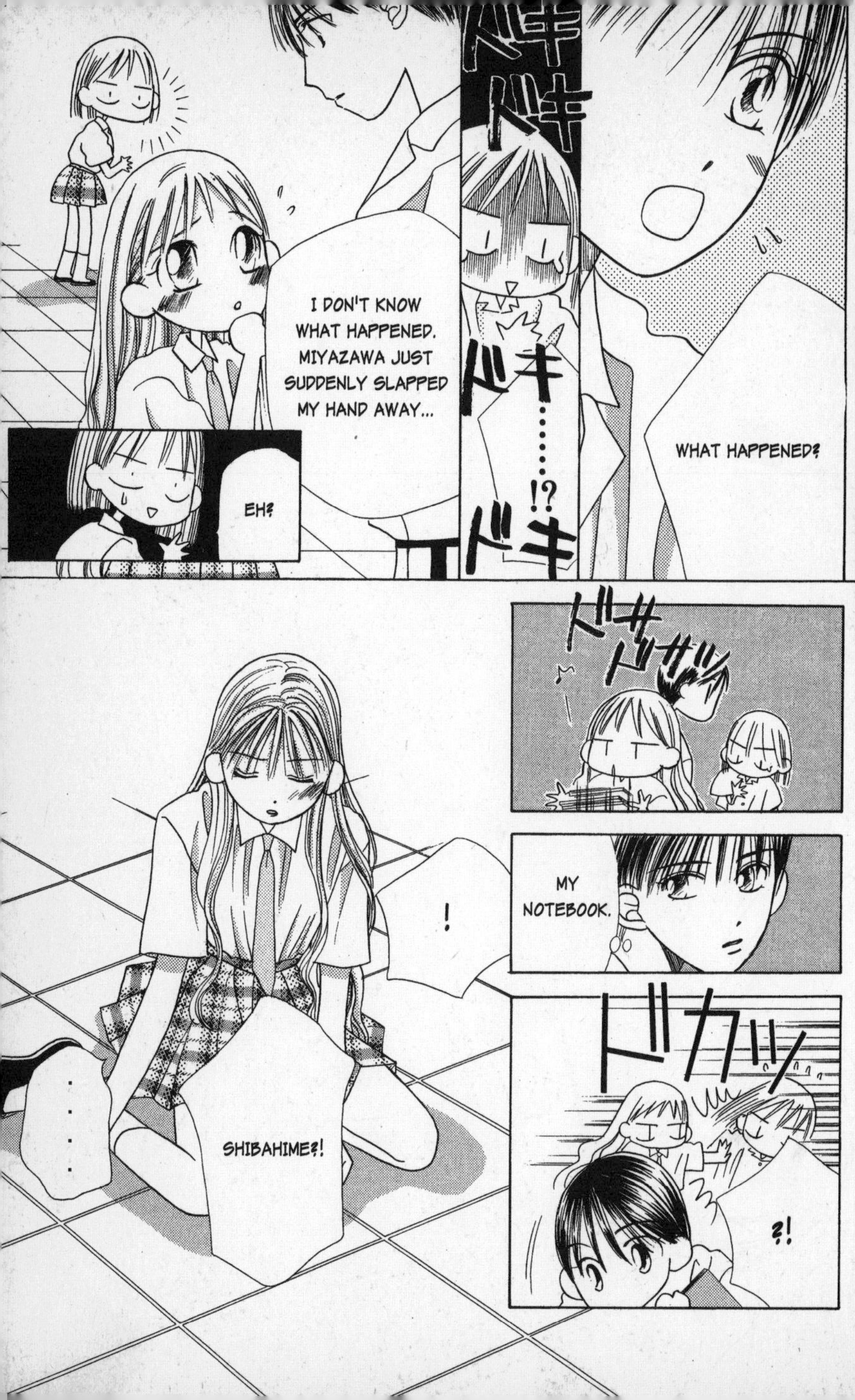
WHAT HAPPENED?
ドキドキ
ドキ……ドキ
!?
I DON'T KNOW WHAT HAPPENED. MIYAZAWA JUST SUDDENLY SLAPPED MY HAND AWAY...
EH?
MY NOTEBOOK.
ドカッ
?!
!
SHIBAHIME?!
....

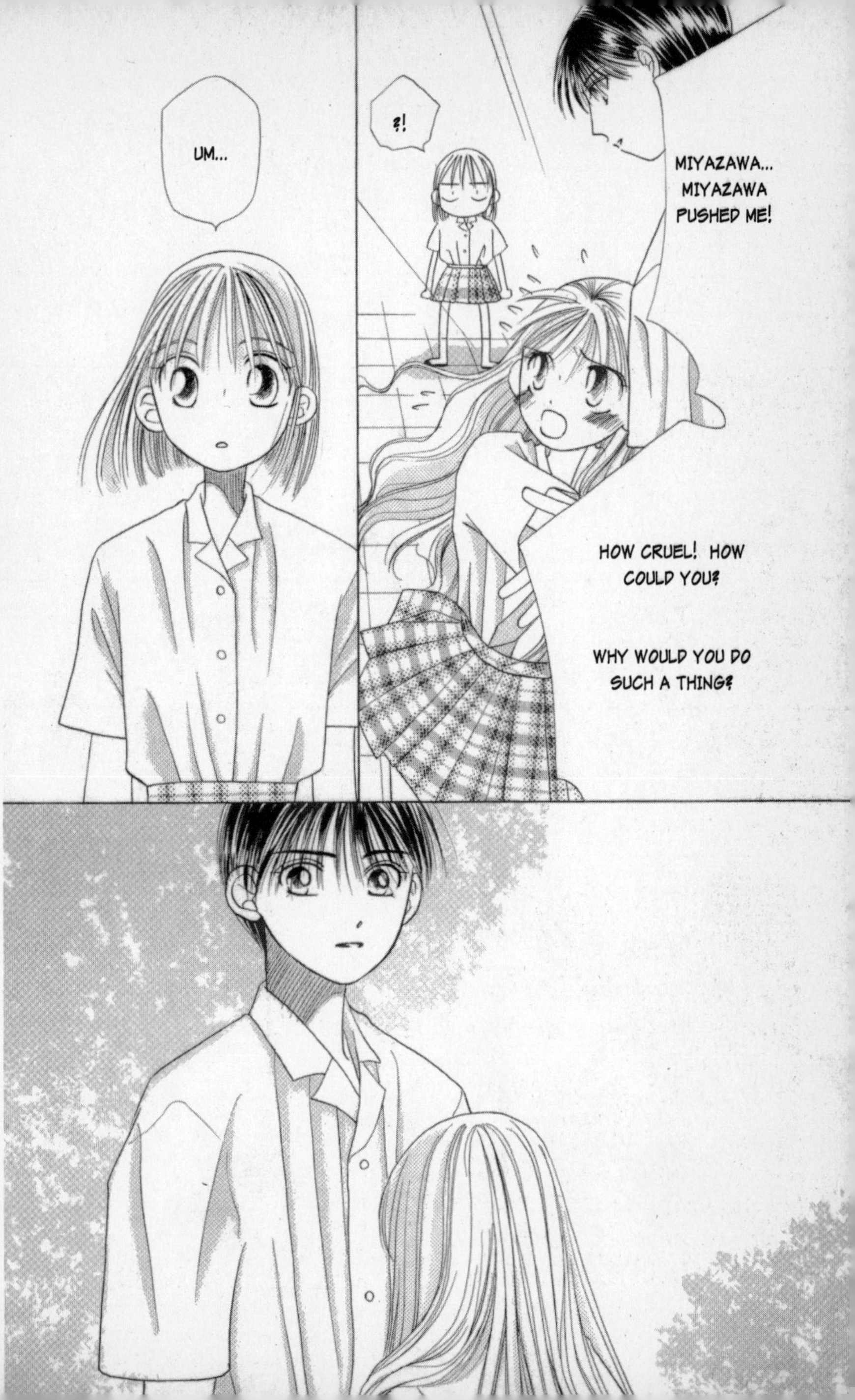
MIYAZAWA... MIYAZAWA PUSHED ME!
?!
HOW CRUEL! HOW COULD YOU?
WHY WOULD YOU DO SUCH A THING?
UM...

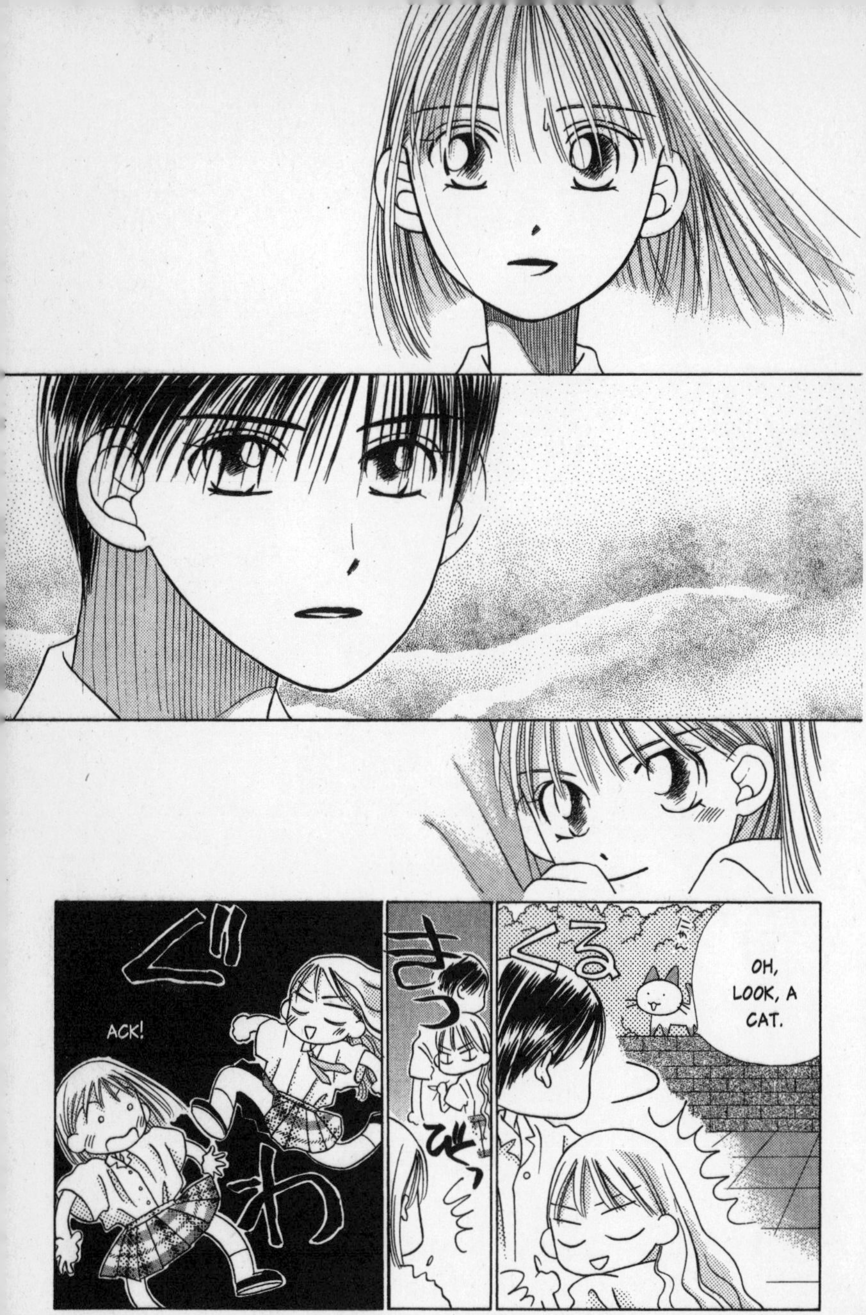

OH, LOOK, A CAT.
くる
きっ
びくっ
ぐわっ
ACK!

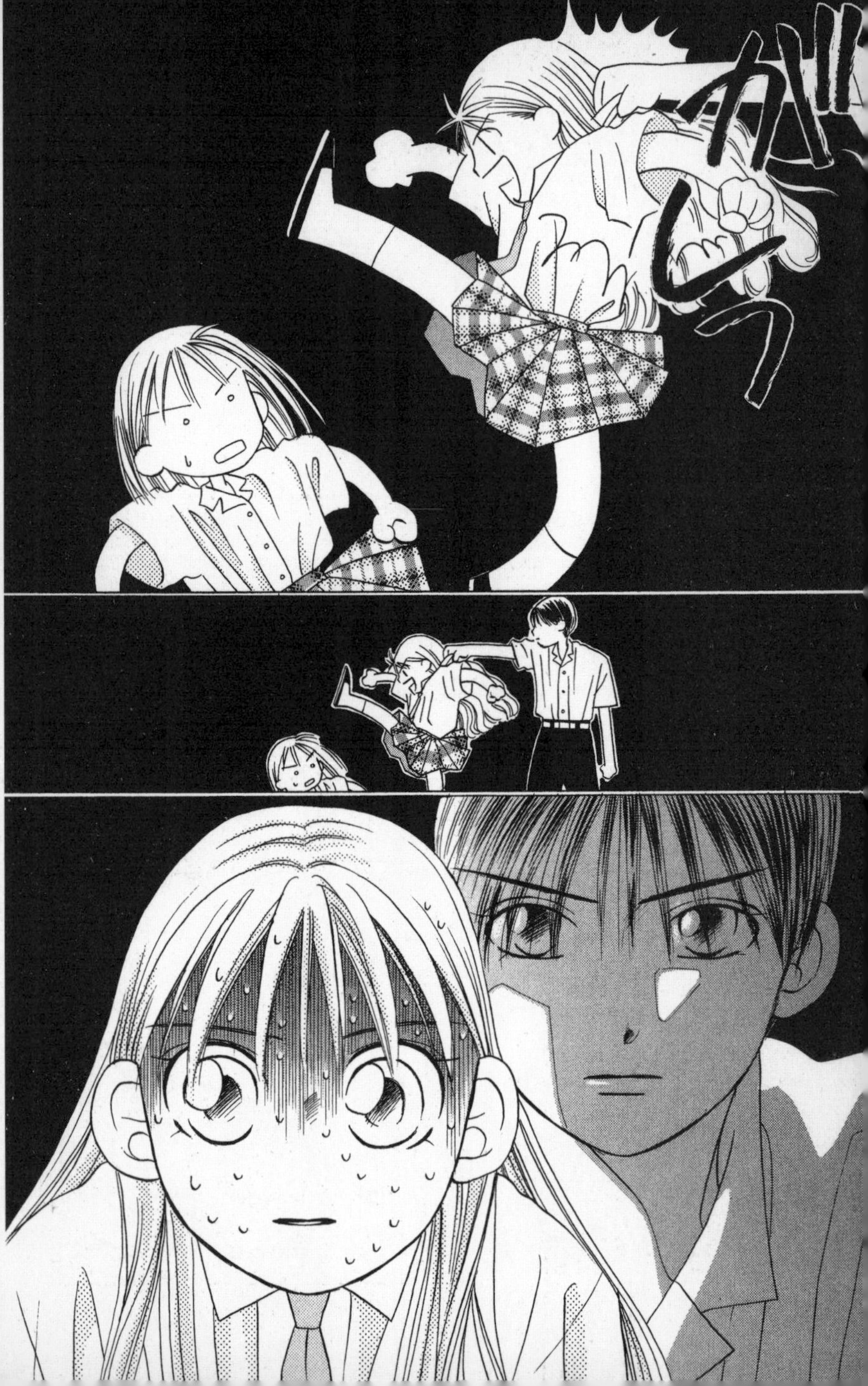
がしっ

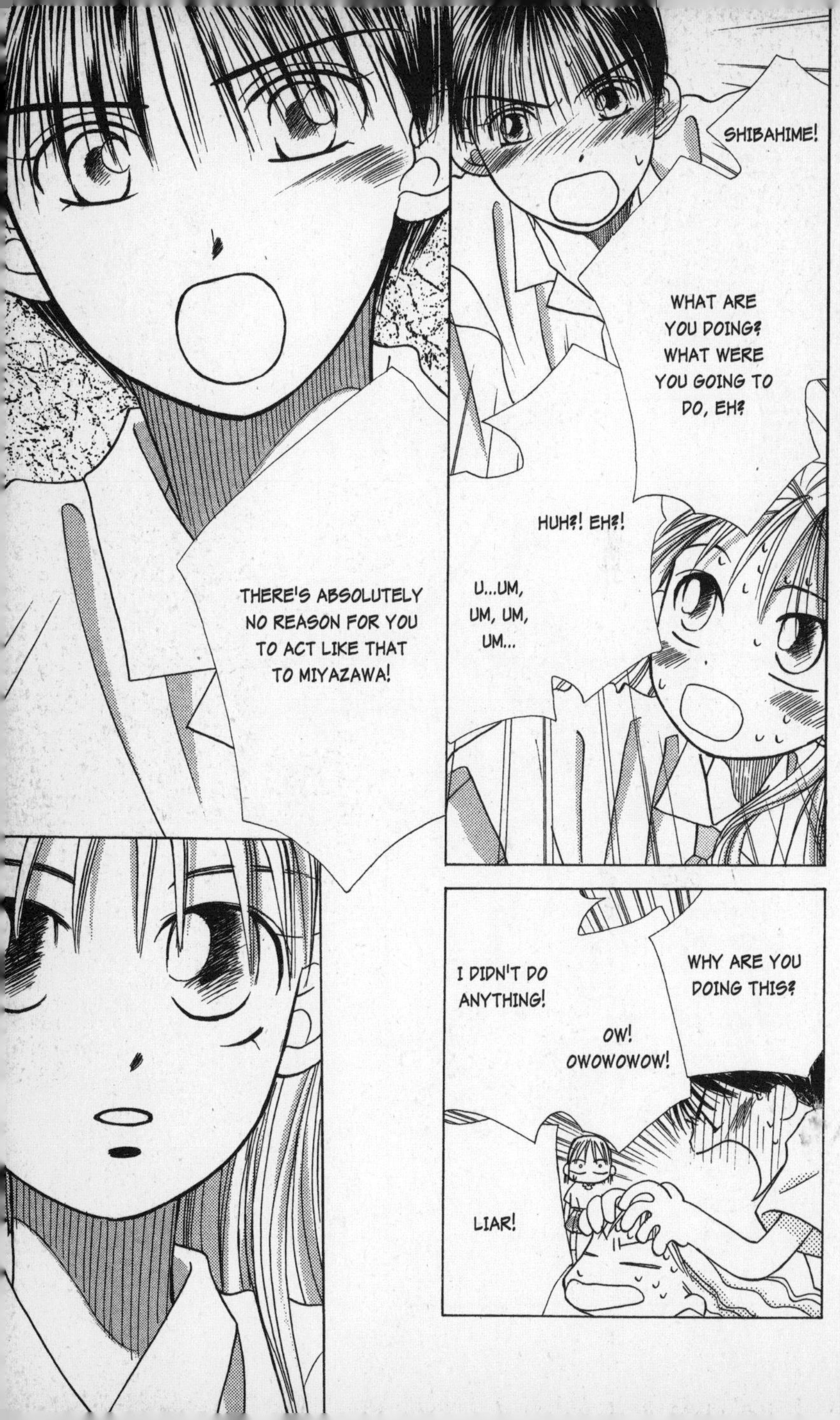
SHIBAHIME!
WHAT ARE YOU DOING? WHAT WERE YOU GOING TO DO, EH?
HUH?! EH?!
U...UM, UM, UM, UM...
THERE'S ABSOLUTELY NO REASON FOR YOU TO ACT LIKE THAT TO MIYAZAWA!
WHY ARE YOU DOING THIS?
I DIDN'T DO ANYTHING!
OW! OWOWOWOW!
LIAR!

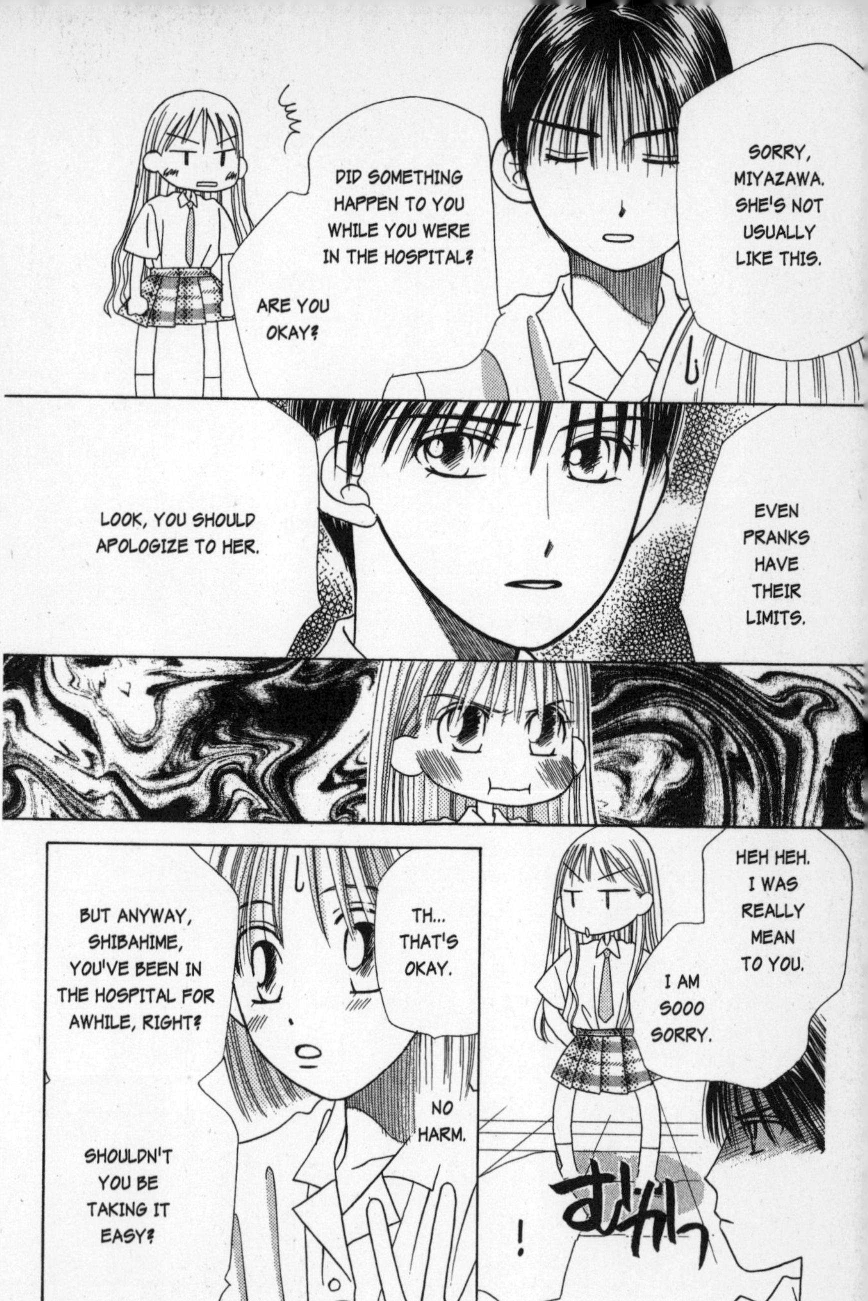
SORRY, MIYAZAWA. SHE'S NOT USUALLY LIKE THIS.
DID SOMETHING HAPPEN TO YOU WHILE YOU WERE IN THE HOSPITAL?
ARE YOU OKAY?
EVEN PRANKS HAVE THEIR LIMITS.
LOOK, YOU SHOULD APOLOGIZE TO HER.
HEH HEH. I WAS REALLY MEAN TO YOU.
I AM SOOO SORRY.
!
TH... THAT'S OKAY.
NO HARM.
BUT ANYWAY, SHIBAHIME, YOU'VE BEEN IN THE HOSPITAL FOR AWHILE, RIGHT?
SHOULDN'T YOU BE TAKING IT EASY?

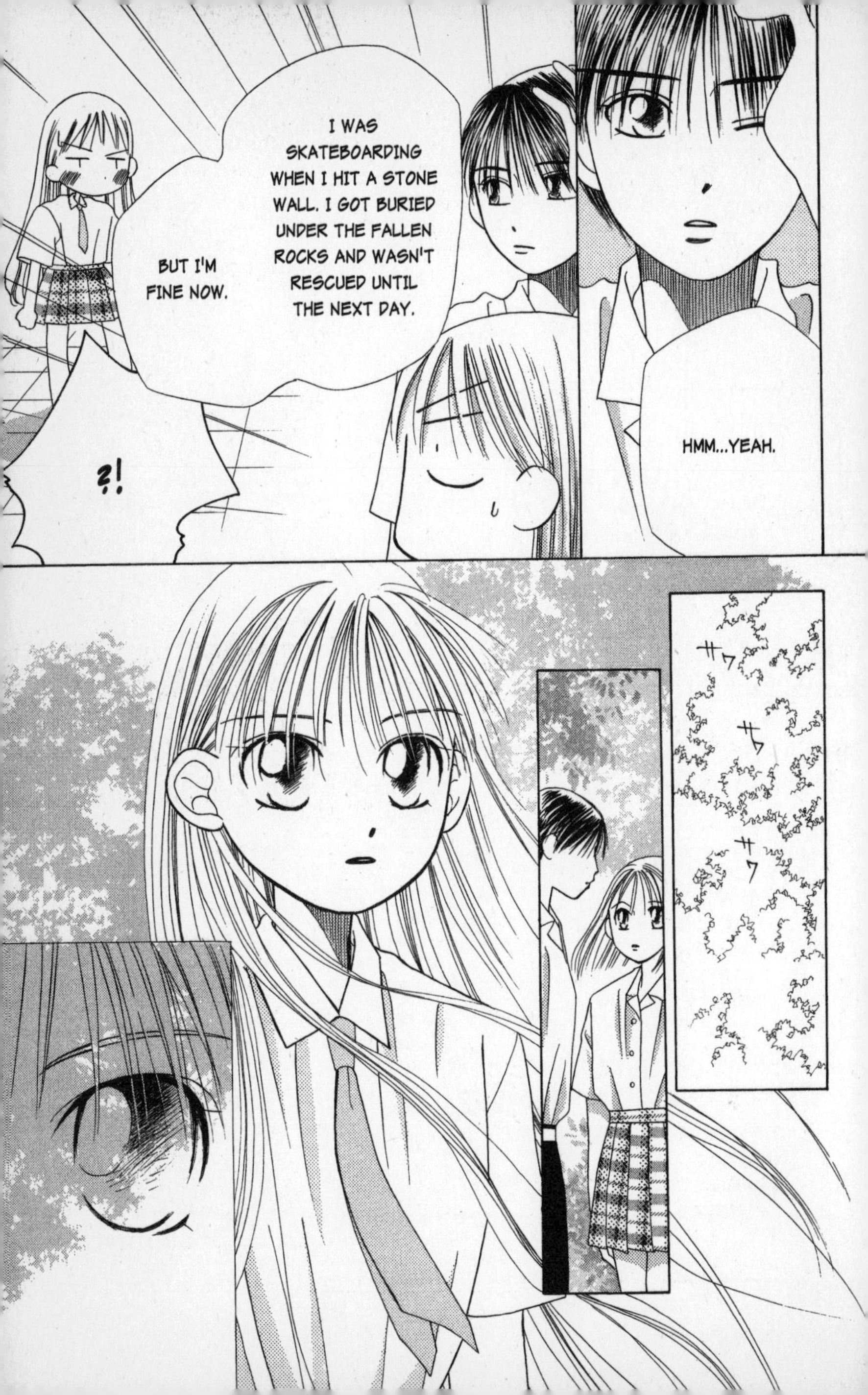
HMM...YEAH.
I WAS SKATEBOARDING WHEN I HIT A STONE WALL. I GOT BURIED UNDER THE FALLEN ROCKS AND WASN'T RESCUED UNTIL THE NEXT DAY.
BUT I'M FINE NOW.
?!
サワ
サワ
サワ

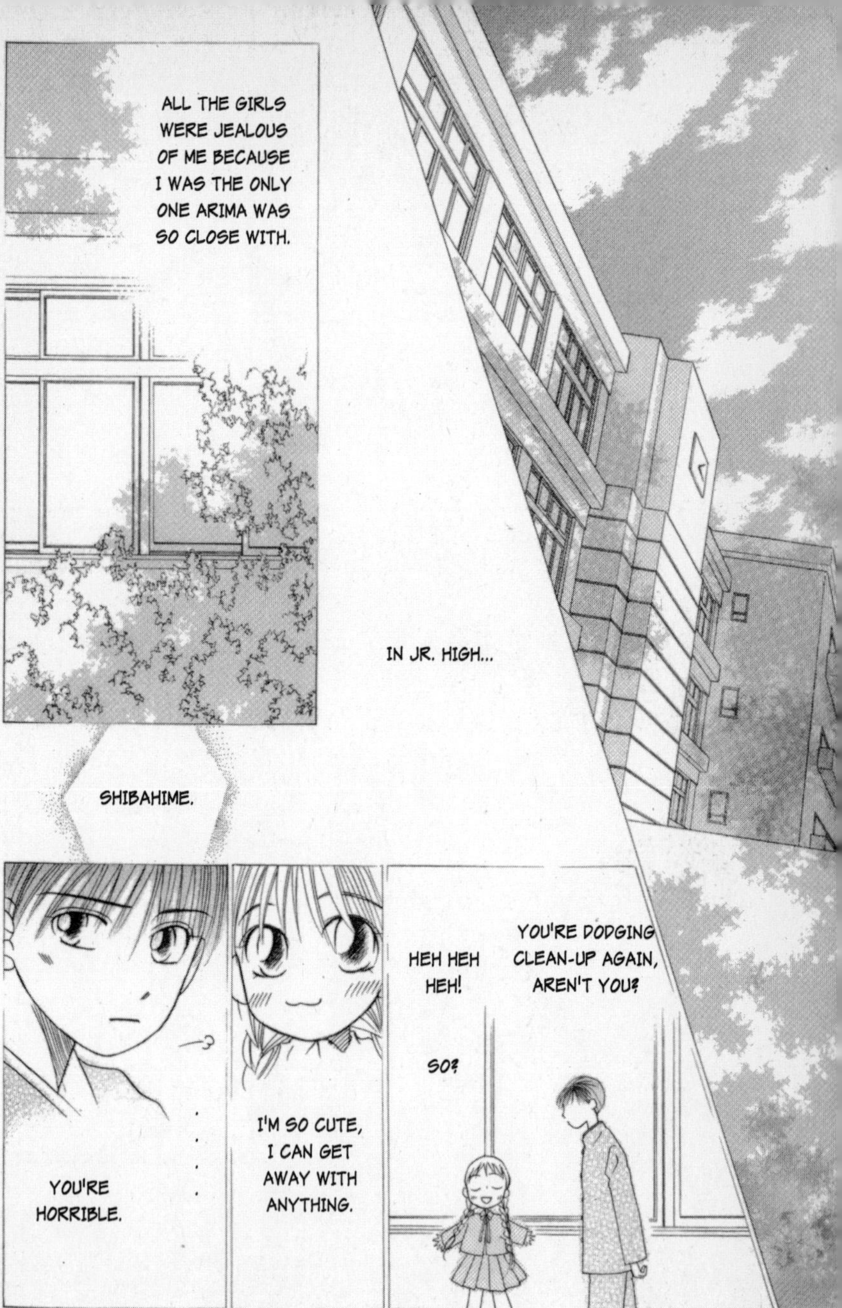
IN JR. HIGH...
ALL THE GIRLS WERE JEALOUS OF ME BECAUSE I WAS THE ONLY ONE ARIMA WAS SO CLOSE WITH.
SHIBAHIME.
YOU'RE DODGING CLEAN-UP AGAIN, AREN'T YOU?
HEH HEH HEH!
SO?
I'M SO CUTE, I CAN GET AWAY WITH ANYTHING.
....
YOU'RE HORRIBLE.

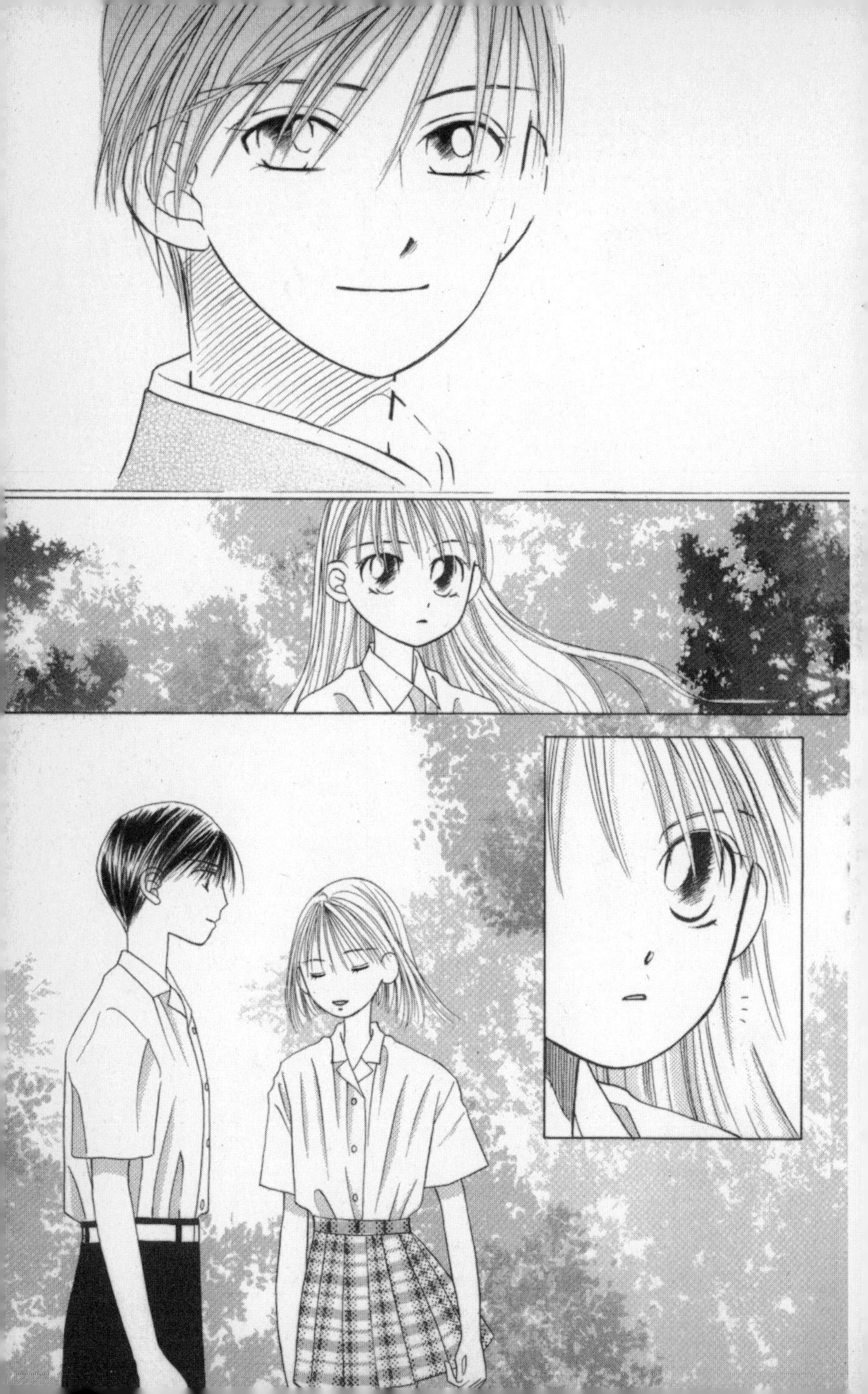

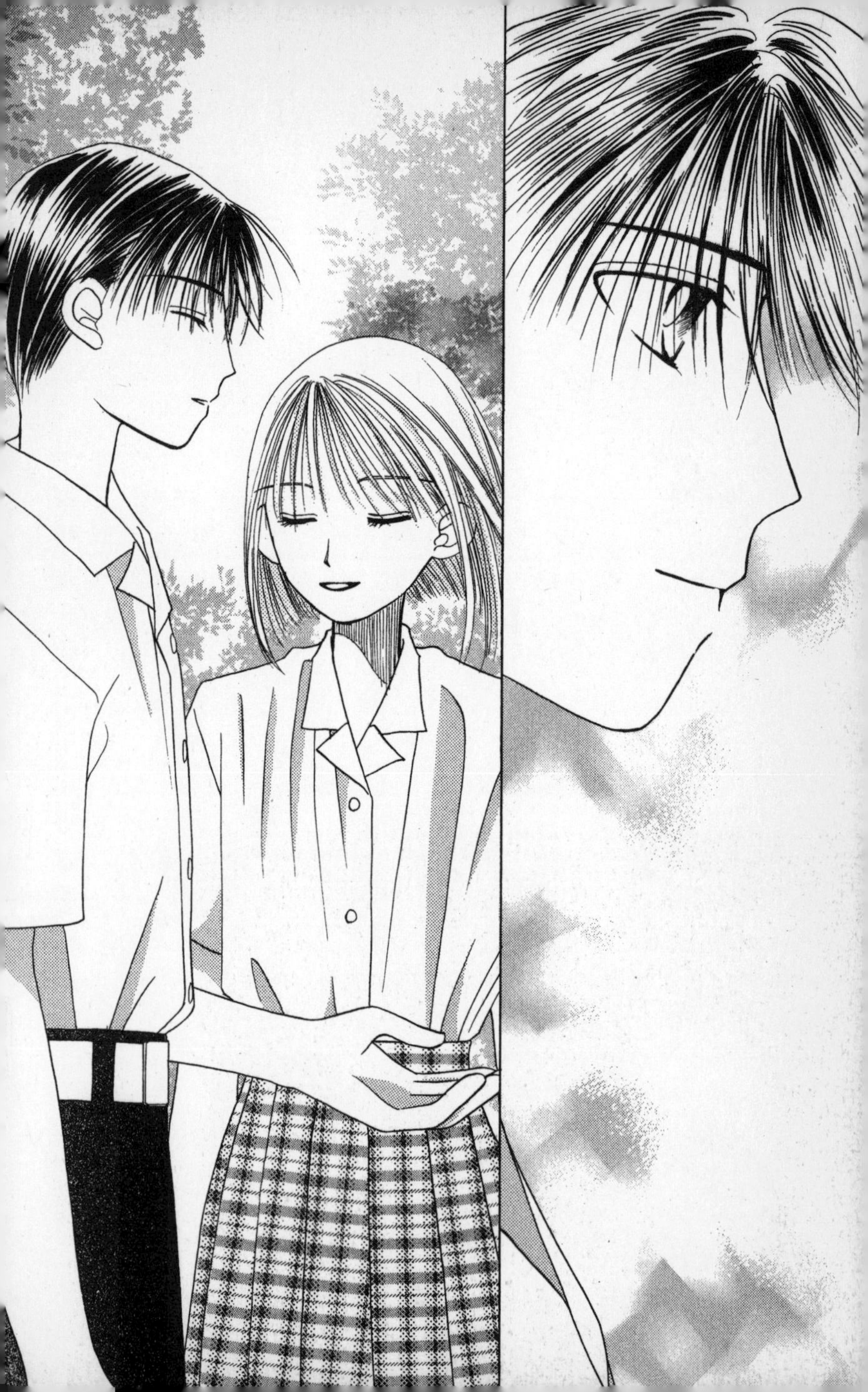

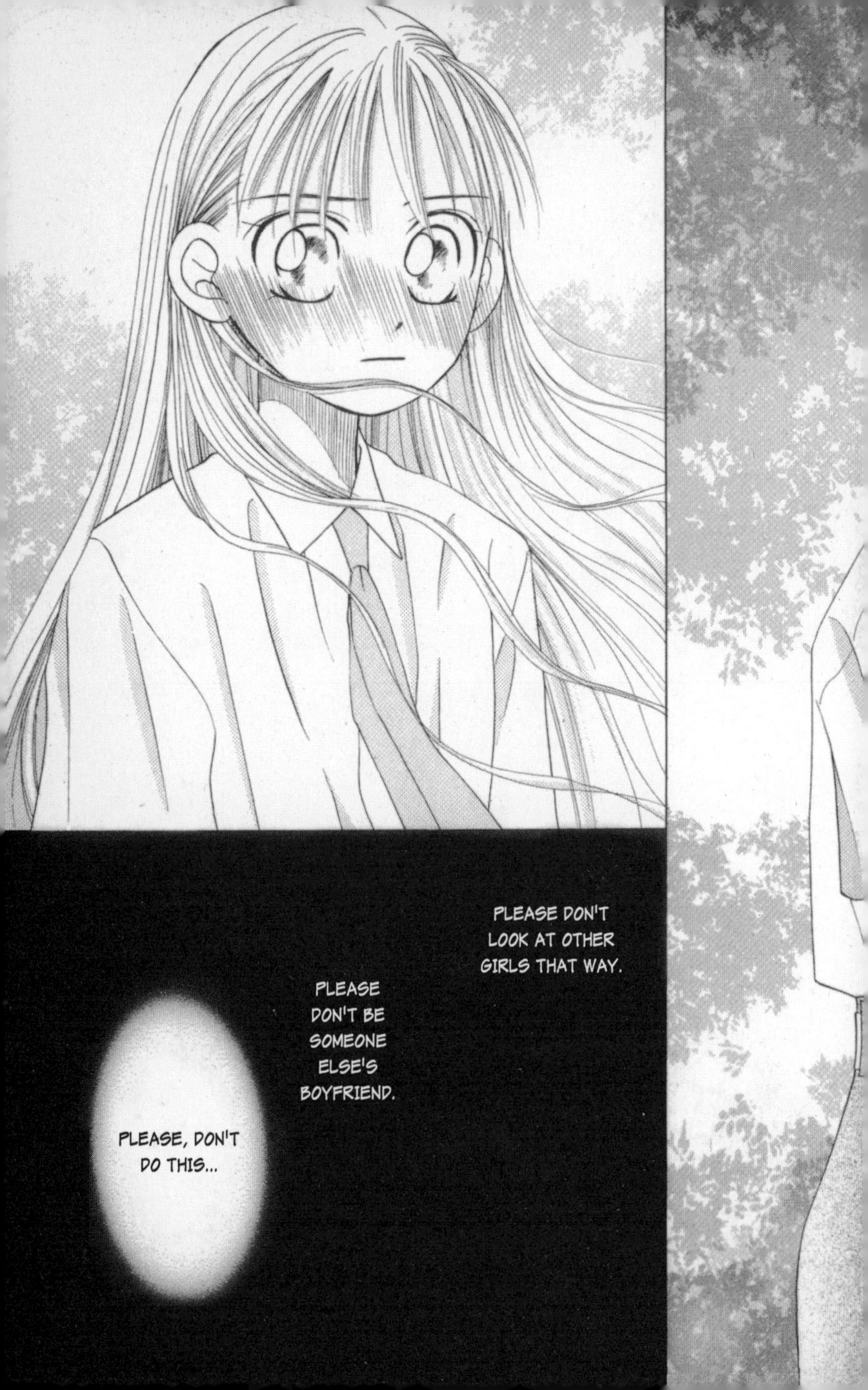
PLEASE DON'T LOOK AT OTHER GIRLS THAT WAY.
PLEASE DON'T BE SOMEONE ELSE'S BOYFRIEND.
PLEASE, DON'T DO THIS...

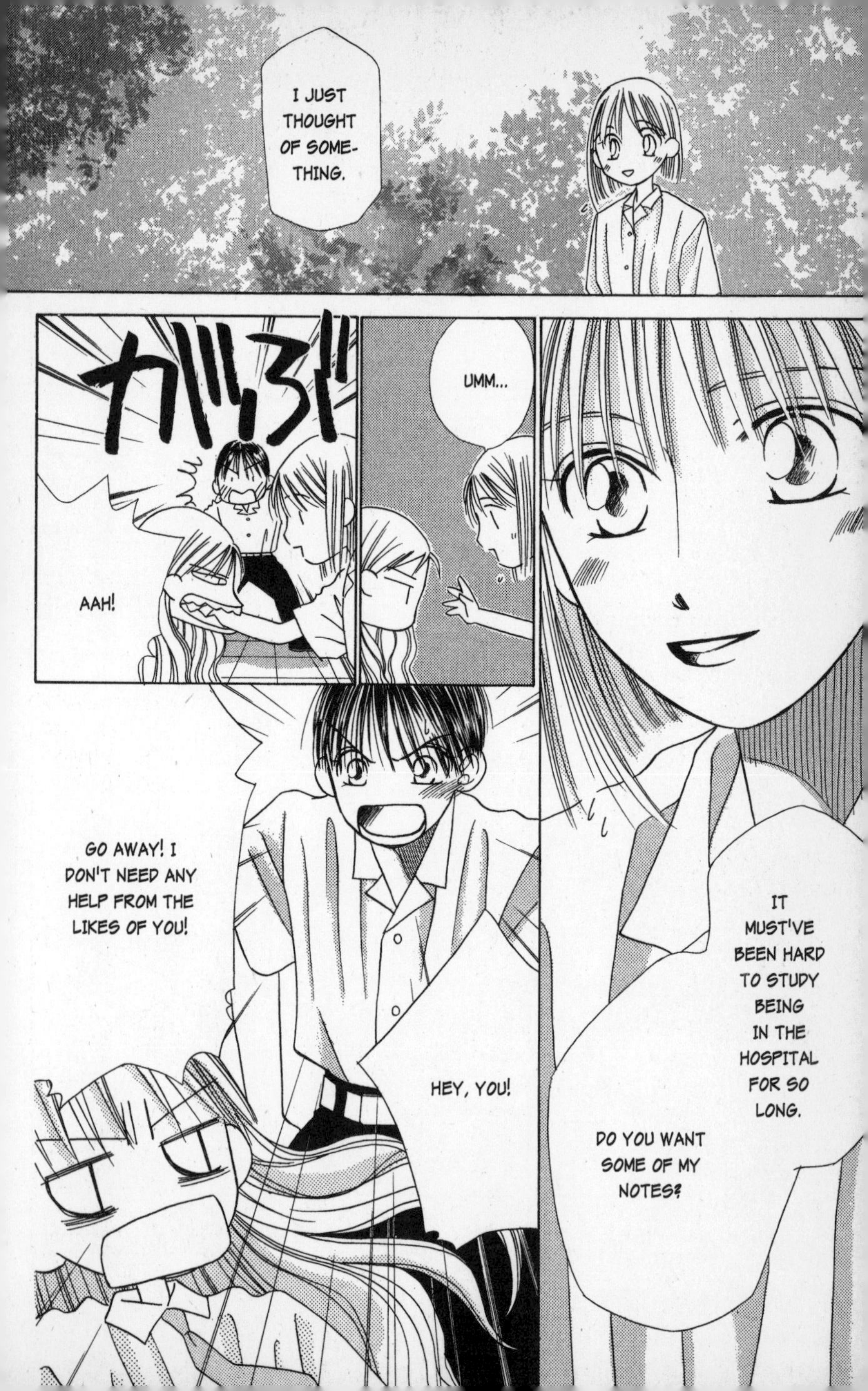
I JUST THOUGHT OF SOME-THING.
IT MUST'VE BEEN HARD TO STUDY BEING IN THE HOSPITAL FOR SO LONG.
DO YOU WANT SOME OF MY NOTES?
UMM...
ガバっ
AAH!
HEY, YOU!
GO AWAY! I DON'T NEED ANY HELP FROM THE LIKES OF YOU!

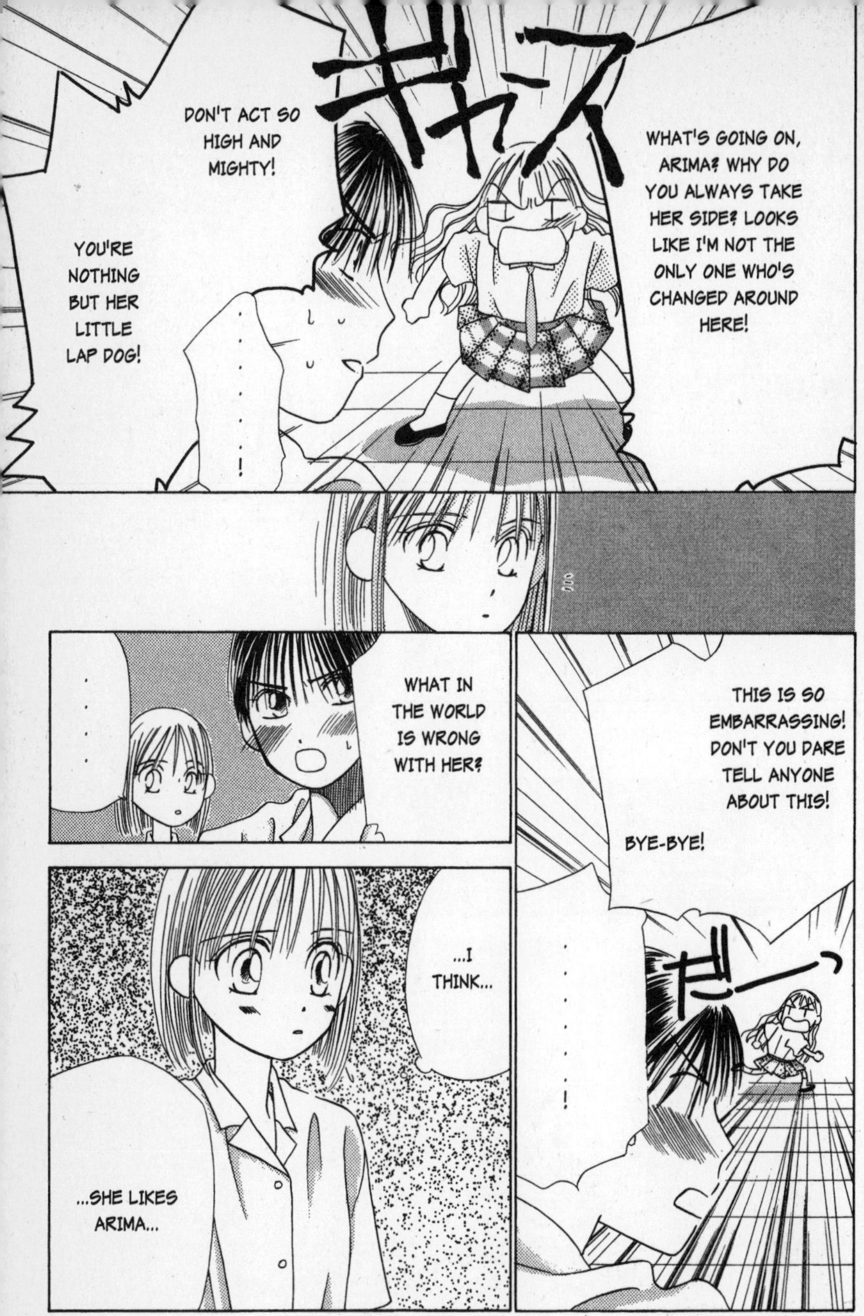
WHAT'S GOING ON, ARIMA? WHY DO YOU ALWAYS TAKE HER SIDE? LOOKS LIKE I'M NOT THE ONLY ONE WHO'S CHANGED AROUND HERE!
ギャース
DON'T ACT SO HIGH AND MIGHTY!
YOU'RE NOTHING BUT HER LITTLE LAP DOG!
......!
THIS IS SO EMBARRASSING! DON'T YOU DARE TELL ANYONE ABOUT THIS!
BYE-BYE!
だーっ
......!
WHAT IN THE WORLD IS WRONG WITH HER?
....
...I THINK...
...SHE LIKES ARIMA...

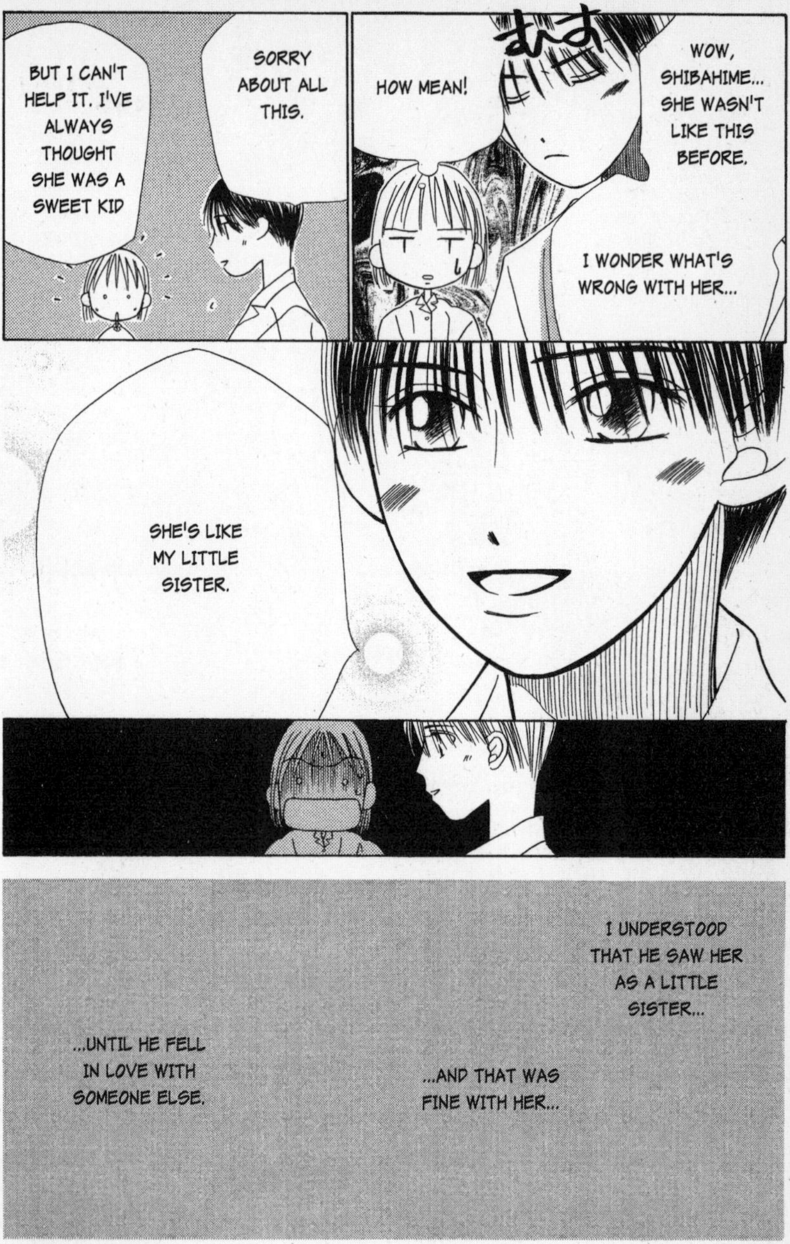
WOW, SHIBAHIME... SHE WASN'T LIKE THIS BEFORE.
HOW MEAN!
I WONDER WHAT'S WRONG WITH HER...
SORRY ABOUT ALL THIS.
BUT I CAN'T HELP IT. I'VE ALWAYS THOUGHT SHE WAS A SWEET KID
SHE'S LIKE MY LITTLE SISTER.
I UNDERSTOOD THAT HE SAW HER AS A LITTLE SISTER...
...AND THAT WAS FINE WITH HER...
...UNTIL HE FELL IN LOVE WITH SOMEONE ELSE.

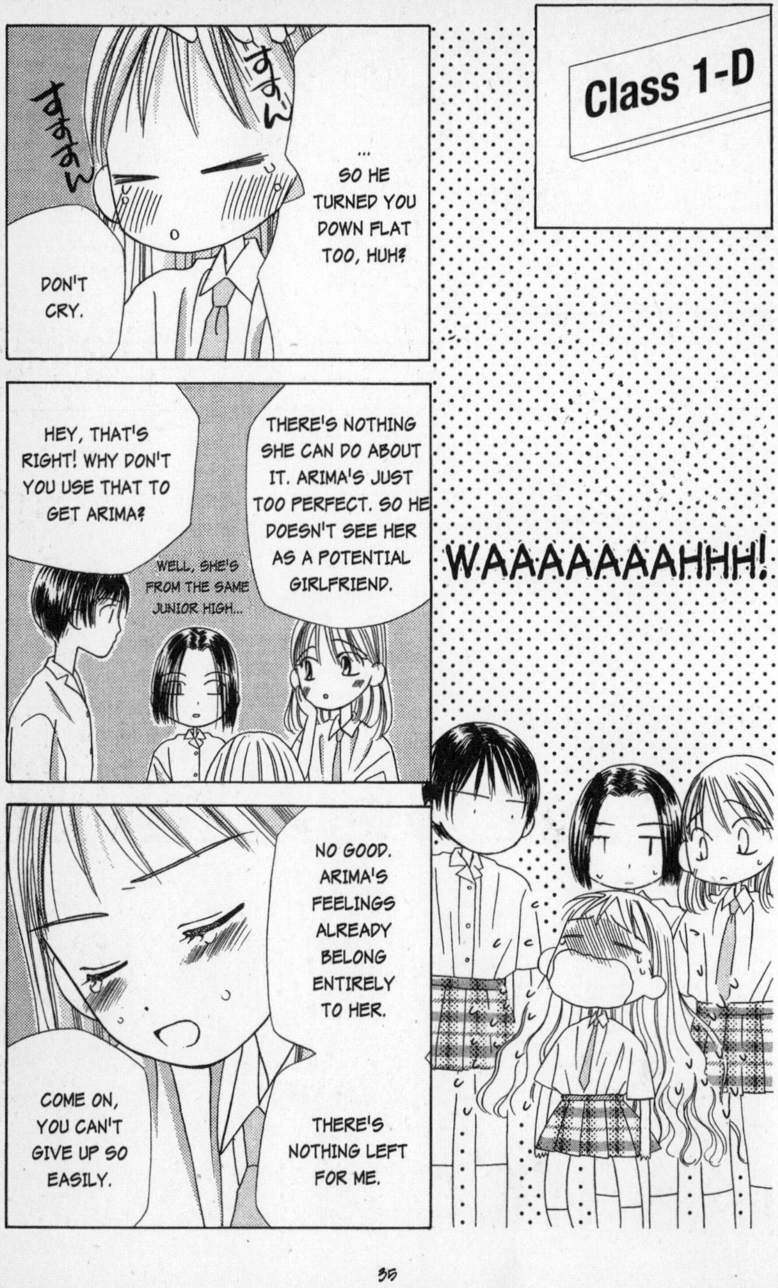
Class 1-D
WAAAAAAAHHH!
すすん
... SO HE TURNED YOU DOWN FLAT TOO, HUH?
すすすん
DON'T CRY.
THERE'S NOTHING SHE CAN DO ABOUT IT. ARIMA'S JUST TOO PERFECT. SO HE DOESN'T SEE HER AS A POTENTIAL GIRLFRIEND.
WELL, SHE'S FROM THE SAME JUNIOR HIGH...
HEY, THAT'S RIGHT! WHY DON'T YOU USE THAT TO GET ARIMA?
NO GOOD. ARIMA'S FEELINGS ALREADY BELONG ENTIRELY TO HER.
COME ON, YOU CAN'T GIVE UP SO EASILY.
THERE'S NOTHING LEFT FOR ME.

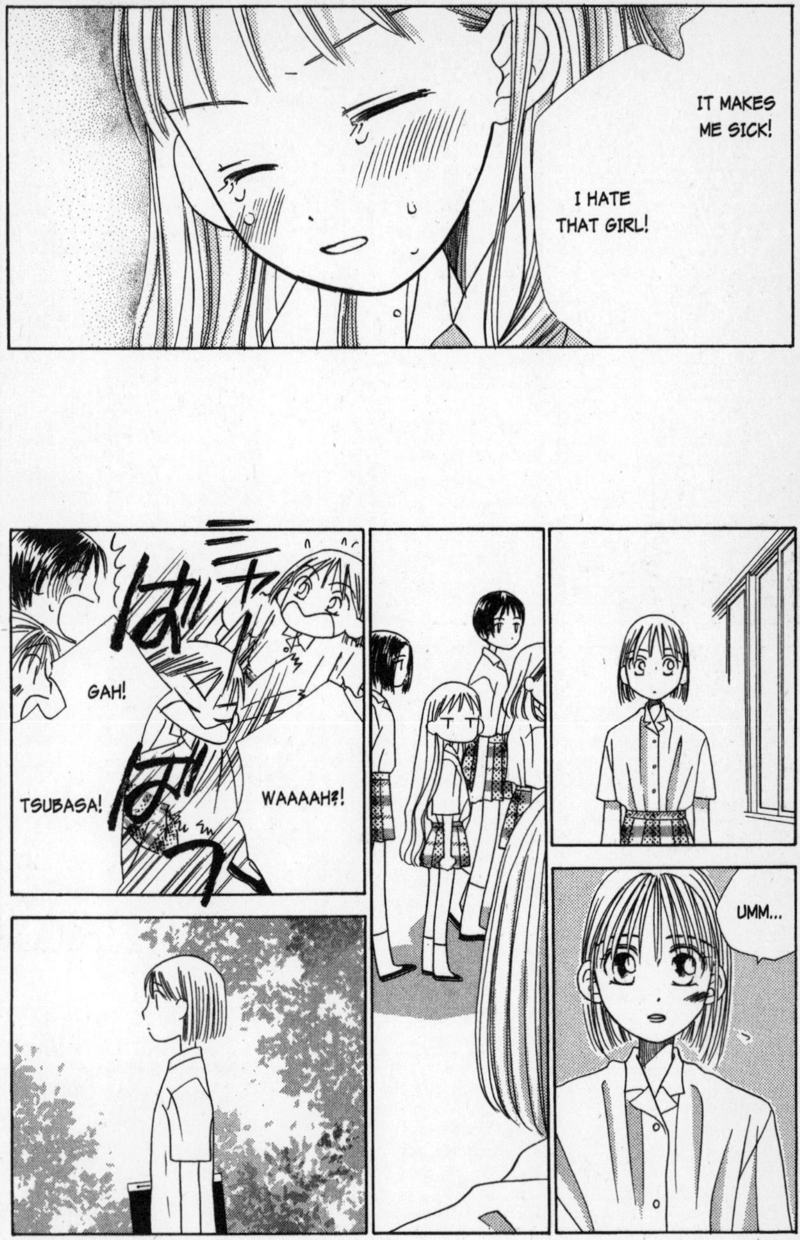
IT MAKES ME SICK!
I HATE THAT GIRL!
UMM...
WAAAAH?!
GAH!
TSUBASA!

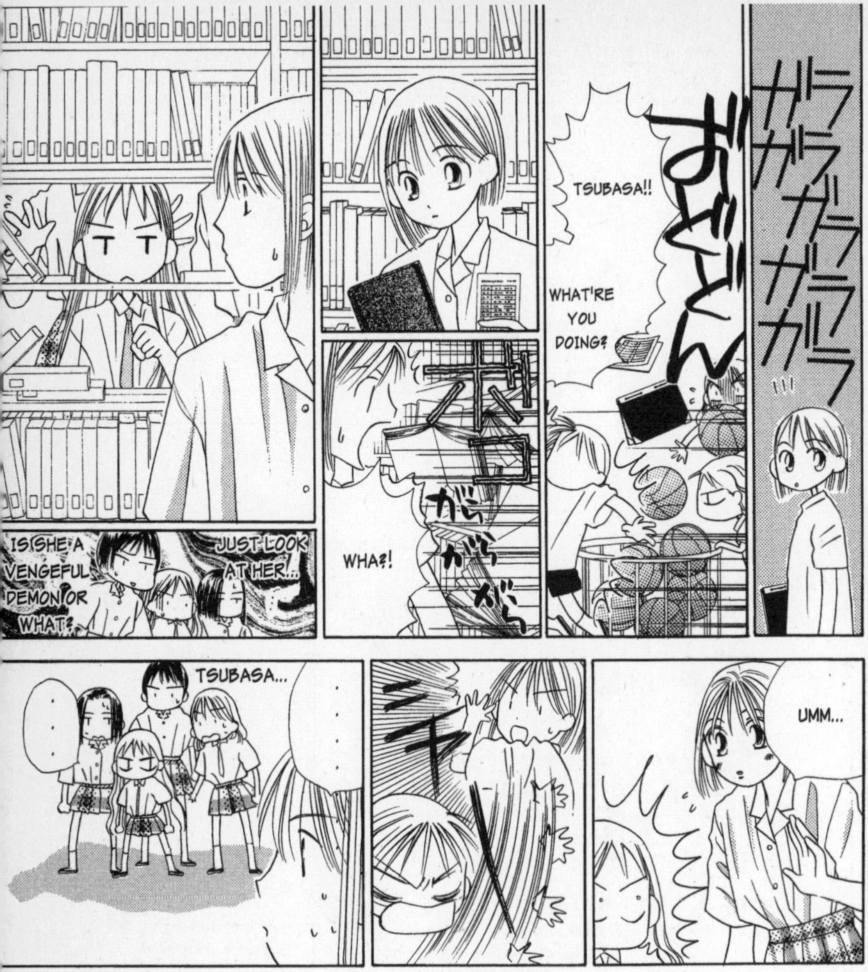
ガラガラガラガラ!!
TSUBASA!!
WHAT'RE YOU DOING?
WHA?!
JUST LOOK AT HER...
IS SHE A VENGEFUL DEMON OR WHAT?
UMM...
TSUBASA...

SHIBAHIME REALLY HATES ME...

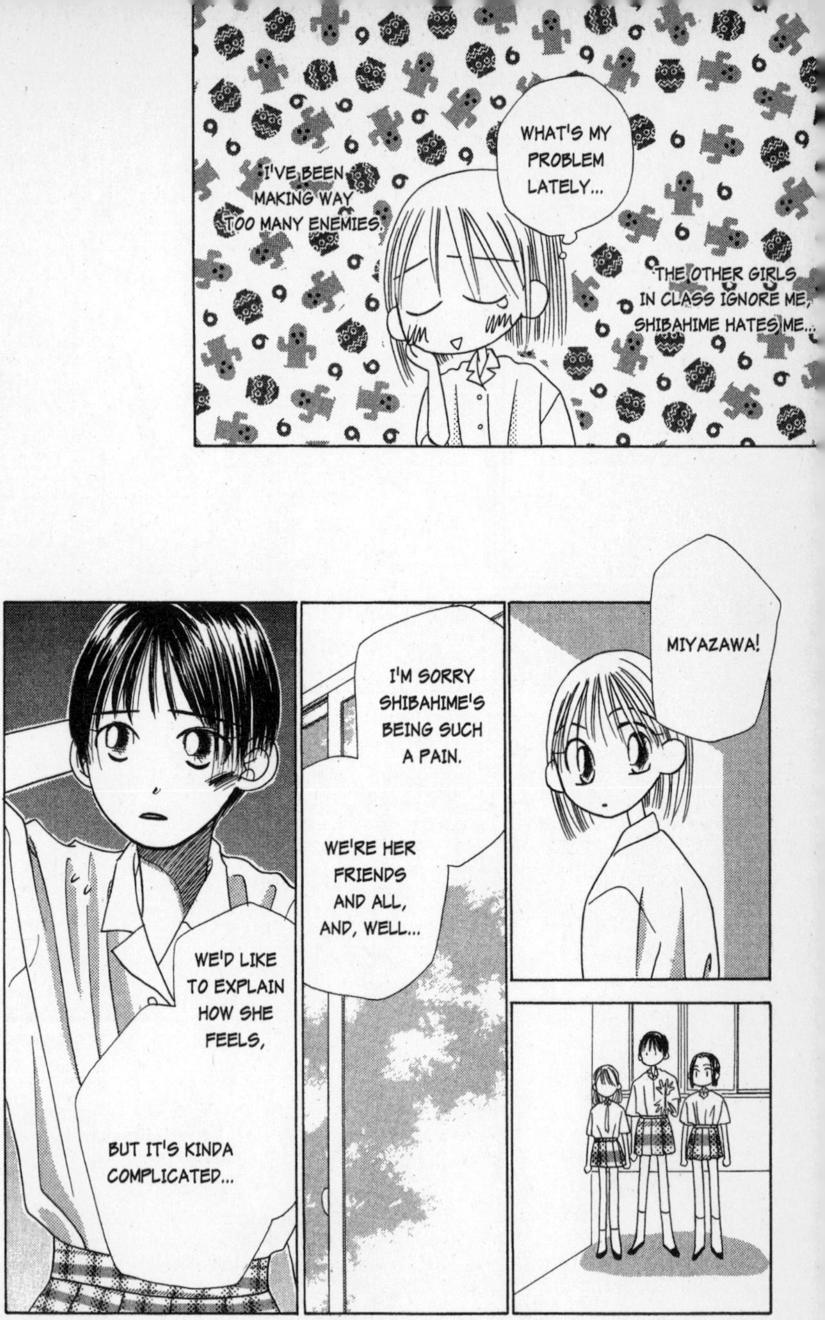
THE OTHER GIRLS IN CLASS IGNORE ME, SHIBAHIME HATES ME...
WHAT'S MY PROBLEM LATELY...
I'VE BEEN MAKING WAY TOO MANY ENEMIES.
MIYAZAWA!
I'M SORRY SHIBAHIME'S BEING SUCH A PAIN.
WE'RE HER FRIENDS AND ALL, AND, WELL...
WE'D LIKE TO EXPLAIN HOW SHE FEELS,
BUT IT'S KINDA COMPLICATED...

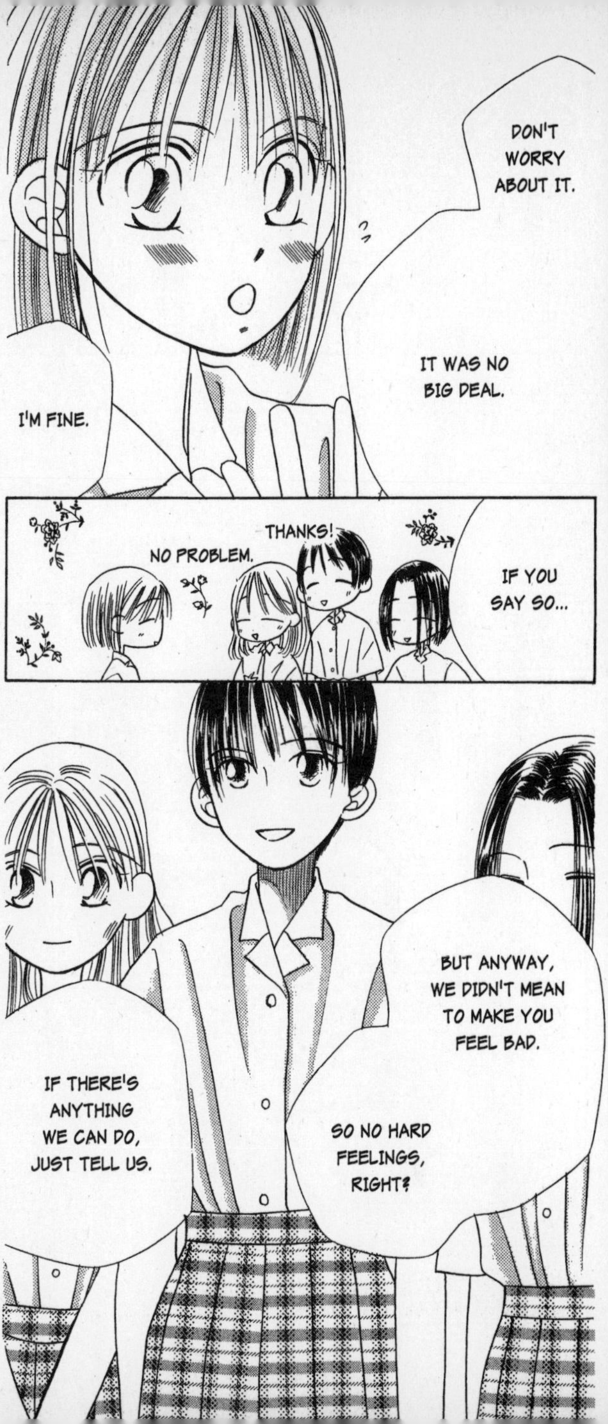
DON'T WORRY ABOUT IT.
IT WAS NO BIG DEAL.
I'M FINE.
IF YOU SAY SO...
THANKS!
NO PROBLEM.
BUT ANYWAY, WE DIDN'T MEAN TO MAKE YOU FEEL BAD.
SO NO HARD FEELINGS, RIGHT?
IF THERE'S ANYTHING WE CAN DO, JUST TELL US.

1

Hello. This is the 4th volume of Kare Kano, Tsuda's manga. I can't believe it got here so quickly! Wow! Well, the previous 3 covers used a flower theme. But this time I'm using fruits all of a sudden*... heh heh... I always thought I would use lily-of-the-valley for Tsukino and Kano's cover. But I couldn't find any good pictures to use. Sigh!

(*on the original Japanese covers)

These are... blueberries.

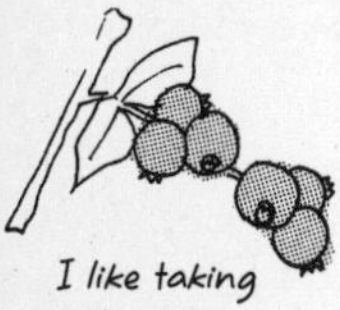

I like taking shortcuts.

Come on, get serious!

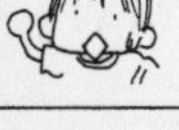

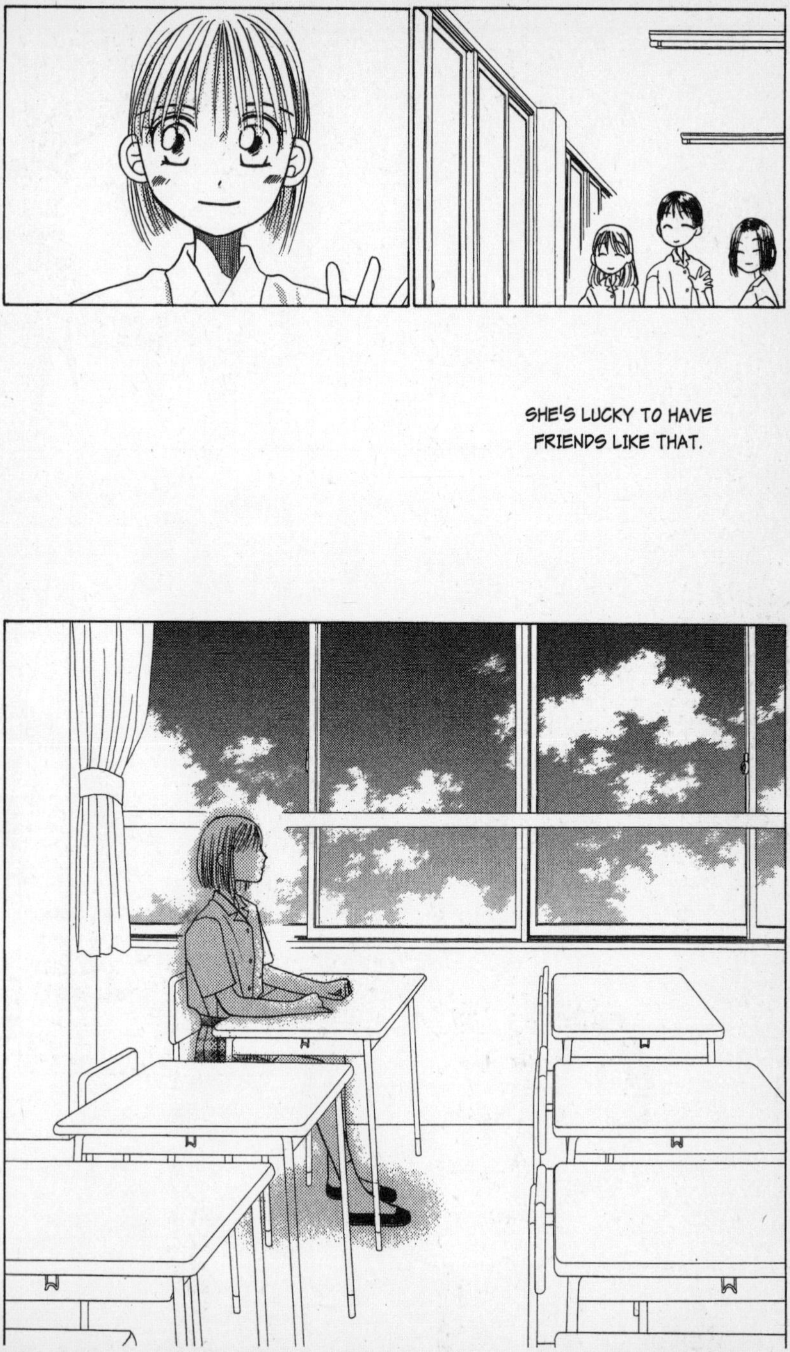
SHE'S LUCKY TO HAVE FRIENDS LIKE THAT.

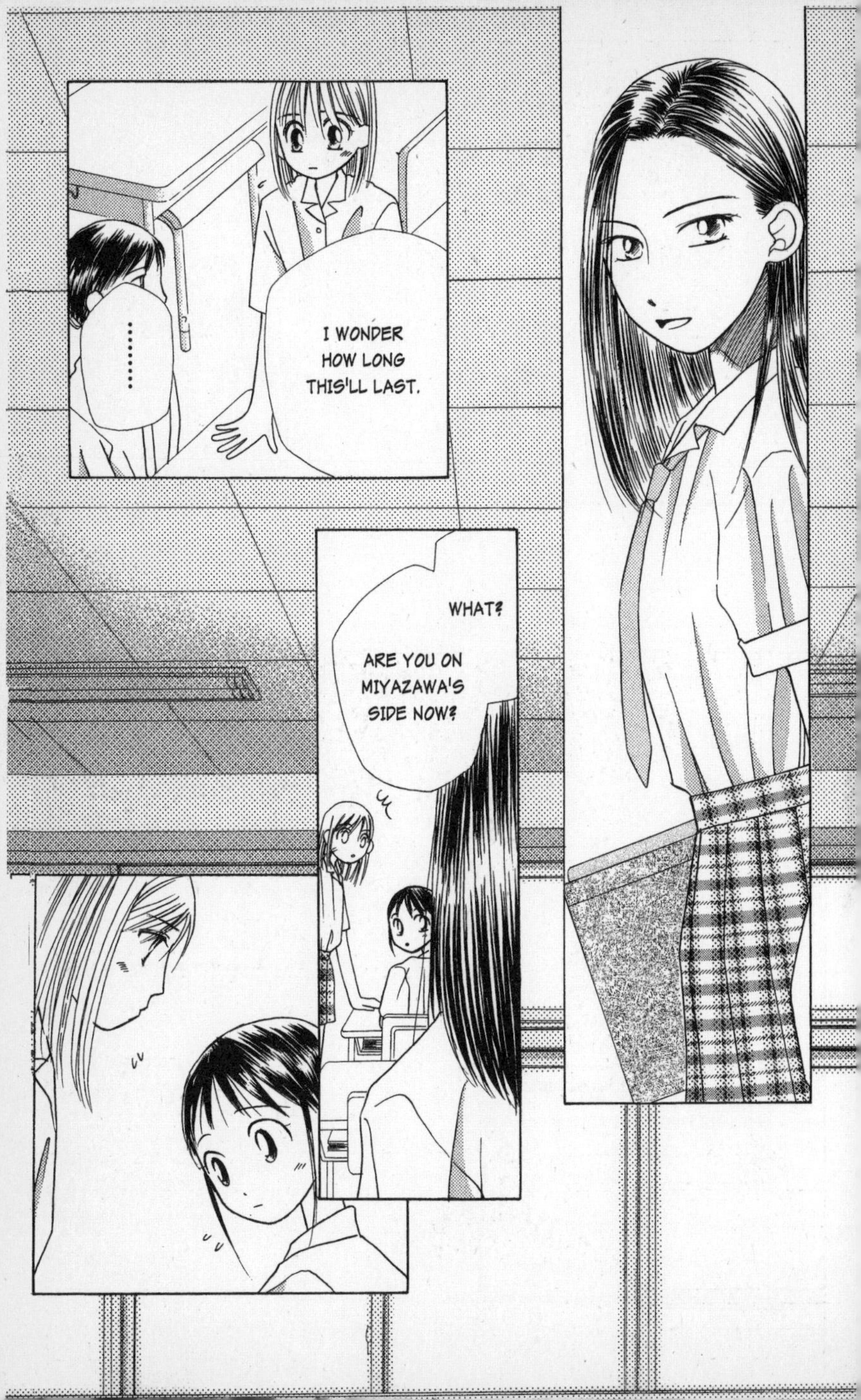
I WONDER HOW LONG THIS'LL LAST.
......
WHAT?
ARE YOU ON MIYAZAWA'S SIDE NOW?

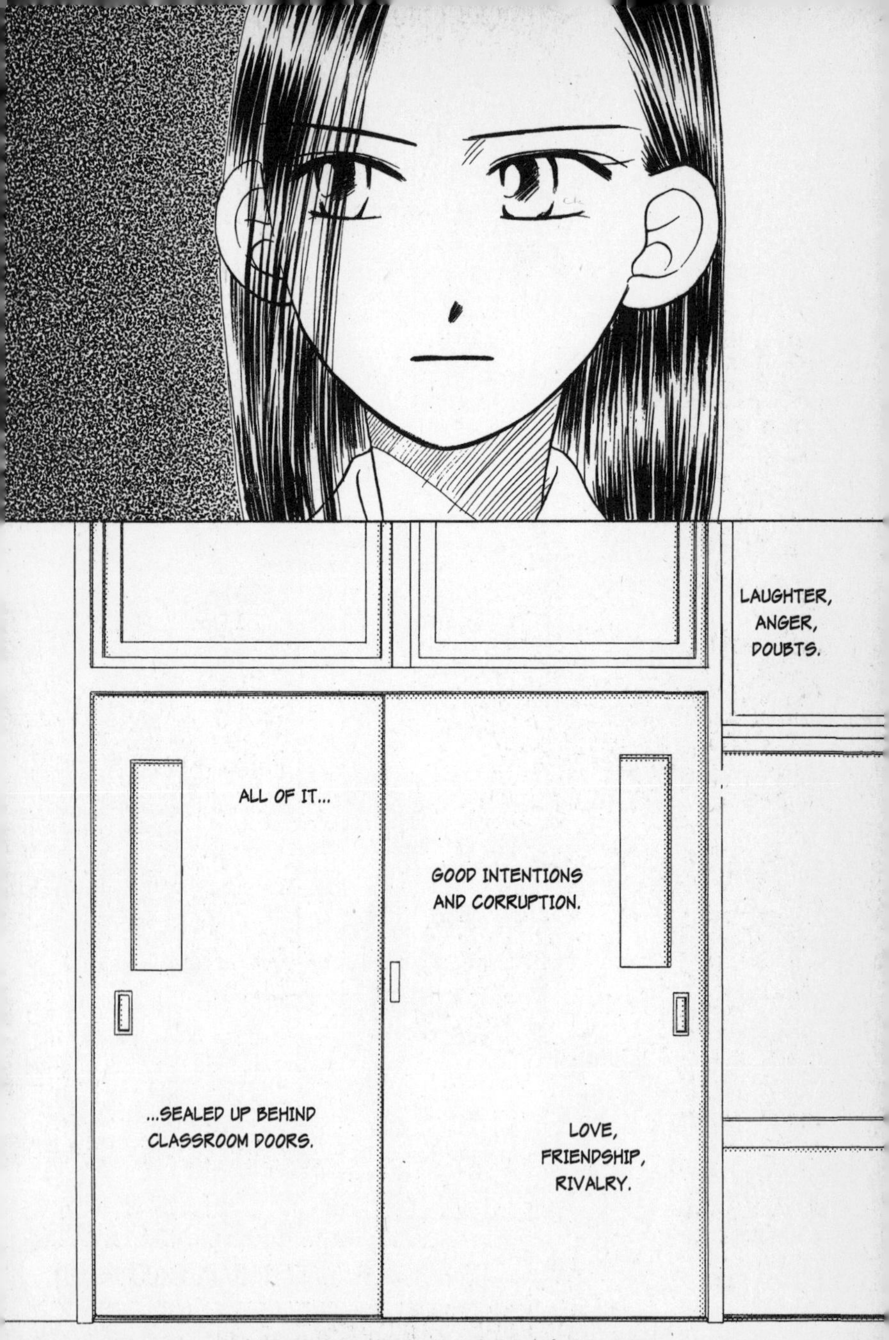
LAUGHTER, ANGER, DOUBTS.
GOOD INTENTIONS AND CORRUPTION.
LOVE, FRIENDSHIP, RIVALRY.
ALL OF IT...
...SEALED UP BEHIND CLASSROOM DOORS.

ACT 13 * FIGHTING WOMAN (2)-THE END

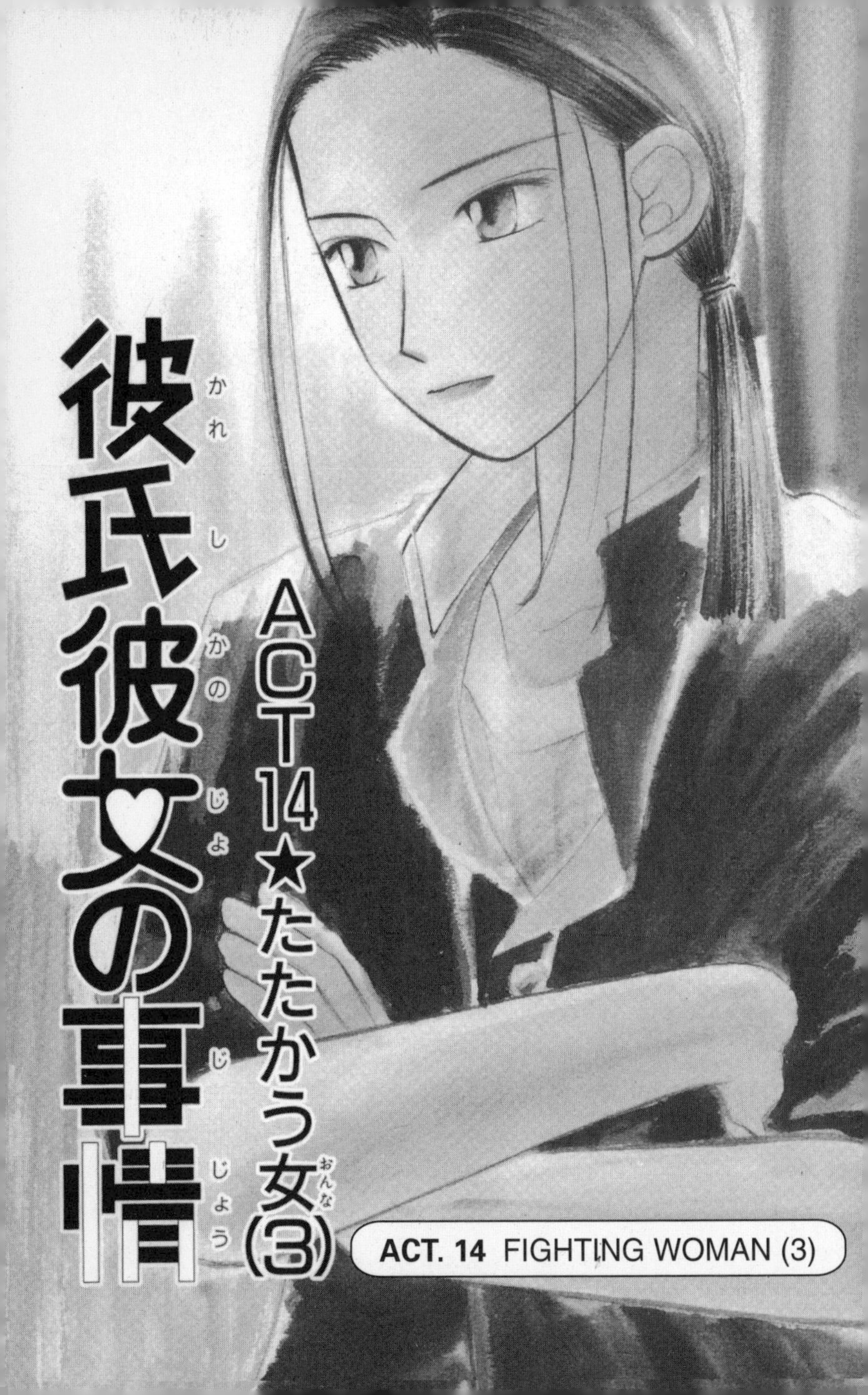
彼氏彼女の事情
ACT14★たたかう女(3)
ACT. 14 FIGHTING WOMAN (3)

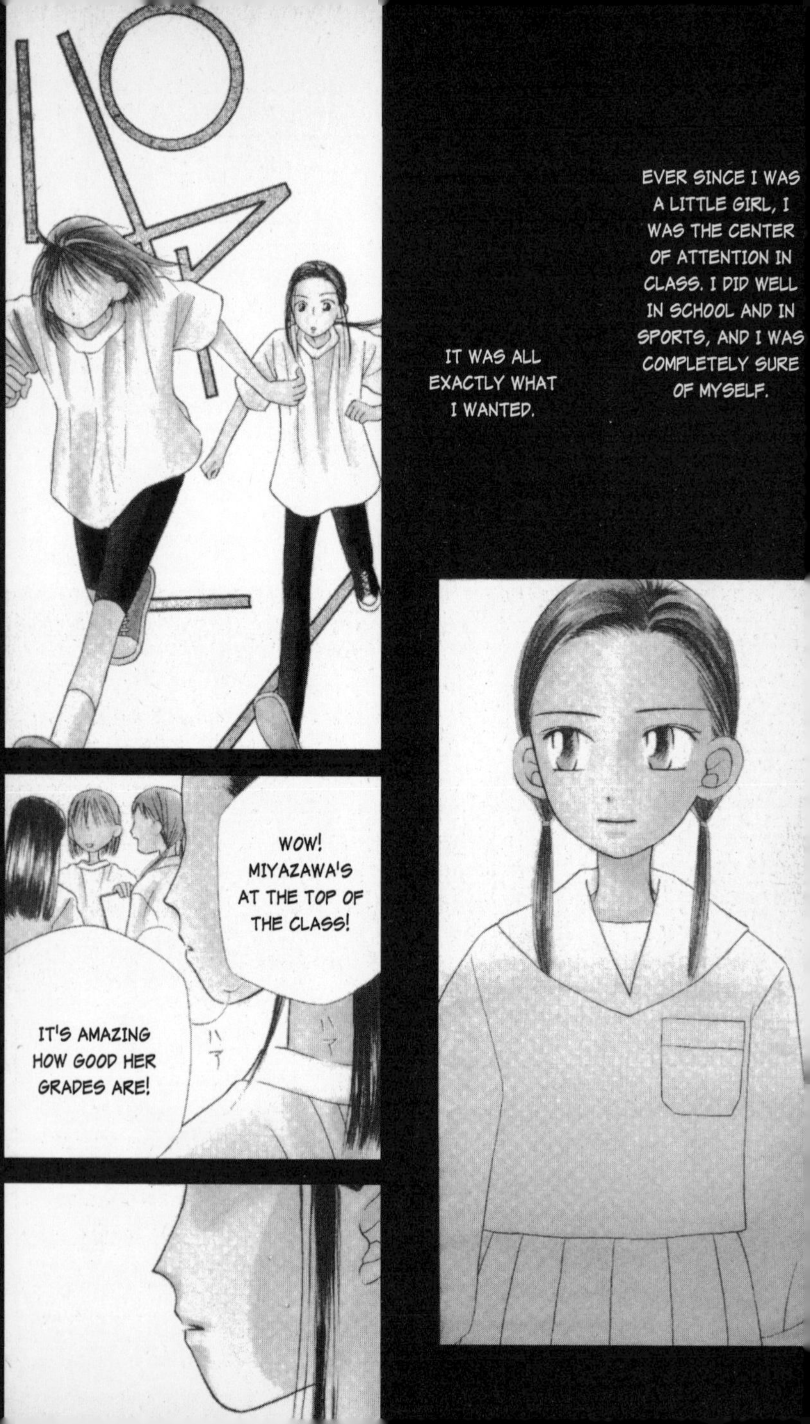
EVER SINCE I WAS A LITTLE GIRL, I WAS THE CENTER OF ATTENTION IN CLASS. I DID WELL IN SCHOOL AND IN SPORTS, AND I WAS COMPLETELY SURE OF MYSELF.
IT WAS ALL EXACTLY WHAT I WANTED.
WOW! MIYAZAWA'S AT THE TOP OF THE CLASS!
IT'S AMAZING HOW GOOD HER GRADES ARE!

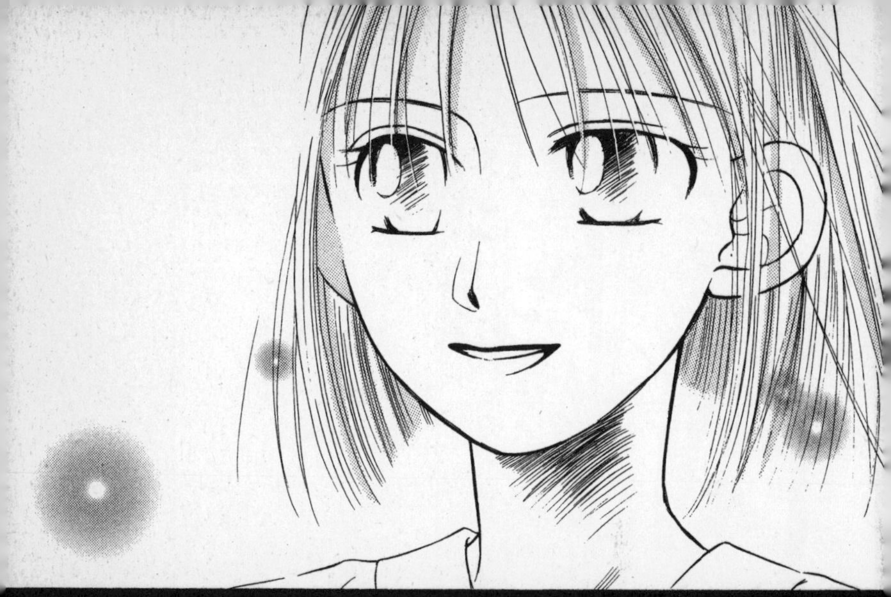

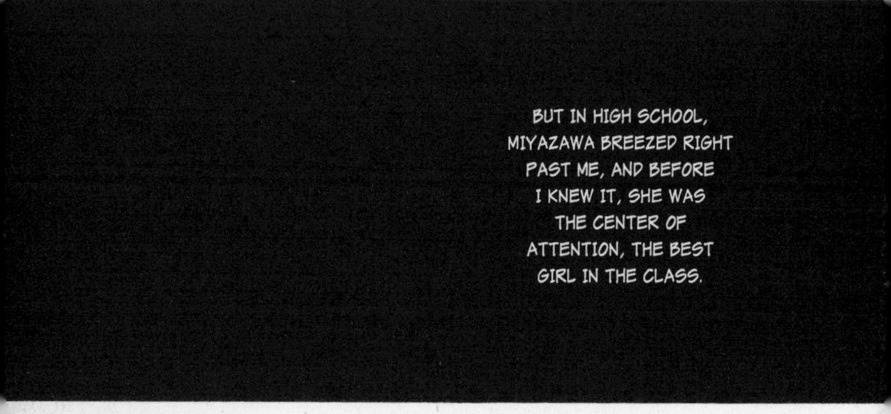
BUT IN HIGH SCHOOL, MIYAZAWA BREEZED RIGHT PAST ME, AND BEFORE I KNEW IT, SHE WAS THE CENTER OF ATTENTION, THE BEST GIRL IN THE CLASS.

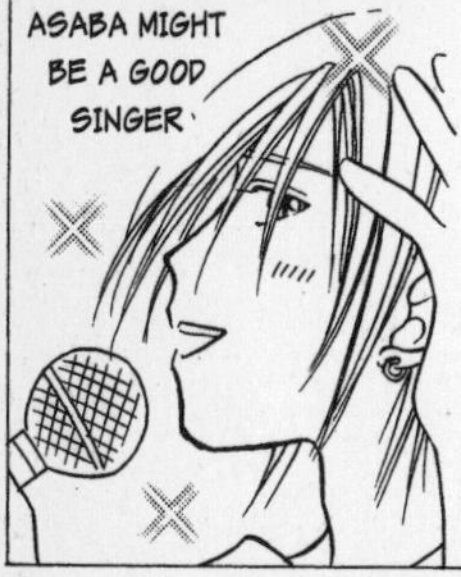
ASABA MIGHT BE A GOOD SINGER

ABOUT MUSIC

I MENTIONED OPERA AND MUSICALS IN THE MANGA, AND I LIKE THEM, BUT I ALSO LISTEN TO REGULAR POP MUSIC. I'VE BEEN GETTING INTO ELECTRONIC GROOVE LATELY. TO GIVE AN EXAMPLE, SHANGRI-LA'S ALBUM "UFO" IS FUN... PARTICULARLY, "IT'S THE BEACH! ELECTRIC GROOVE."

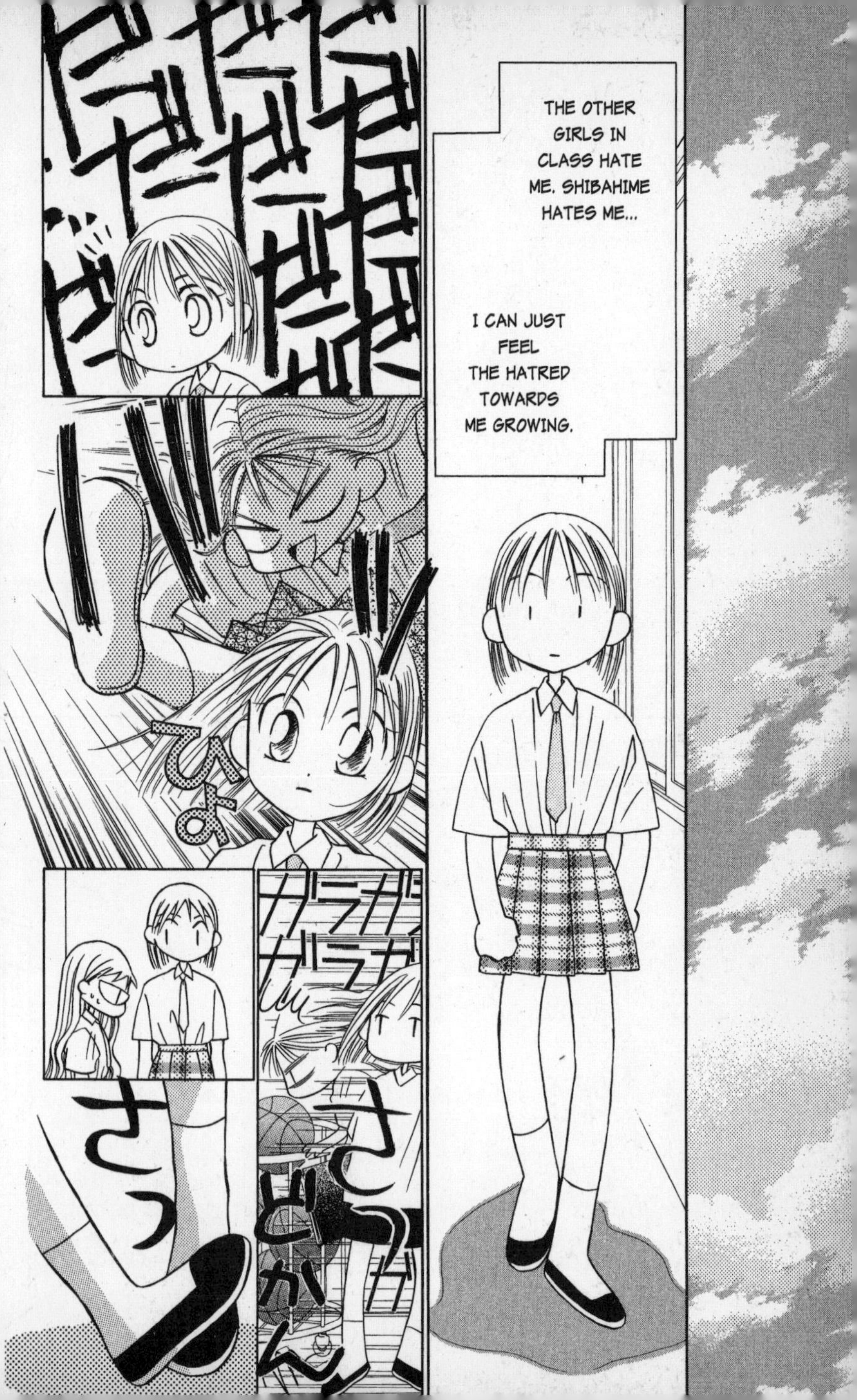
THE OTHER GIRLS IN CLASS HATE ME. SHIBAHIME HATES ME...
I CAN JUST FEEL THE HATRED TOWARDS ME GROWING.

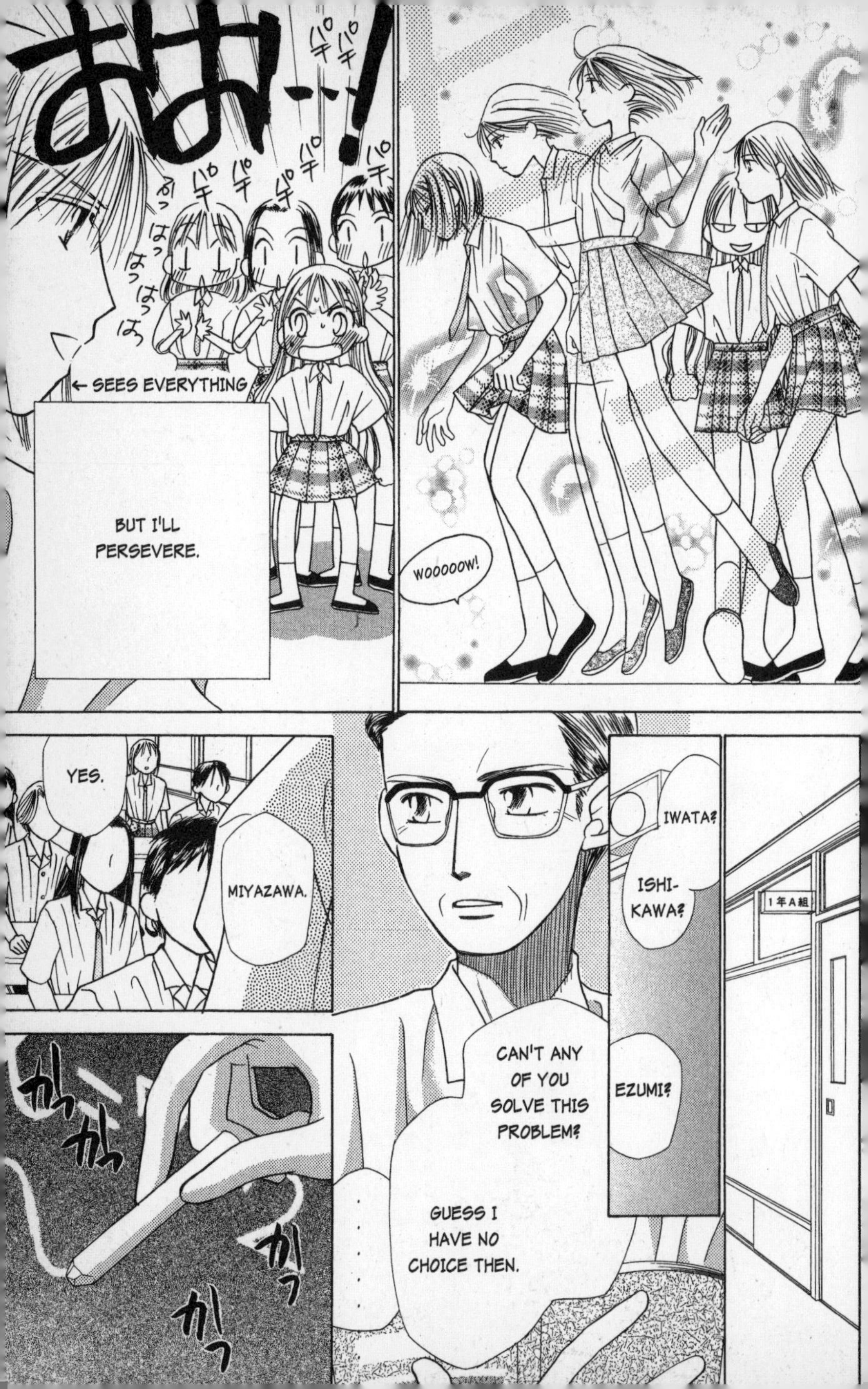

WOOOOOW!
おお〜!
パチパチ
パチパチ
パチパチ
はっはっはっはっ
← SEES EVERYTHING
BUT I'LL PERSEVERE.
1年A組
IWATA?
ISHI-KAWA?
EZUMI?
CAN'T ANY OF YOU SOLVE THIS PROBLEM?
GUESS I HAVE NO CHOICE THEN.
MIYAZAWA.
YES.
カッカッ
カッ
カッ

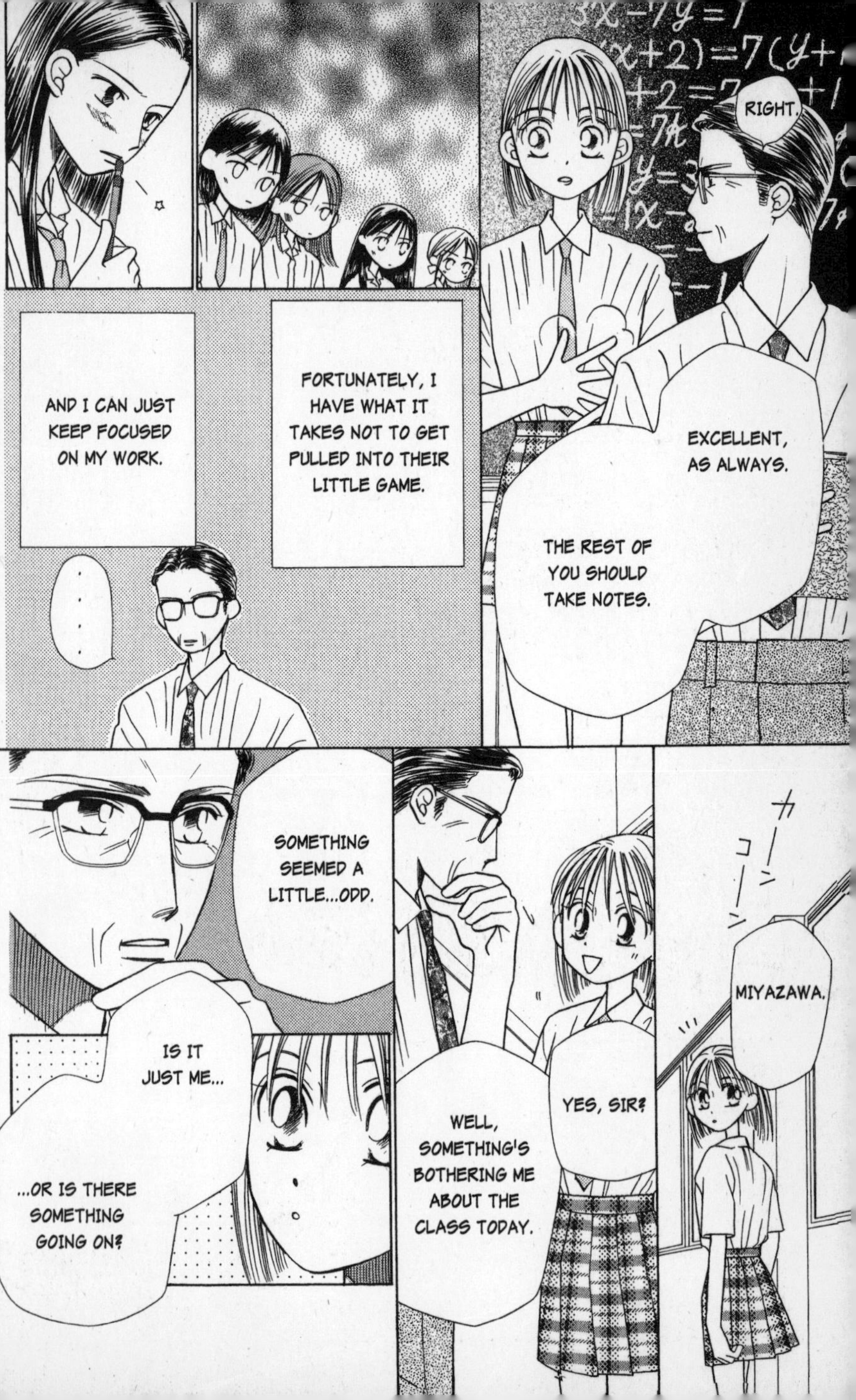

RIGHT.
EXCELLENT, AS ALWAYS.
THE REST OF YOU SHOULD TAKE NOTES.
FORTUNATELY, I HAVE WHAT IT TAKES NOT TO GET PULLED INTO THEIR LITTLE GAME.
AND I CAN JUST KEEP FOCUSED ON MY WORK.
....
カーンコーン
MIYAZAWA.
YES, SIR?
WELL, SOMETHING'S BOTHERING ME ABOUT THE CLASS TODAY.
SOMETHING SEEMED A LITTLE...ODD.
IS IT JUST ME...
...OR IS THERE SOMETHING GOING ON?

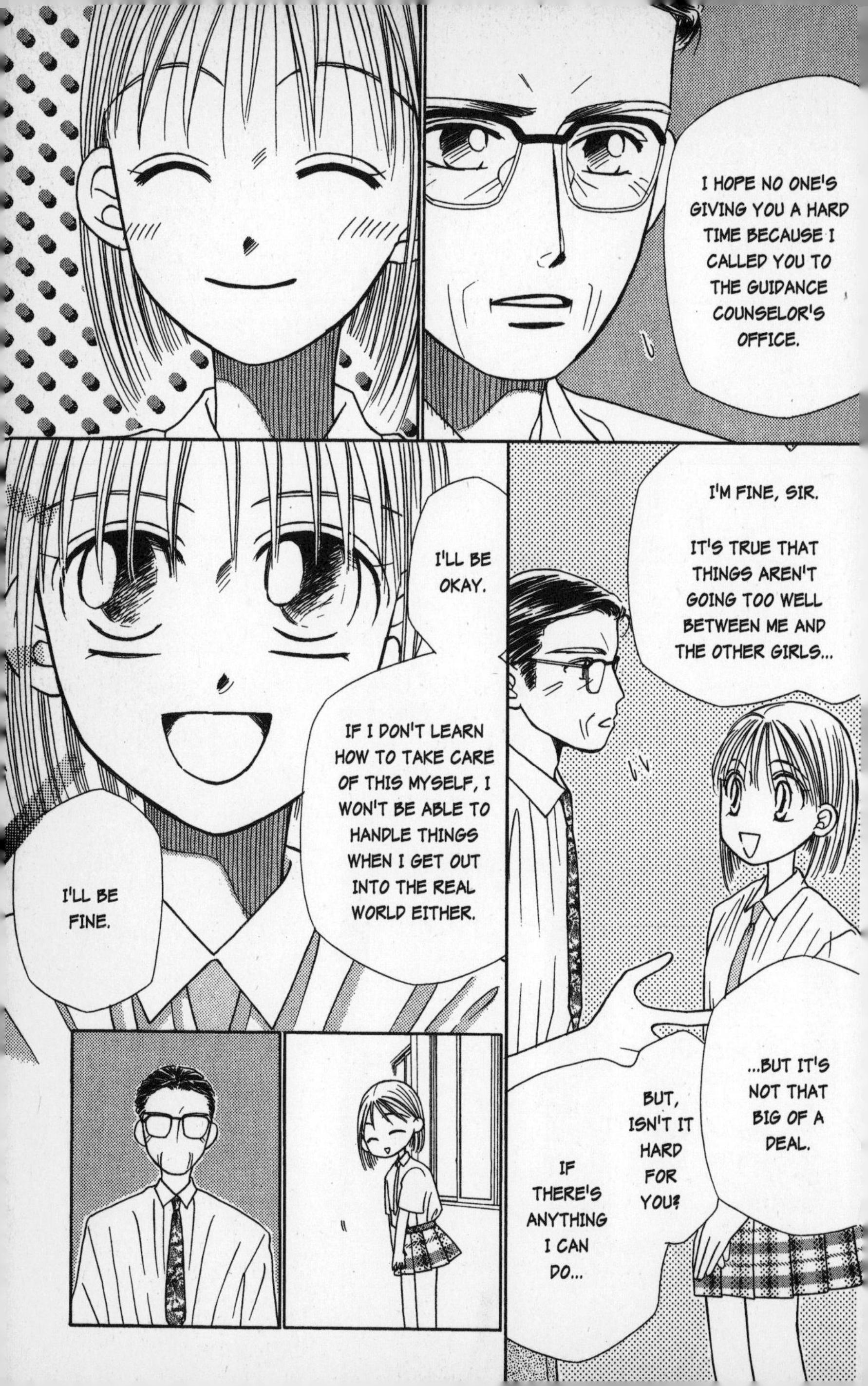
I HOPE NO ONE'S GIVING YOU A HARD TIME BECAUSE I CALLED YOU TO THE GUIDANCE COUNSELOR'S OFFICE.
I'M FINE, SIR.
IT'S TRUE THAT THINGS AREN'T GOING TOO WELL BETWEEN ME AND THE OTHER GIRLS...
...BUT IT'S NOT THAT BIG OF A DEAL.
BUT, ISN'T IT HARD FOR YOU?
IF THERE'S ANYTHING I CAN DO...
I'LL BE OKAY.
IF I DON'T LEARN HOW TO TAKE CARE OF THIS MYSELF, I WON'T BE ABLE TO HANDLE THINGS WHEN I GET OUT INTO THE REAL WORLD EITHER.
I'LL BE FINE.

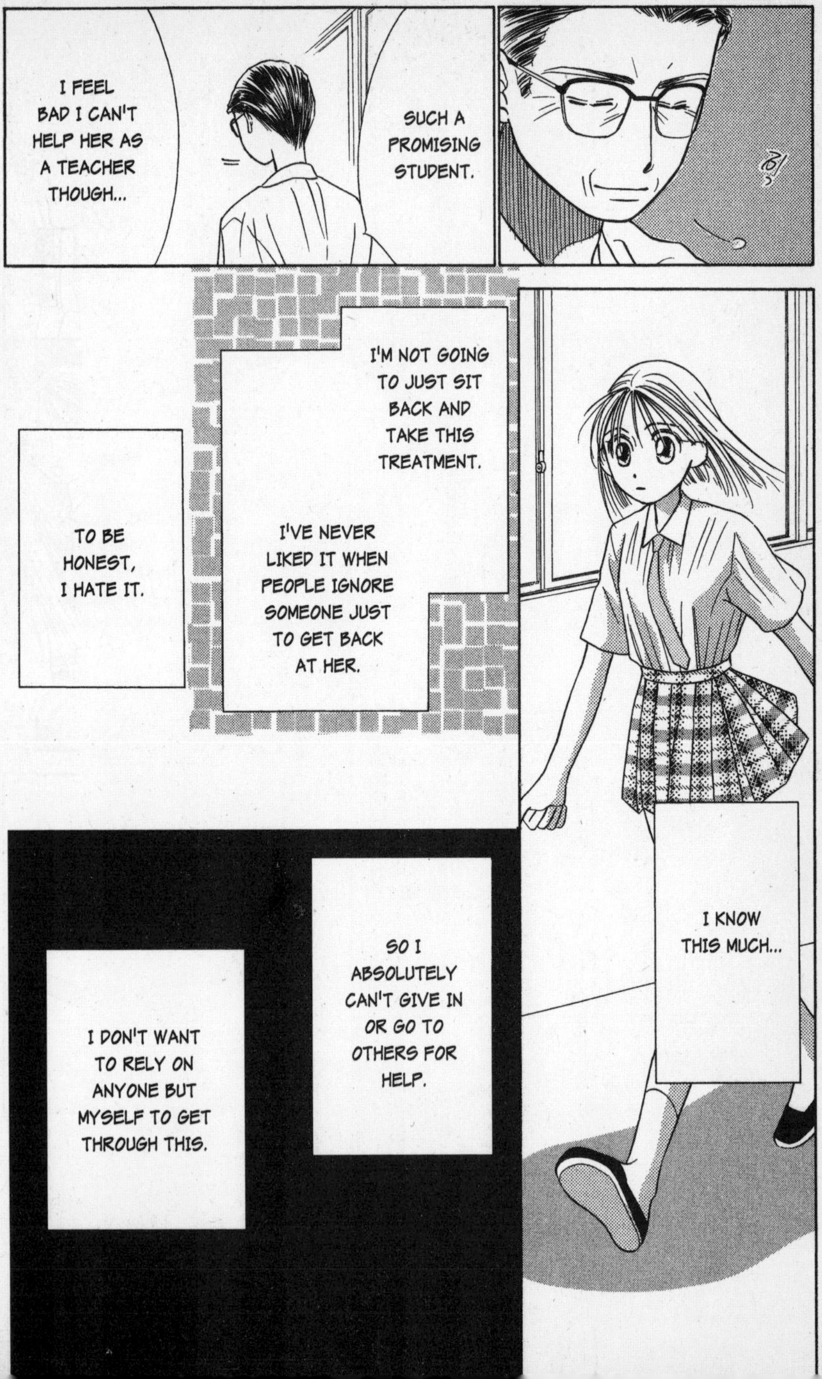
SUCH A PROMISING STUDENT.
I FEEL BAD I CAN'T HELP HER AS A TEACHER THOUGH...
I KNOW THIS MUCH...
I'M NOT GOING TO JUST SIT BACK AND TAKE THIS TREATMENT.
I'VE NEVER LIKED IT WHEN PEOPLE IGNORE SOMEONE JUST TO GET BACK AT HER.
TO BE HONEST, I HATE IT.
SO I ABSOLUTELY CAN'T GIVE IN OR GO TO OTHERS FOR HELP.
I DON'T WANT TO RELY ON ANYONE BUT MYSELF TO GET THROUGH THIS.

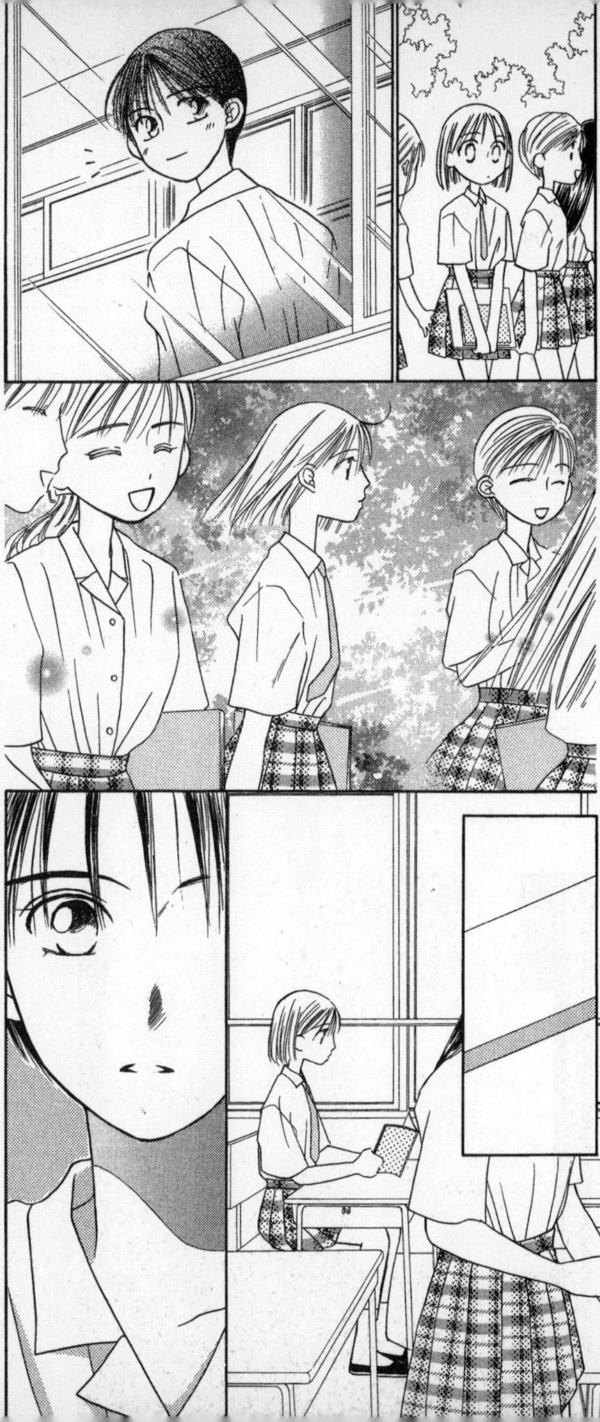

2

Morning
Routines

* Watering
the plants

* Radio exercises

Her joints are
crying out.

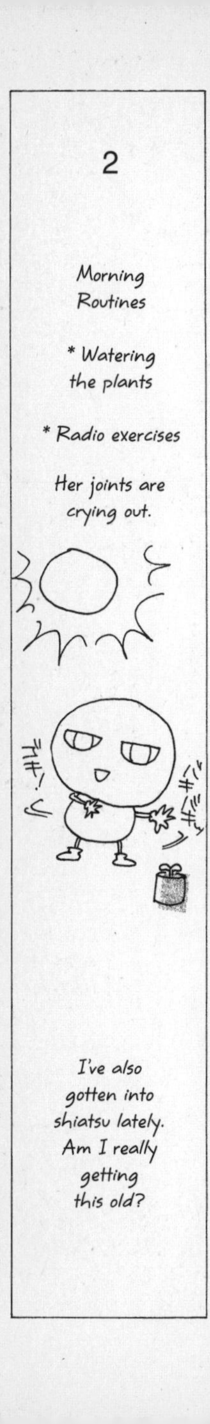

I've also
gotten into
shiatsu lately.
Am I really
getting
this old?

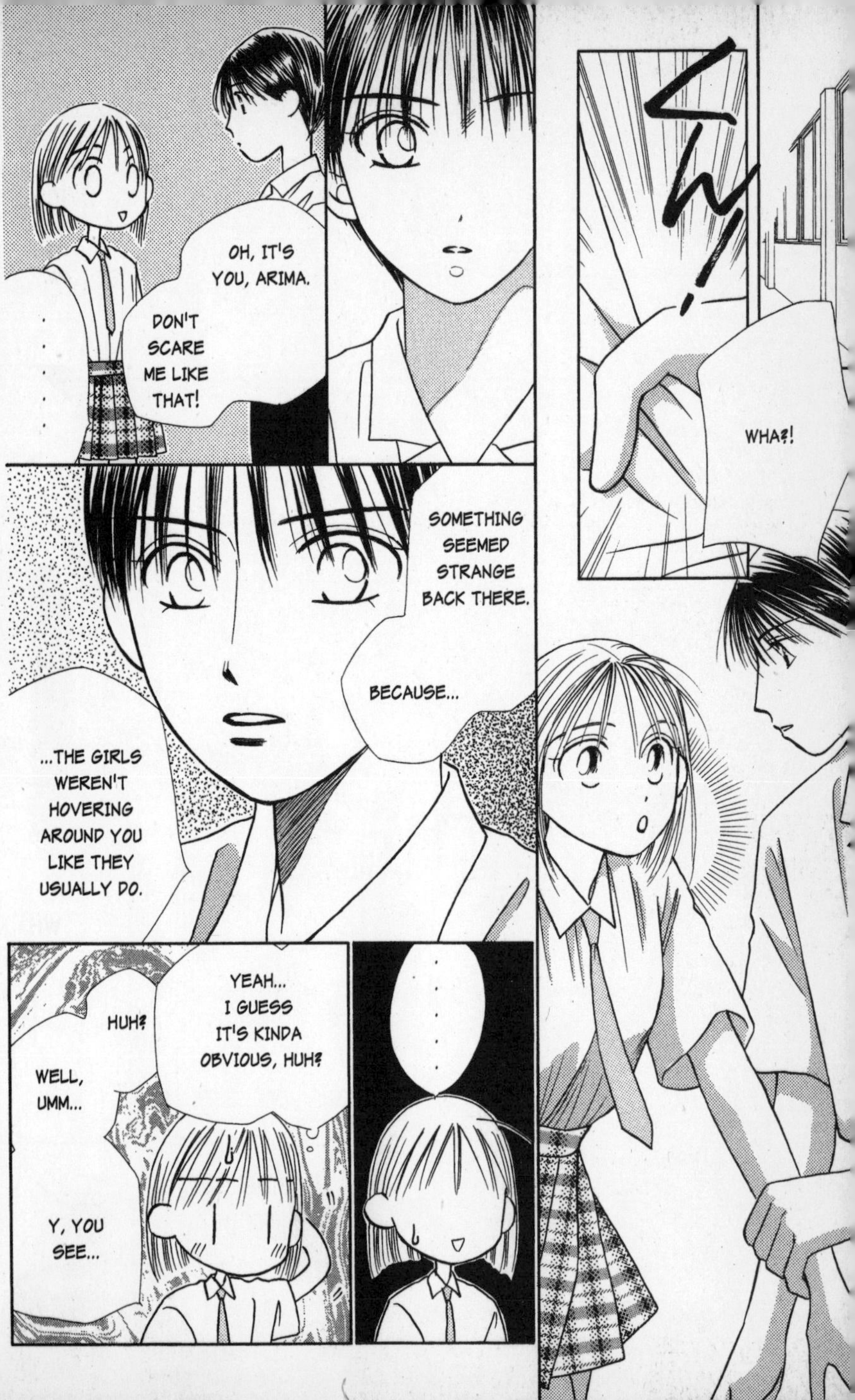
くん!
WHA?!
OH, IT'S YOU, ARIMA.
DON'T SCARE ME LIKE THAT!
.....
SOMETHING SEEMED STRANGE BACK THERE.
BECAUSE...
...THE GIRLS WEREN'T HOVERING AROUND YOU LIKE THEY USUALLY DO.
......
YEAH... I GUESS IT'S KINDA OBVIOUS, HUH?
HUH?
WELL, UMM...
Y, YOU SEE...

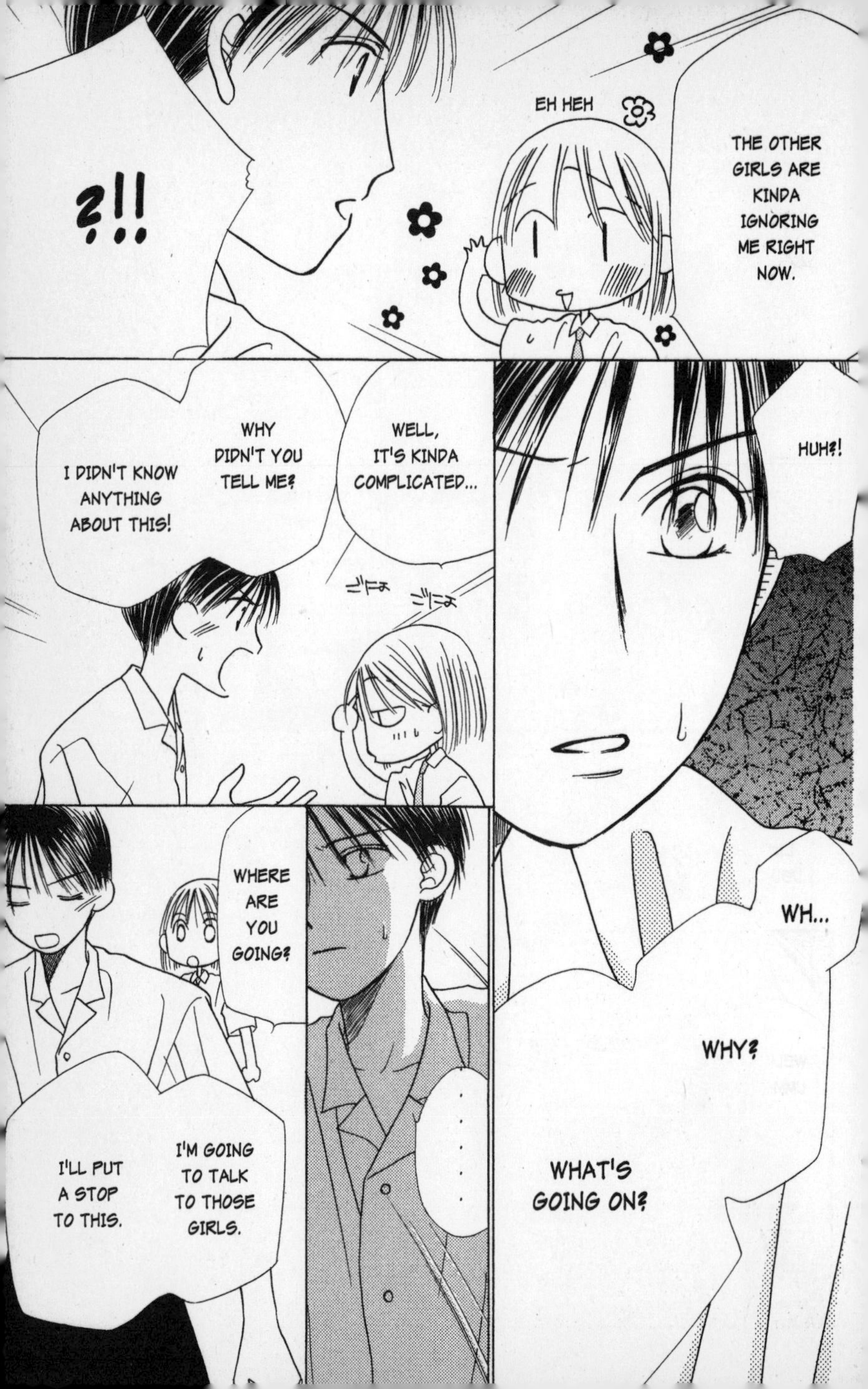
THE OTHER GIRLS ARE KINDA IGNORING ME RIGHT NOW.
EH HEH
?!!
HUH?!
WH...
WHY?
WHAT'S GOING ON?
WELL, IT'S KINDA COMPLICATED...
WHY DIDN'T YOU TELL ME?
I DIDN'T KNOW ANYTHING ABOUT THIS!
ごにょ
ごにょ
......
WHERE ARE YOU GOING?
I'M GOING TO TALK TO THOSE GIRLS.
I'LL PUT A STOP TO THIS.

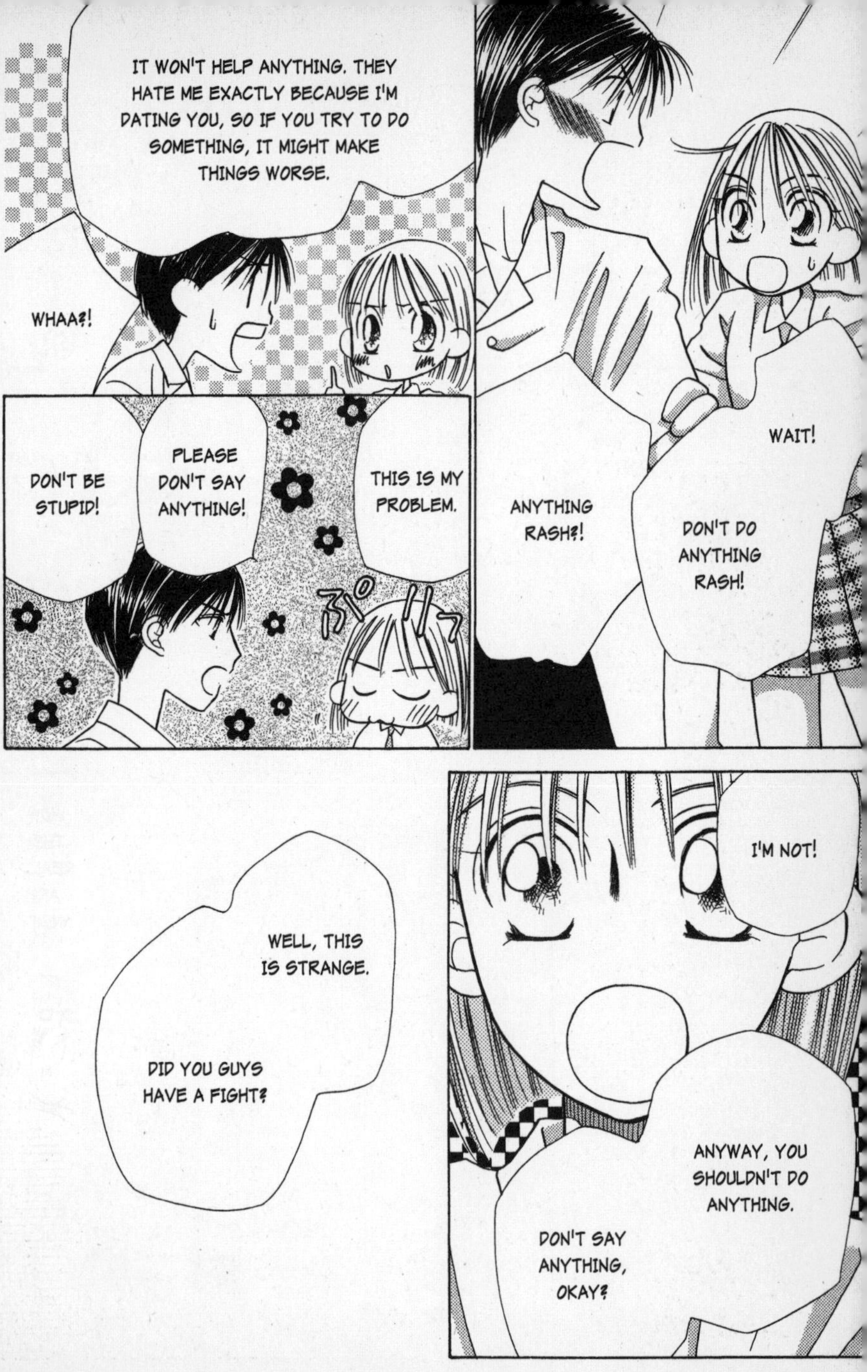

WAIT!
DON'T DO ANYTHING RASH!
ANYTHING RASH?!
IT WON'T HELP ANYTHING. THEY HATE ME EXACTLY BECAUSE I'M DATING YOU, SO IF YOU TRY TO DO SOMETHING, IT MIGHT MAKE THINGS WORSE.
WHAA?!
THIS IS MY PROBLEM.
PLEASE DON'T SAY ANYTHING!
ぷいっ
DON'T BE STUPID!
I'M NOT!
ANYWAY, YOU SHOULDN'T DO ANYTHING.
DON'T SAY ANYTHING, OKAY?
WELL, THIS IS STRANGE.
DID YOU GUYS HAVE A FIGHT?

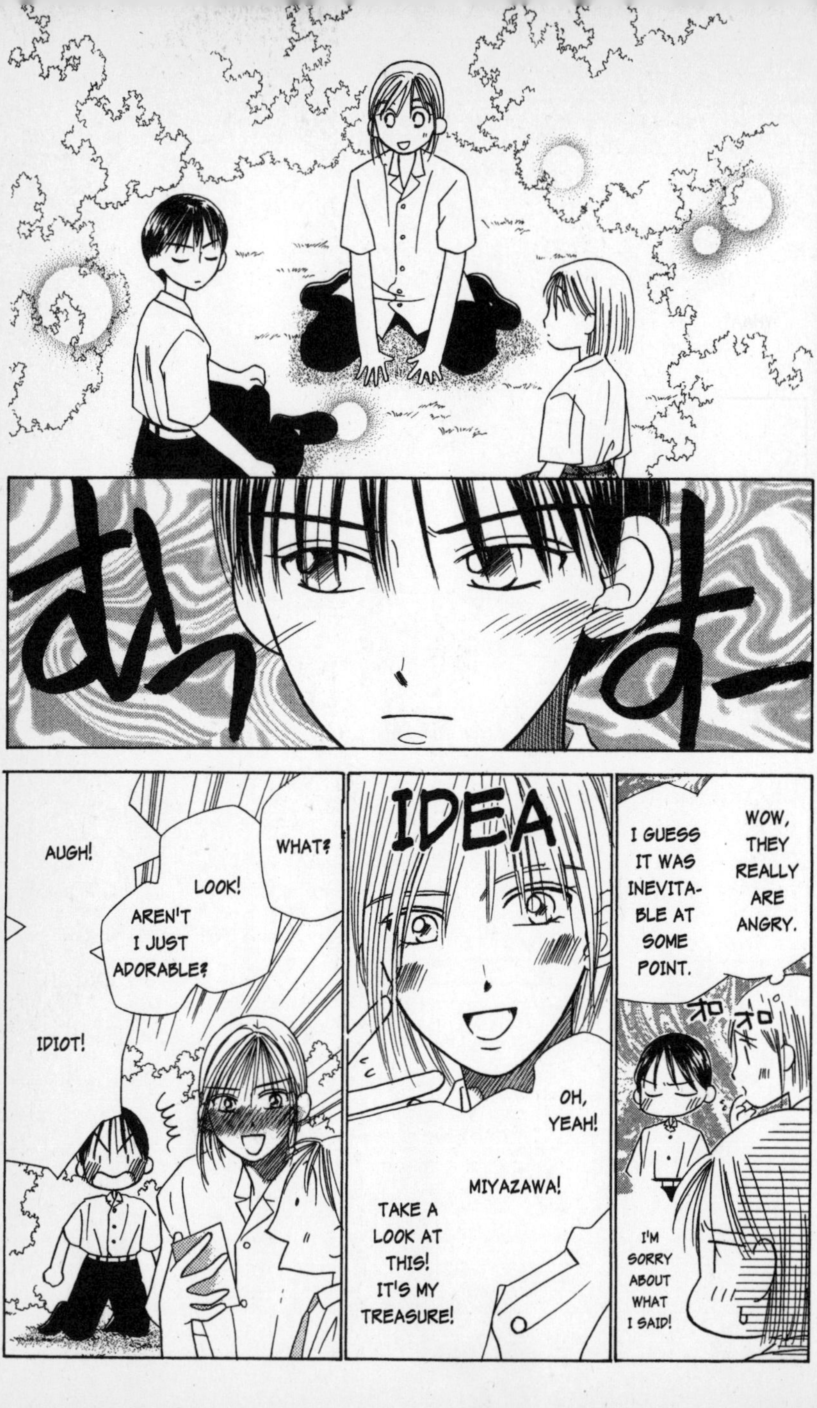
むっすー
WOW, THEY REALLY ARE ANGRY.
I GUESS IT WAS INEVITABLE AT SOME POINT.
オロオロ
I'M SORRY ABOUT WHAT I SAID!
IDEA
OH, YEAH!
MIYAZAWA!
TAKE A LOOK AT THIS! IT'S MY TREASURE!
WHAT?
LOOK!
AREN'T I JUST ADORABLE?
AUGH!
IDIOT!

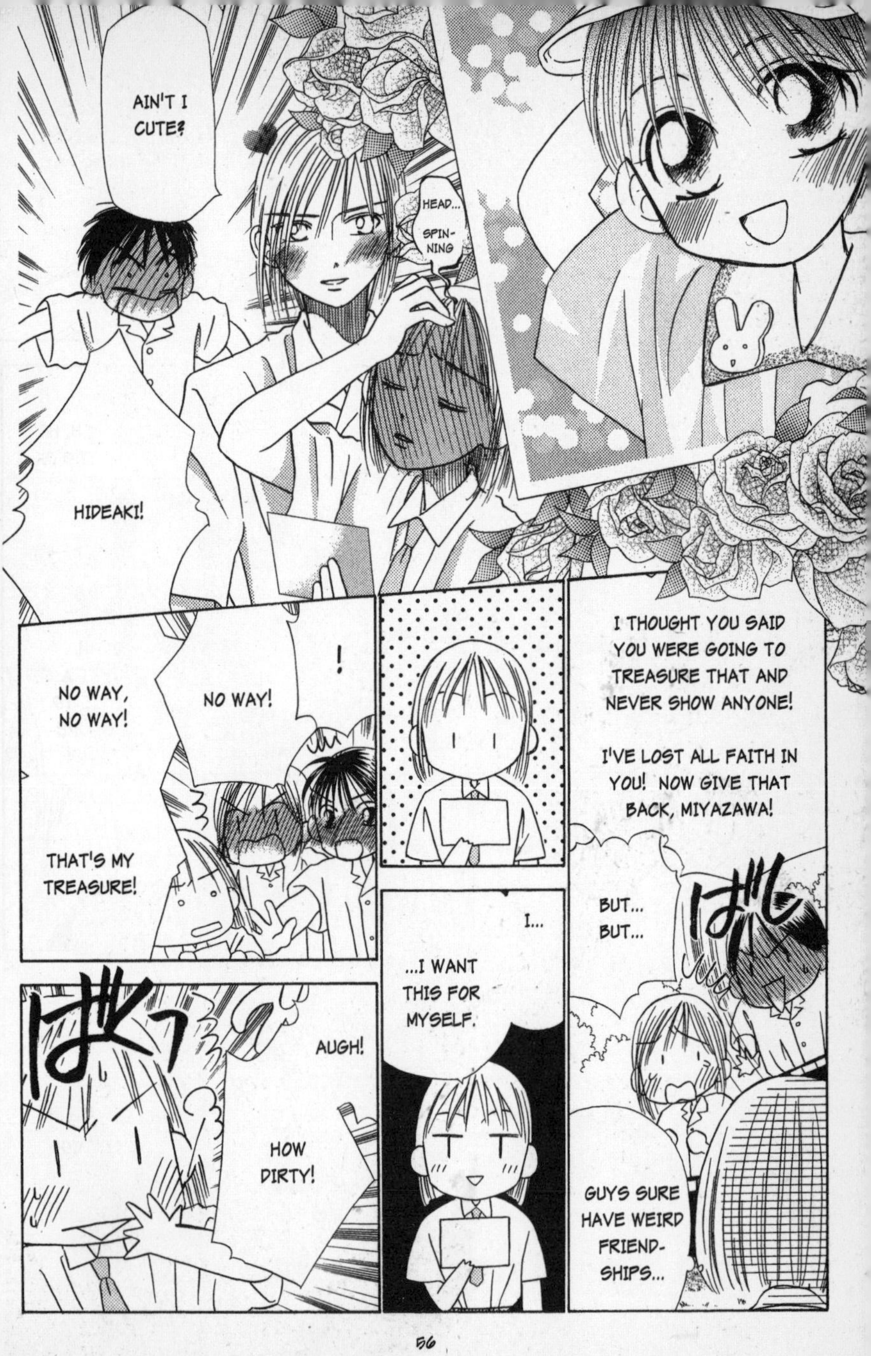
HEAD... SPINNING
AIN'T I CUTE?
HIDEAKI!
I THOUGHT YOU SAID YOU WERE GOING TO TREASURE THAT AND NEVER SHOW ANYONE!
I'VE LOST ALL FAITH IN YOU! NOW GIVE THAT BACK, MIYAZAWA!
BUT... BUT...
GUYS SURE HAVE WEIRD FRIEND-SHIPS...
!
NO WAY!
NO WAY, NO WAY!
THAT'S MY TREASURE!
I...
...I WANT THIS FOR MYSELF.
ばくっ
AUGH!
HOW DIRTY!

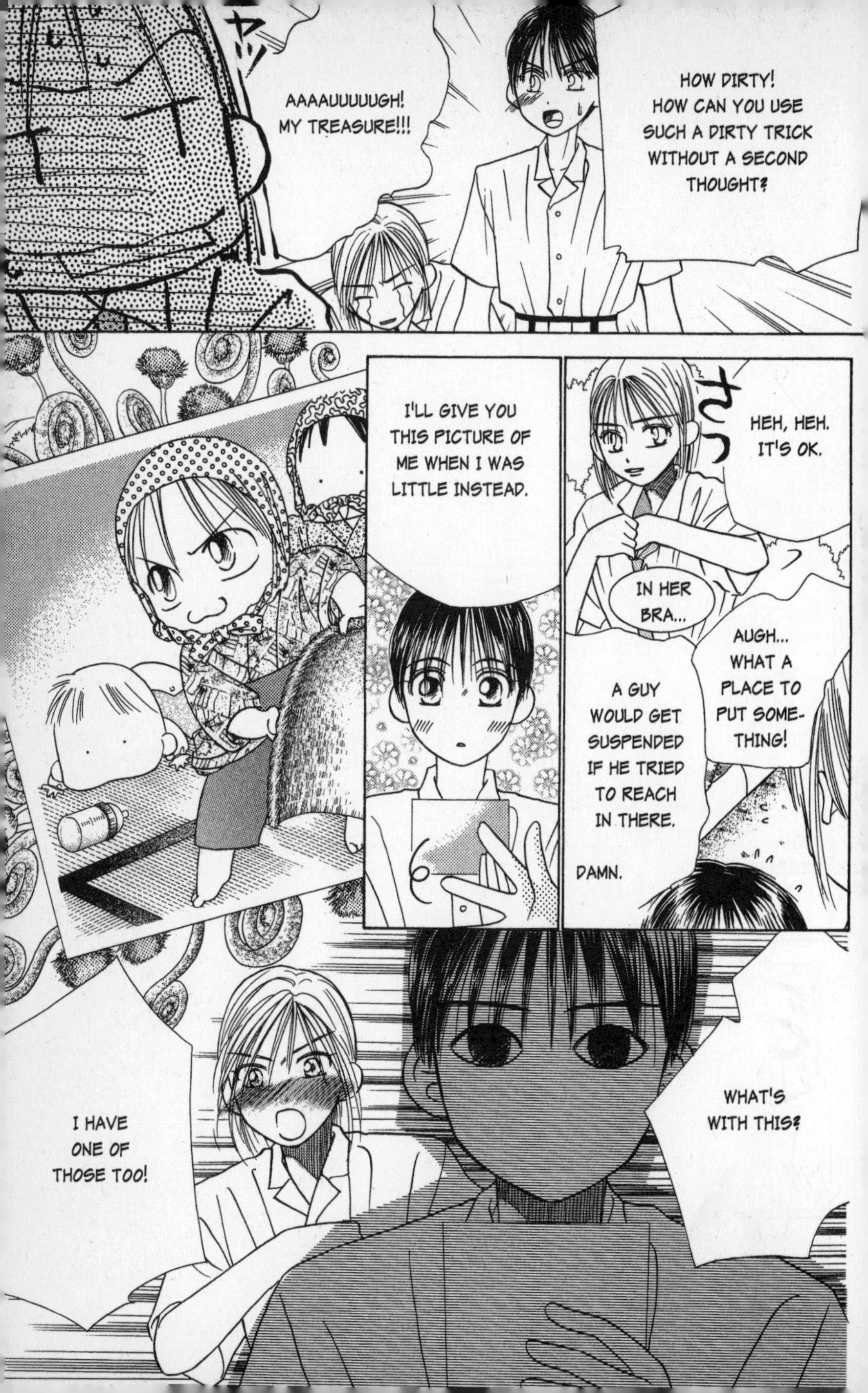

HOW DIRTY! HOW CAN YOU USE SUCH A DIRTY TRICK WITHOUT A SECOND THOUGHT?
ヤッ
AAAAUUUUUGH! MY TREASURE!!!
さっ
HEH, HEH. IT'S OK.
IN HER BRA...
AUGH... WHAT A PLACE TO PUT SOME-THING!
A GUY WOULD GET SUSPENDED IF HE TRIED TO REACH IN THERE.
DAMN.
I'LL GIVE YOU THIS PICTURE OF ME WHEN I WAS LITTLE INSTEAD.
WHAT'S WITH THIS?
I HAVE ONE OF THOSE TOO!

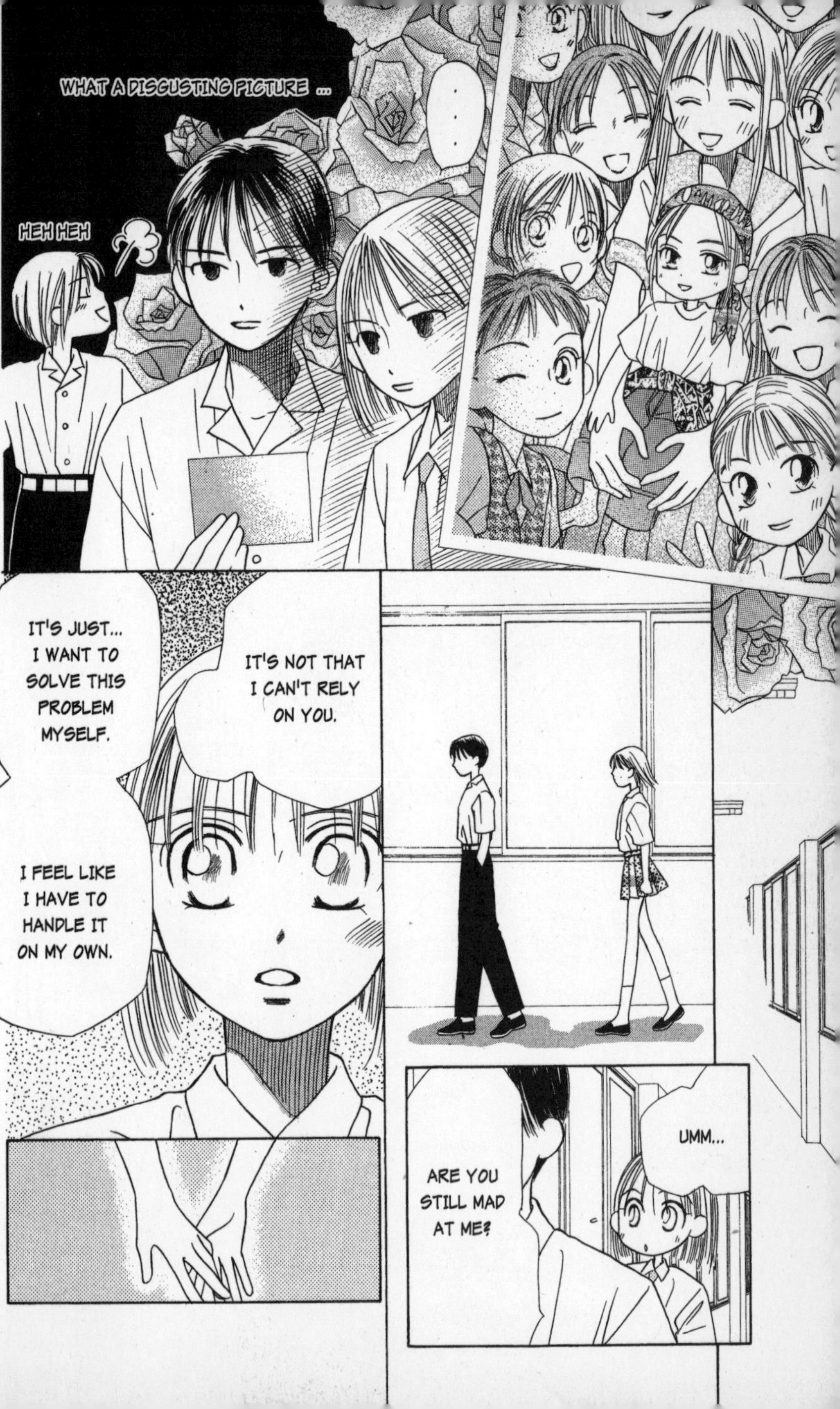
. . .
WHAT A DISGUSTING PICTURE ...
HEH HEH
UMM...
ARE YOU STILL MAD AT ME?
IT'S NOT THAT I CAN'T RELY ON YOU.
IT'S JUST... I WANT TO SOLVE THIS PROBLEM MYSELF.
I FEEL LIKE I HAVE TO HANDLE IT ON MY OWN.

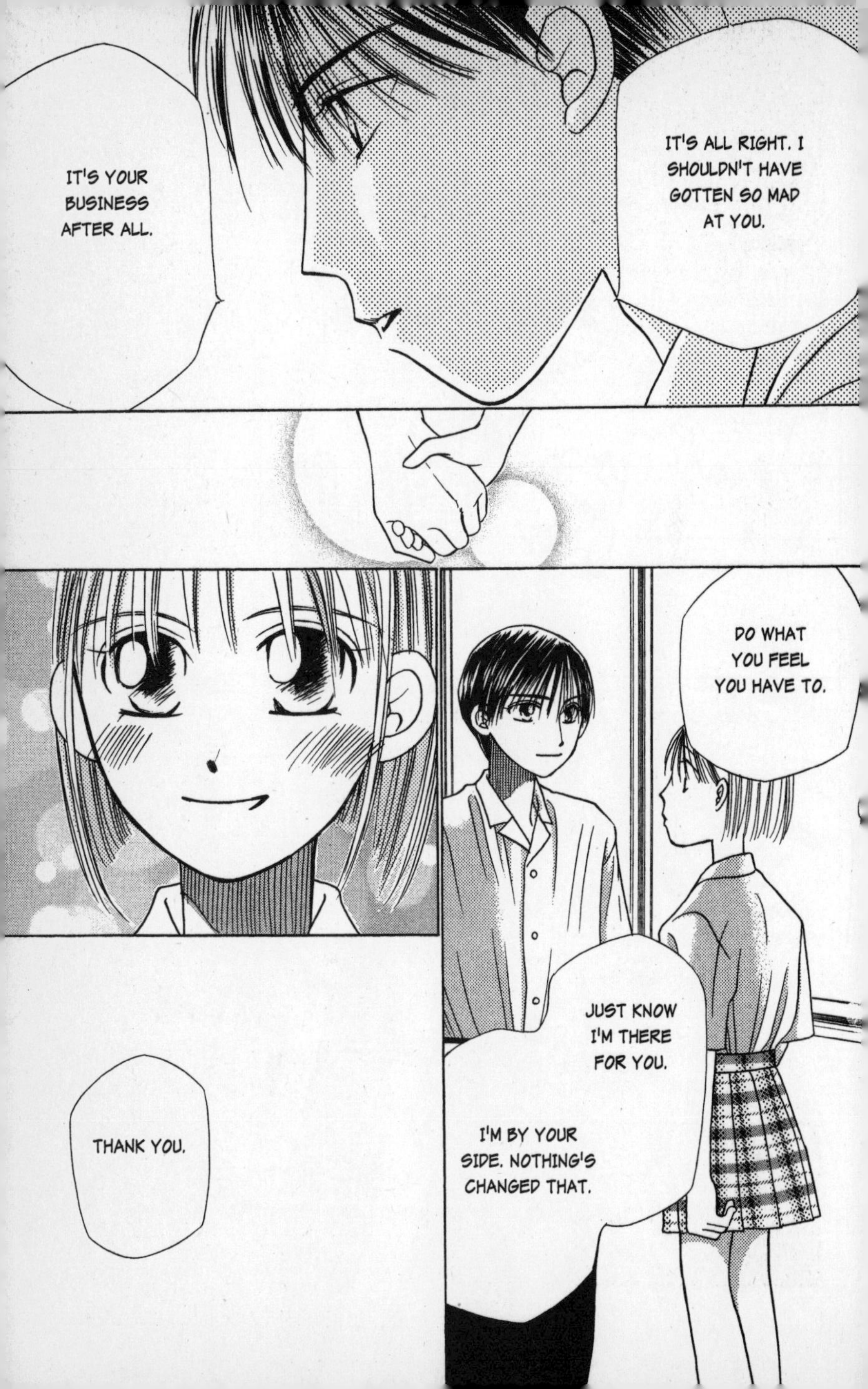
IT'S ALL RIGHT. I SHOULDN'T HAVE GOTTEN SO MAD AT YOU.
IT'S YOUR BUSINESS AFTER ALL.
DO WHAT YOU FEEL YOU HAVE TO.
JUST KNOW I'M THERE FOR YOU.
I'M BY YOUR SIDE. NOTHING'S CHANGED THAT.
THANK YOU.

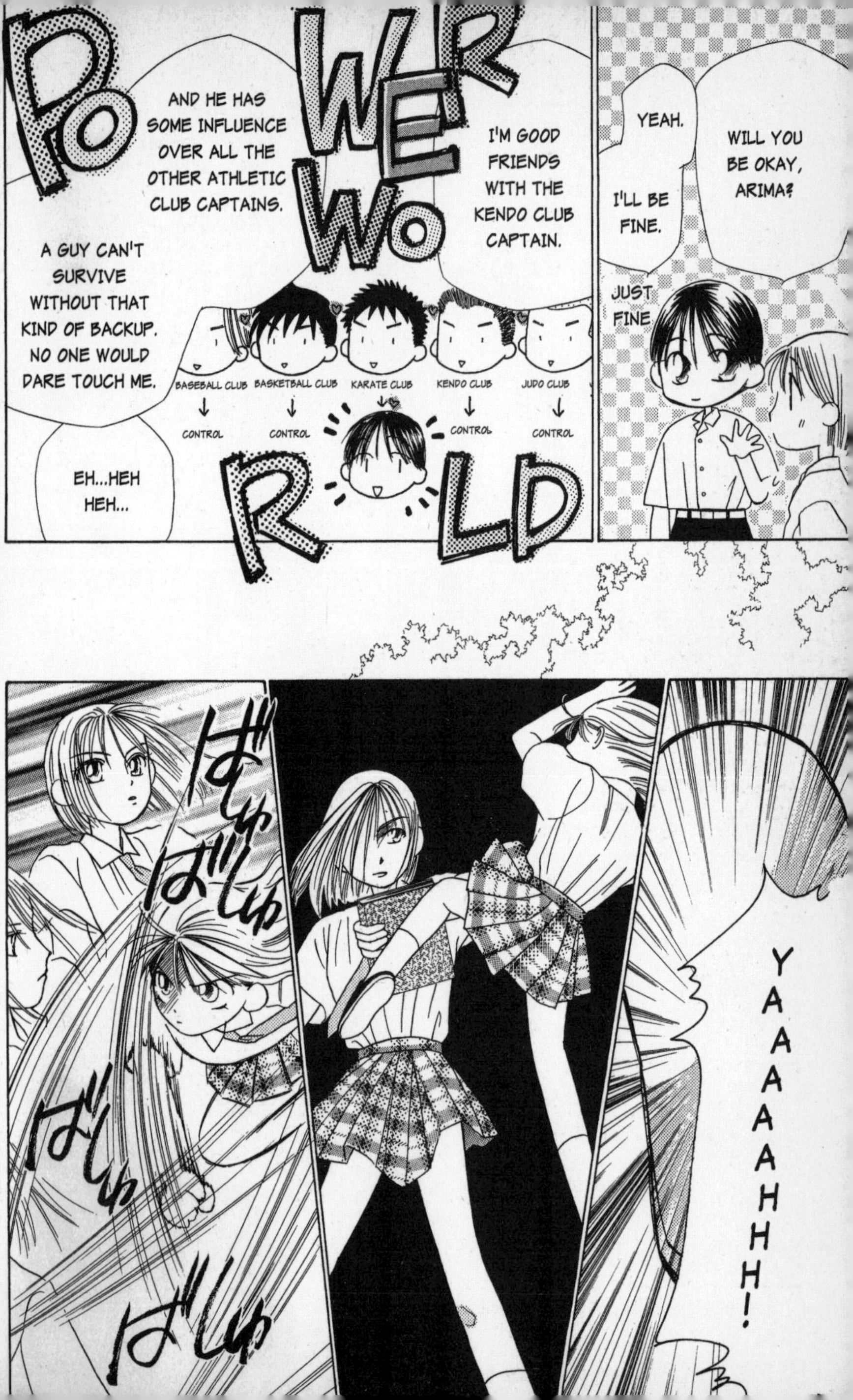

WILL YOU BE OKAY, ARIMA?
YEAH.
I'LL BE FINE.
JUST FINE
I'M GOOD FRIENDS WITH THE KENDO CLUB CAPTAIN.
AND HE HAS SOME INFLUENCE OVER ALL THE OTHER ATHLETIC CLUB CAPTAINS.
POWER WORLD
BASEBALL CLUB
BASKETBALL CLUB
KARATE CLUB
KENDO CLUB
JUDO CLUB
CONTROL
CONTROL
CONTROL
CONTROL
A GUY CAN'T SURVIVE WITHOUT THAT KIND OF BACKUP. NO ONE WOULD DARE TOUCH ME.
EH...HEH HEH...
YAAAAAAHHH!
ばしゅ
ばしゅ
ばしゅ
ばしゅ

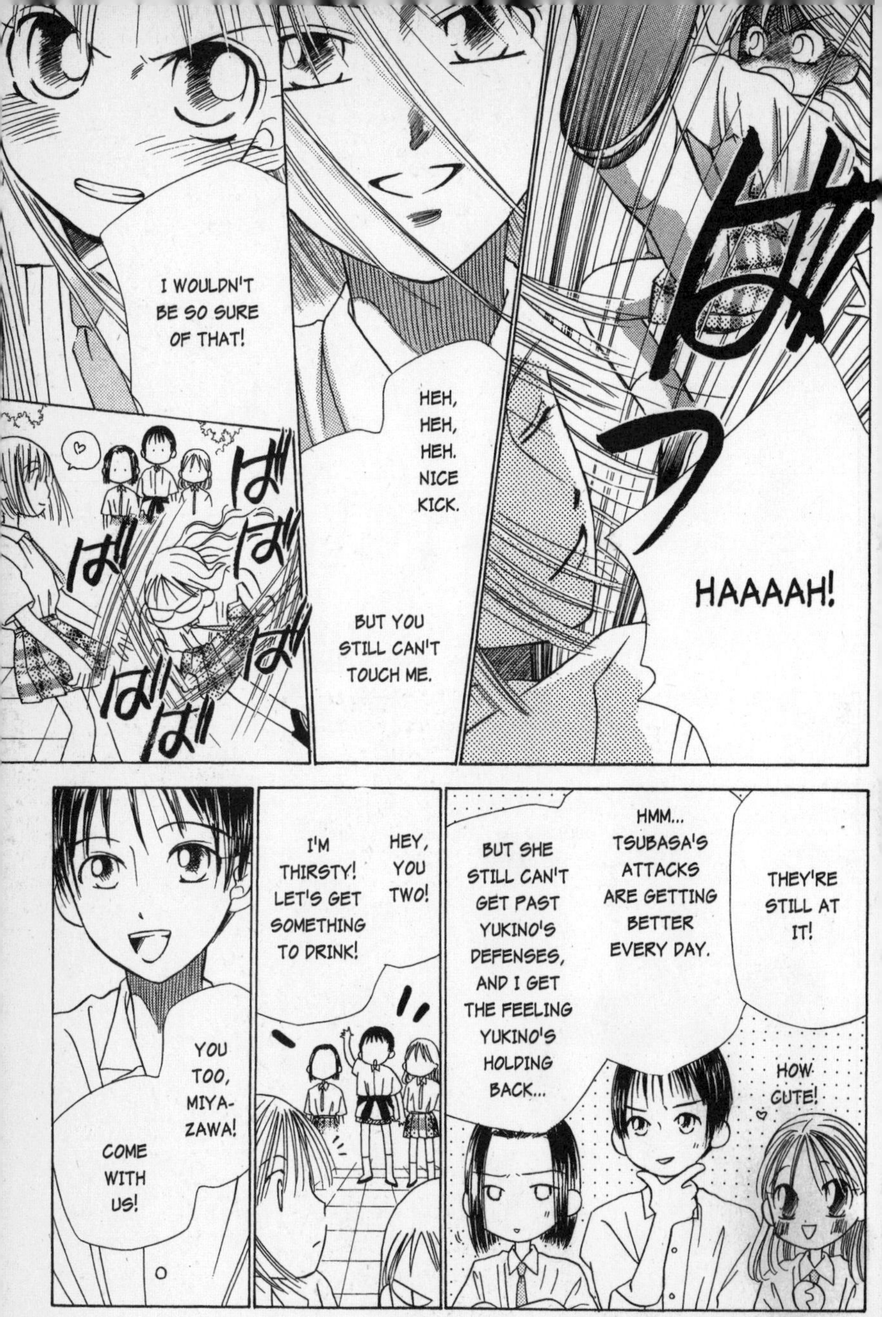

はっ!!
HAAAAH!
HEH, HEH, HEH. NICE KICK.
BUT YOU STILL CAN'T TOUCH ME.
I WOULDN'T BE SO SURE OF THAT!
ばばばばばば
THEY'RE STILL AT IT!
HMM... TSUBASA'S ATTACKS ARE GETTING BETTER EVERY DAY.
BUT SHE STILL CAN'T GET PAST YUKINO'S DEFENSES, AND I GET THE FEELING YUKINO'S HOLDING BACK...
HOW CUTE!
HEY, YOU TWO!
I'M THIRSTY! LET'S GET SOMETHING TO DRINK!
YOU TOO, MIYAZAWA!
COME WITH US!

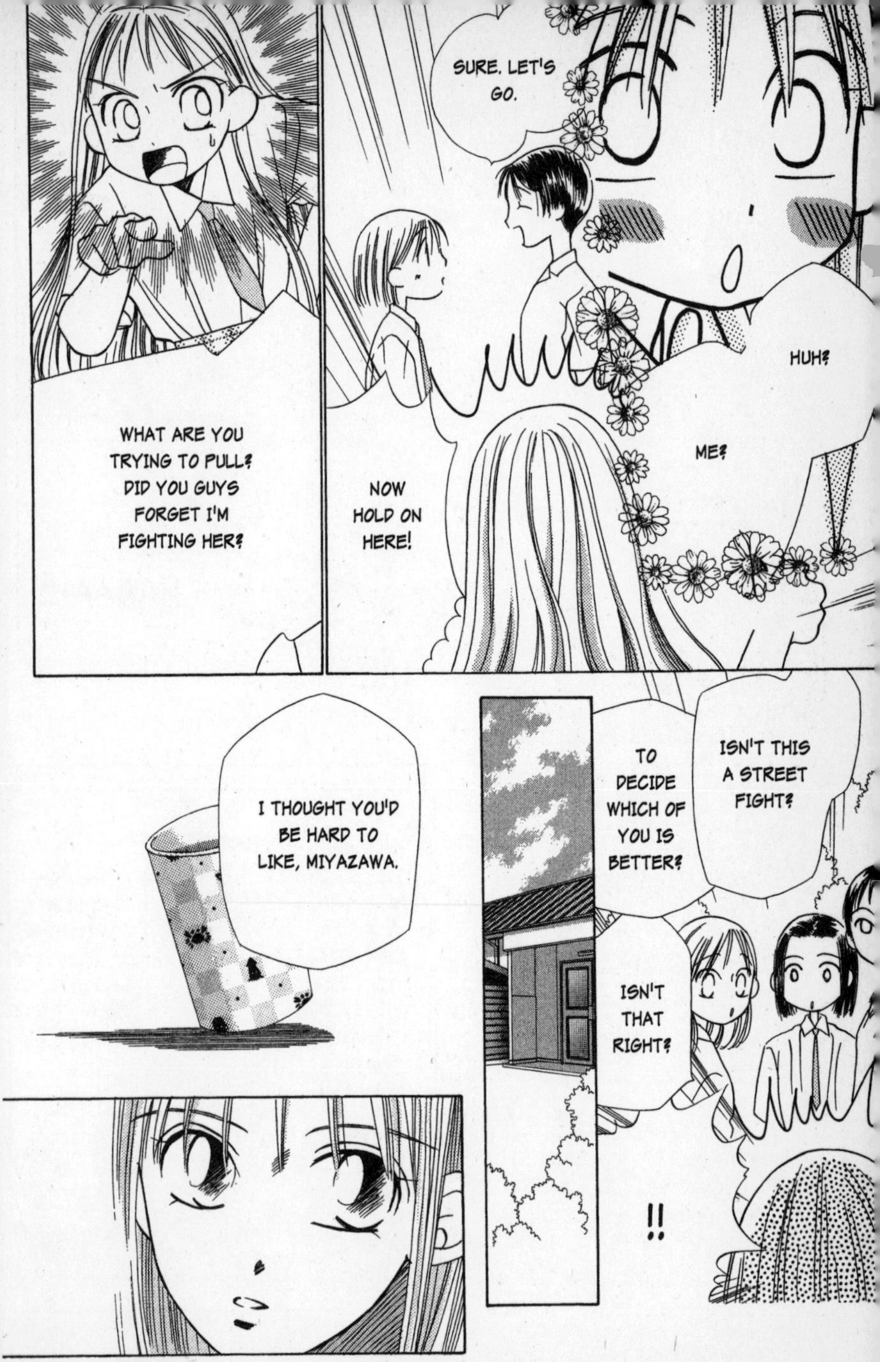
HUH?
ME?
SURE. LET'S GO.
NOW HOLD ON HERE!
WHAT ARE YOU TRYING TO PULL? DID YOU GUYS FORGET I'M FIGHTING HER?
ISN'T THIS A STREET FIGHT?
TO DECIDE WHICH OF YOU IS BETTER?
ISN'T THAT RIGHT?
!!
I THOUGHT YOU'D BE HARD TO LIKE, MIYAZAWA.

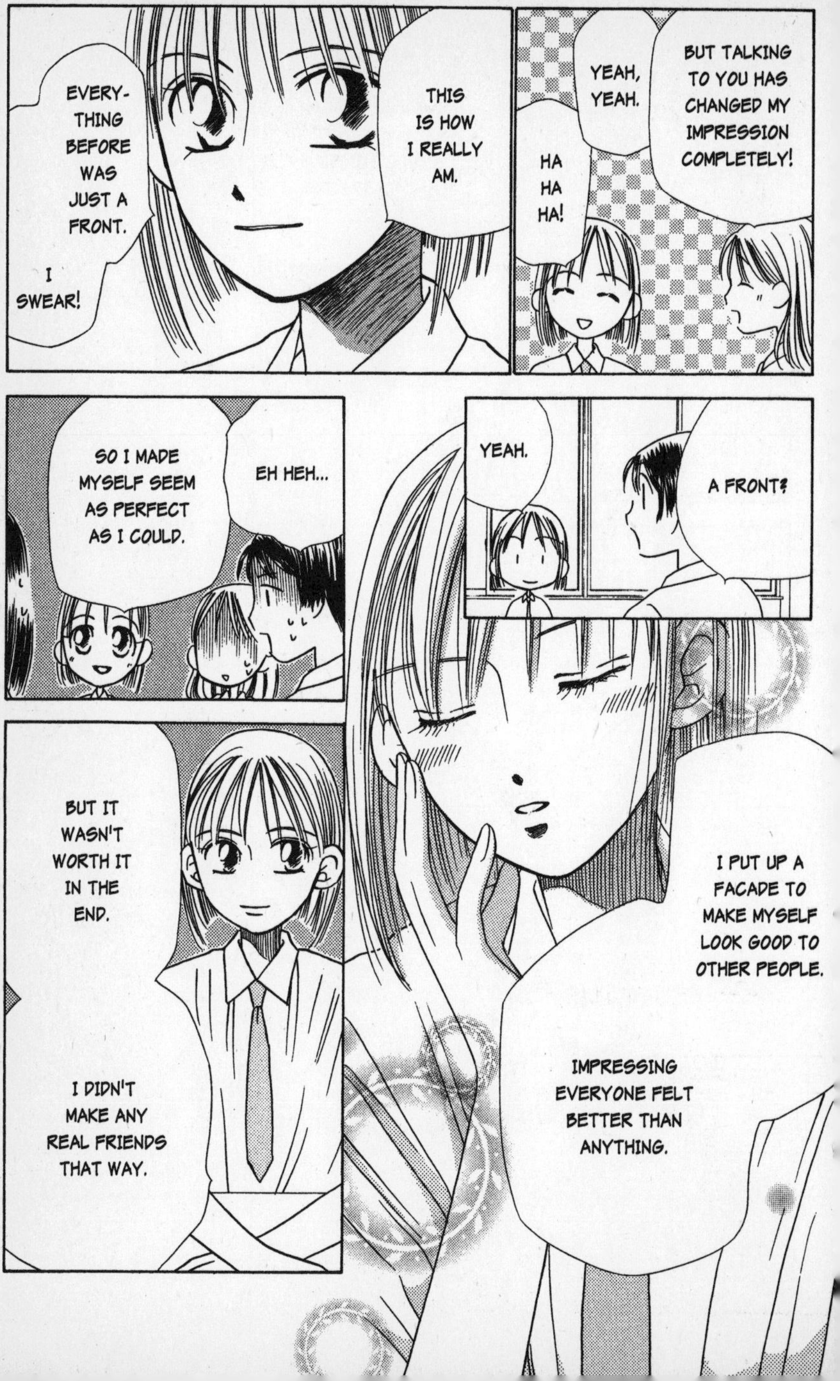
BUT TALKING TO YOU HAS CHANGED MY IMPRESSION COMPLETELY!
YEAH, YEAH.
HA HA HA!
THIS IS HOW I REALLY AM.
EVERY-THING BEFORE WAS JUST A FRONT.
I SWEAR!
A FRONT?
YEAH.
I PUT UP A FACADE TO MAKE MYSELF LOOK GOOD TO OTHER PEOPLE.
IMPRESSING EVERYONE FELT BETTER THAN ANYTHING.
EH HEH...
SO I MADE MYSELF SEEM AS PERFECT AS I COULD.
BUT IT WASN'T WORTH IT IN THE END.
I DIDN'T MAKE ANY REAL FRIENDS THAT WAY.

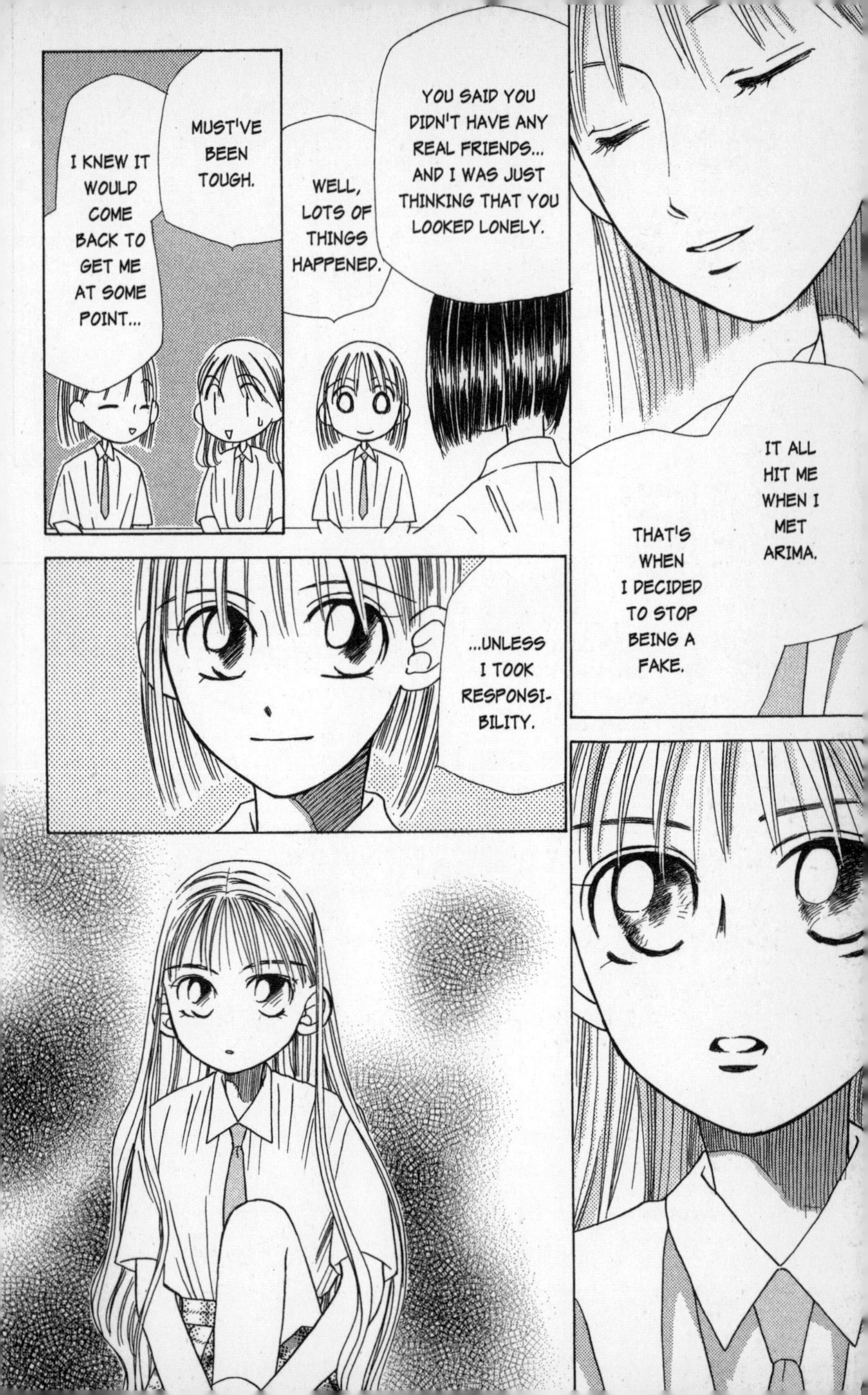
IT ALL HIT ME WHEN I MET ARIMA.
THAT'S WHEN I DECIDED TO STOP BEING A FAKE.
YOU SAID YOU DIDN'T HAVE ANY REAL FRIENDS... AND I WAS JUST THINKING THAT YOU LOOKED LONELY.
WELL, LOTS OF THINGS HAPPENED.
MUST'VE BEEN TOUGH.
I KNEW IT WOULD COME BACK TO GET ME AT SOME POINT...
...UNLESS I TOOK RESPONSI-BILITY.

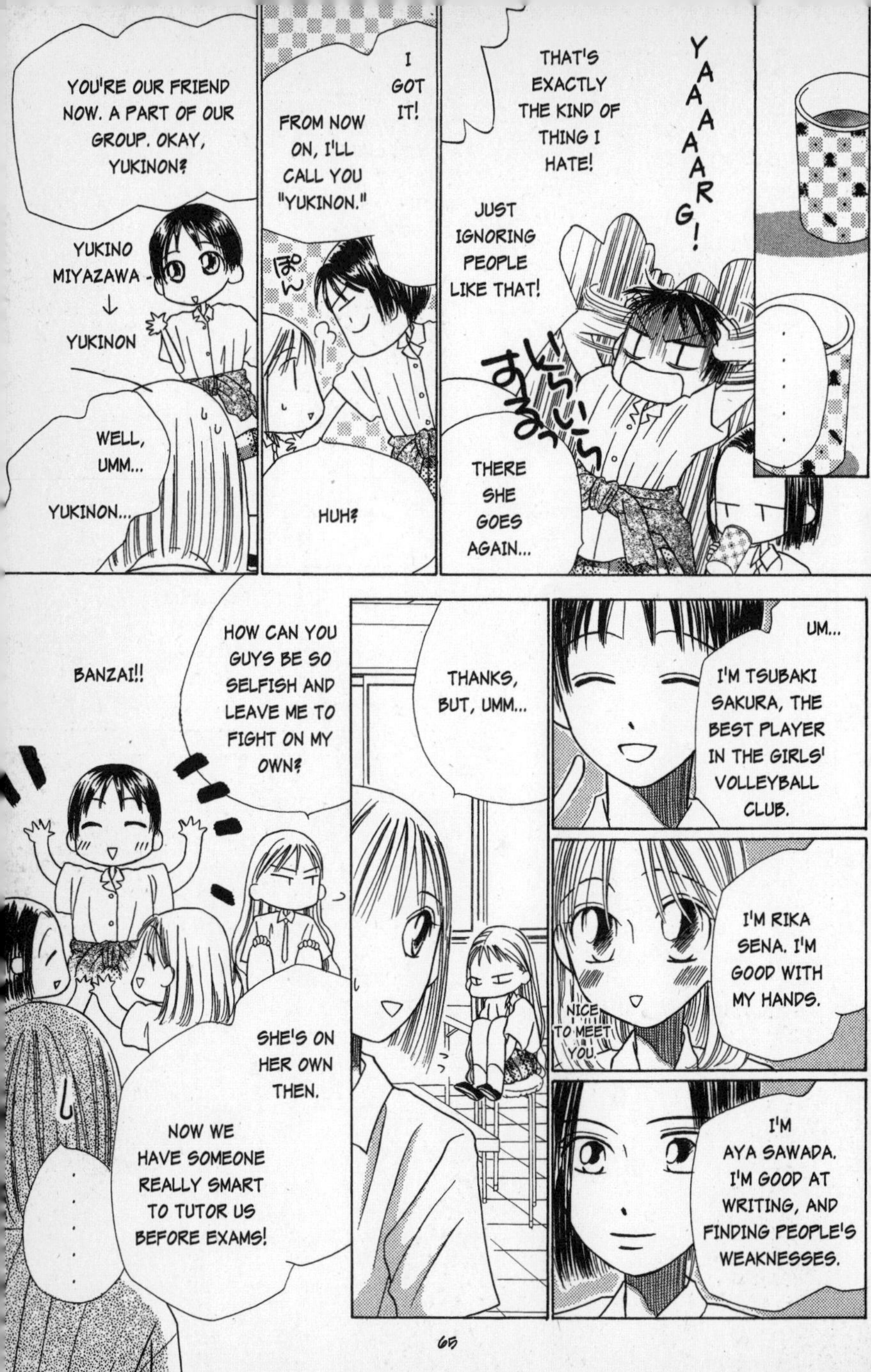

.....
YAAAAARG!
THAT'S EXACTLY THE KIND OF THING I HATE!
JUST IGNORING PEOPLE LIKE THAT!
いらいら
THERE SHE GOES AGAIN...
I GOT IT!
FROM NOW ON, I'LL CALL YOU "YUKINON."
ぽん
HUH?
YOU'RE OUR FRIEND NOW. A PART OF OUR GROUP. OKAY, YUKINON?
YUKINO MIYAZAWA ↓ YUKINON
WELL, UMM...
YUKINON...
UM...
I'M TSUBAKI SAKURA, THE BEST PLAYER IN THE GIRLS' VOLLEYBALL CLUB.
I'M RIKA SENA. I'M GOOD WITH MY HANDS.
NICE TO MEET YOU.
I'M AYA SAWADA. I'M GOOD AT WRITING, AND FINDING PEOPLE'S WEAKNESSES.
THANKS, BUT, UMM...
HOW CAN YOU GUYS BE SO SELFISH AND LEAVE ME TO FIGHT ON MY OWN?
BANZAI!!
SHE'S ON HER OWN THEN.
NOW WE HAVE SOMEONE REALLY SMART TO TUTOR US BEFORE EXAMS!
.....

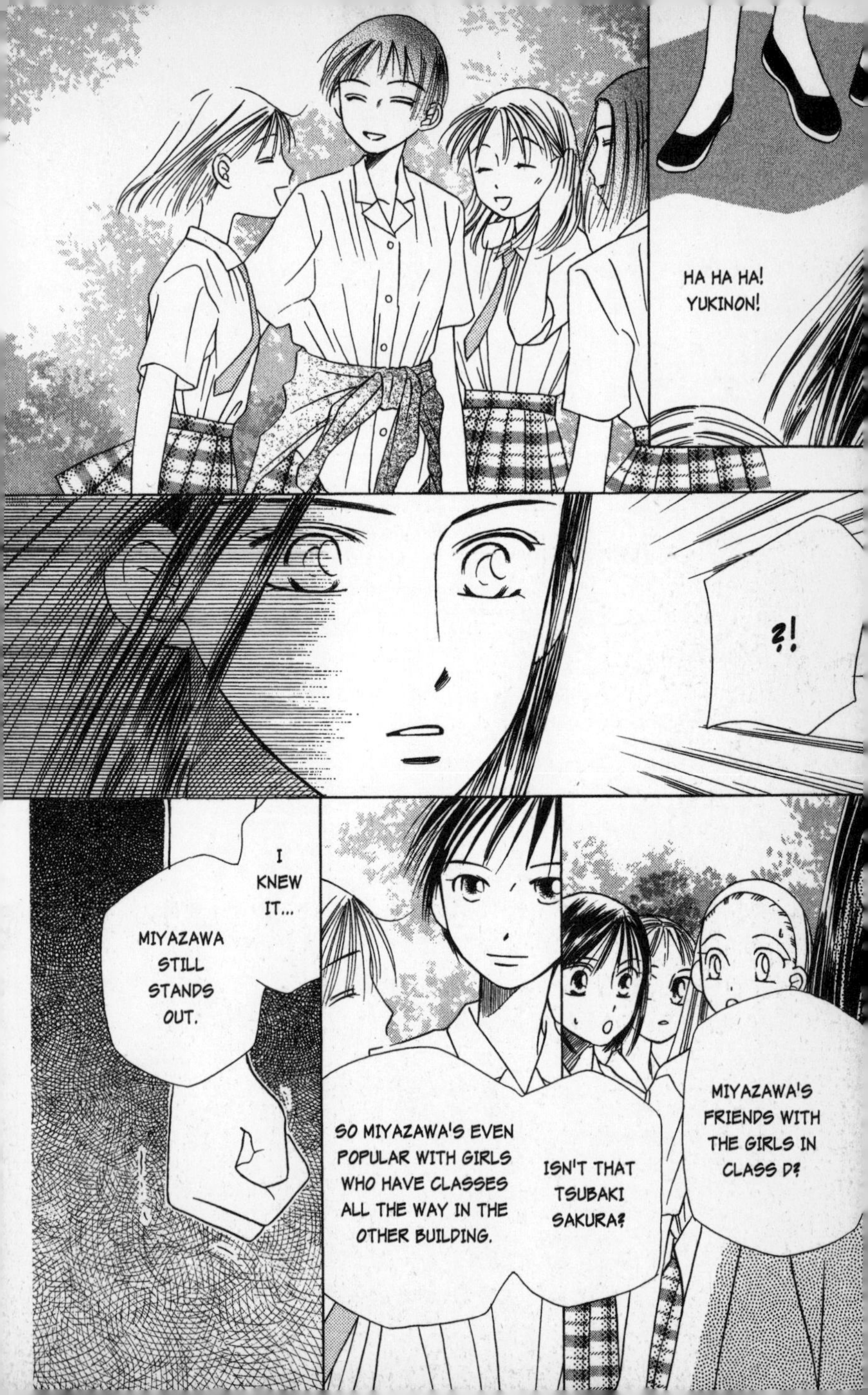
HA HA HA! YUKINON!
?!
MIYAZAWA'S FRIENDS WITH THE GIRLS IN CLASS D?
ISN'T THAT TSUBAKI SAKURA?
SO MIYAZAWA'S EVEN POPULAR WITH GIRLS WHO HAVE CLASSES ALL THE WAY IN THE OTHER BUILDING.
I KNEW IT...
MIYAZAWA STILL STANDS OUT.

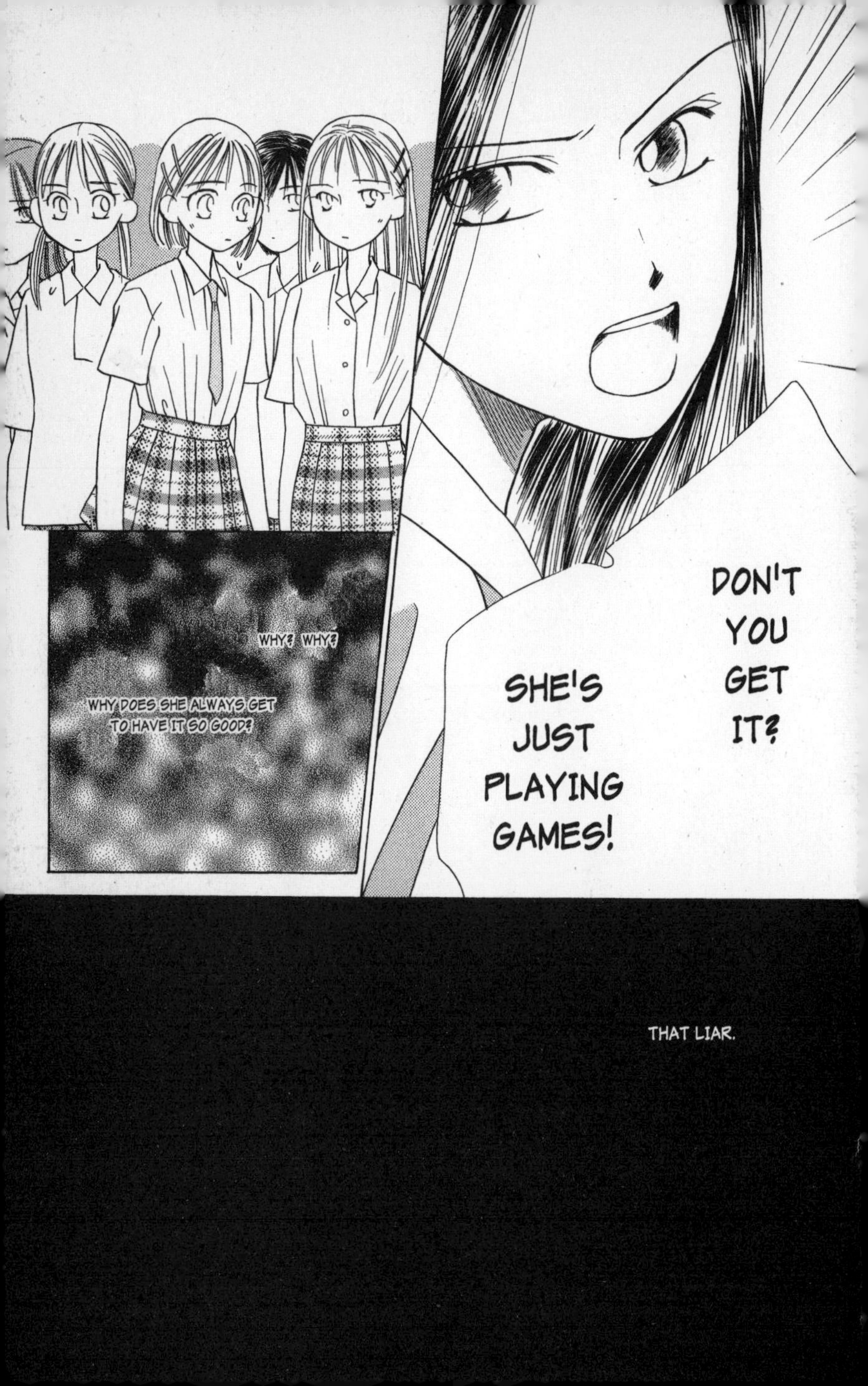
DON'T YOU GET IT?
SHE'S JUST PLAYING GAMES!
WHY? WHY?
WHY DOES SHE ALWAYS GET TO HAVE IT SO GOOD?
THAT LIAR.

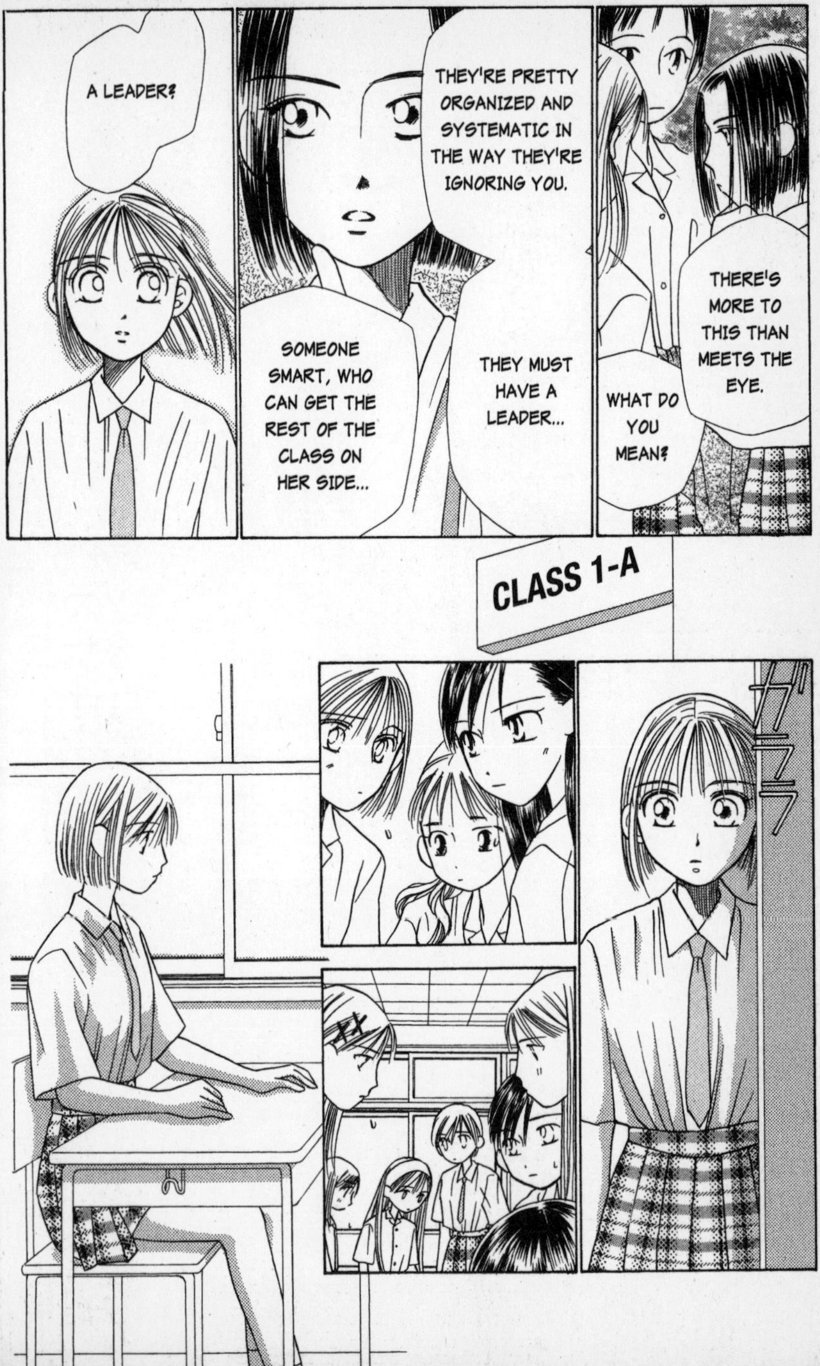
THERE'S MORE TO THIS THAN MEETS THE EYE.
WHAT DO YOU MEAN?
THEY'RE PRETTY ORGANIZED AND SYSTEMATIC IN THE WAY THEY'RE IGNORING YOU.
THEY MUST HAVE A LEADER...
SOMEONE SMART, WHO CAN GET THE REST OF THE CLASS ON HER SIDE...
A LEADER?
CLASS 1-A

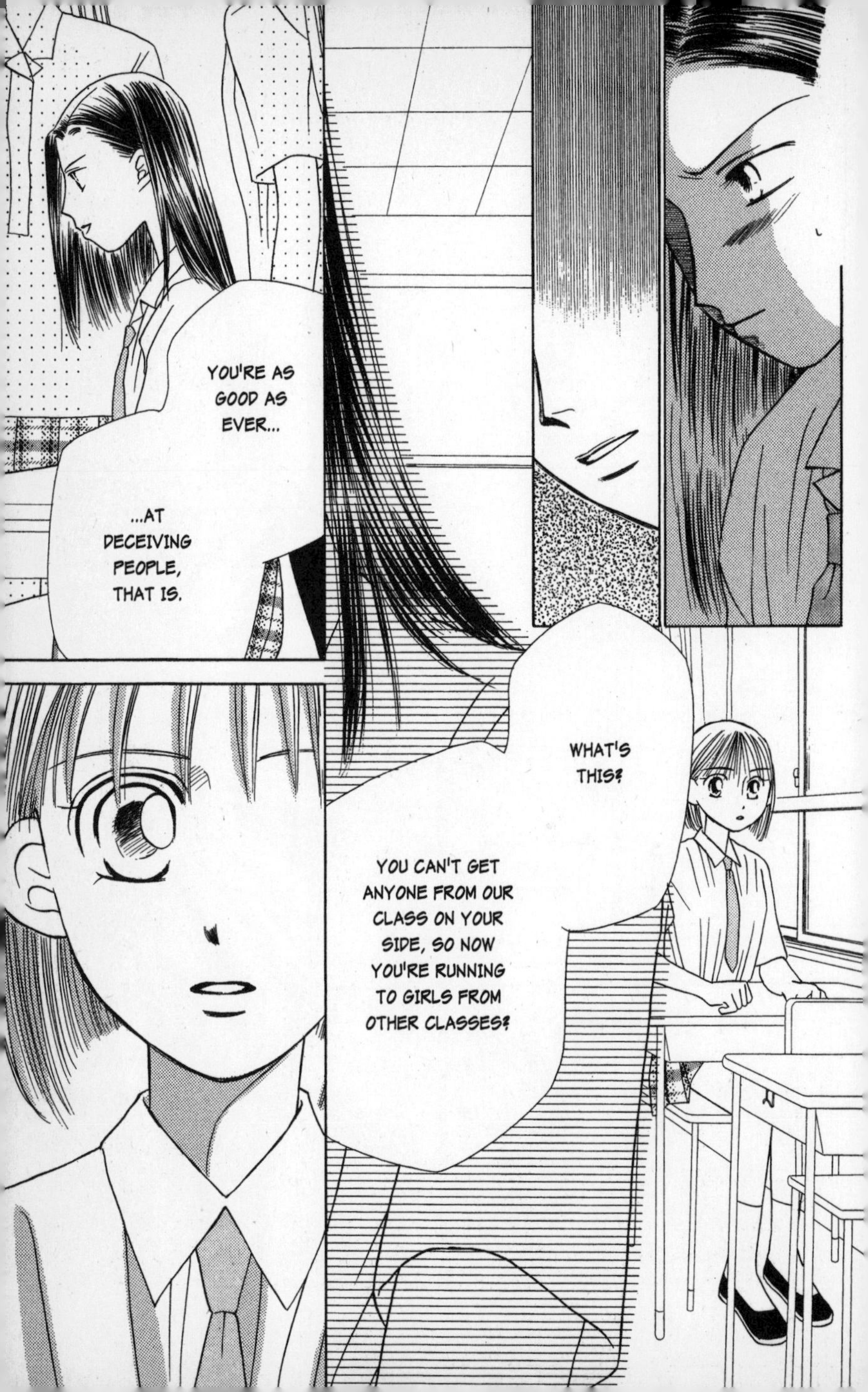
YOU'RE AS GOOD AS EVER...
...AT DECEIVING PEOPLE, THAT IS.
WHAT'S THIS?
YOU CAN'T GET ANYONE FROM OUR CLASS ON YOUR SIDE, SO NOW YOU'RE RUNNING TO GIRLS FROM OTHER CLASSES?

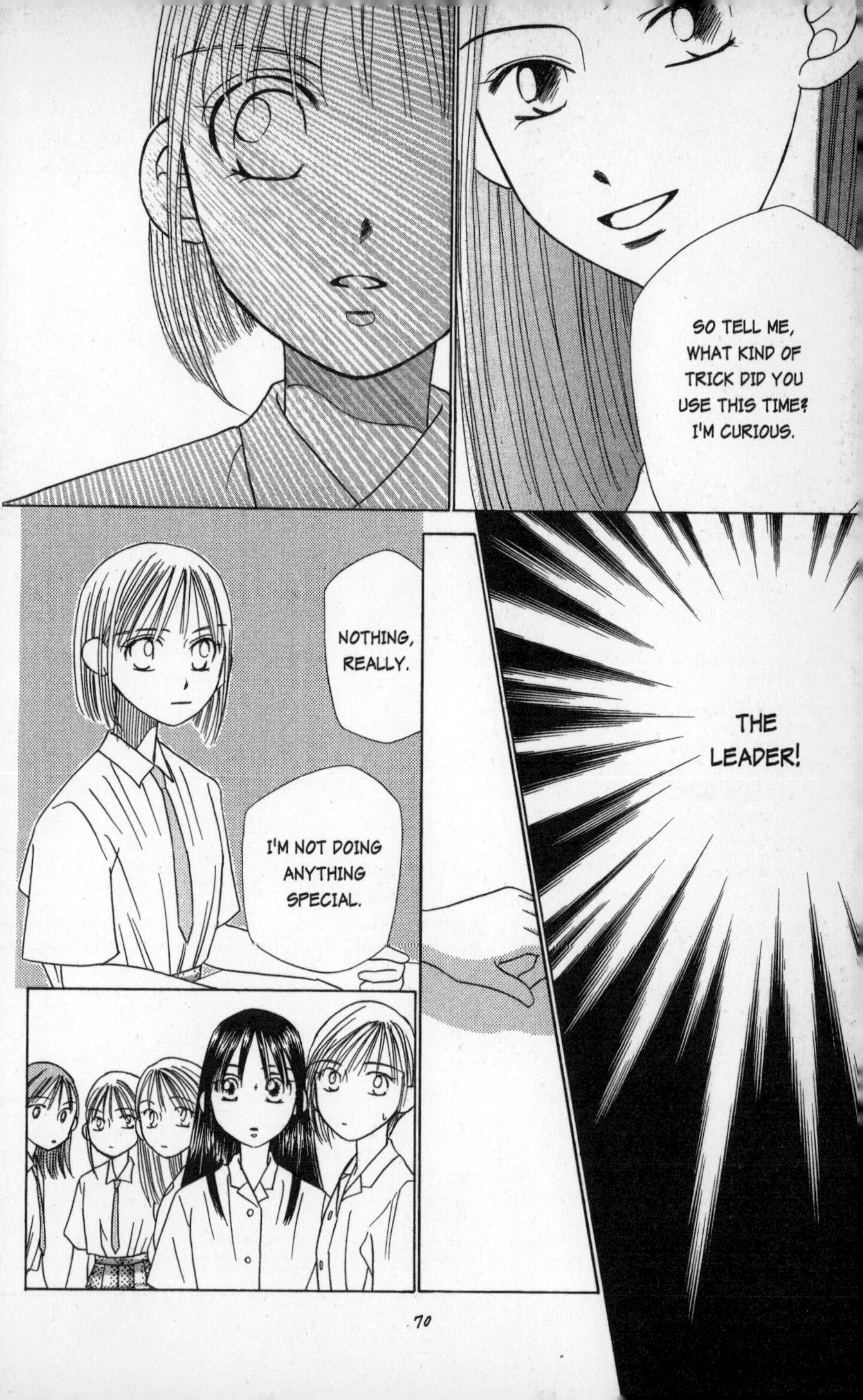
SO TELL ME, WHAT KIND OF TRICK DID YOU USE THIS TIME? I'M CURIOUS.
THE LEADER!
NOTHING, REALLY.
I'M NOT DOING ANYTHING SPECIAL.

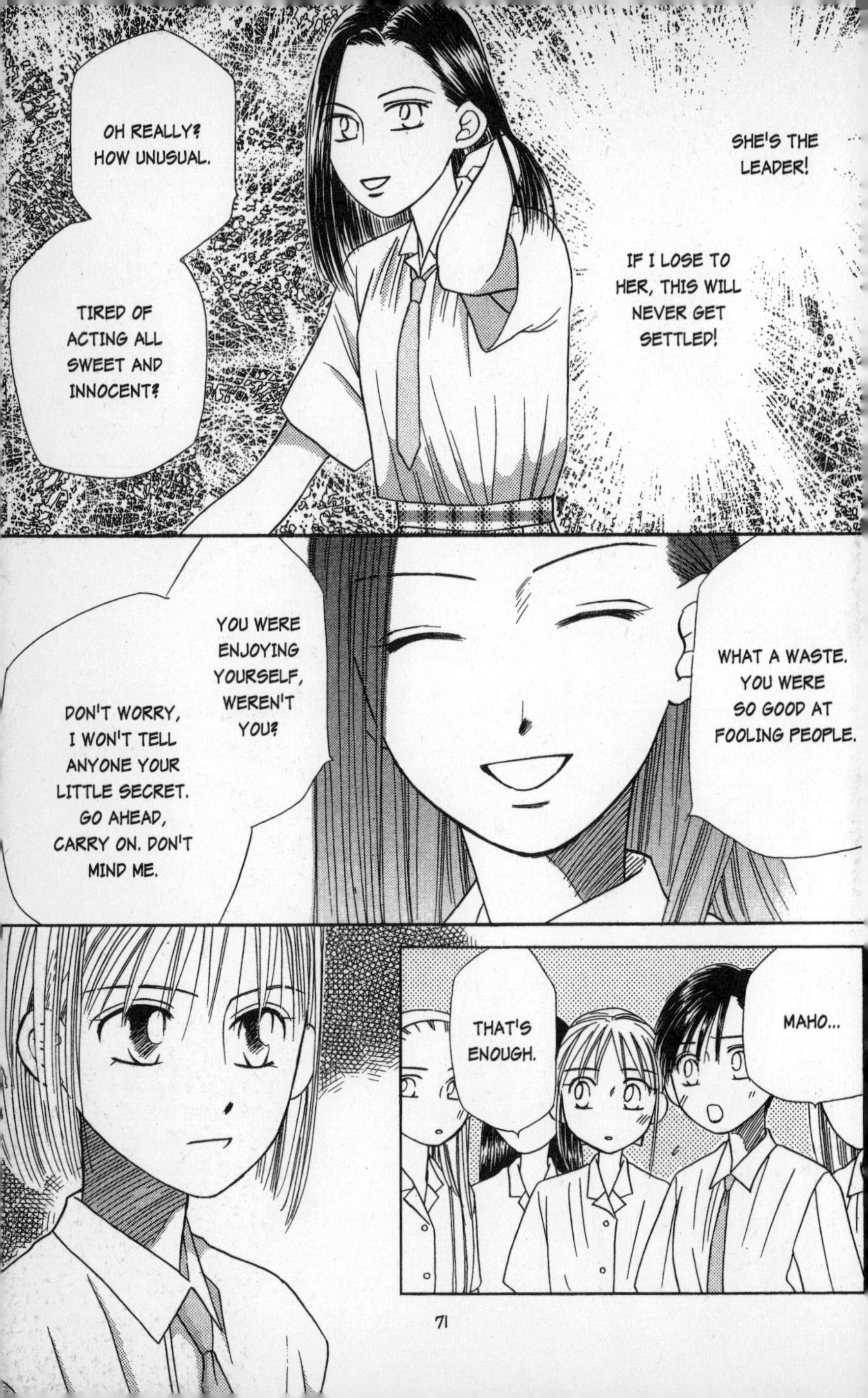
SHE'S THE LEADER!
IF I LOSE TO HER, THIS WILL NEVER GET SETTLED!
OH REALLY? HOW UNUSUAL.
TIRED OF ACTING ALL SWEET AND INNOCENT?
WHAT A WASTE. YOU WERE SO GOOD AT FOOLING PEOPLE.
YOU WERE ENJOYING YOURSELF, WEREN'T YOU?
DON'T WORRY, I WON'T TELL ANYONE YOUR LITTLE SECRET. GO AHEAD, CARRY ON. DON'T MIND ME.
MAHO...
THAT'S ENOUGH.

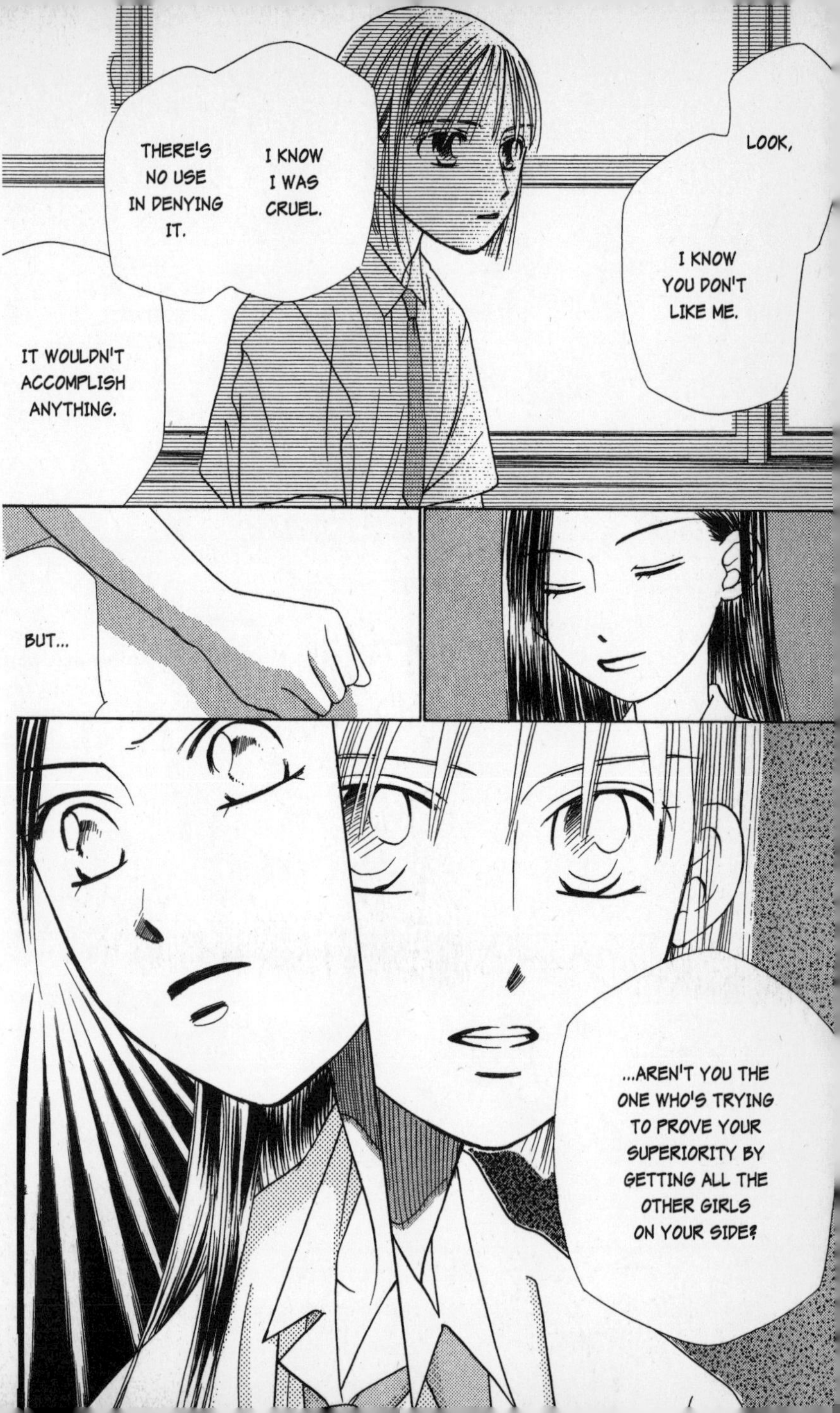
LOOK,
I KNOW YOU DON'T LIKE ME.
I KNOW I WAS CRUEL.
THERE'S NO USE IN DENYING IT.
IT WOULDN'T ACCOMPLISH ANYTHING.
BUT...
...AREN'T YOU THE ONE WHO'S TRYING TO PROVE YOUR SUPERIORITY BY GETTING ALL THE OTHER GIRLS ON YOUR SIDE?

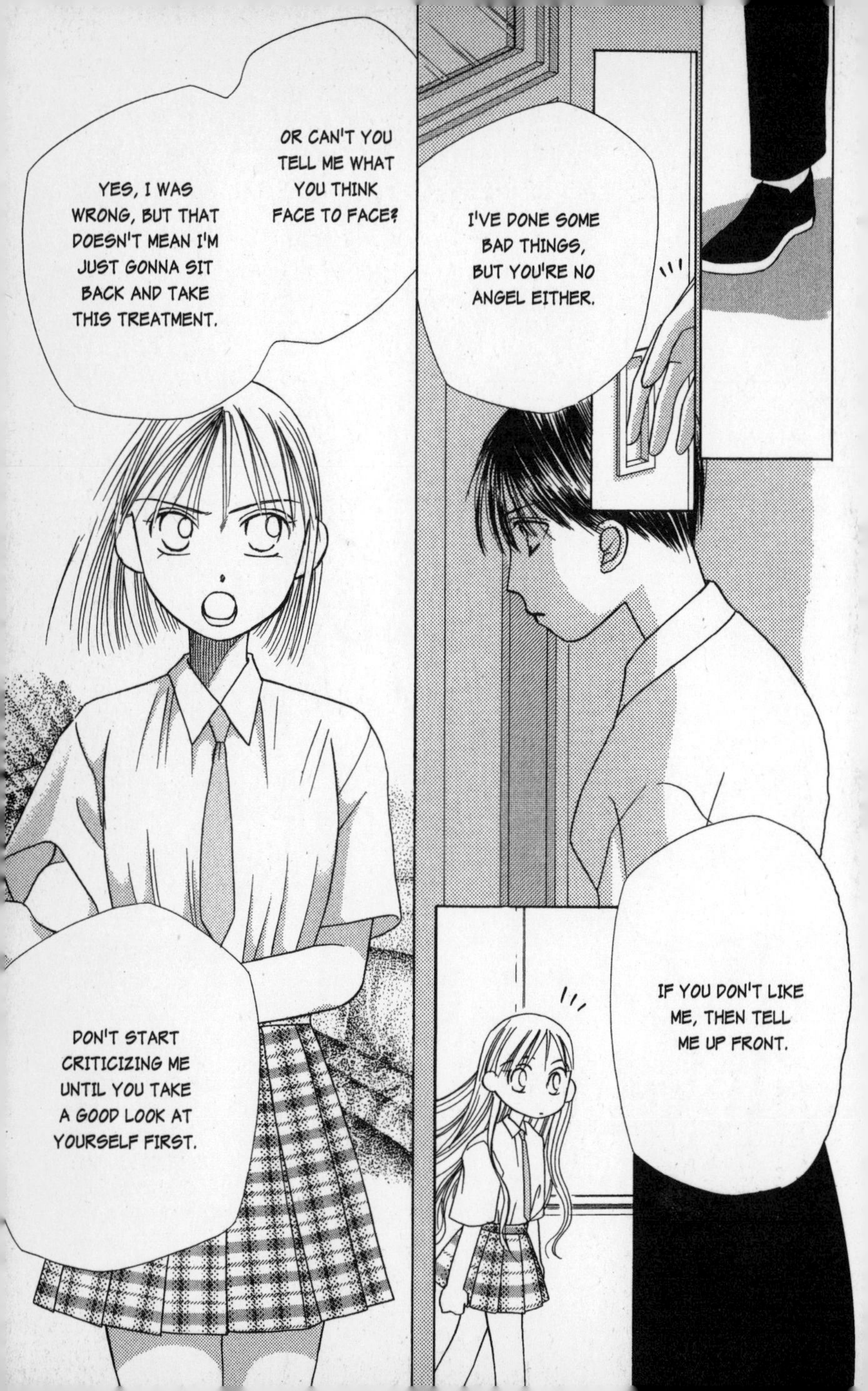
I'VE DONE SOME BAD THINGS, BUT YOU'RE NO ANGEL EITHER.
IF YOU DON'T LIKE ME, THEN TELL ME UP FRONT.
OR CAN'T YOU TELL ME WHAT YOU THINK FACE TO FACE?
YES, I WAS WRONG, BUT THAT DOESN'T MEAN I'M JUST GONNA SIT BACK AND TAKE THIS TREATMENT.
DON'T START CRITICIZING ME UNTIL YOU TAKE A GOOD LOOK AT YOURSELF FIRST.

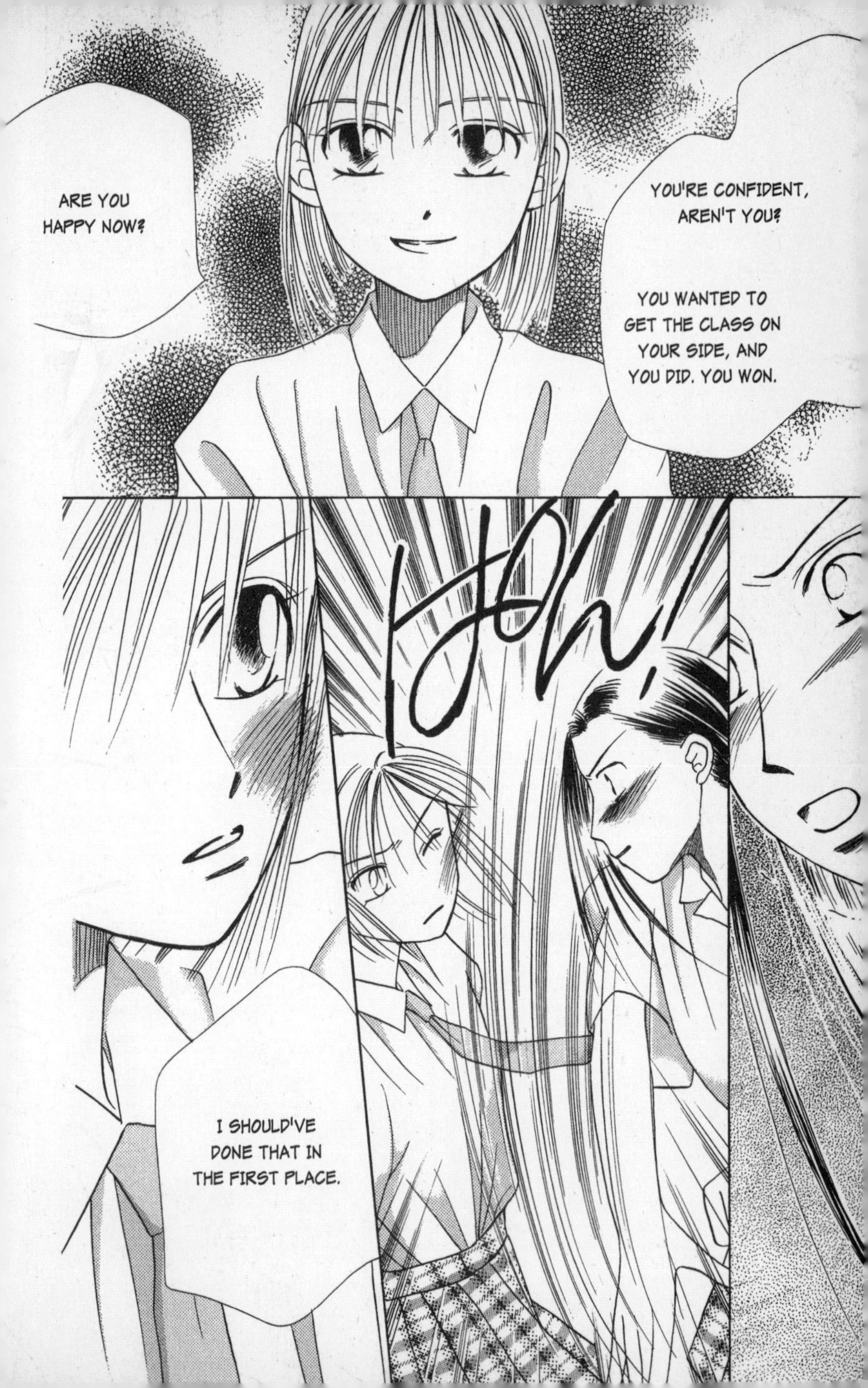
YOU'RE CONFIDENT, AREN'T YOU?
YOU WANTED TO GET THE CLASS ON YOUR SIDE, AND YOU DID. YOU WON.
ARE YOU HAPPY NOW?
I SHOULD'VE DONE THAT IN THE FIRST PLACE.

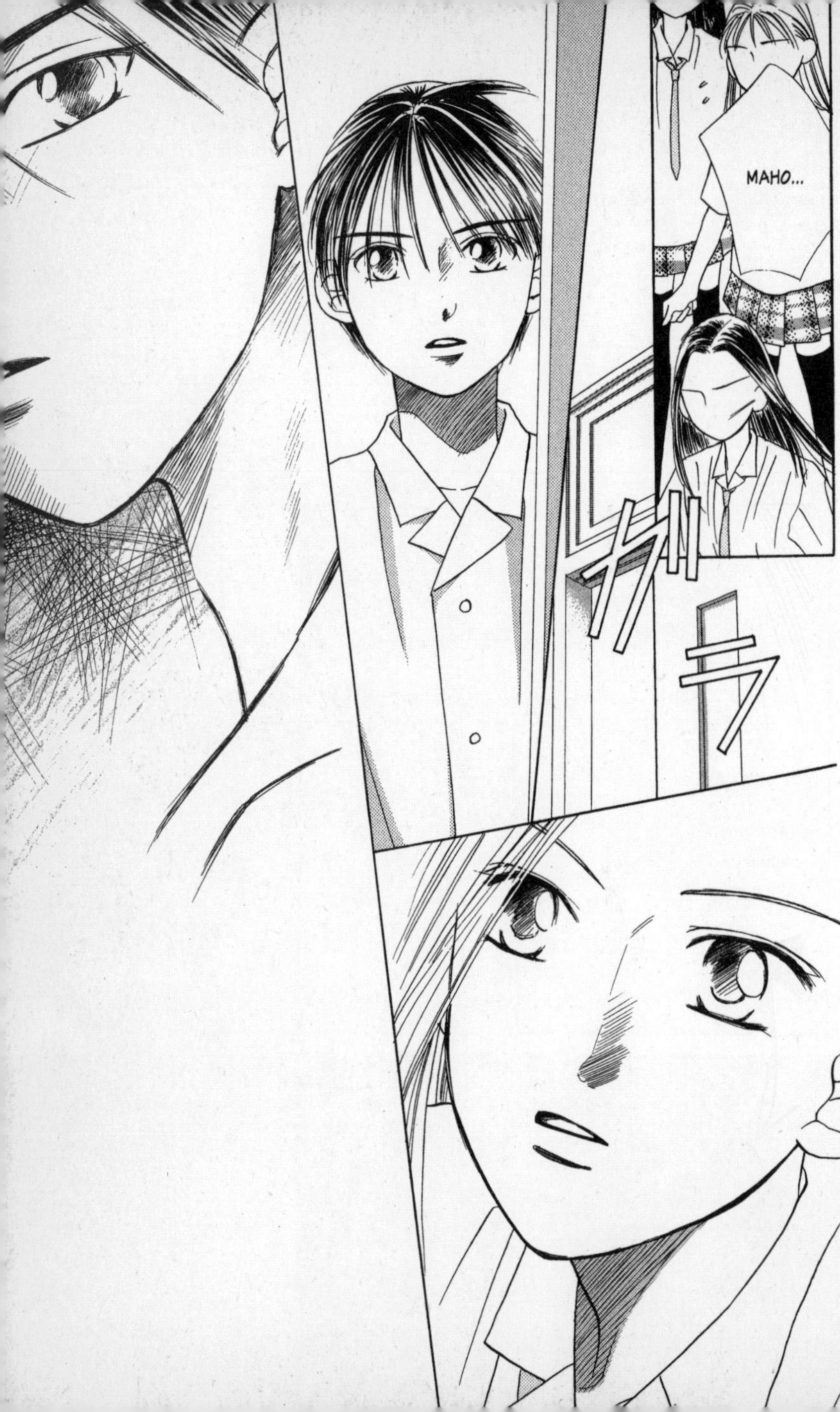
MAHO...
ガラ

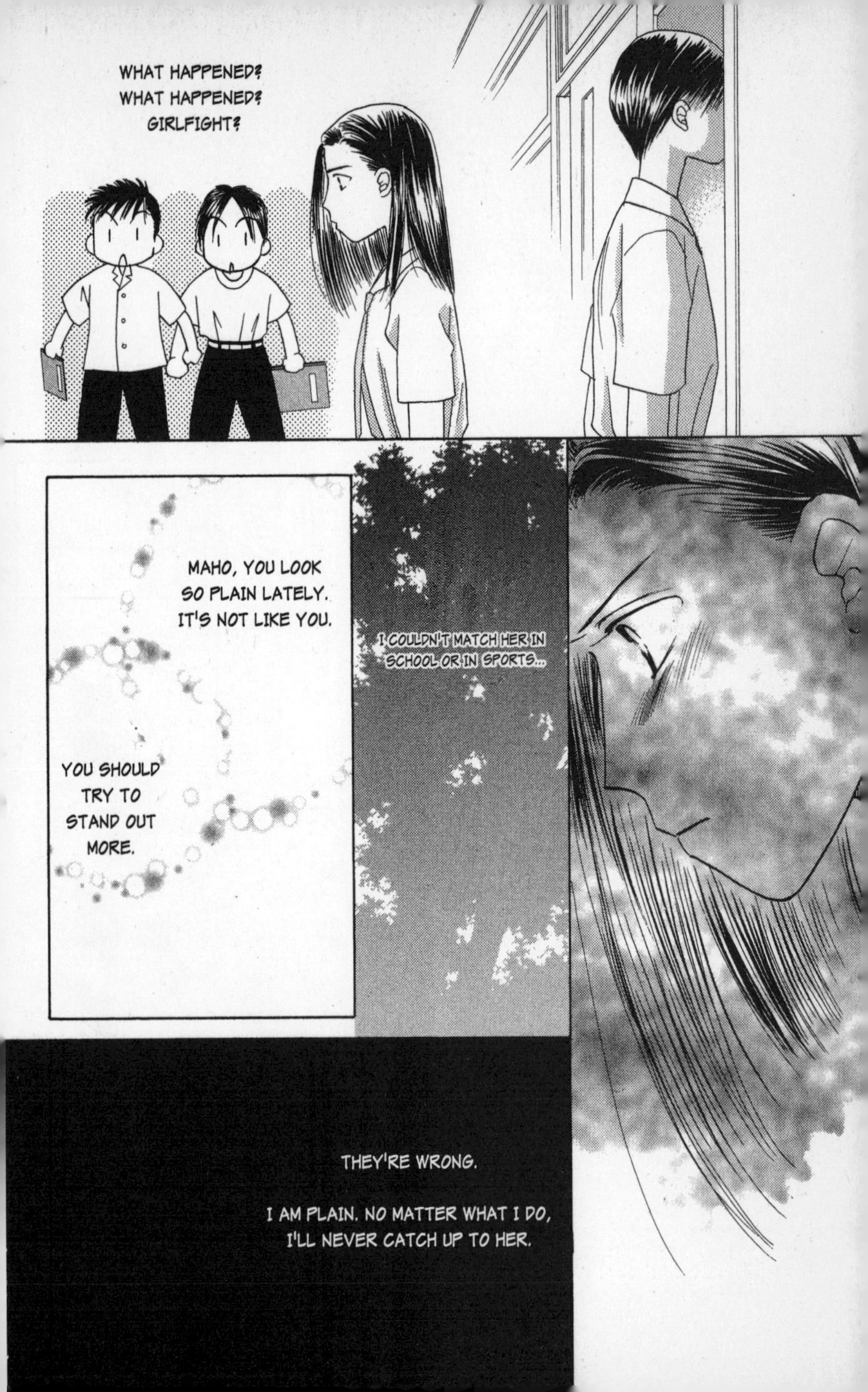
WHAT HAPPENED? WHAT HAPPENED? GIRLFIGHT?
I COULDN'T MATCH HER IN SCHOOL OR IN SPORTS...
MAHO, YOU LOOK SO PLAIN LATELY. IT'S NOT LIKE YOU.
YOU SHOULD TRY TO STAND OUT MORE.
THEY'RE WRONG.
I AM PLAIN. NO MATTER WHAT I DO, I'LL NEVER CATCH UP TO HER.

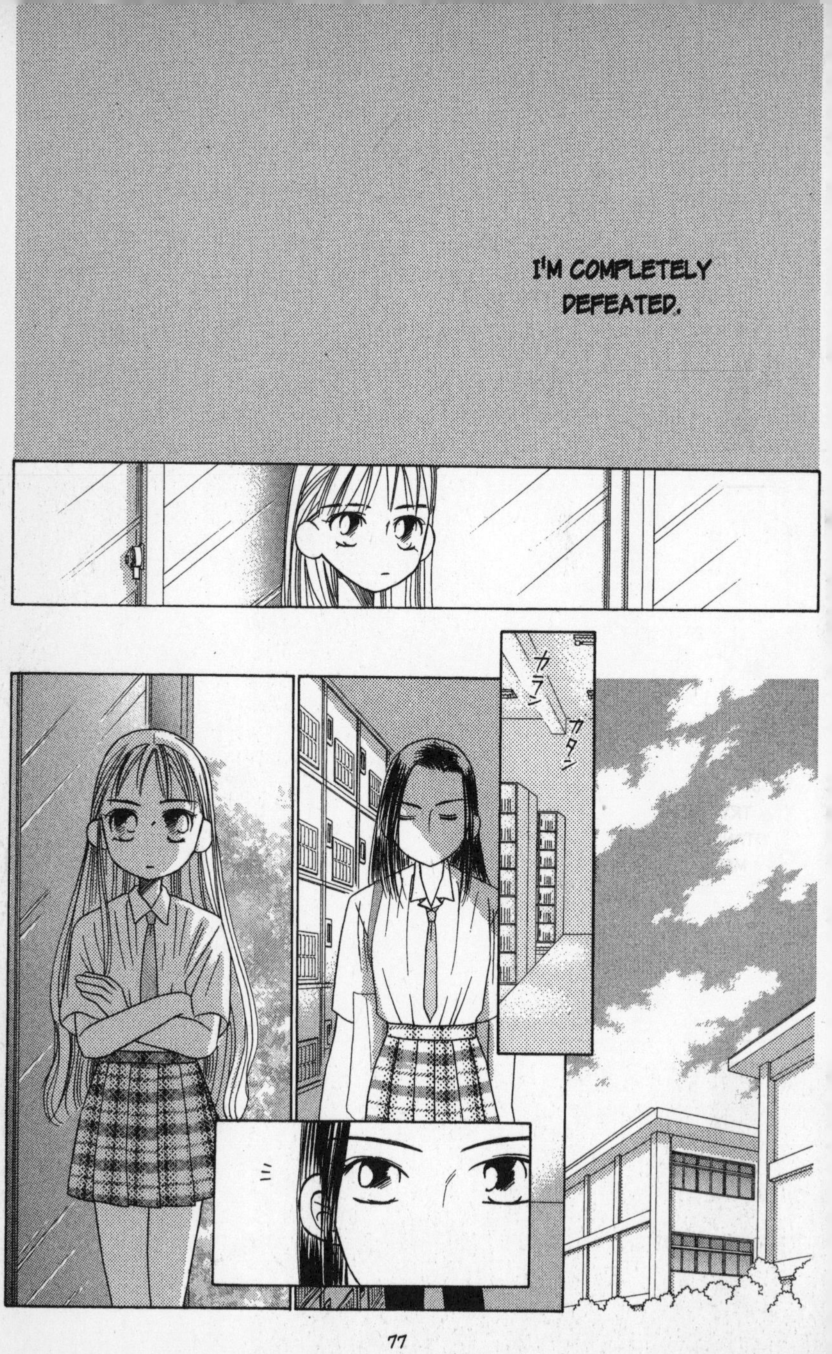
I'M COMPLETELY DEFEATED.
カラン
カタン

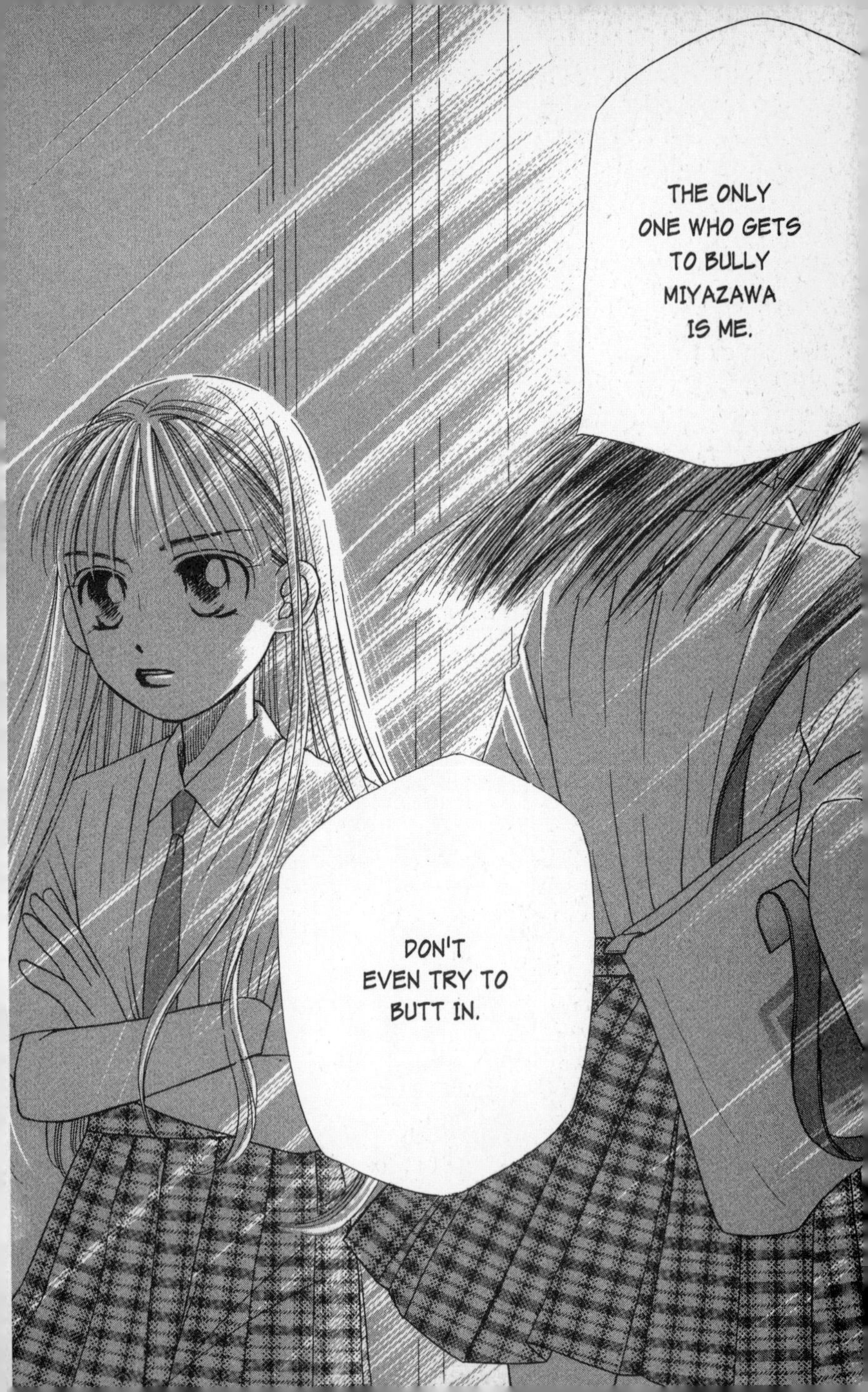
THE ONLY ONE WHO GETS TO BULLY MIYAZAWA IS ME.
DON'T EVEN TRY TO BUTT IN.

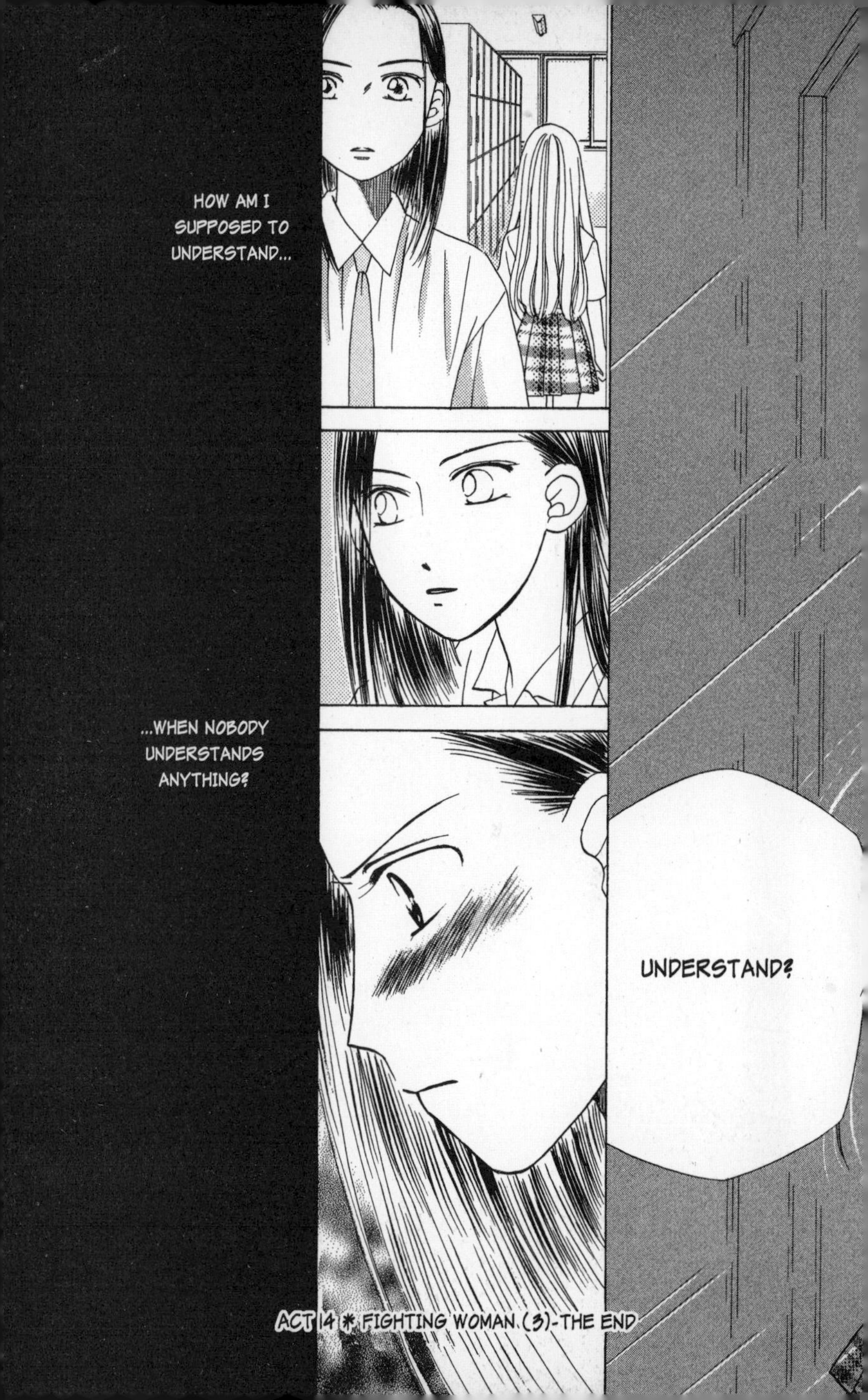
UNDERSTAND?
HOW AM I SUPPOSED TO UNDERSTAND...
...WHEN NOBODY UNDERSTANDS ANYTHING?
ACT 14 * FIGHTING WOMAN (3)-THE END

LATELY I'VE BEEN READING SERIOUS BOOKS WHILE STANDING ON A FOOT MASSAGE PLATFORM.

IF WE TAKE A LOOK AT...
...THE OFFENDER'S MENTALITY...

FOOT MASSAGES FEEL SOOOO GOOD!

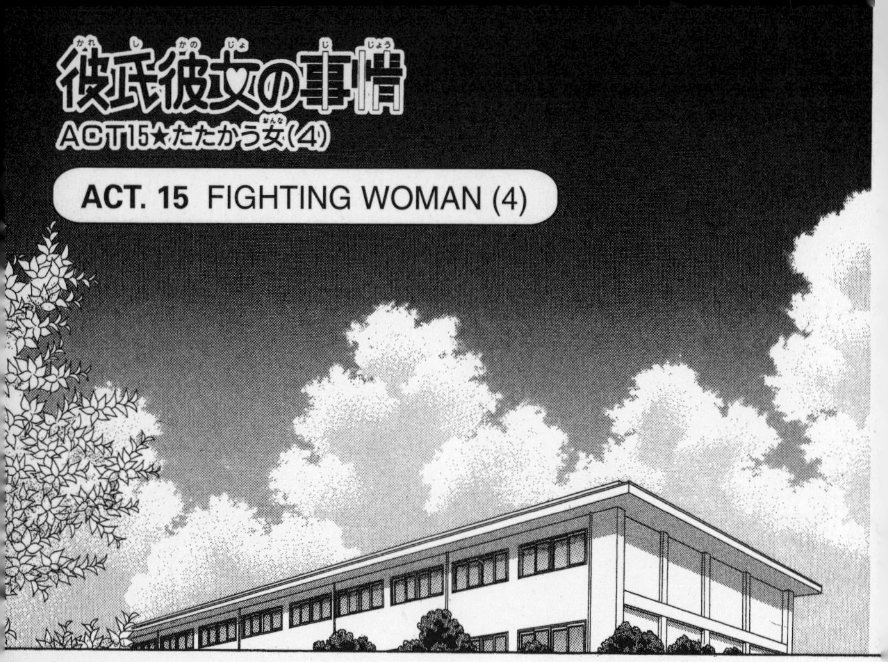
彼氏彼女の事情
ACT15★たたかう女(4)
ACT. 15 FIGHTING WOMAN (4)

WHO IS TO BLAME?

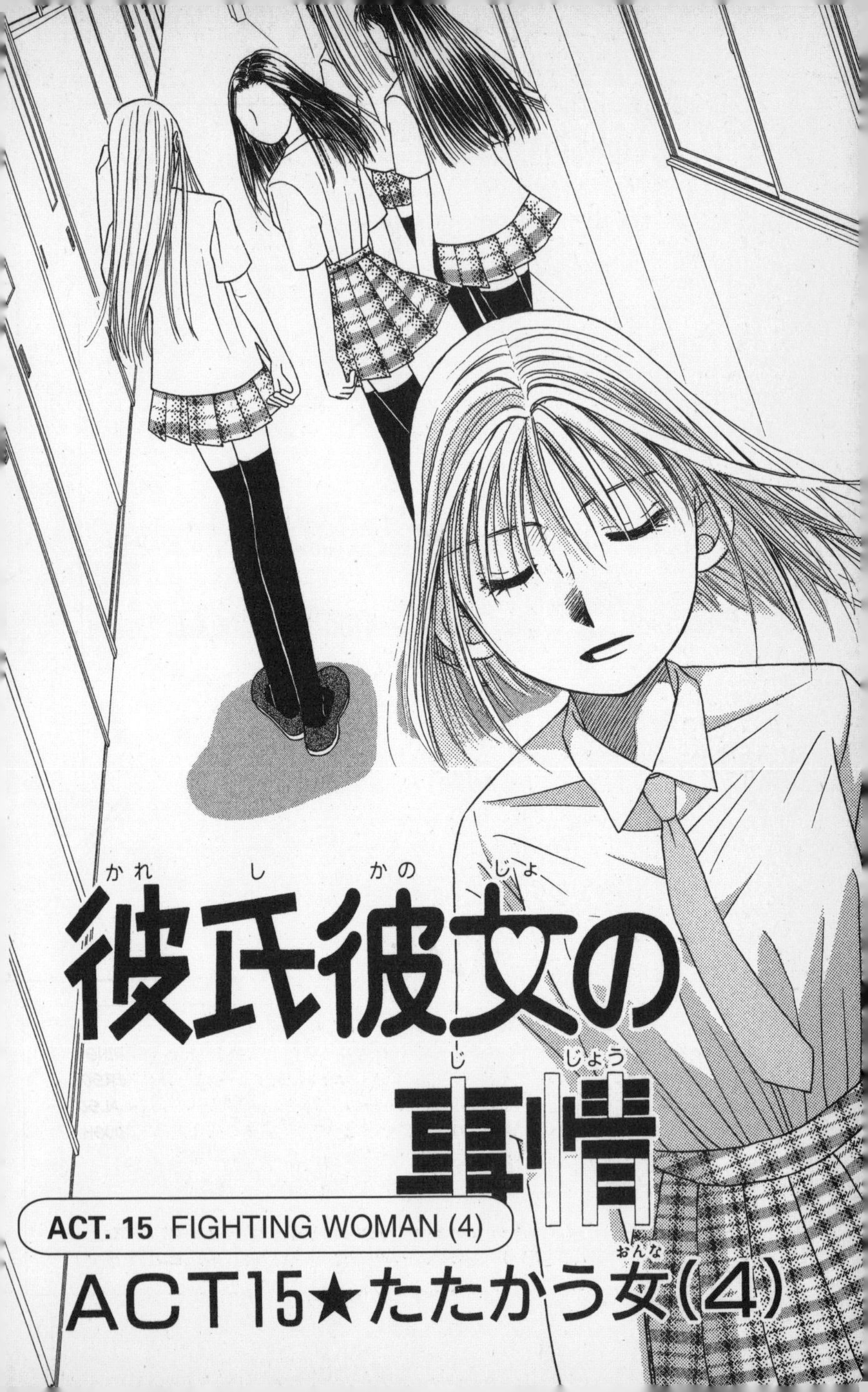
彼氏彼女の事情
ACT. 15 FIGHTING WOMAN (4)
ACT15★たたかう女(4)

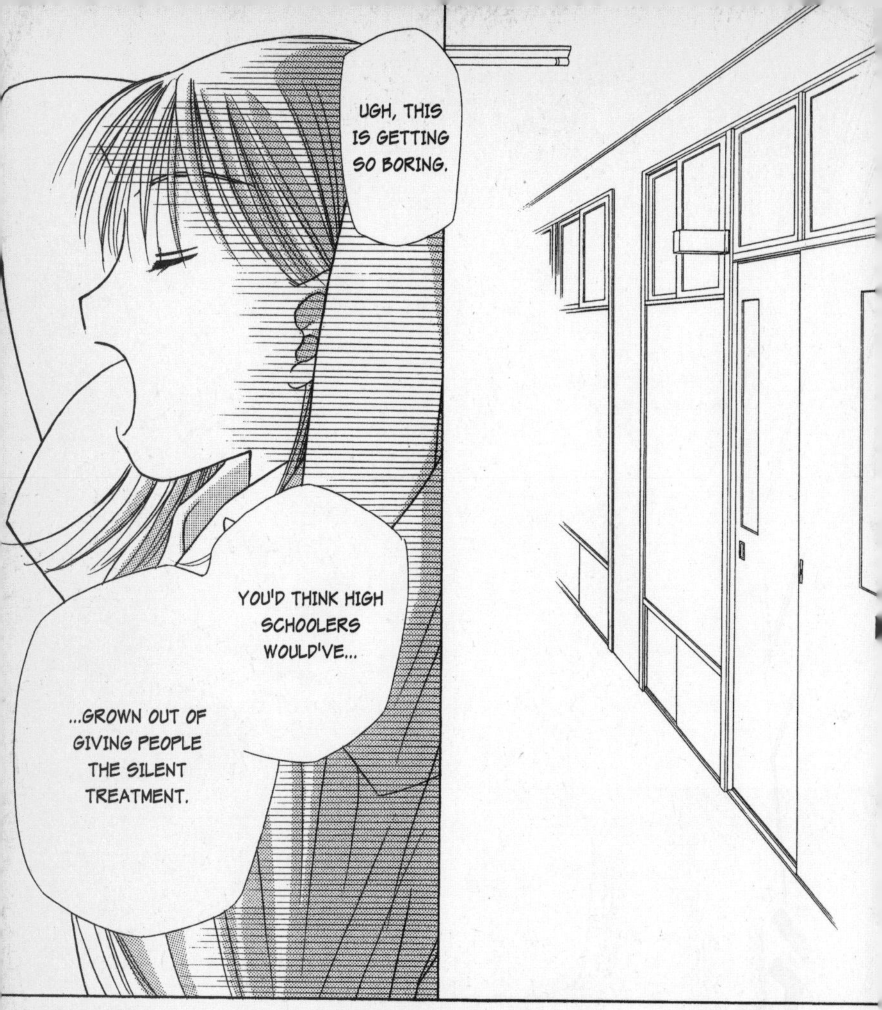
UGH, THIS IS GETTING SO BORING.
YOU'D THINK HIGH SCHOOLERS WOULD'VE...
...GROWN OUT OF GIVING PEOPLE THE SILENT TREATMENT.

ABOUT "SOFIES VERDEN"

"SOFIES VERDEN" WAS A BESTSELLER NOT TOO LONG AGO. TSUDA'S BEEN READING IT, LITTLE BY LITTLE, FOR ABOUT A YEAR NOW. THE REASON IS, IT'S NOT IN MY PERSONALITY TO READ A BOOK FAST, AND ALTHOUGH THE BOOK IS INTERESTING, I'M ALSO READING OTHER BOOKS AT THE SAME TIME. I'M ABOUT 2/3 OF THE WAY THROUGH. I WANT TO FINISH IT SOME TIME THIS YEAR, ABOUT THE TIME THIS MANGA COMES OUT.

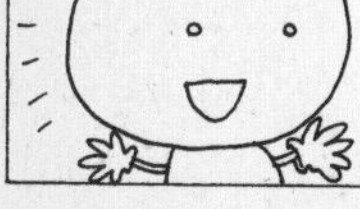

OH, GIMME A BREAK. I WONDER WHAT THIS IDEA IS HERE... SHE CAN'T RECALL FROM THE LAST TIME SHE READ IT ⑦

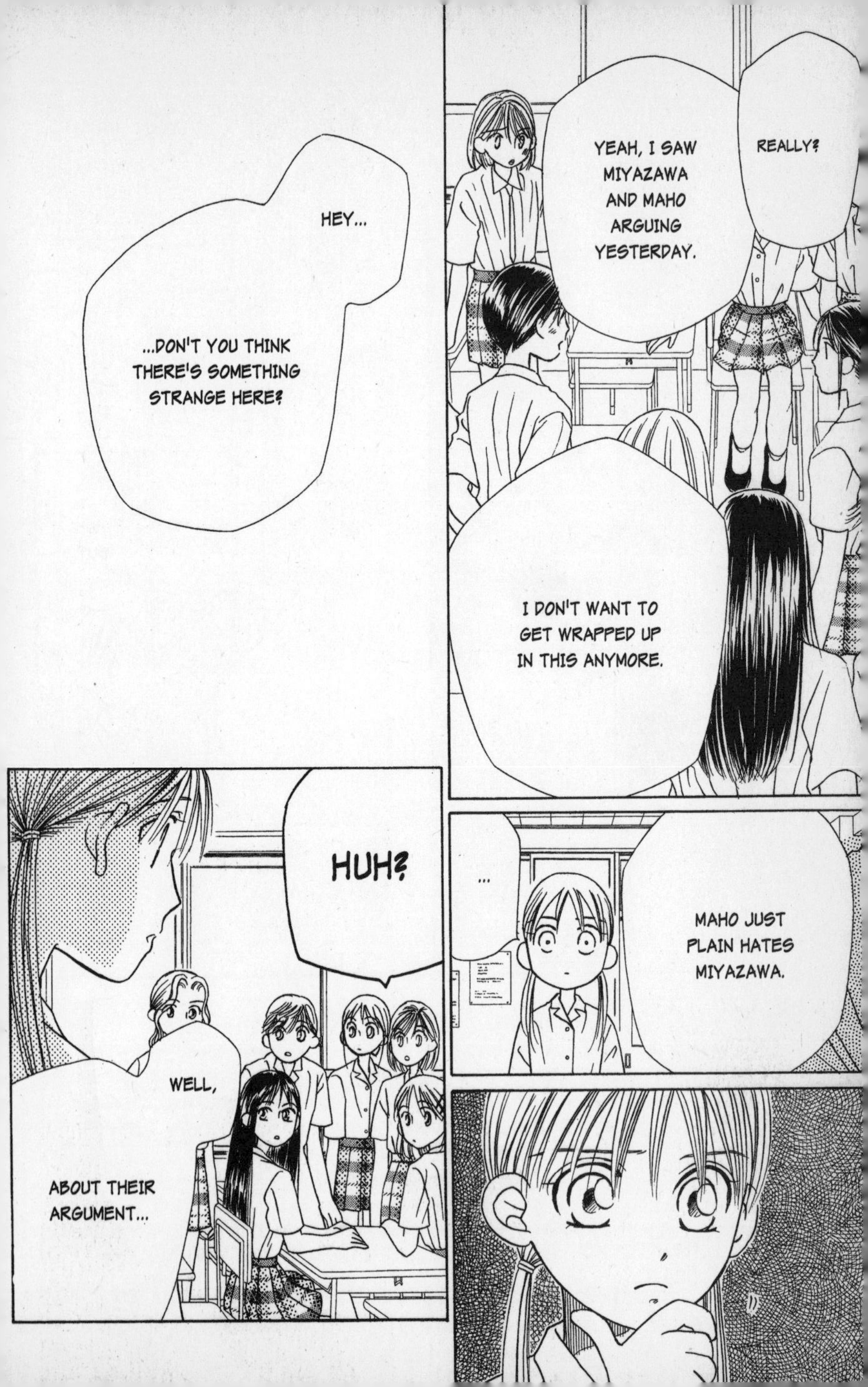
REALLY?
YEAH, I SAW MIYAZAWA AND MAHO ARGUING YESTERDAY.
I DON'T WANT TO GET WRAPPED UP IN THIS ANYMORE.
HEY...
...DON'T YOU THINK THERE'S SOMETHING STRANGE HERE?
MAHO JUST PLAIN HATES MIYAZAWA.
...
HUH?
WELL,
ABOUT THEIR ARGUMENT...

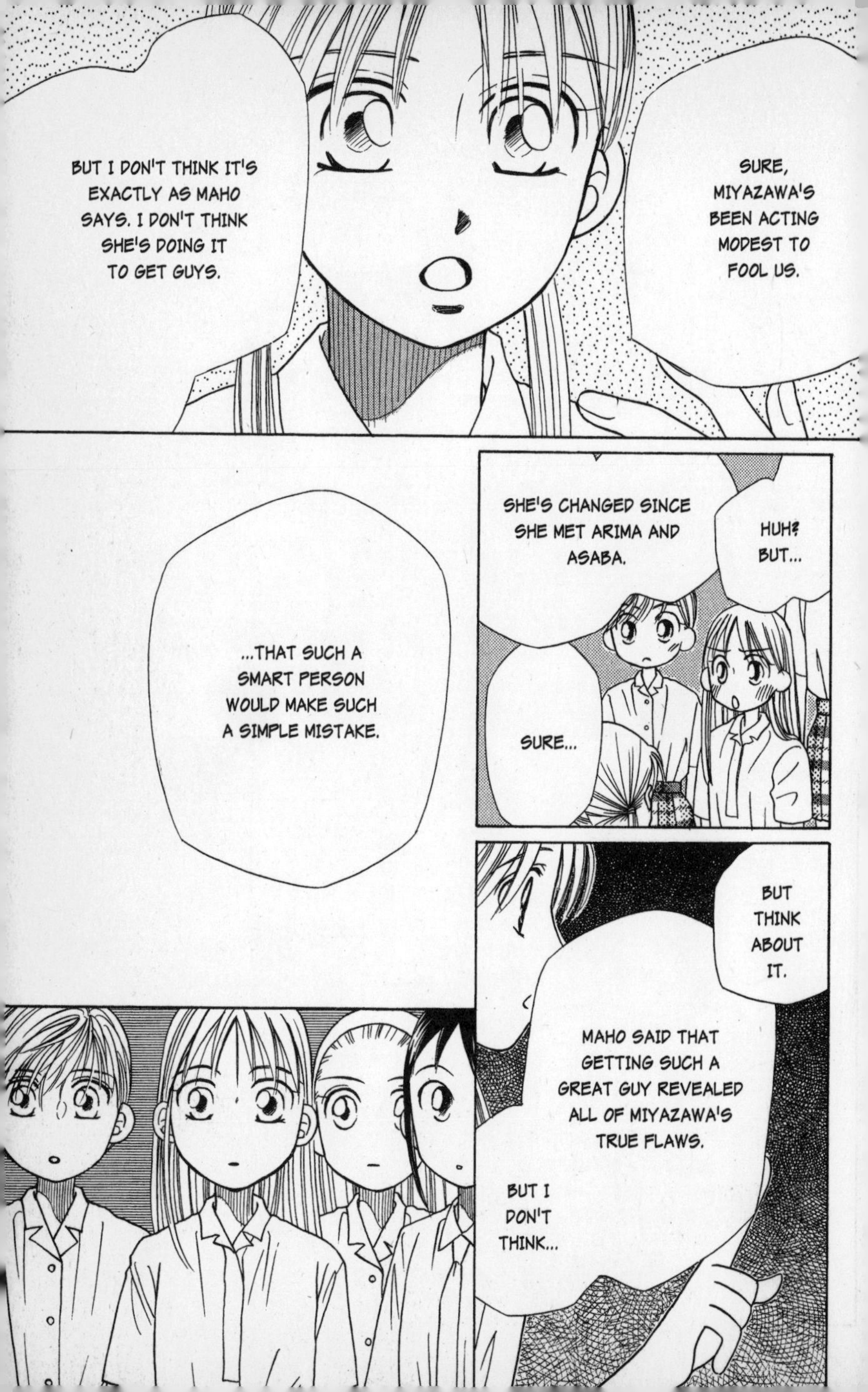
SURE, MIYAZAWA'S BEEN ACTING MODEST TO FOOL US.
BUT I DON'T THINK IT'S EXACTLY AS MAHO SAYS. I DON'T THINK SHE'S DOING IT TO GET GUYS.
HUH? BUT...
SHE'S CHANGED SINCE SHE MET ARIMA AND ASABA.
SURE...
BUT THINK ABOUT IT.
MAHO SAID THAT GETTING SUCH A GREAT GUY REVEALED ALL OF MIYAZAWA'S TRUE FLAWS.
BUT I DON'T THINK...
...THAT SUCH A SMART PERSON WOULD MAKE SUCH A SIMPLE MISTAKE.

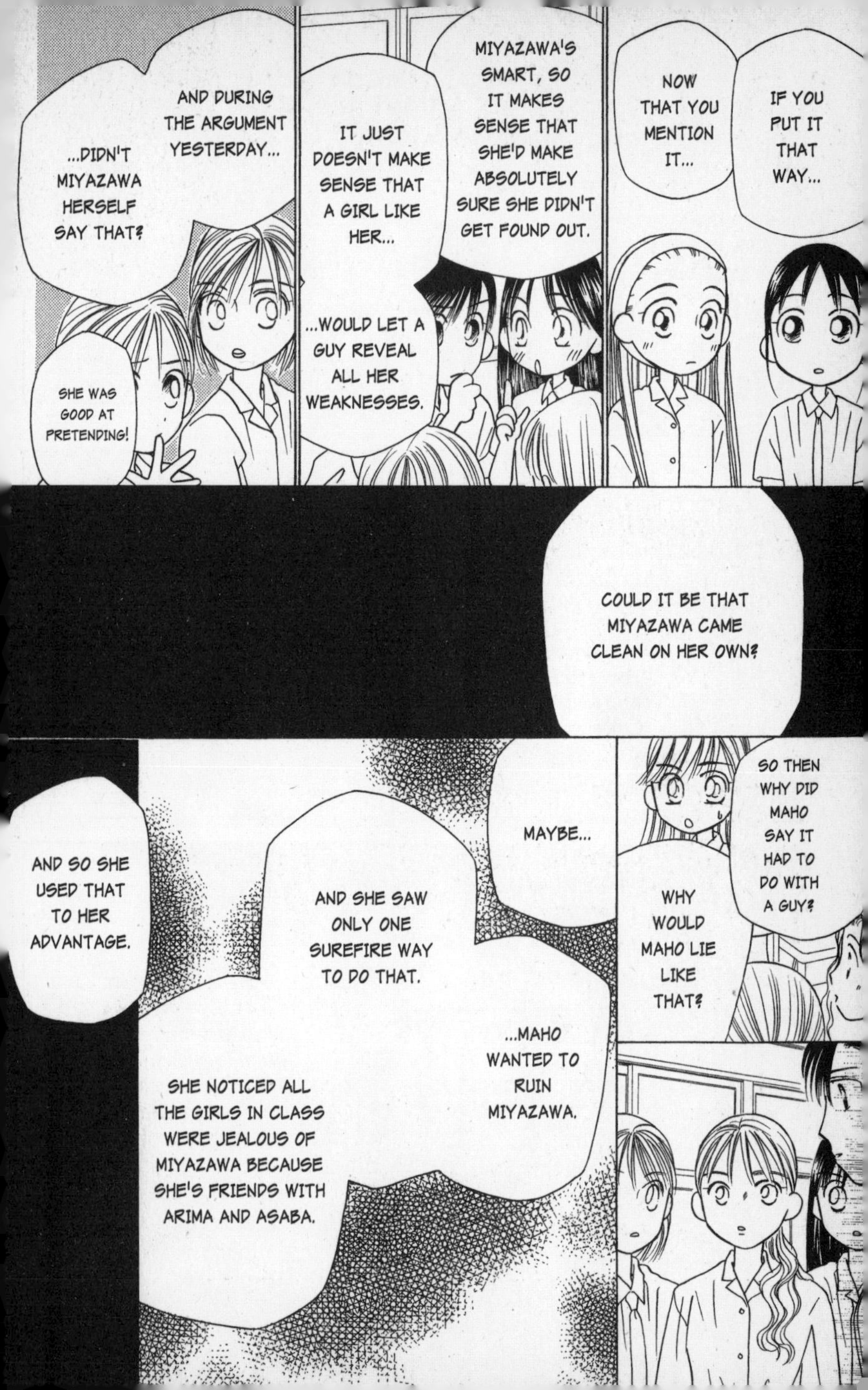
IF YOU PUT IT THAT WAY...
NOW THAT YOU MENTION IT...
MIYAZAWA'S SMART, SO IT MAKES SENSE THAT SHE'D MAKE ABSOLUTELY SURE SHE DIDN'T GET FOUND OUT.
IT JUST DOESN'T MAKE SENSE THAT A GIRL LIKE HER...
...WOULD LET A GUY REVEAL ALL HER WEAKNESSES.
AND DURING THE ARGUMENT YESTERDAY...
...DIDN'T MIYAZAWA HERSELF SAY THAT?
SHE WAS GOOD AT PRETENDING!
COULD IT BE THAT MIYAZAWA CAME CLEAN ON HER OWN?
SO THEN WHY DID MAHO SAY IT HAD TO DO WITH A GUY?
WHY WOULD MAHO LIE LIKE THAT?
MAYBE...
...MAHO WANTED TO RUIN MIYAZAWA.
AND SHE SAW ONLY ONE SUREFIRE WAY TO DO THAT.
SHE NOTICED ALL THE GIRLS IN CLASS WERE JEALOUS OF MIYAZAWA BECAUSE SHE'S FRIENDS WITH ARIMA AND ASABA.
AND SO SHE USED THAT TO HER ADVANTAGE.

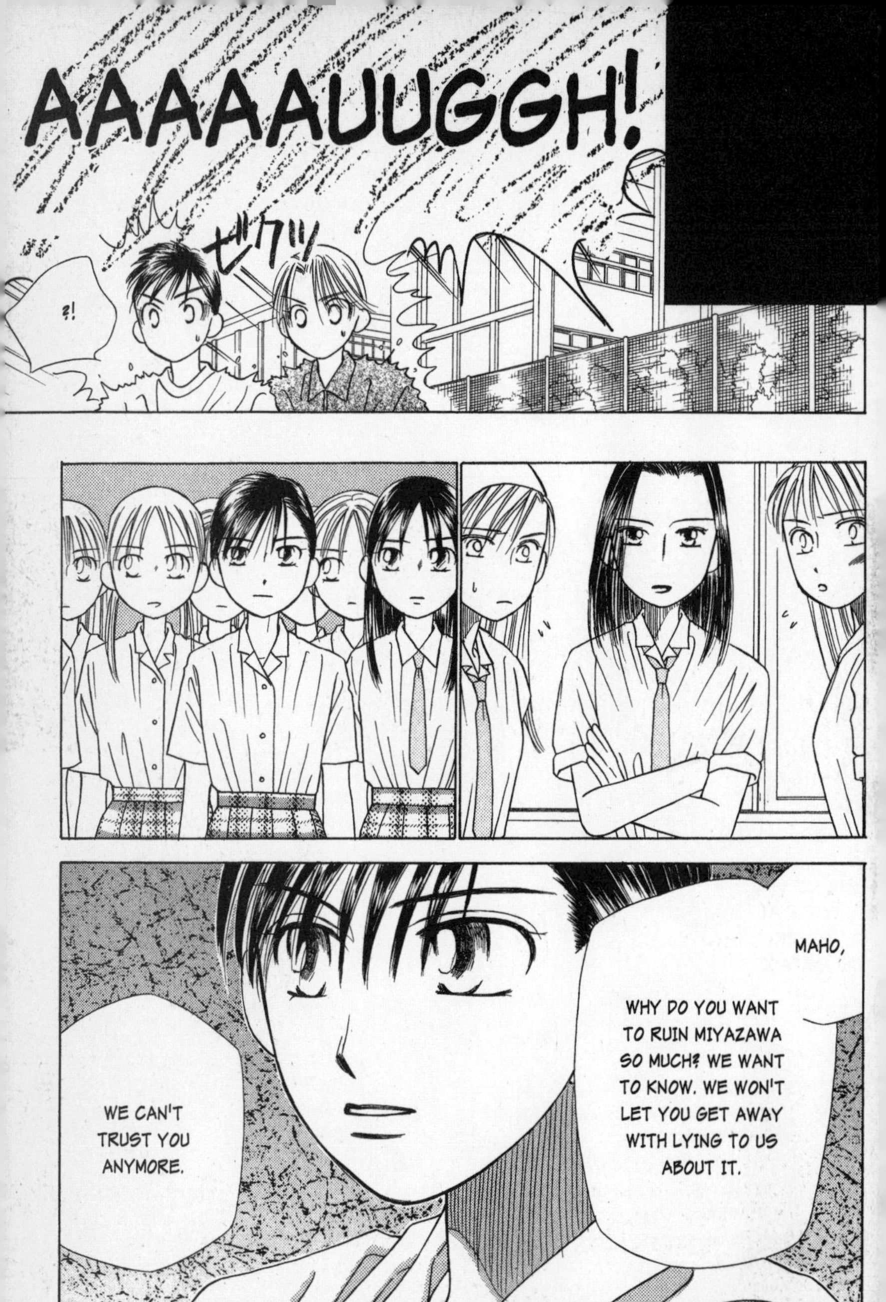
AAAAAUUGGH!
ゾクッ
?!
MAHO,
WHY DO YOU WANT TO RUIN MIYAZAWA SO MUCH? WE WANT TO KNOW. WE WON'T LET YOU GET AWAY WITH LYING TO US ABOUT IT.
WE CAN'T TRUST YOU ANYMORE.

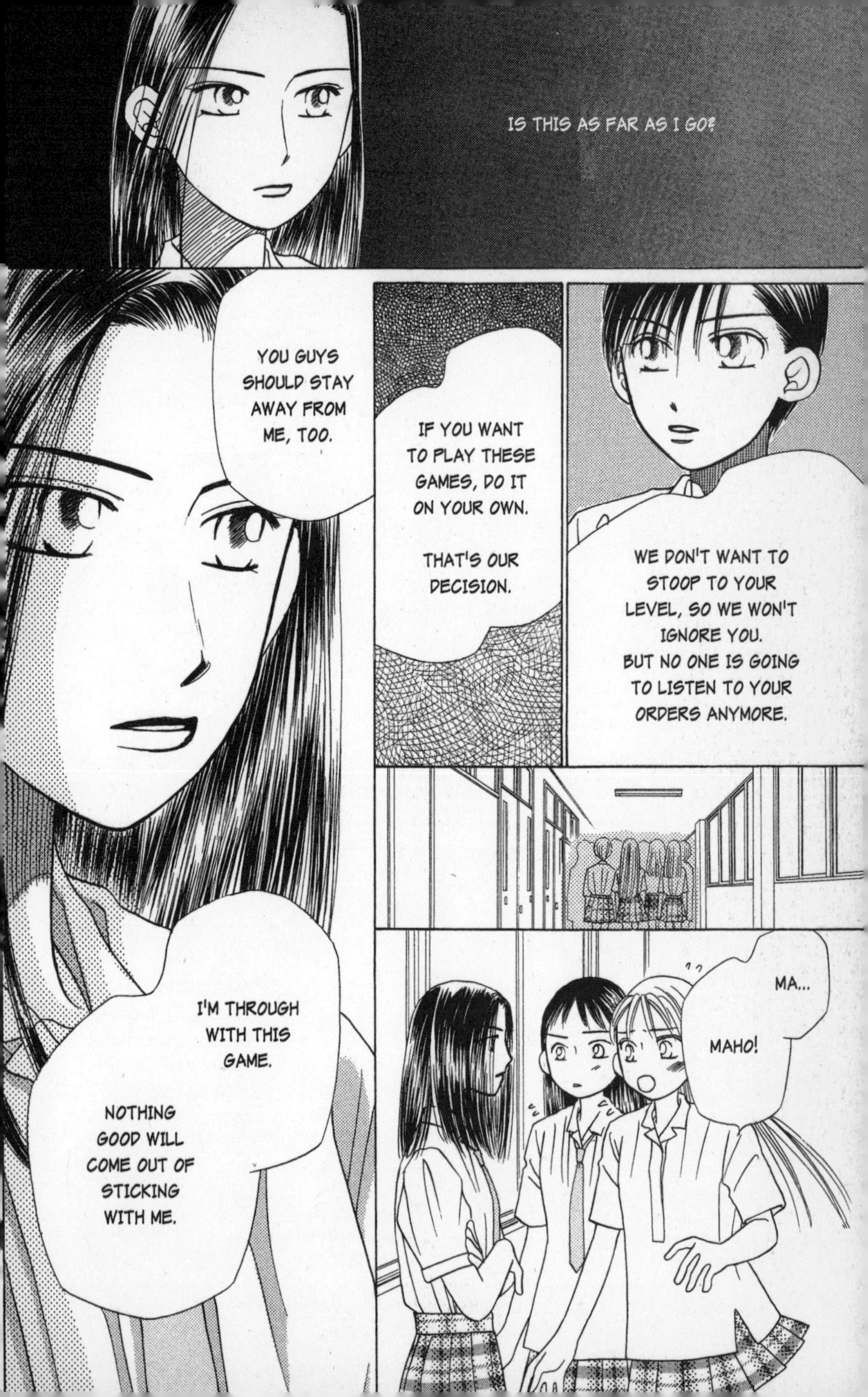
IS THIS AS FAR AS I GO?
WE DON'T WANT TO STOOP TO YOUR LEVEL, SO WE WON'T IGNORE YOU. BUT NO ONE IS GOING TO LISTEN TO YOUR ORDERS ANYMORE.
IF YOU WANT TO PLAY THESE GAMES, DO IT ON YOUR OWN.
THAT'S OUR DECISION.
MA...
MAHO!
YOU GUYS SHOULD STAY AWAY FROM ME, TOO.
I'M THROUGH WITH THIS GAME.
NOTHING GOOD WILL COME OUT OF STICKING WITH ME.

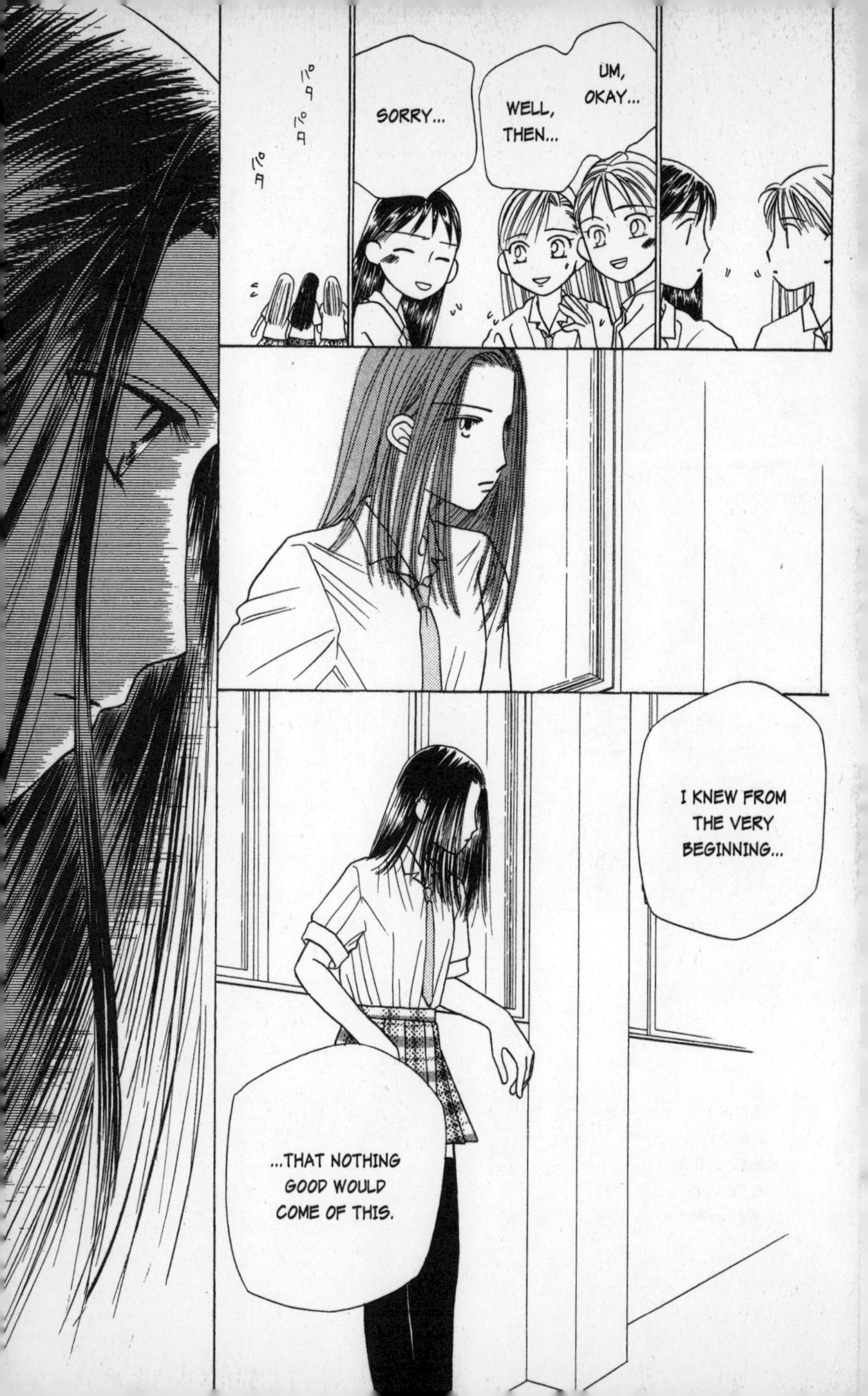
UM, OKAY...
WELL, THEN...
SORRY...
パタパタパタ
I KNEW FROM THE VERY BEGINNING...
...THAT NOTHING GOOD WOULD COME OF THIS.

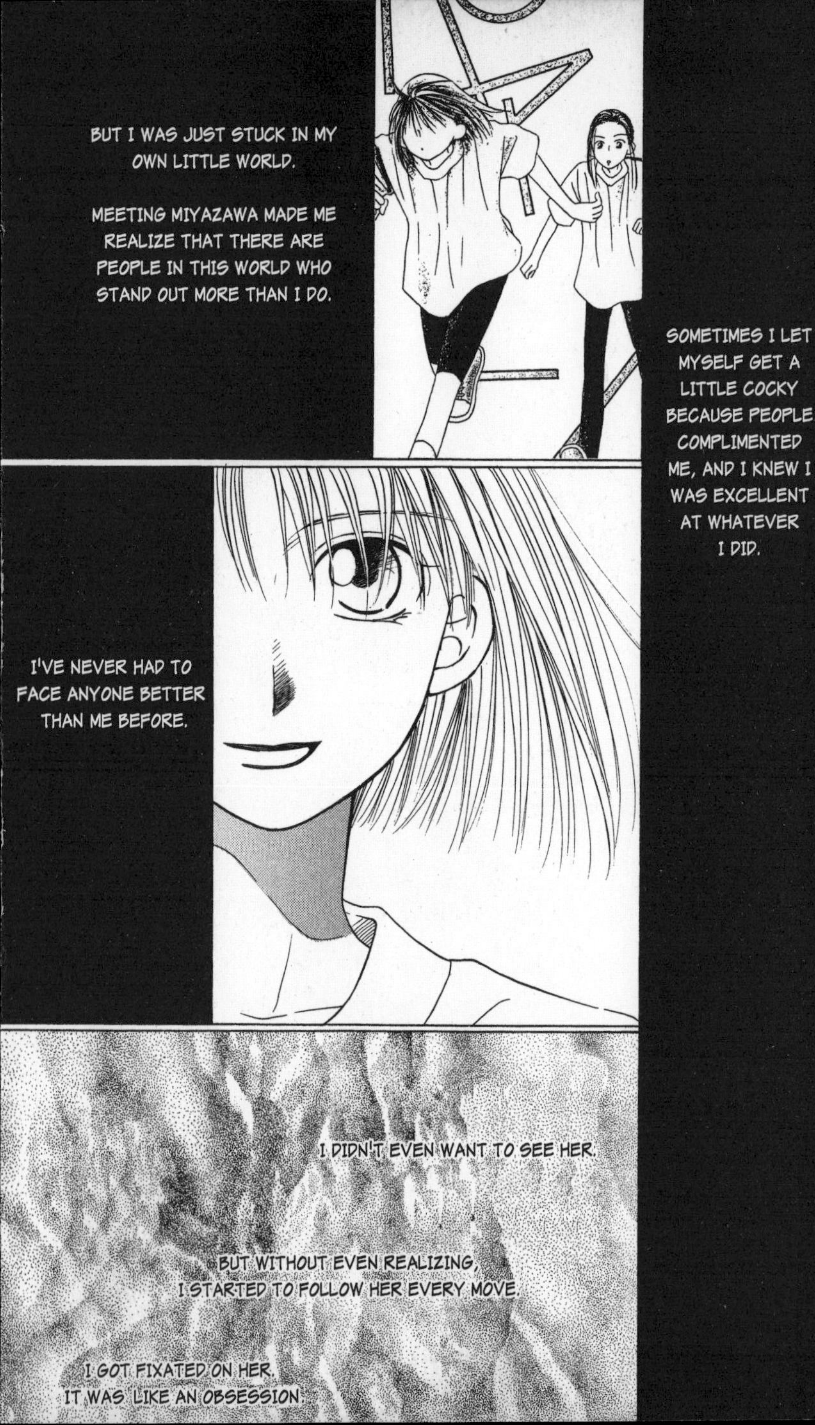
SOMETIMES I LET MYSELF GET A LITTLE COCKY BECAUSE PEOPLE COMPLIMENTED ME, AND I KNEW I WAS EXCELLENT AT WHATEVER I DID.
BUT I WAS JUST STUCK IN MY OWN LITTLE WORLD.
MEETING MIYAZAWA MADE ME REALIZE THAT THERE ARE PEOPLE IN THIS WORLD WHO STAND OUT MORE THAN I DO.
I'VE NEVER HAD TO FACE ANYONE BETTER THAN ME BEFORE.
I DIDN'T EVEN WANT TO SEE HER.
BUT WITHOUT EVEN REALIZING, I STARTED TO FOLLOW HER EVERY MOVE.
I GOT FIXATED ON HER. IT WAS LIKE AN OBSESSION.

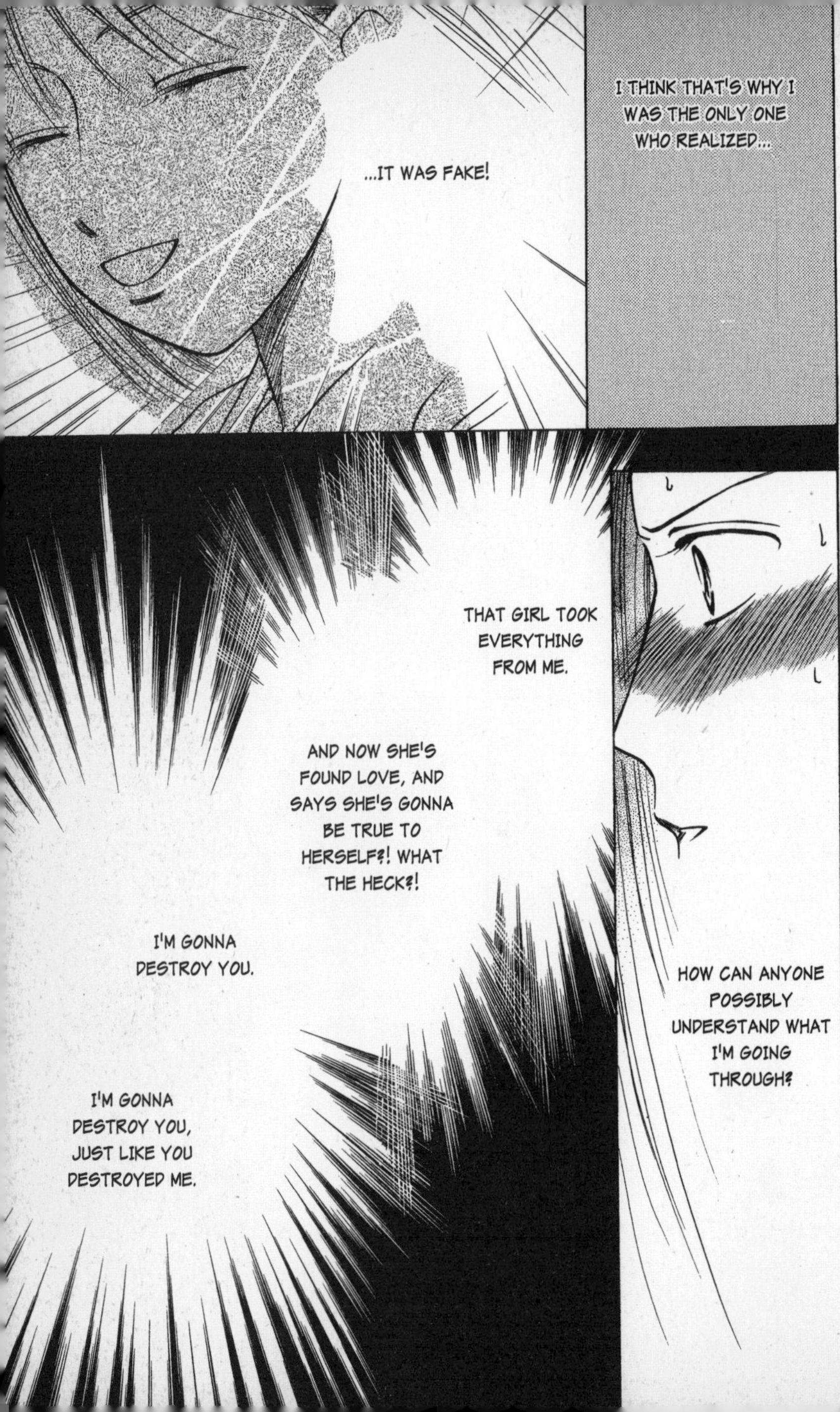
I THINK THAT'S WHY I WAS THE ONLY ONE WHO REALIZED...
...IT WAS FAKE!
HOW CAN ANYONE POSSIBLY UNDERSTAND WHAT I'M GOING THROUGH?
THAT GIRL TOOK EVERYTHING FROM ME.
AND NOW SHE'S FOUND LOVE, AND SAYS SHE'S GONNA BE TRUE TO HERSELF?! WHAT THE HECK?!
I'M GONNA DESTROY YOU.
I'M GONNA DESTROY YOU, JUST LIKE YOU DESTROYED ME.

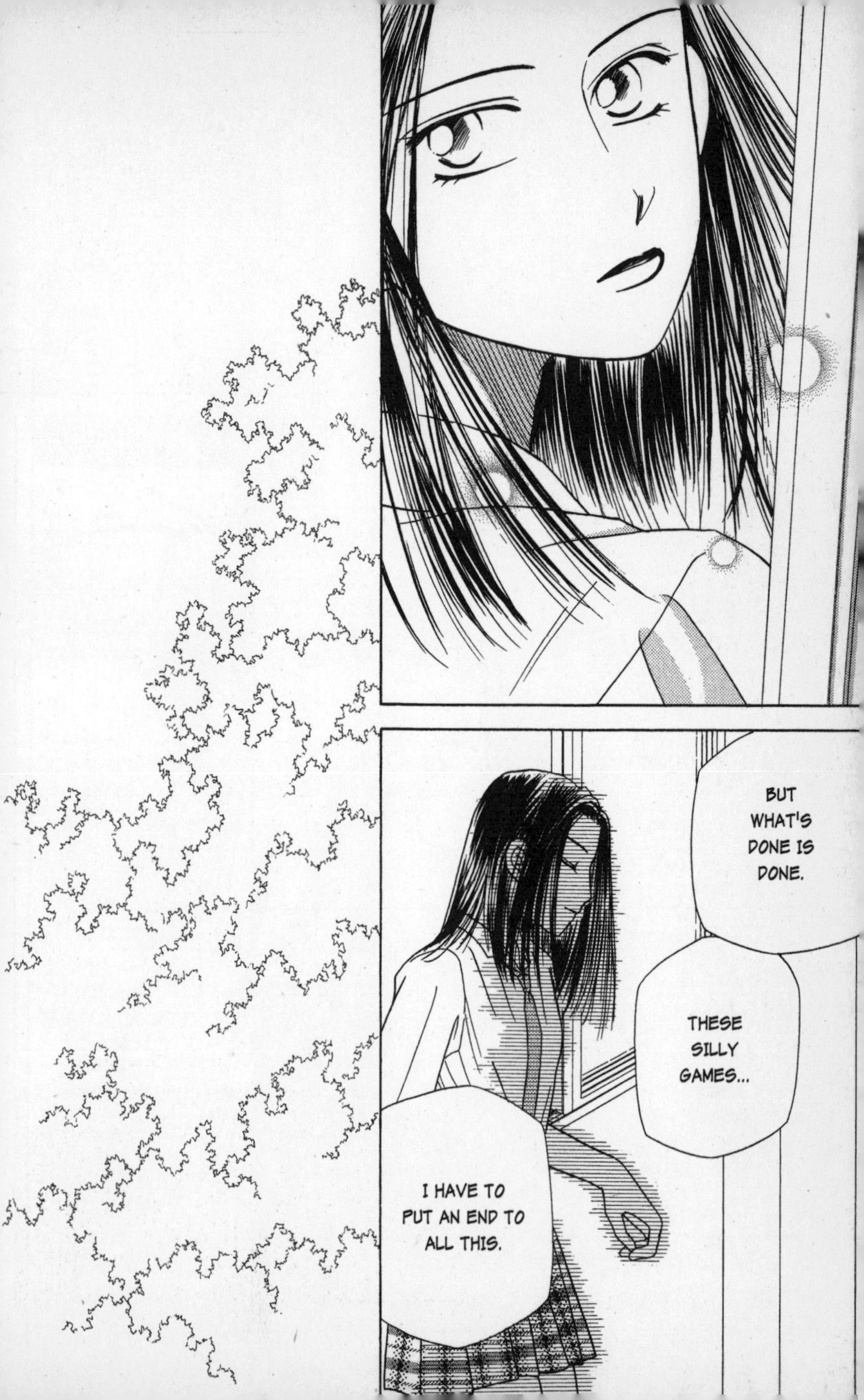
BUT WHAT'S DONE IS DONE.
THESE SILLY GAMES...
I HAVE TO PUT AN END TO ALL THIS.

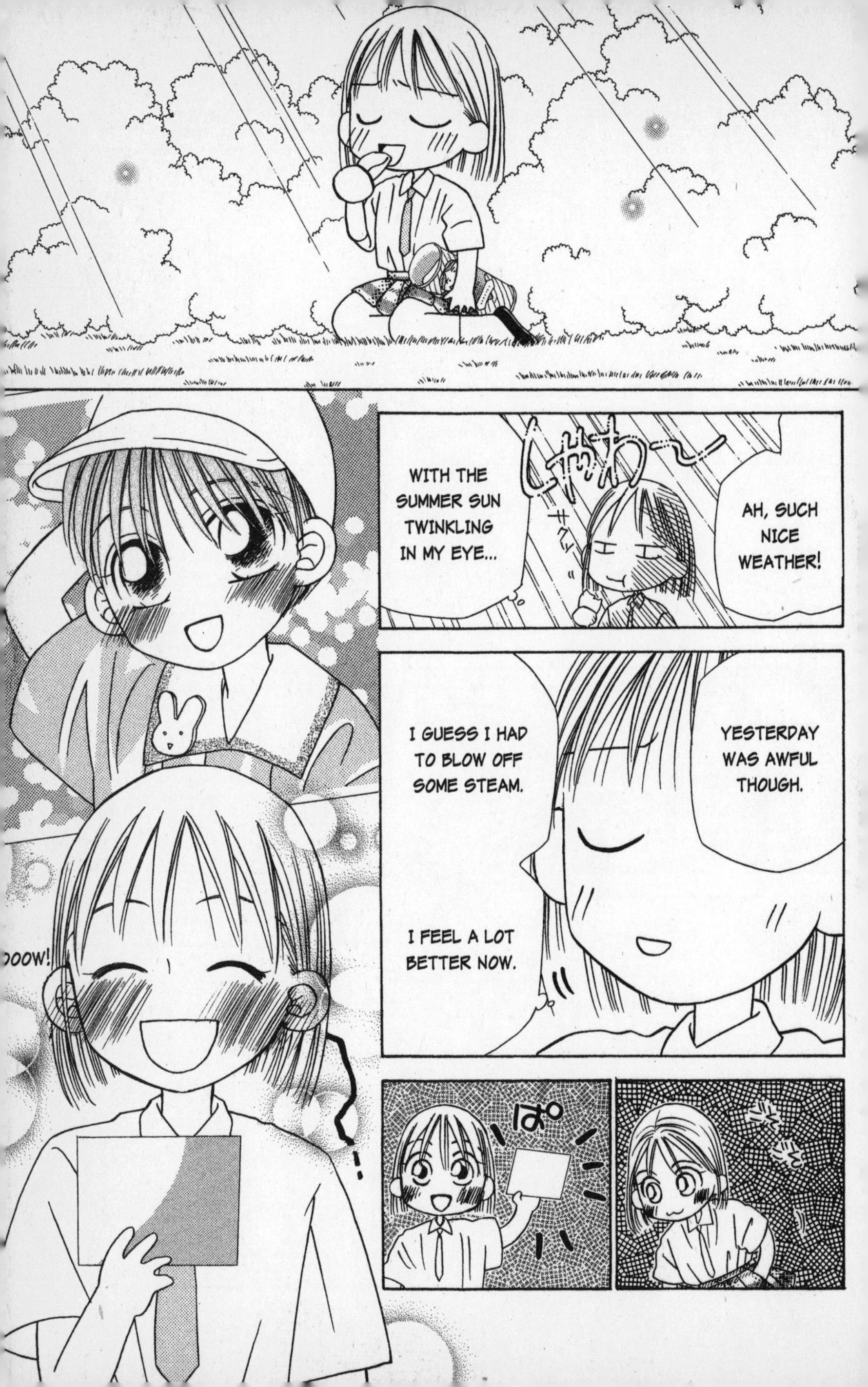
AH, SUCH NICE WEATHER!
しゃわ〜〜
WITH THE SUMMER SUN TWINKLING IN MY EYE...
YESTERDAY WAS AWFUL THOUGH.
I GUESS I HAD TO BLOW OFF SOME STEAM.
I FEEL A LOT BETTER NOW.
ぱ
OOOW!

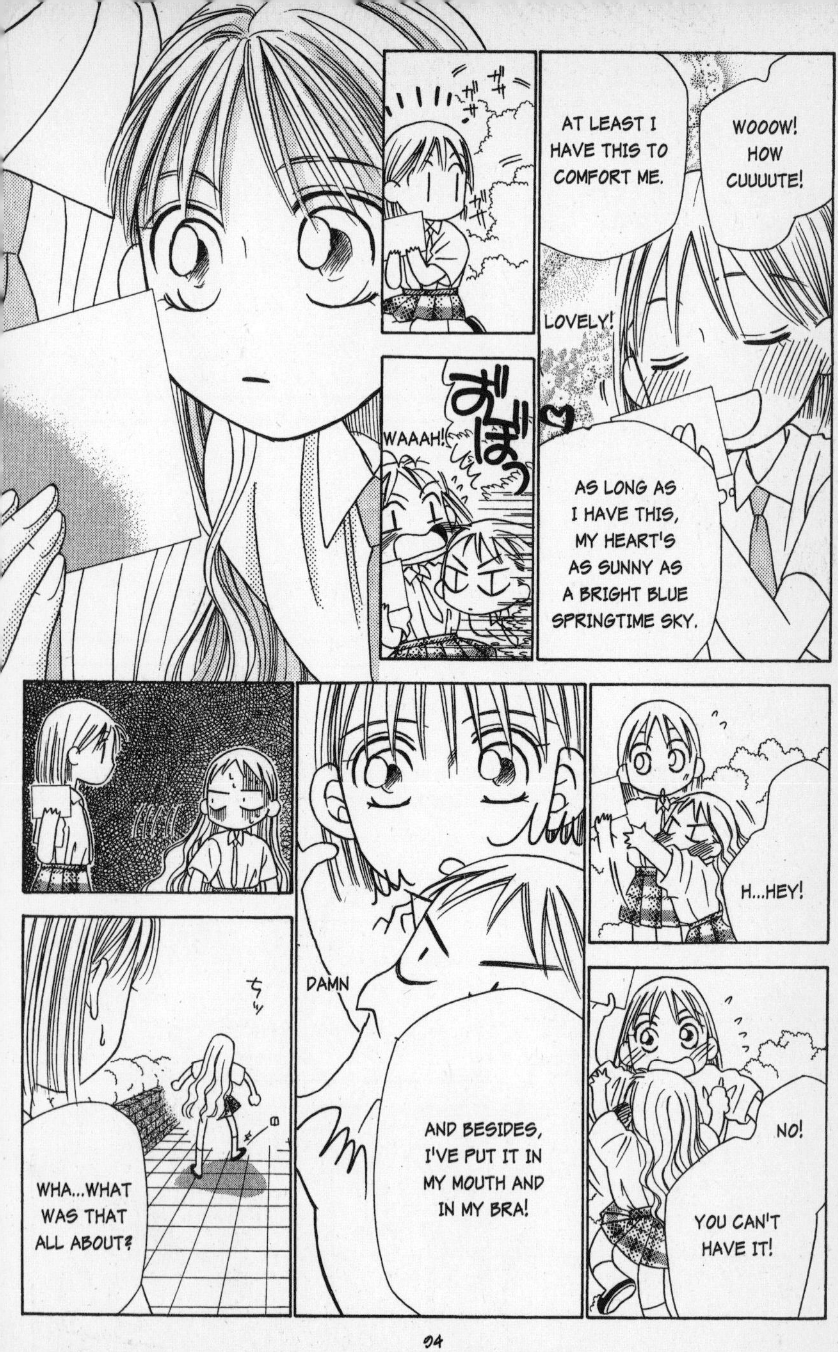
WOOOW! HOW CUUUUTE!
AT LEAST I HAVE THIS TO COMFORT ME.
LOVELY!
AS LONG AS I HAVE THIS, MY HEART'S AS SUNNY AS A BRIGHT BLUE SPRINGTIME SKY.
ガサ ガサ
おんぼっ
WAAAH!
H...HEY!
NO!
YOU CAN'T HAVE IT!
DAMN
AND BESIDES, I'VE PUT IT IN MY MOUTH AND IN MY BRA!
ちッ
WHA...WHAT WAS THAT ALL ABOUT?

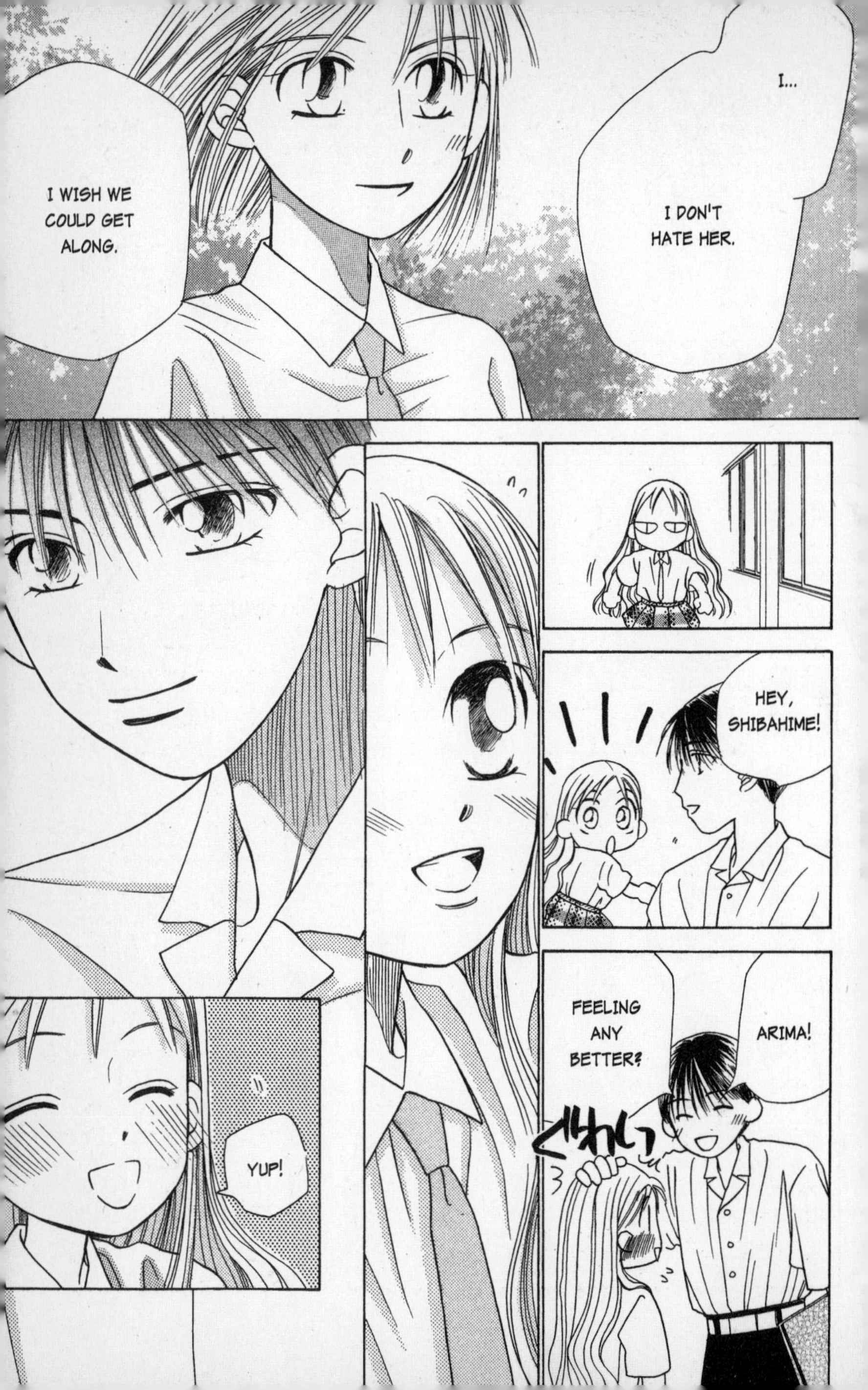
I...
I DON'T HATE HER.
I WISH WE COULD GET ALONG.
HEY, SHIBAHIME!
ARIMA!
FEELING ANY BETTER?
YUP!

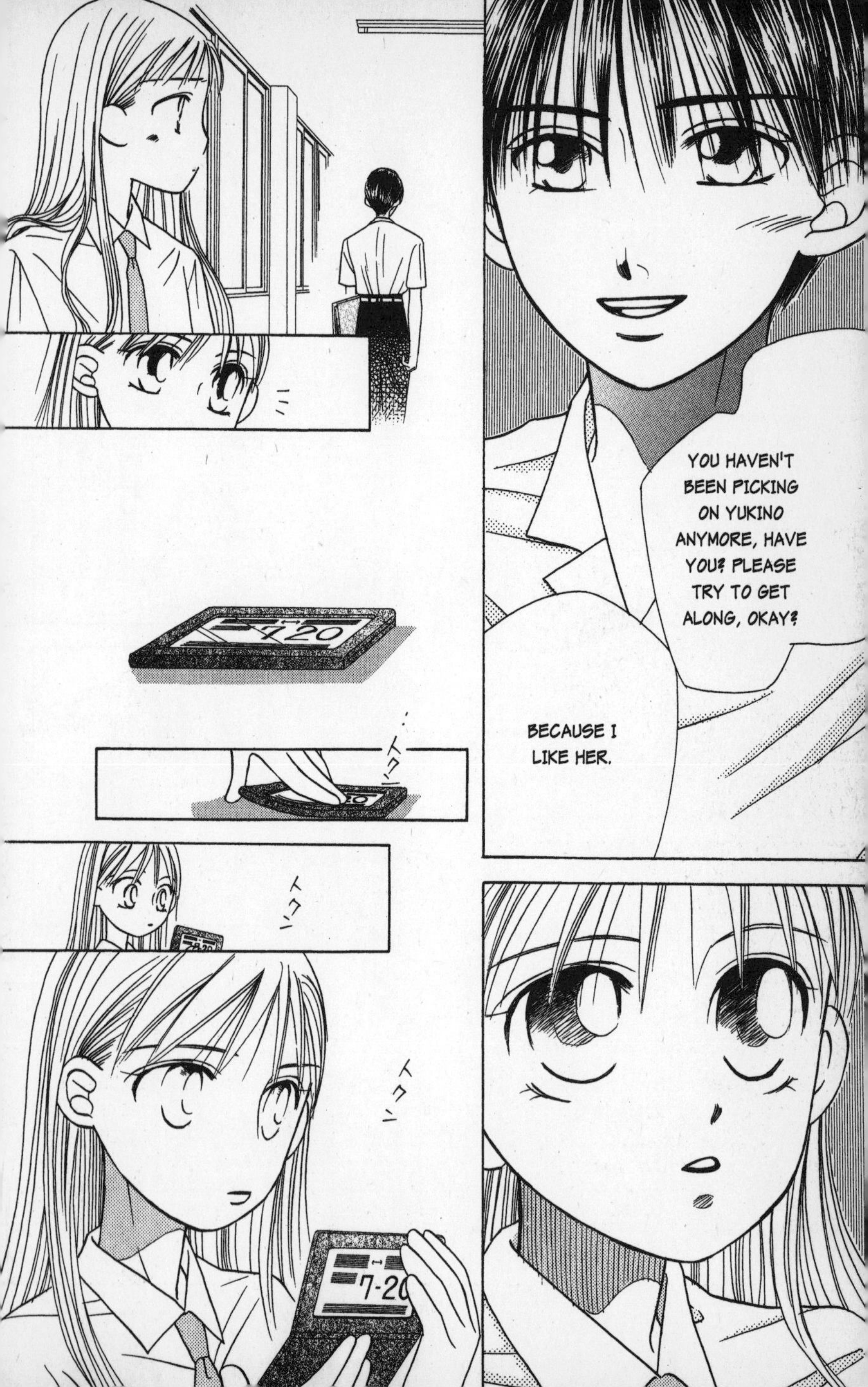
YOU HAVEN'T BEEN PICKING ON YUKINO ANYMORE, HAVE YOU? PLEASE TRY TO GET ALONG, OKAY?
BECAUSE I LIKE HER.
トクン
トクン
トクン

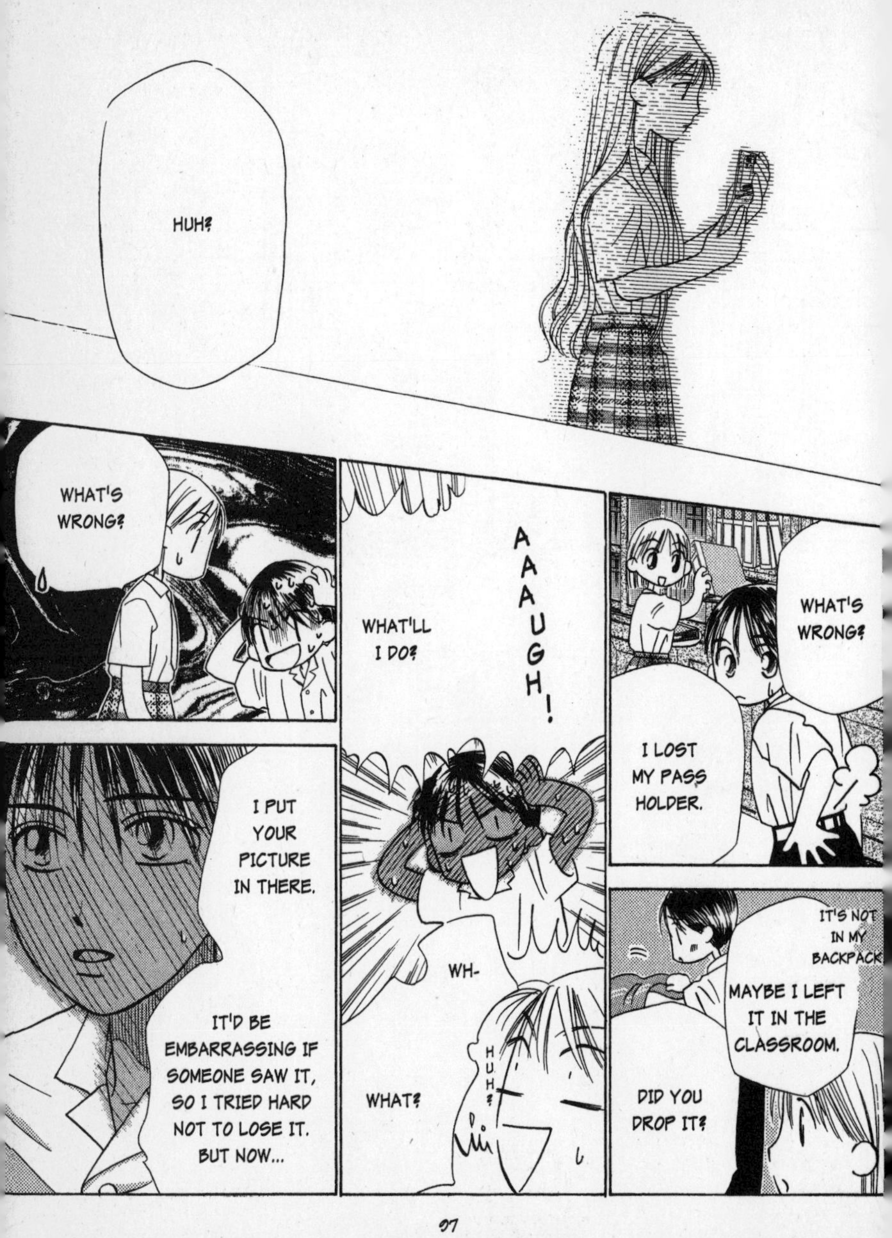
HUH?
WHAT'S WRONG?
I LOST MY PASS HOLDER.
IT'S NOT IN MY BACKPACK
MAYBE I LEFT IT IN THE CLASSROOM.
DID YOU DROP IT?
AAAUGH!
WHAT'LL I DO?
WH-
HUH?
WHAT?
WHAT'S WRONG?
I PUT YOUR PICTURE IN THERE.
IT'D BE EMBARRASSING IF SOMEONE SAW IT, SO I TRIED HARD NOT TO LOSE IT. BUT NOW...

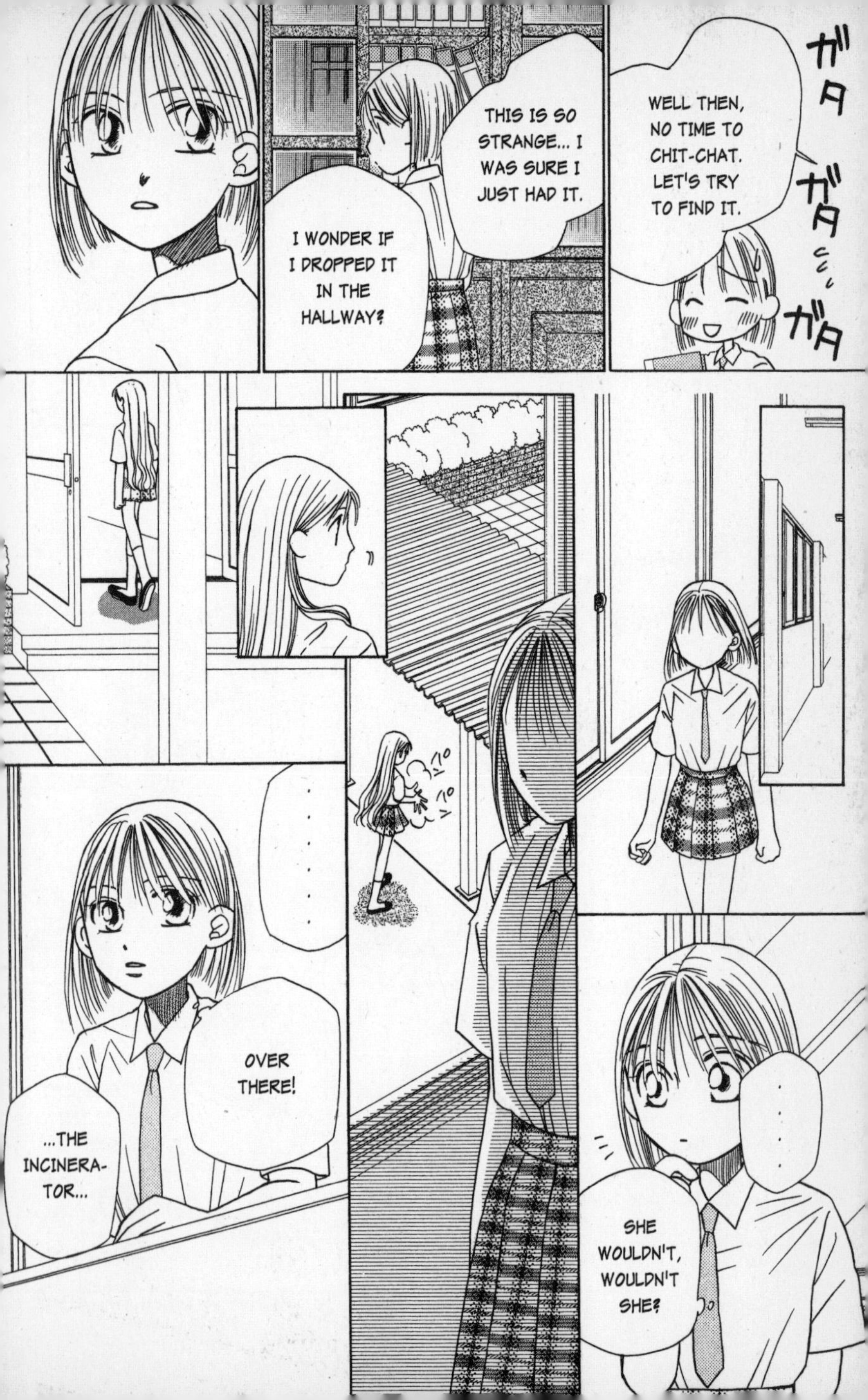
ガタ
ガタ
ガタ
WELL THEN, NO TIME TO CHIT-CHAT. LET'S TRY TO FIND IT.
THIS IS SO STRANGE... I WAS SURE I JUST HAD IT.
I WONDER IF I DROPPED IT IN THE HALLWAY?
SHE WOULDN'T, WOULDN'T SHE?
OVER THERE!
...THE INCINERATOR...

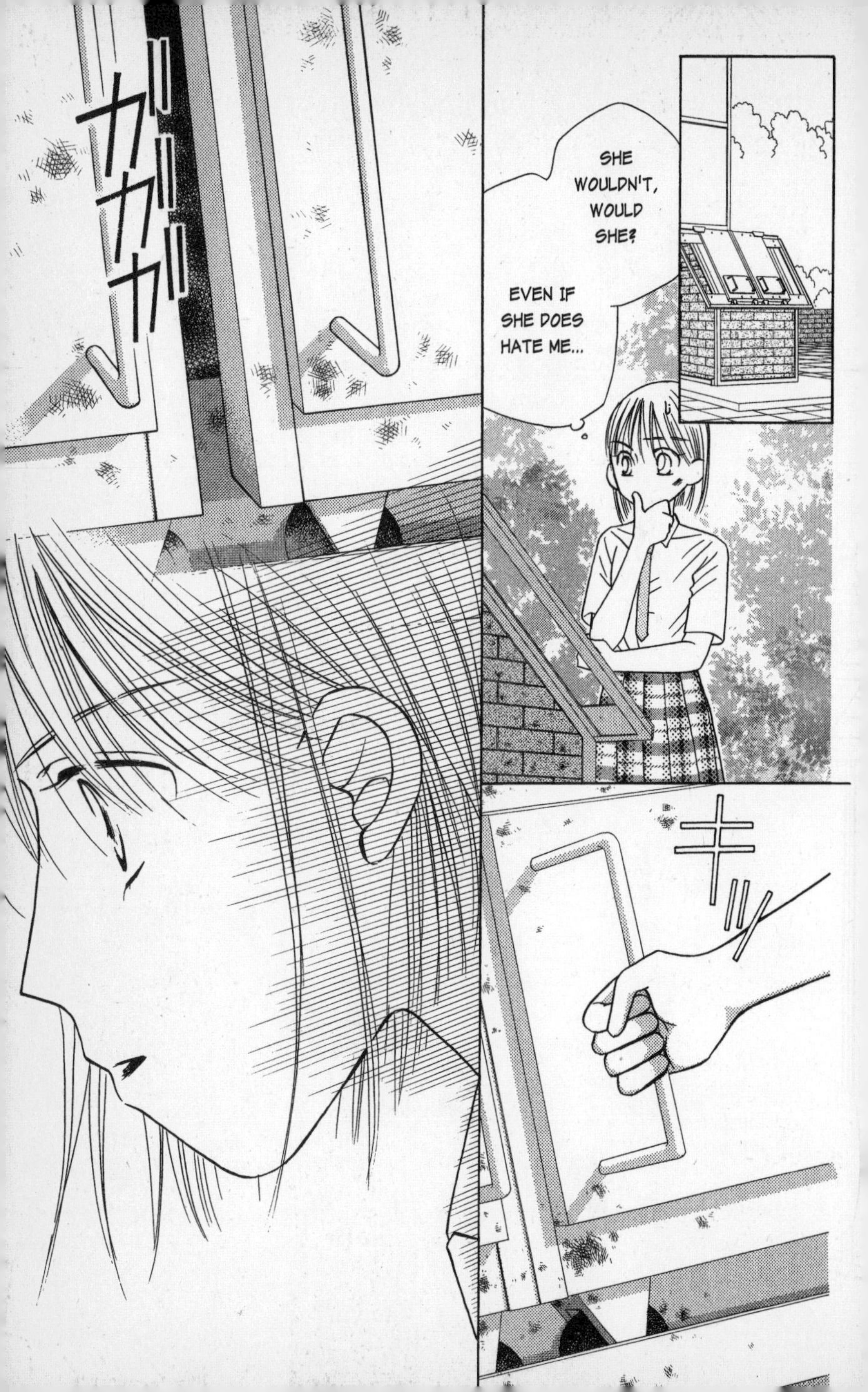
SHE WOULDN'T, WOULD SHE?
EVEN IF SHE DOES HATE ME...
ガガガ

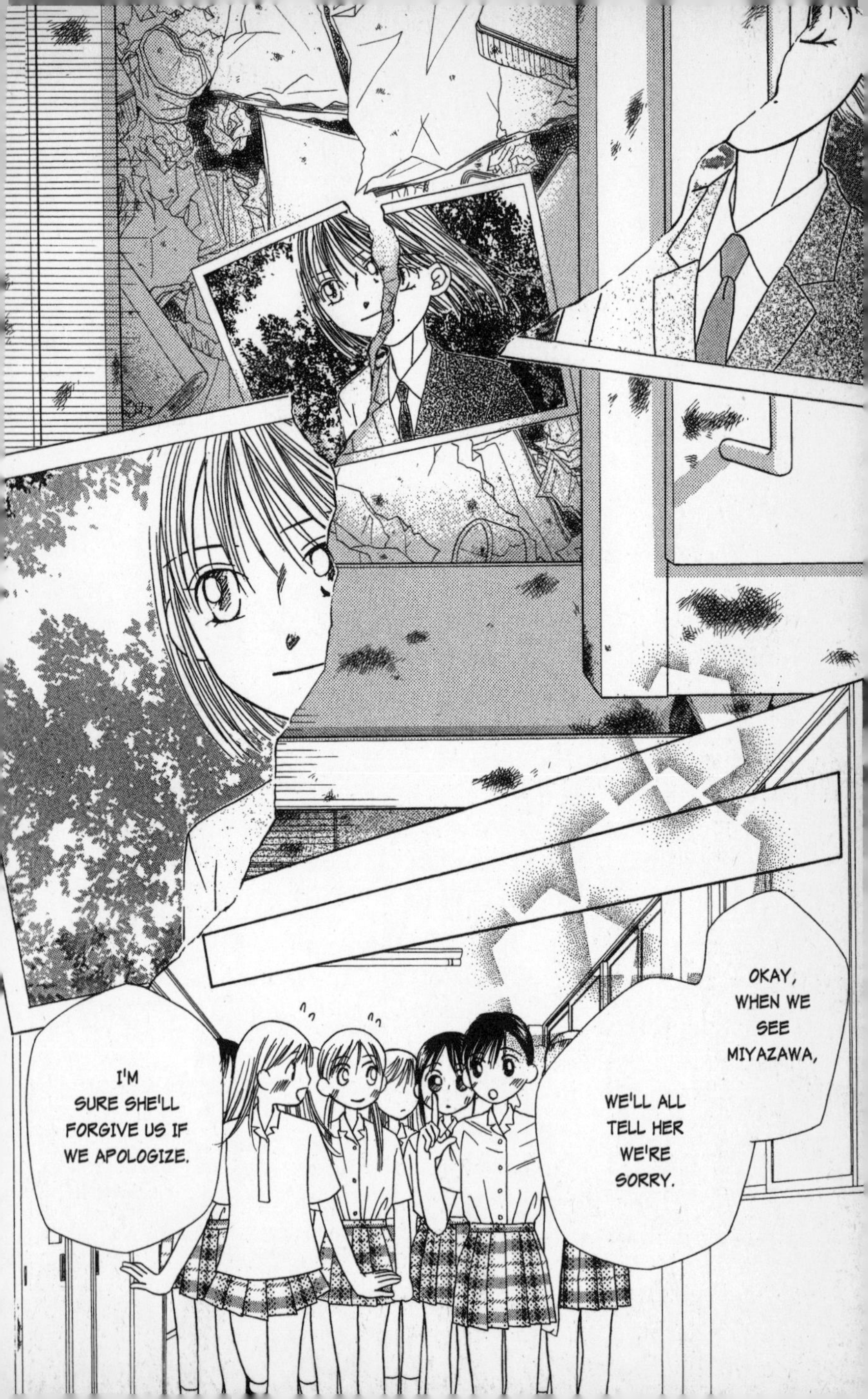
OKAY, WHEN WE SEE MIYAZAWA,
WE'LL ALL TELL HER WE'RE SORRY.
I'M SURE SHE'LL FORGIVE US IF WE APOLOGIZE.

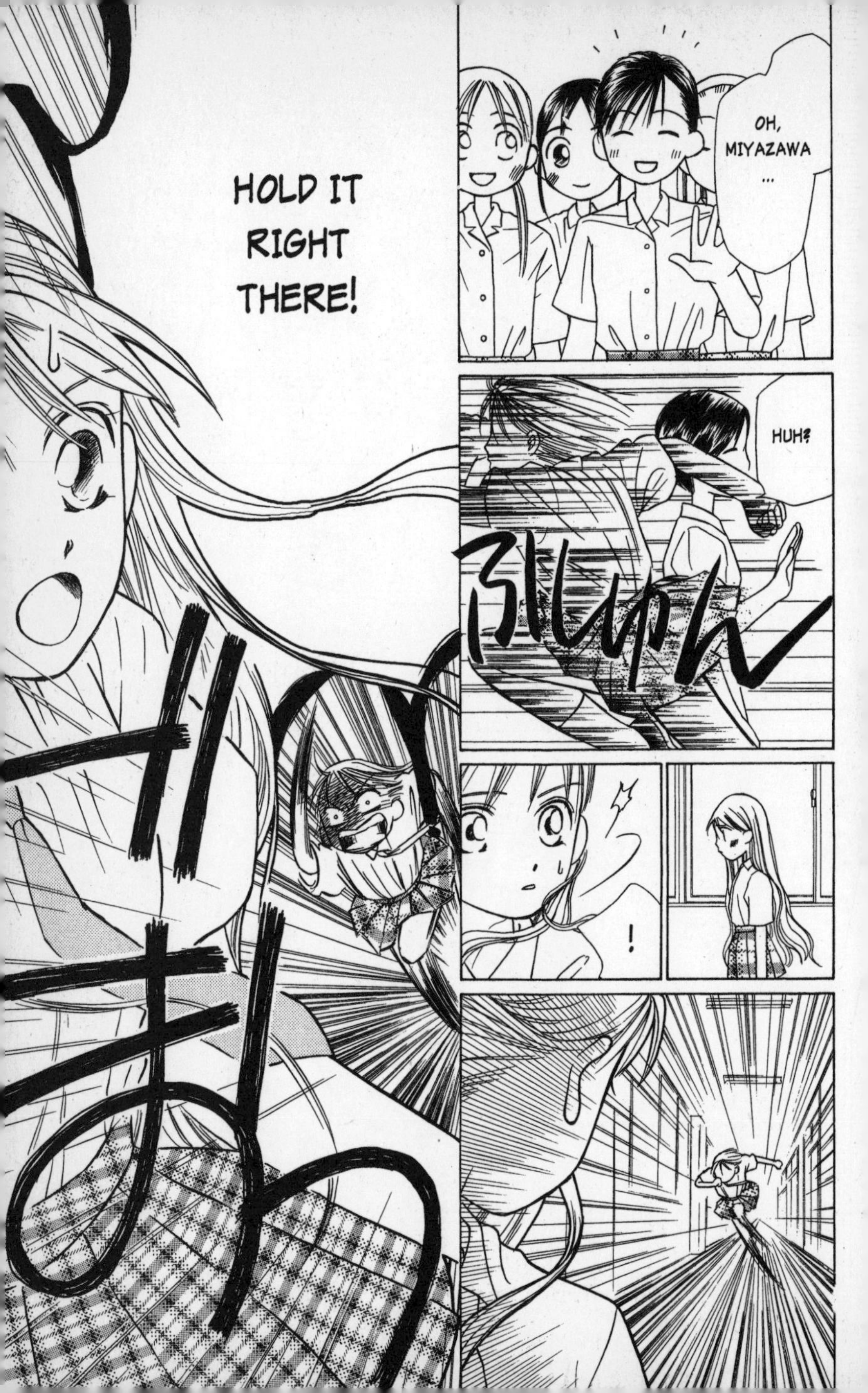
OH, MIYAZAWA ...
HUH?
!
HOLD IT RIGHT THERE!

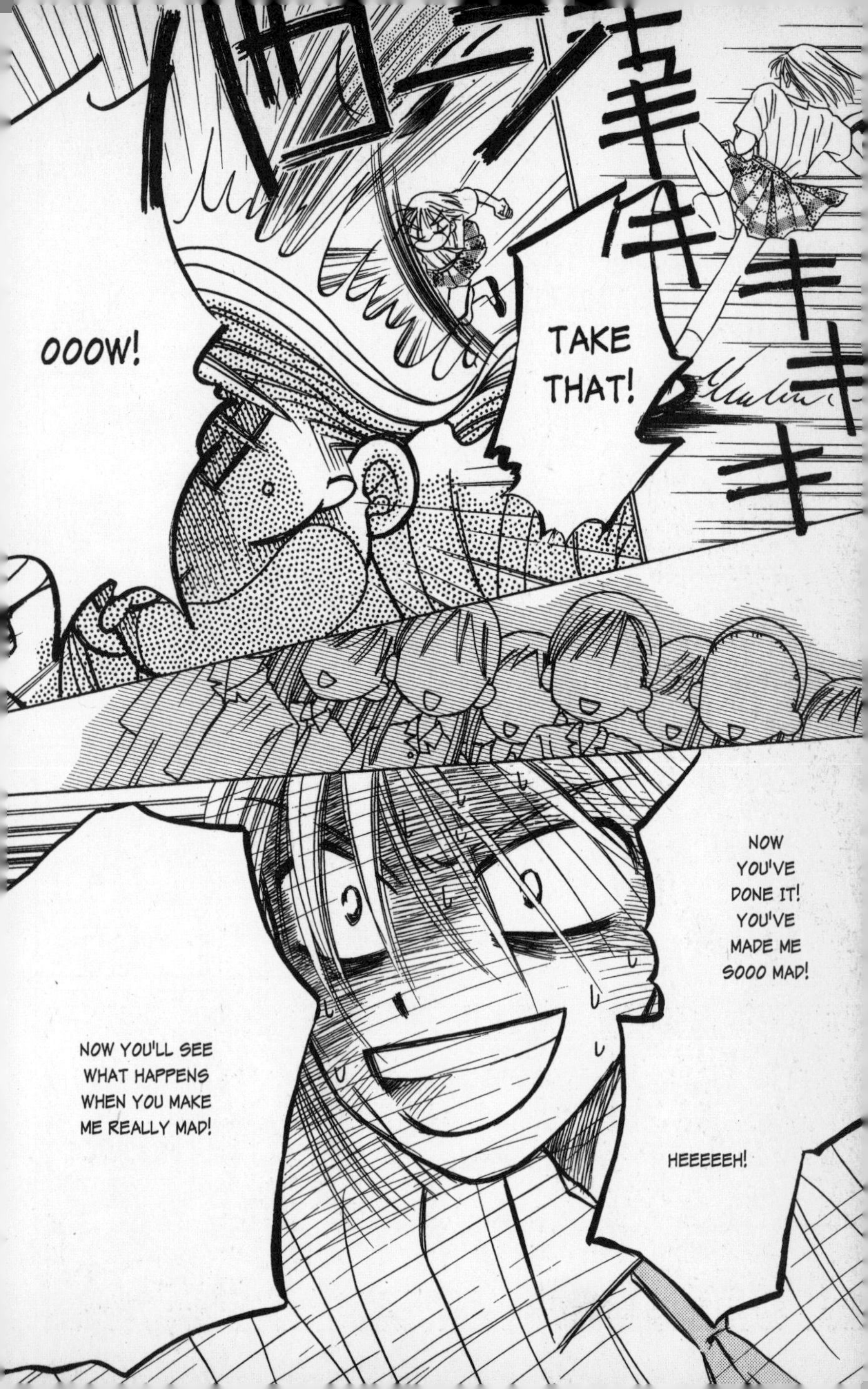
TAKE THAT!
OOOW!
NOW YOU'VE DONE IT! YOU'VE MADE ME SOOO MAD!
HEEEEEH!
NOW YOU'LL SEE WHAT HAPPENS WHEN YOU MAKE ME REALLY MAD!

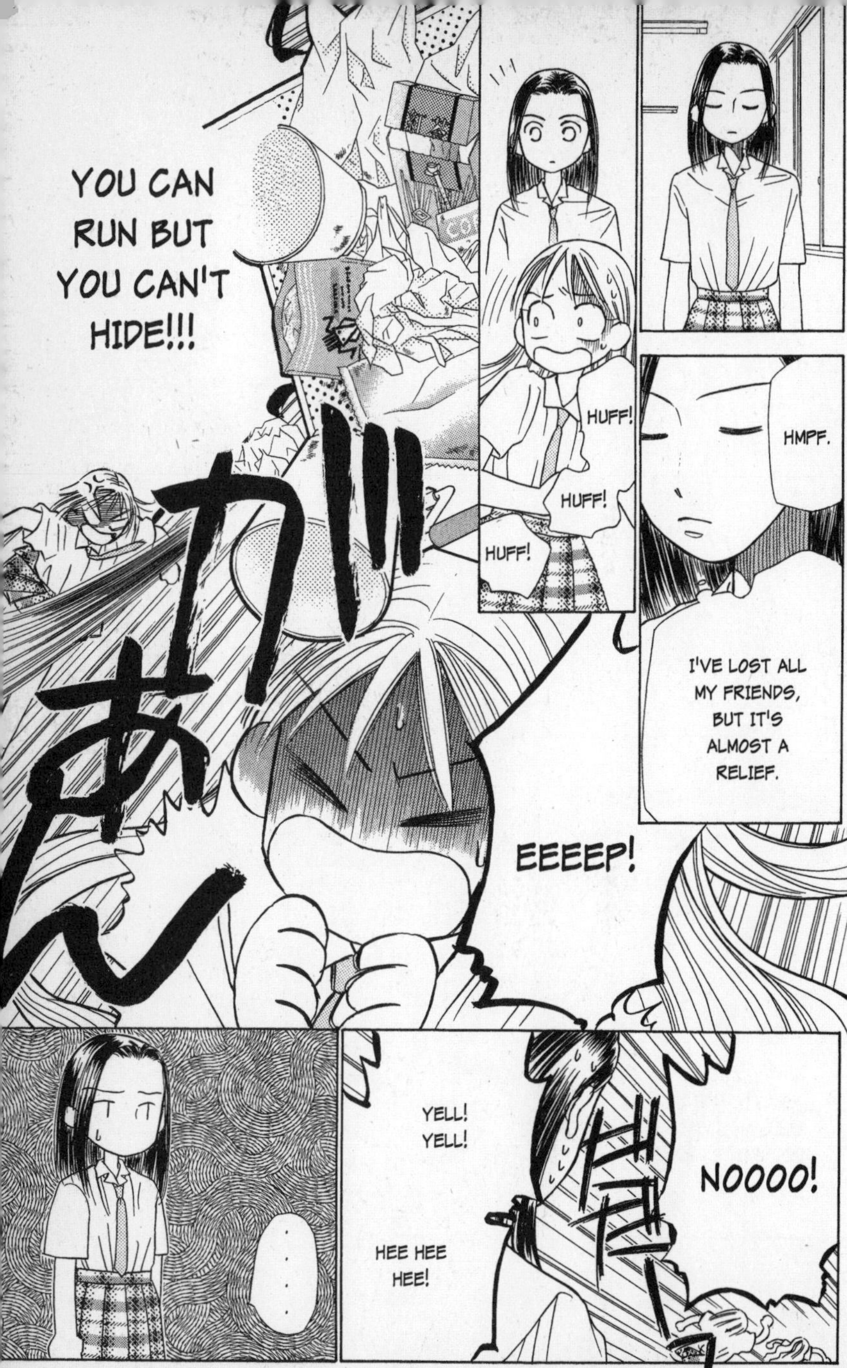
HUFF!
HUFF!
HUFF!
HMPF.
I'VE LOST ALL MY FRIENDS, BUT IT'S ALMOST A RELIEF.
YOU CAN RUN BUT YOU CAN'T HIDE!!!
EEEEP!
NOOOO!
YELL! YELL!
HEE HEE HEE!
. . .

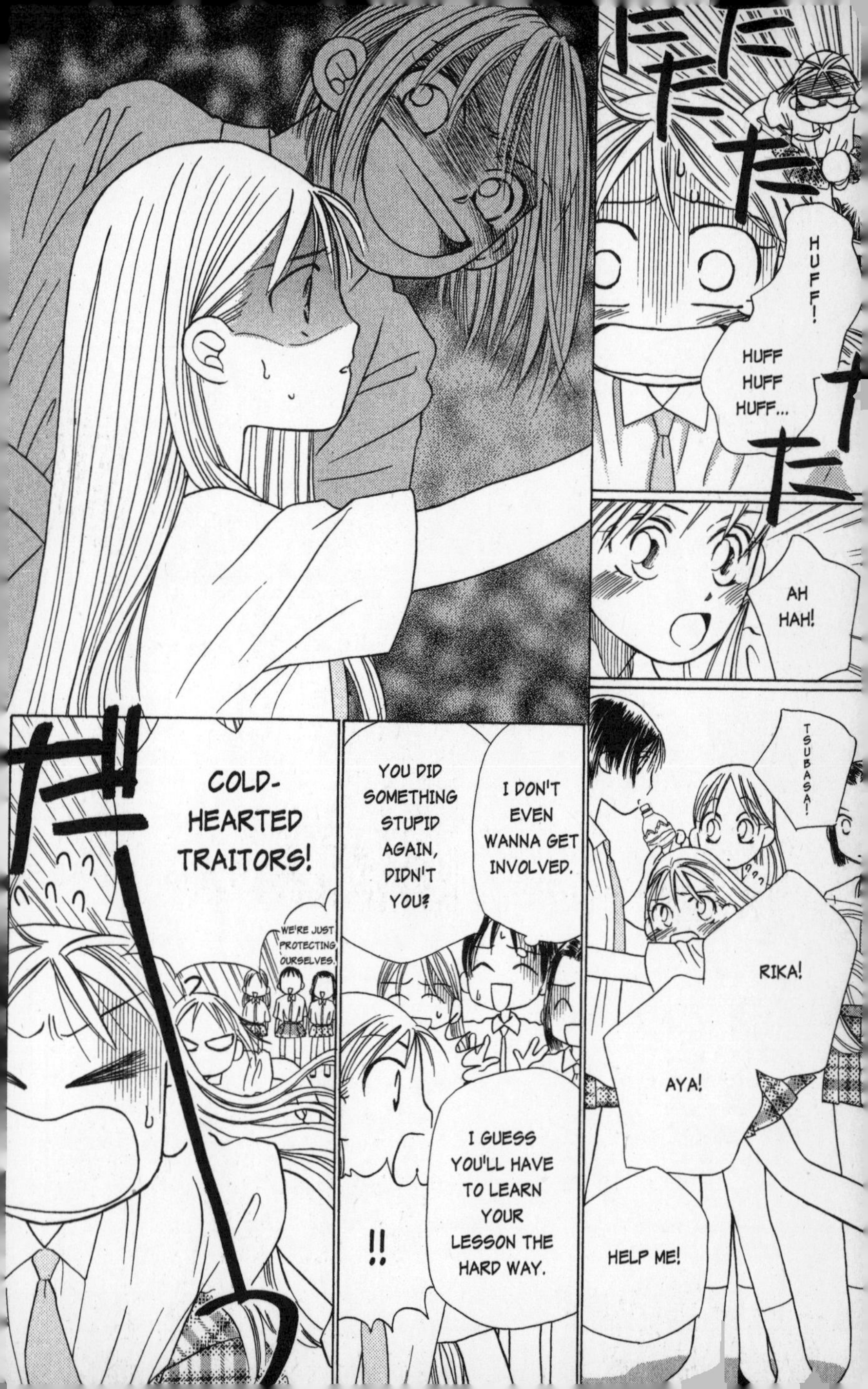
HUFF!
HUFF HUFF HUFF...
AH HAH!
TSUBASA!
RIKA!
AYA!
HELP ME!
I DON'T EVEN WANNA GET INVOLVED.
YOU DID SOMETHING STUPID AGAIN, DIDN'T YOU?
I GUESS YOU'LL HAVE TO LEARN YOUR LESSON THE HARD WAY.
!!
COLD-HEARTED TRAITORS!
WE'RE JUST PROTECTING OURSELVES.

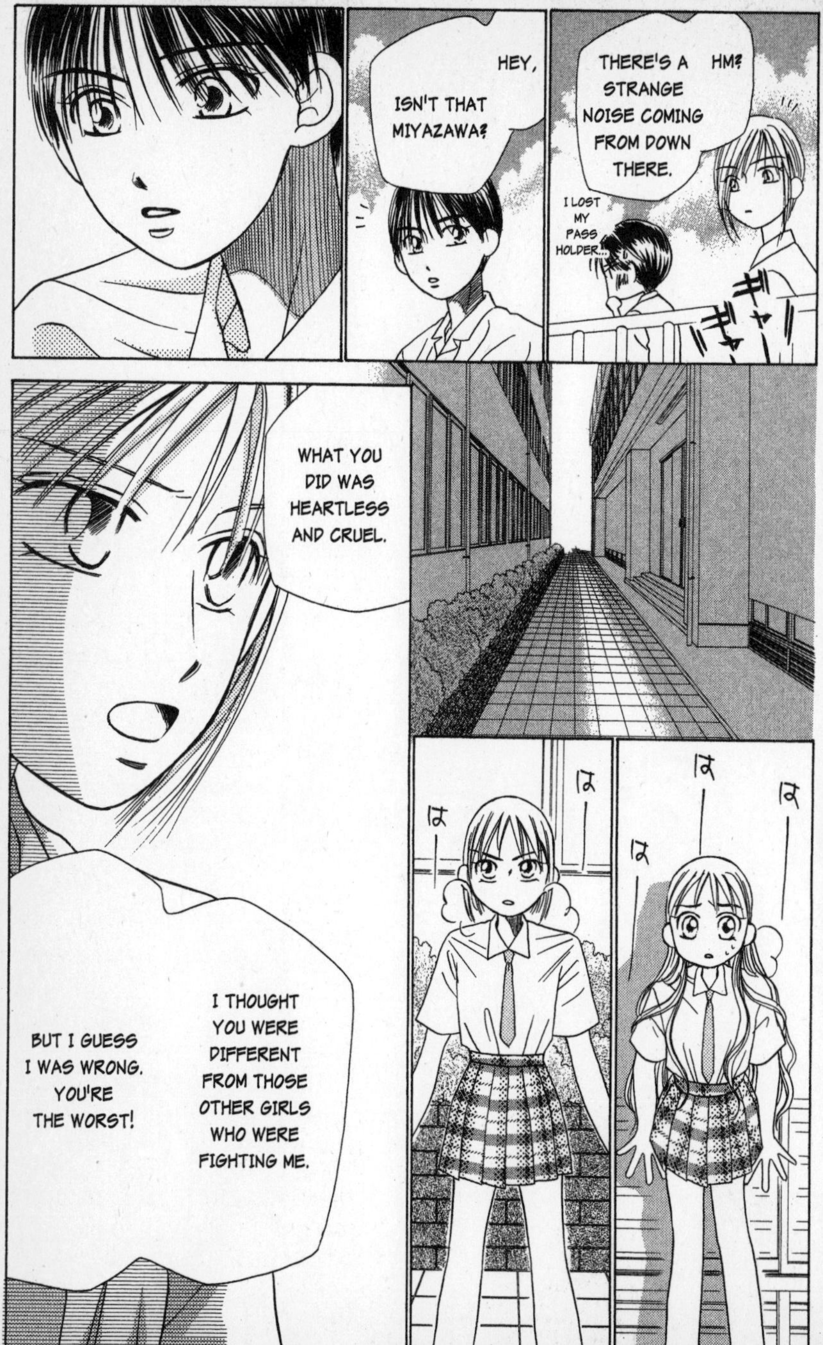
THERE'S A STRANGE NOISE COMING FROM DOWN THERE.
HM?
I LOST MY PASS HOLDER...
ギャ ぎゃ
HEY, ISN'T THAT MIYAZAWA?
はー はー
はー はー
WHAT YOU DID WAS HEARTLESS AND CRUEL.
I THOUGHT YOU WERE DIFFERENT FROM THOSE OTHER GIRLS WHO WERE FIGHTING ME.
BUT I GUESS I WAS WRONG. YOU'RE THE WORST!

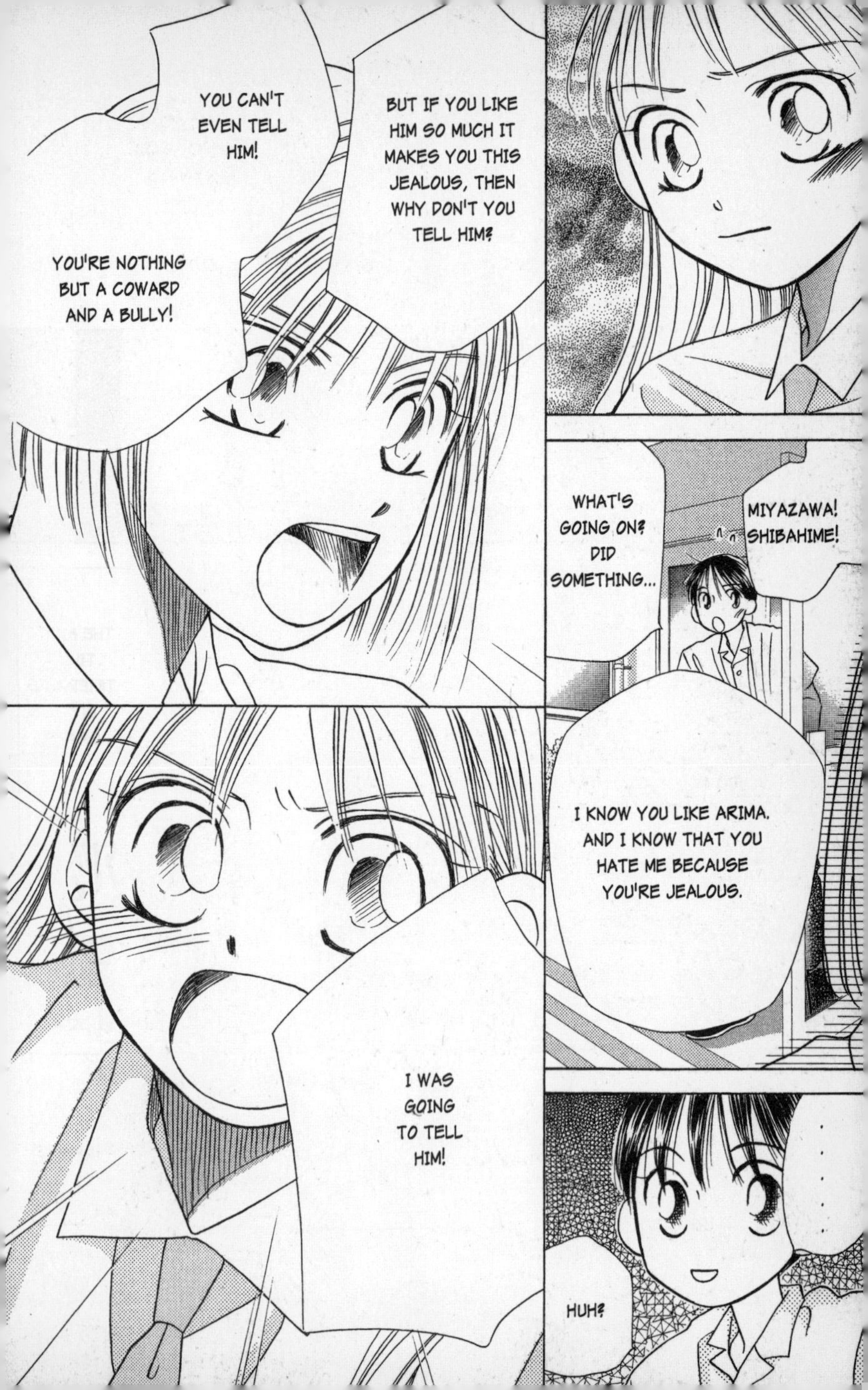
MIYAZAWA! SHIBAHIME!
WHAT'S GOING ON? DID SOMETHING...
BUT IF YOU LIKE HIM SO MUCH IT MAKES YOU THIS JEALOUS, THEN WHY DON'T YOU TELL HIM?
YOU CAN'T EVEN TELL HIM!
YOU'RE NOTHING BUT A COWARD AND A BULLY!
I KNOW YOU LIKE ARIMA. AND I KNOW THAT YOU HATE ME BECAUSE YOU'RE JEALOUS.
....
HUH?
I WAS GOING TO TELL HIM!

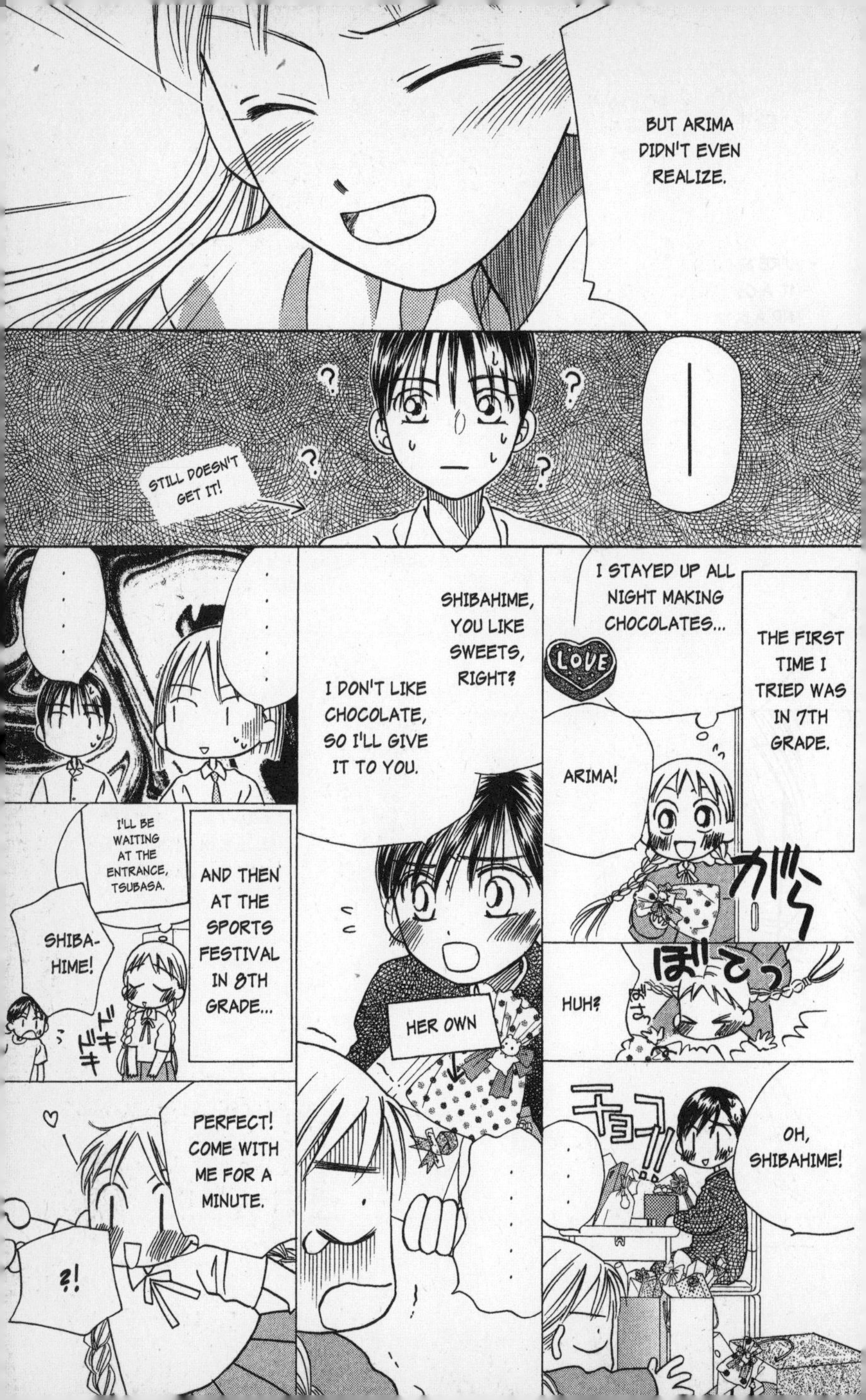
BUT ARIMA DIDN'T EVEN REALIZE.
—
STILL DOESN'T GET IT!
THE FIRST TIME I TRIED WAS IN 7TH GRADE.
I STAYED UP ALL NIGHT MAKING CHOCOLATES...
LOVE
ARIMA!
ぼてっ
HUH?
OH, SHIBAHIME!
チョコ!!
SHIBAHIME, YOU LIKE SWEETS, RIGHT?
I DON'T LIKE CHOCOLATE, SO I'LL GIVE IT TO YOU.
HER OWN
......
......
......
AND THEN AT THE SPORTS FESTIVAL IN 8TH GRADE...
I'LL BE WAITING AT THE ENTRANCE, TSUBASA.
SHIBA-HIME!
ドキドキ
PERFECT! COME WITH ME FOR A MINUTE.
?!

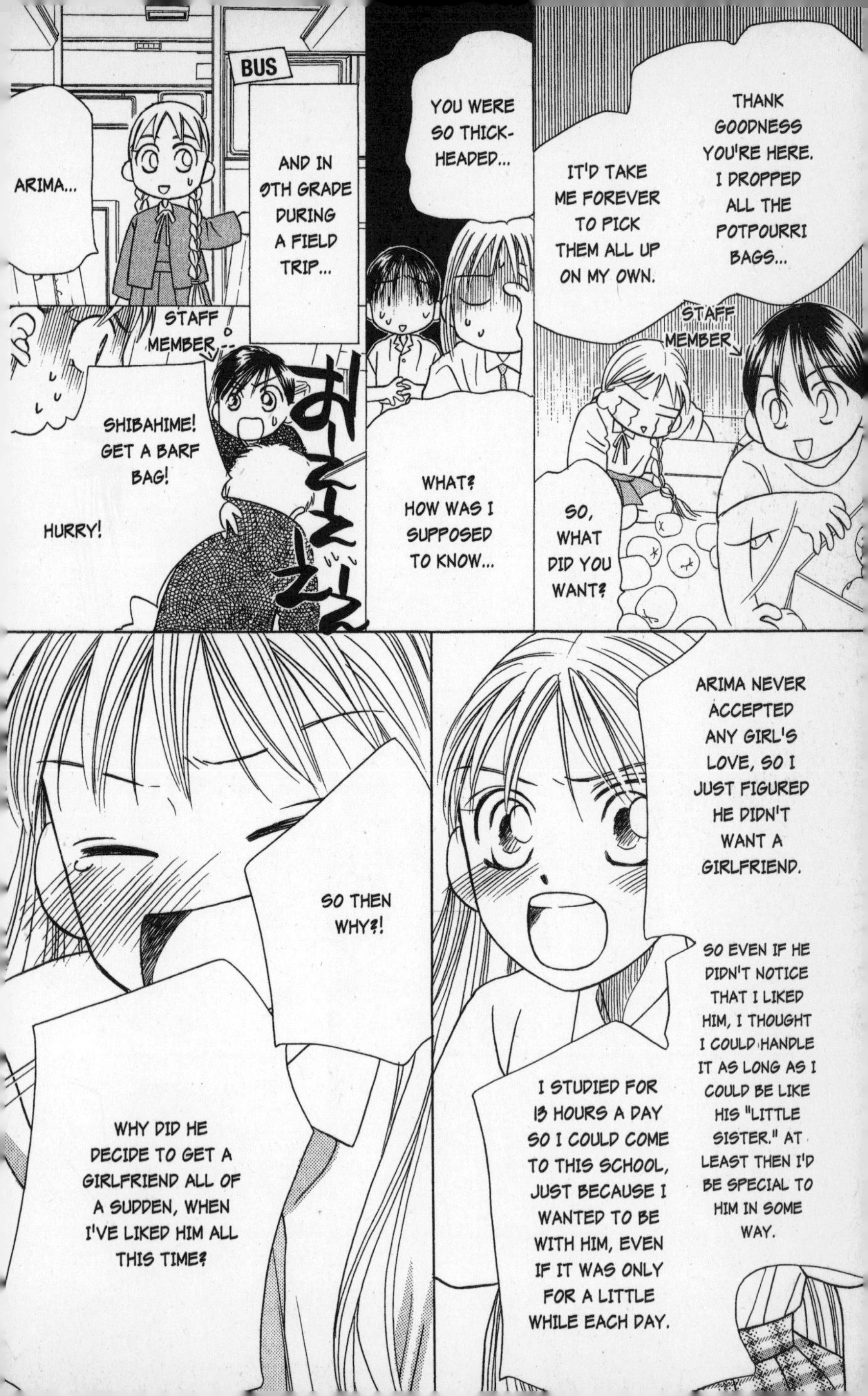
THANK GOODNESS YOU'RE HERE. I DROPPED ALL THE POTPOURRI BAGS...
IT'D TAKE ME FOREVER TO PICK THEM ALL UP ON MY OWN.
STAFF MEMBER
SO, WHAT DID YOU WANT?
YOU WERE SO THICK-HEADED...
WHAT? HOW WAS I SUPPOSED TO KNOW...
BUS
AND IN 9TH GRADE DURING A FIELD TRIP...
ARIMA...
STAFF MEMBER
SHIBAHIME! GET A BARF BAG!
HURRY!
ARIMA NEVER ACCEPTED ANY GIRL'S LOVE, SO I JUST FIGURED HE DIDN'T WANT A GIRLFRIEND.
SO EVEN IF HE DIDN'T NOTICE THAT I LIKED HIM, I THOUGHT I COULD HANDLE IT AS LONG AS I COULD BE LIKE HIS "LITTLE SISTER." AT LEAST THEN I'D BE SPECIAL TO HIM IN SOME WAY.
I STUDIED FOR 13 HOURS A DAY SO I COULD COME TO THIS SCHOOL, JUST BECAUSE I WANTED TO BE WITH HIM, EVEN IF IT WAS ONLY FOR A LITTLE WHILE EACH DAY.
SO THEN WHY?!
WHY DID HE DECIDE TO GET A GIRLFRIEND ALL OF A SUDDEN, WHEN I'VE LIKED HIM ALL THIS TIME?

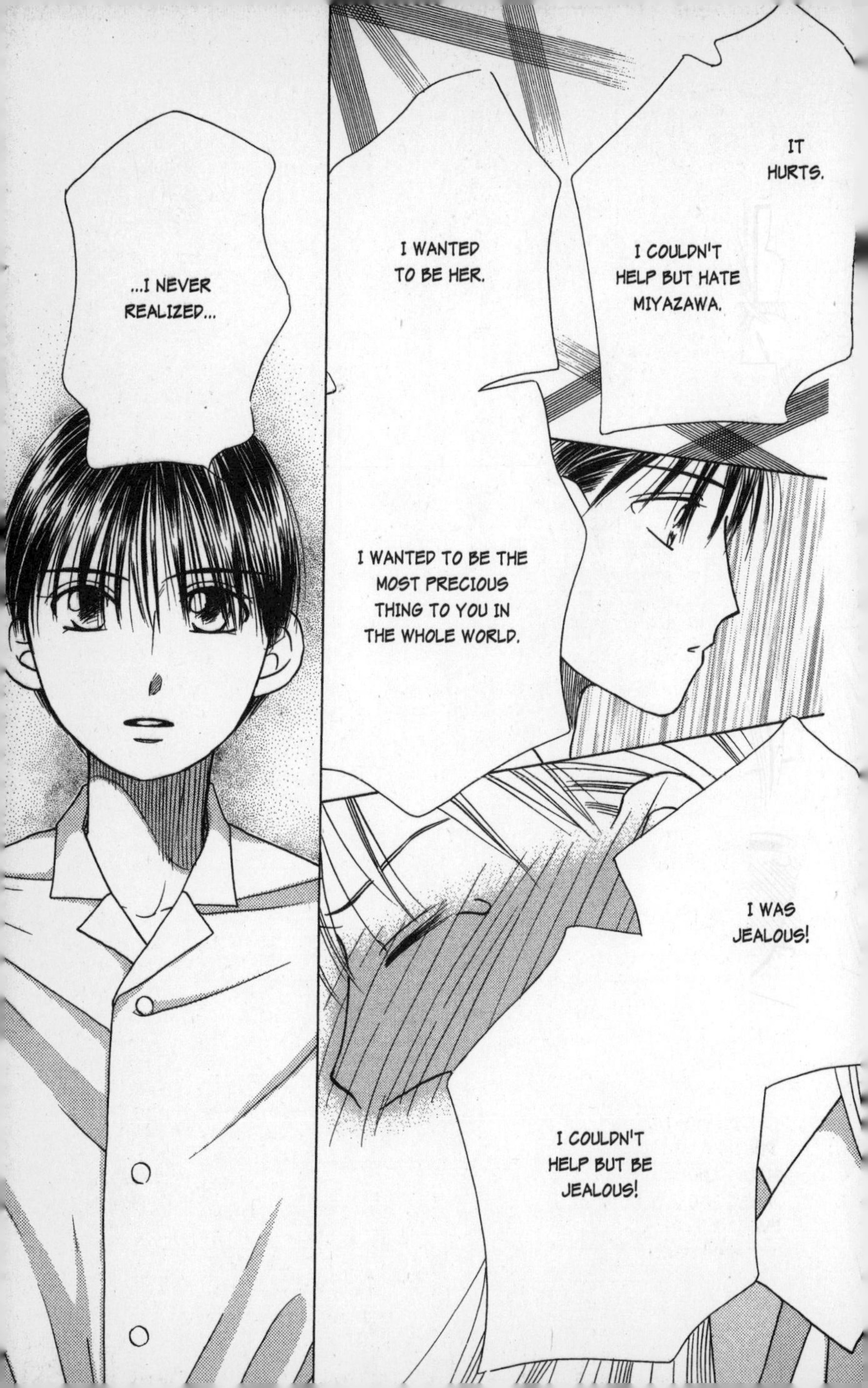
IT HURTS.
I COULDN'T HELP BUT HATE MIYAZAWA.
I WANTED TO BE HER.
I WANTED TO BE THE MOST PRECIOUS THING TO YOU IN THE WHOLE WORLD.
I WAS JEALOUS!
I COULDN'T HELP BUT BE JEALOUS!
...I NEVER REALIZED...

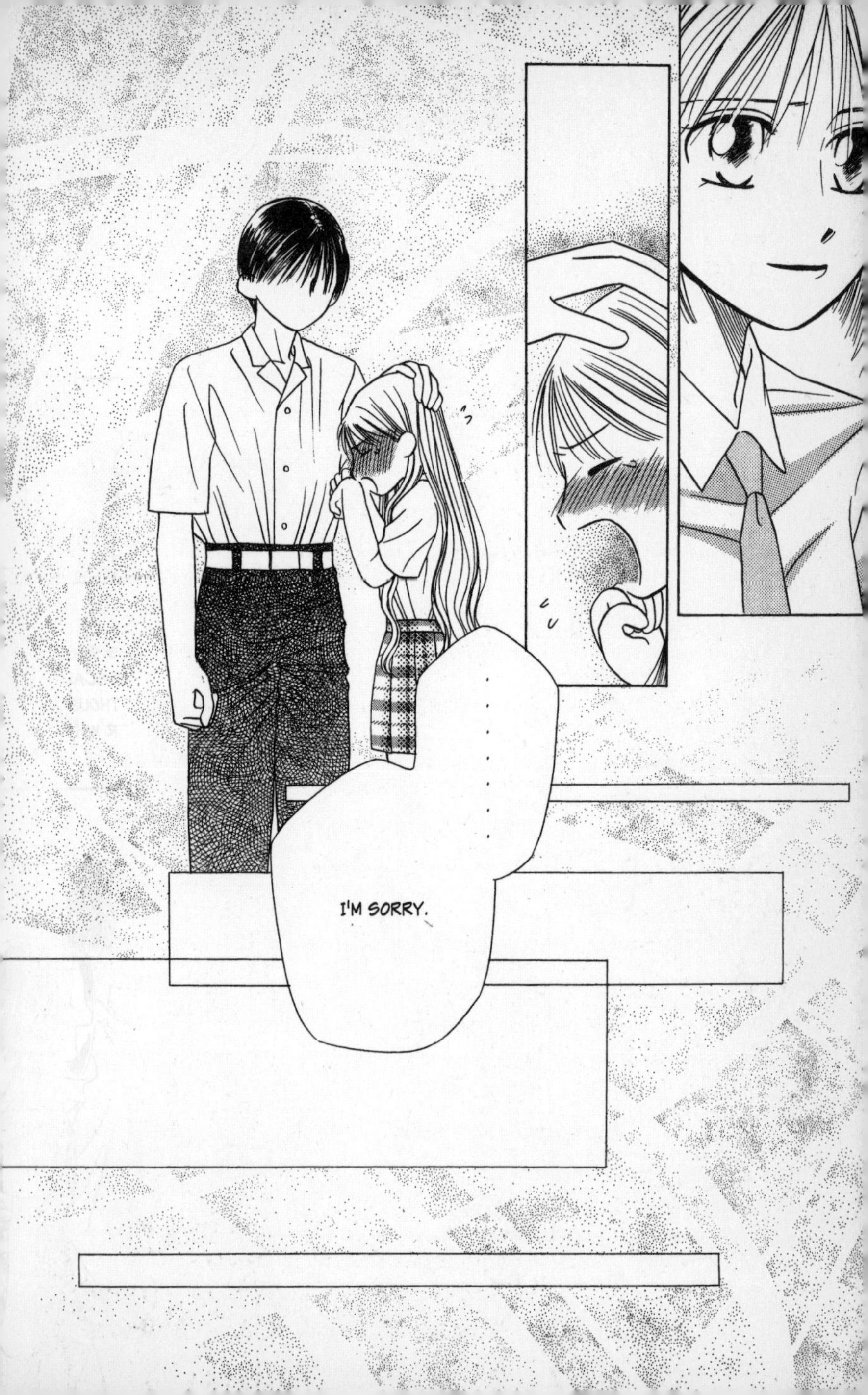
......
I'M SORRY.

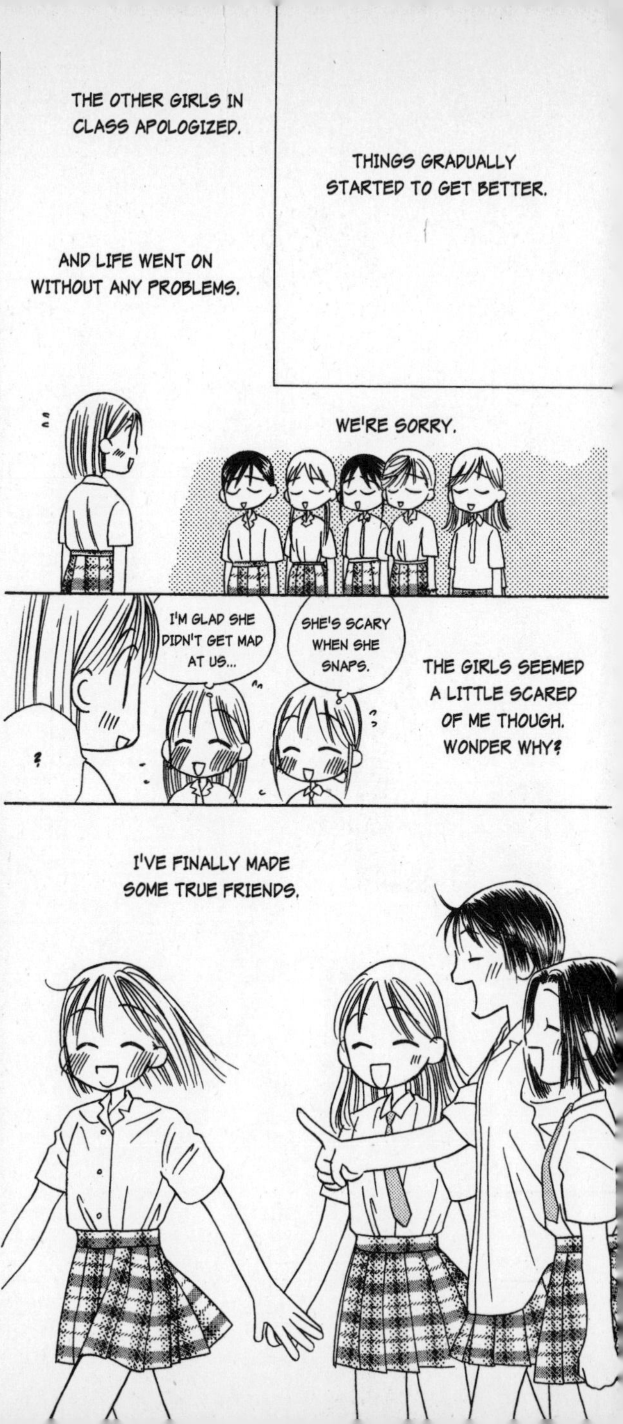
THINGS GRADUALLY STARTED TO GET BETTER.
THE OTHER GIRLS IN CLASS APOLOGIZED.
AND LIFE WENT ON WITHOUT ANY PROBLEMS.
WE'RE SORRY.
THE GIRLS SEEMED A LITTLE SCARED OF ME THOUGH. WONDER WHY?
SHE'S SCARY WHEN SHE SNAPS.
I'M GLAD SHE DIDN'T GET MAD AT US...
I'VE FINALLY MADE SOME TRUE FRIENDS.

3

Once Tsuda finishes drawing a book, she won't look over it again. Sometimes she'll even forget what she drew. If she does, she'll get so embarrassed by the bad drawings it'll drive her crazy. But having said that, I'm still including a manga that I drew in my first year as a manga artist.

It stinks!

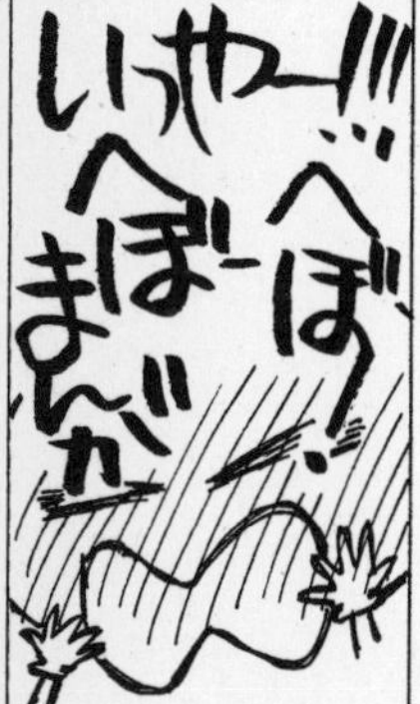
いっやー!!!
へぼへぼー
まんが

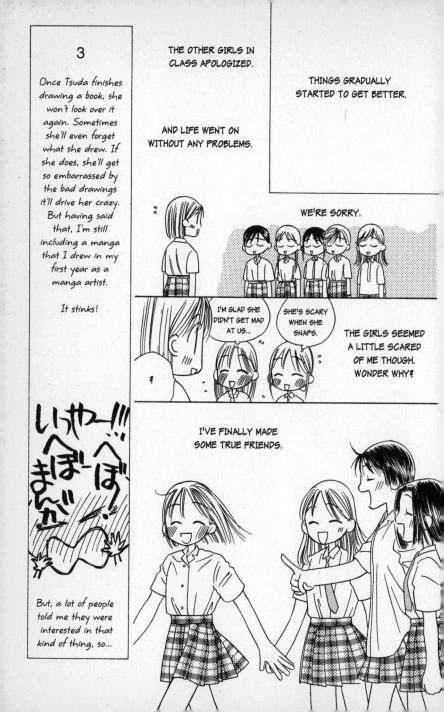

But, a lot of people told me they were interested in that kind of thing, so...

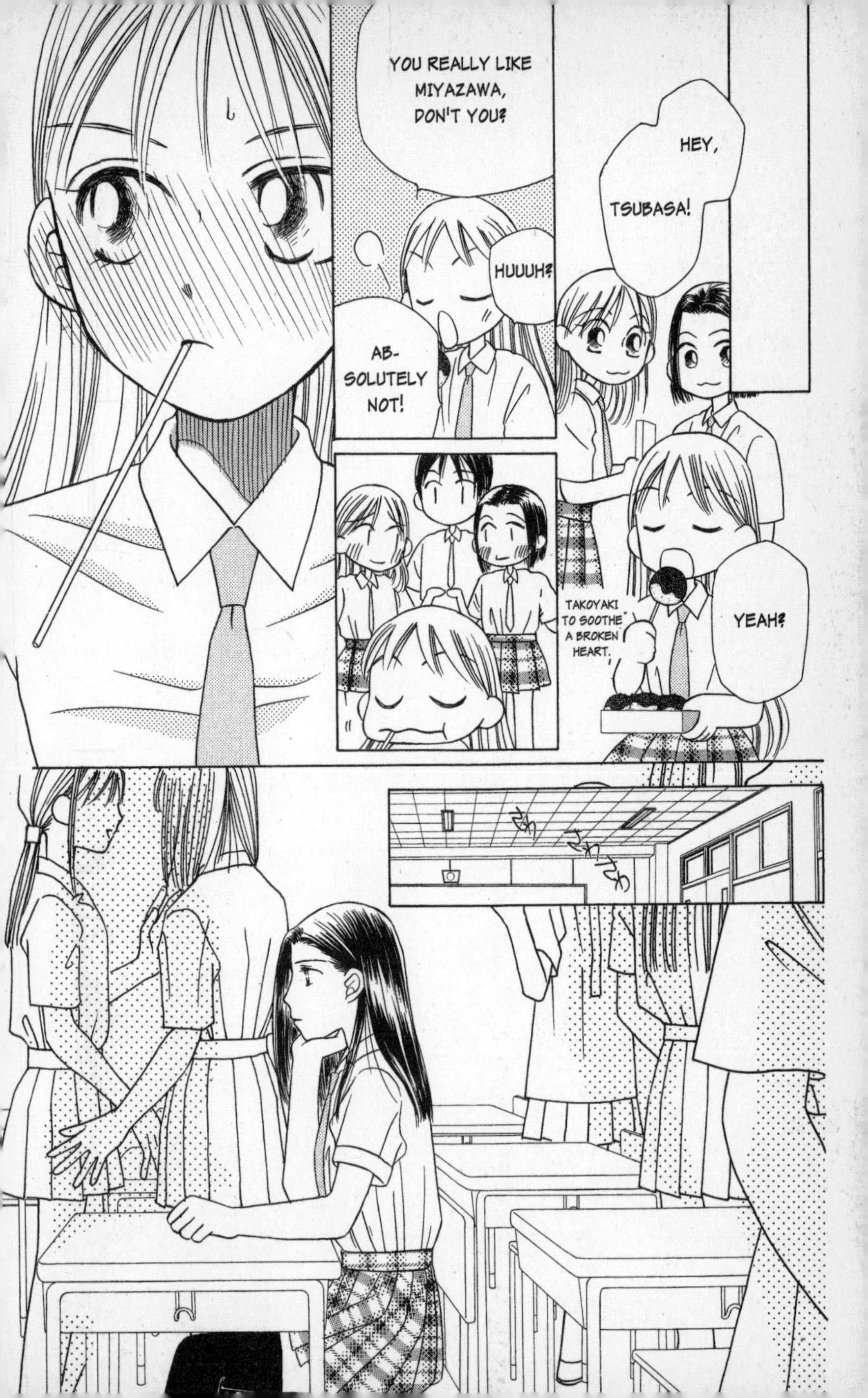
HEY,
TSUBASA!
YOU REALLY LIKE MIYAZAWA, DON'T YOU?
HUUUH?
AB-SOLUTELY NOT!
YEAH?
TAKOYAKI TO SOOTHE A BROKEN HEART.

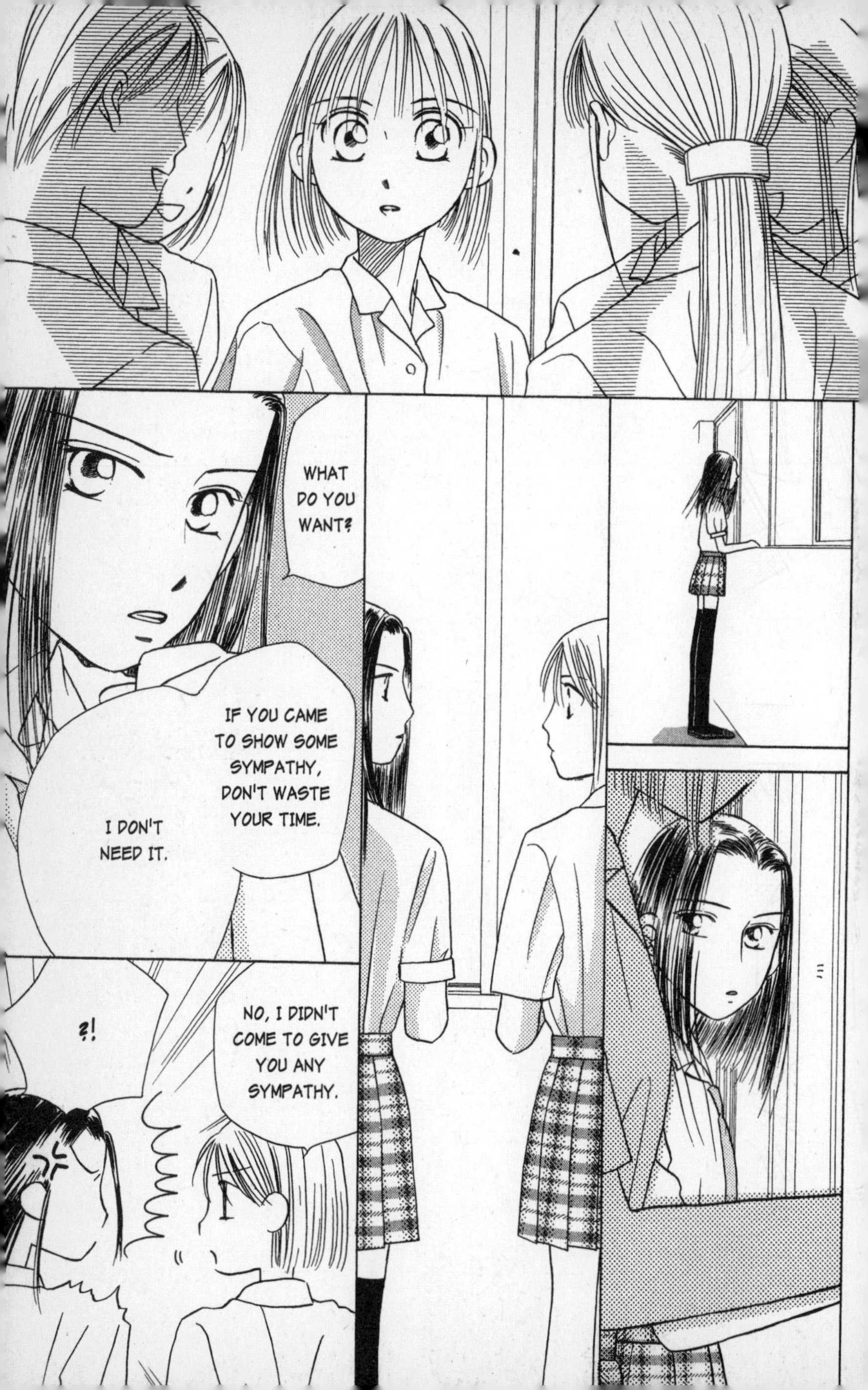
WHAT DO YOU WANT?
IF YOU CAME TO SHOW SOME SYMPATHY, DON'T WASTE YOUR TIME.
I DON'T NEED IT.
NO, I DIDN'T COME TO GIVE YOU ANY SYMPATHY.
?!

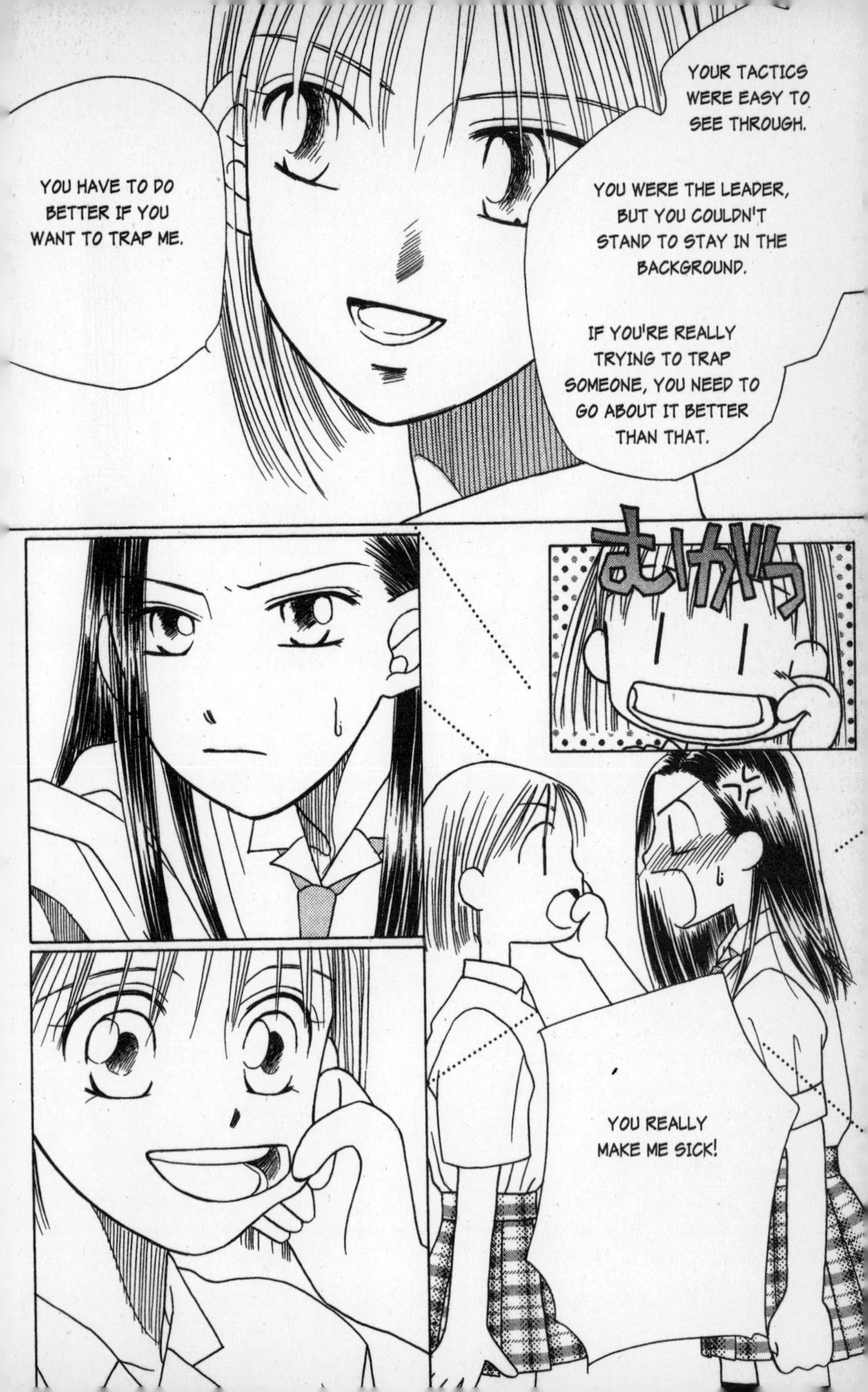
YOUR TACTICS WERE EASY TO SEE THROUGH.
YOU WERE THE LEADER, BUT YOU COULDN'T STAND TO STAY IN THE BACKGROUND.
IF YOU'RE REALLY TRYING TO TRAP SOMEONE, YOU NEED TO GO ABOUT IT BETTER THAN THAT.
YOU HAVE TO DO BETTER IF YOU WANT TO TRAP ME.
YOU REALLY MAKE ME SICK!

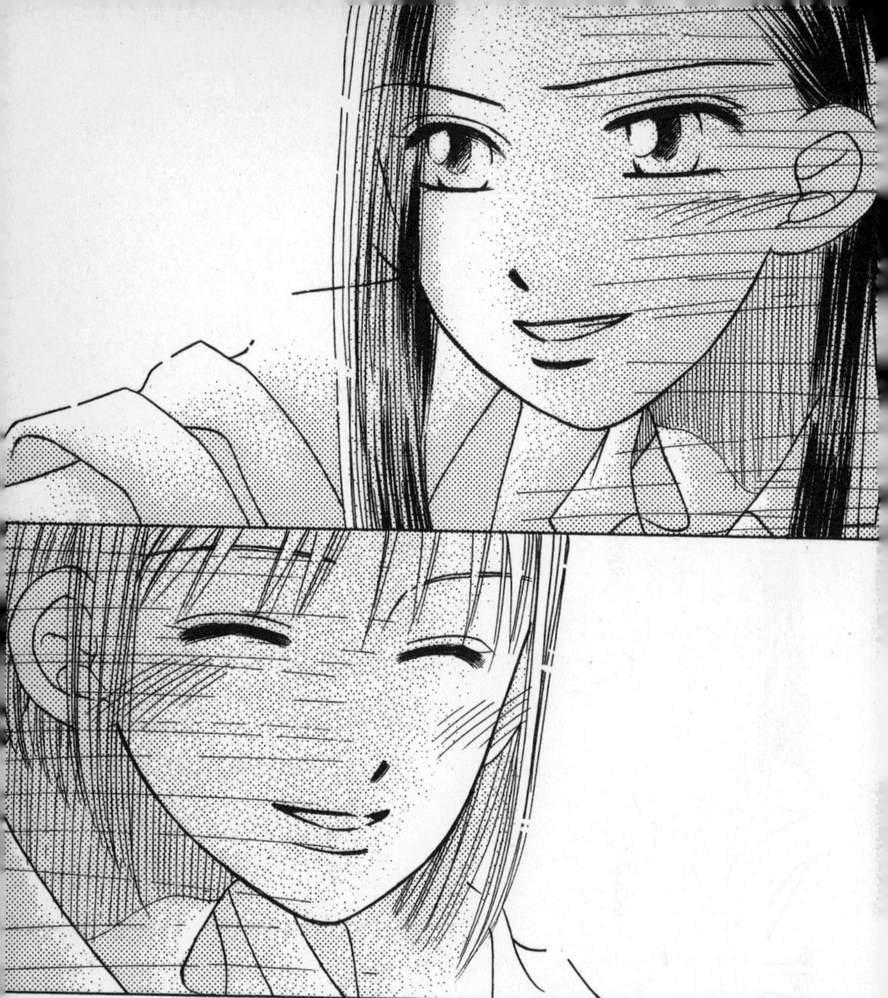

BEFORE I KNEW IT, IT WAS TIME FOR SUMMER VACATION.

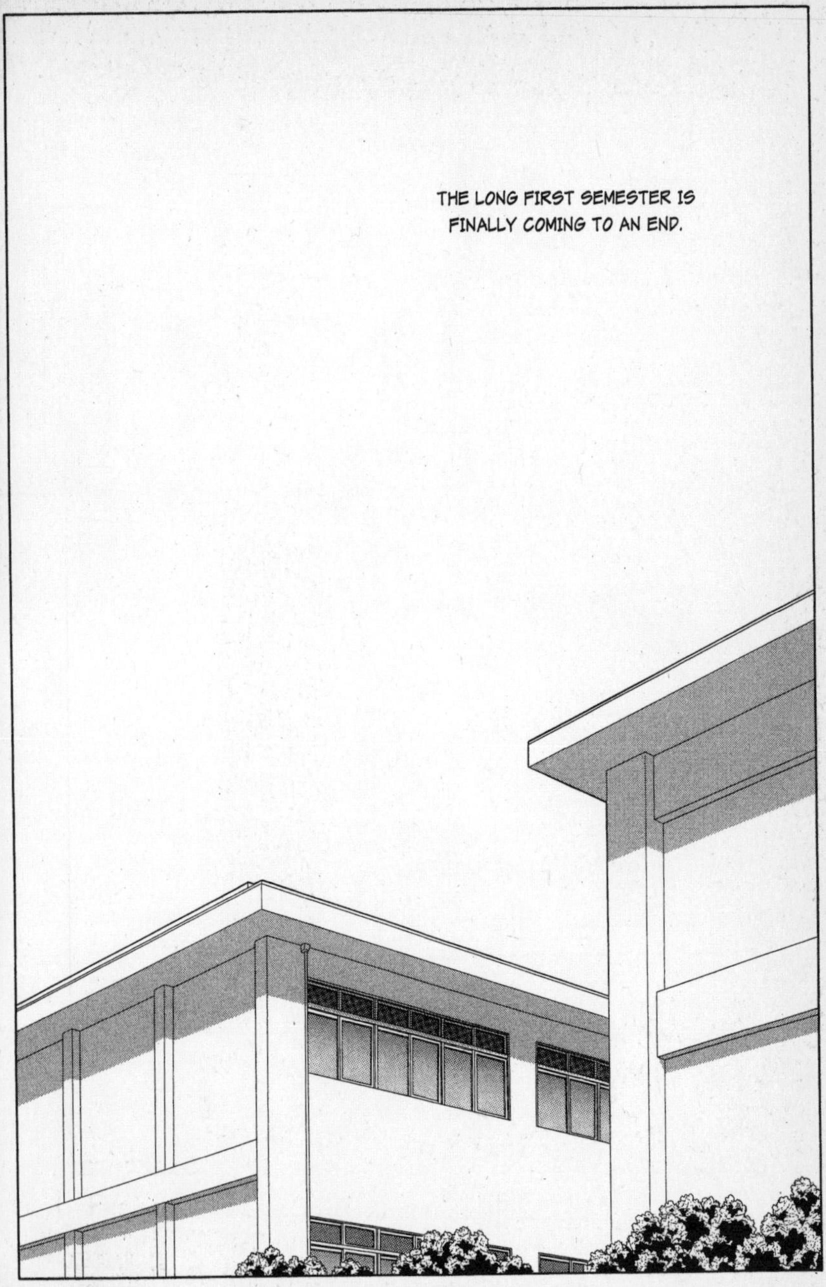
THE LONG FIRST SEMESTER IS FINALLY COMING TO AN END.

ACT 15 * FIGHTING WOMAN (4)-THE END

ACT16★一学期の終わりに

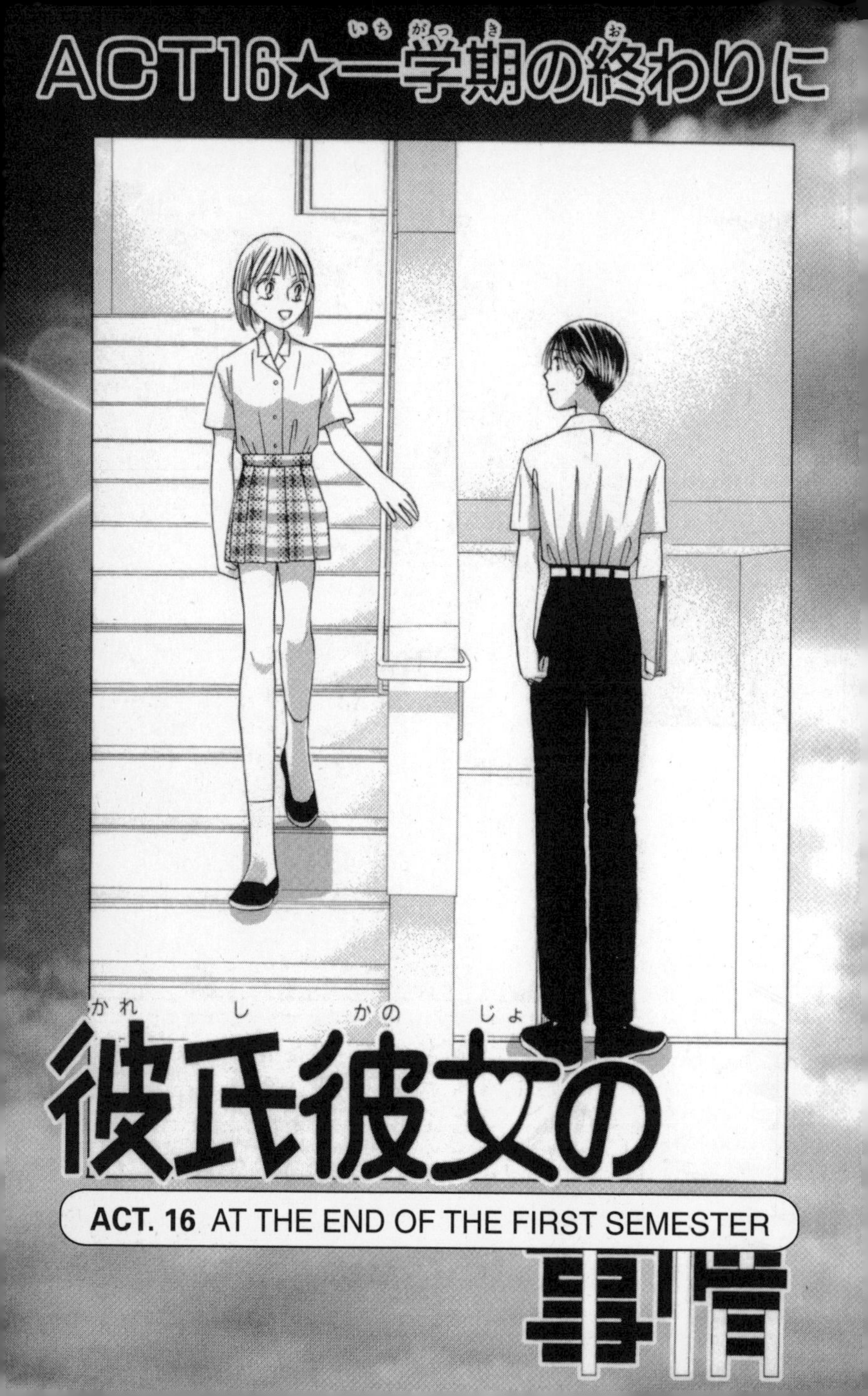

彼氏彼女の事情

ACT. 16 AT THE END OF THE FIRST SEMESTER

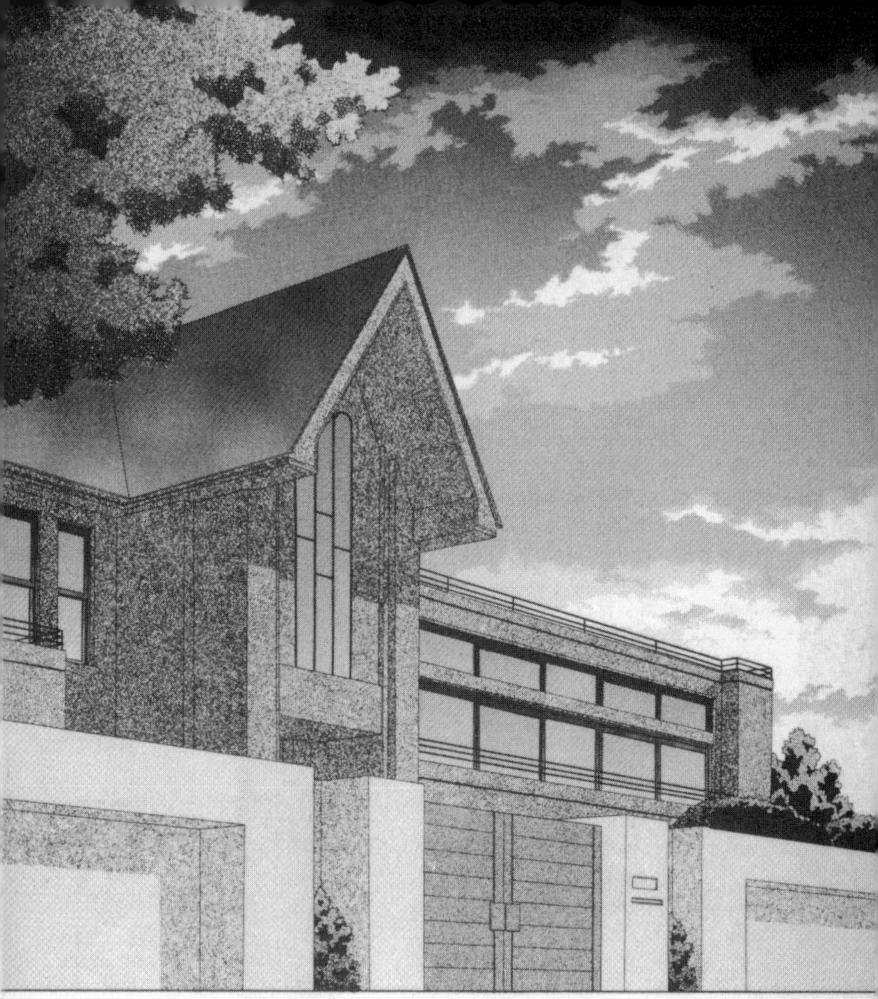

ABOUT THE PERSON KNOWN AS TSUDA

TSUDA ALWAYS LOOKS CASUAL AND RELAXED, AS IF SHE COULDN'T CARE LESS. BUT LATELY (OR MAYBE BEFORE), WHENEVER SHE LOOKS INTO PEOPLE'S EYES, PEOPLE THINK SHE'S SCARY. I WONDER WHAT IT IS. MAYBE BECAUSE MY EYES SPARKLE? I'VE BEEN THINKING LIKE A GUY. YO! I'M A GUY!

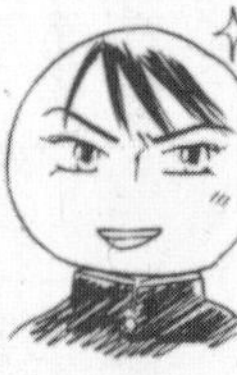

I'VE BEEN SWITCHING BACK AND FORTH BETWEEN THINKING, "WOMEN ARE CUTE" AND "ALL WOMEN DO IS NAG." I DON'T UNDERSTAND HOW WOMEN THINK...OR MEN, FOR THAT MATTER.

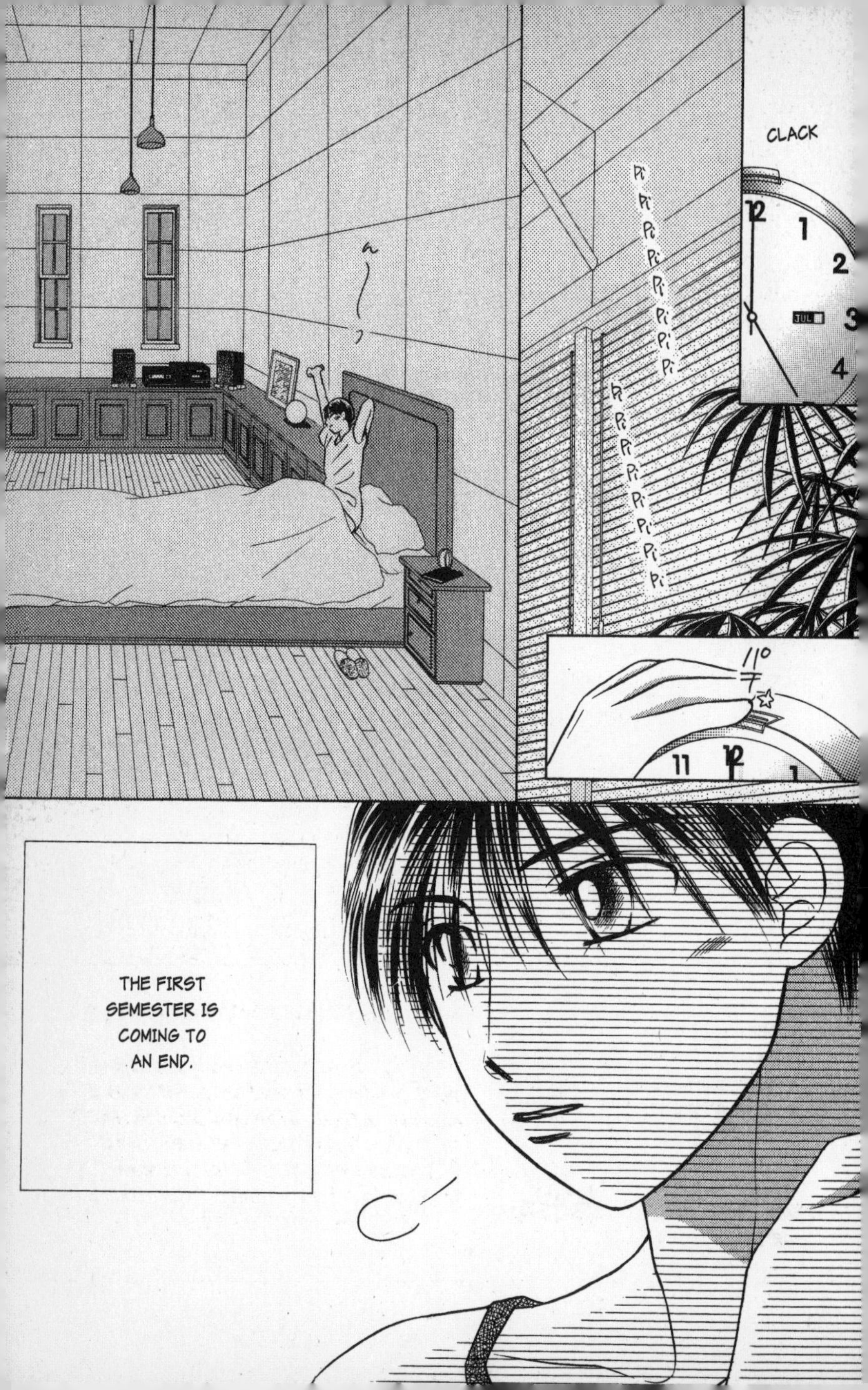
CLACK
Pi Pi Pi Pi Pi Pi Pi Pi Pi
Pi Pi Pi Pi Pi Pi Pi Pi Pi
THE FIRST SEMESTER IS COMING TO AN END.

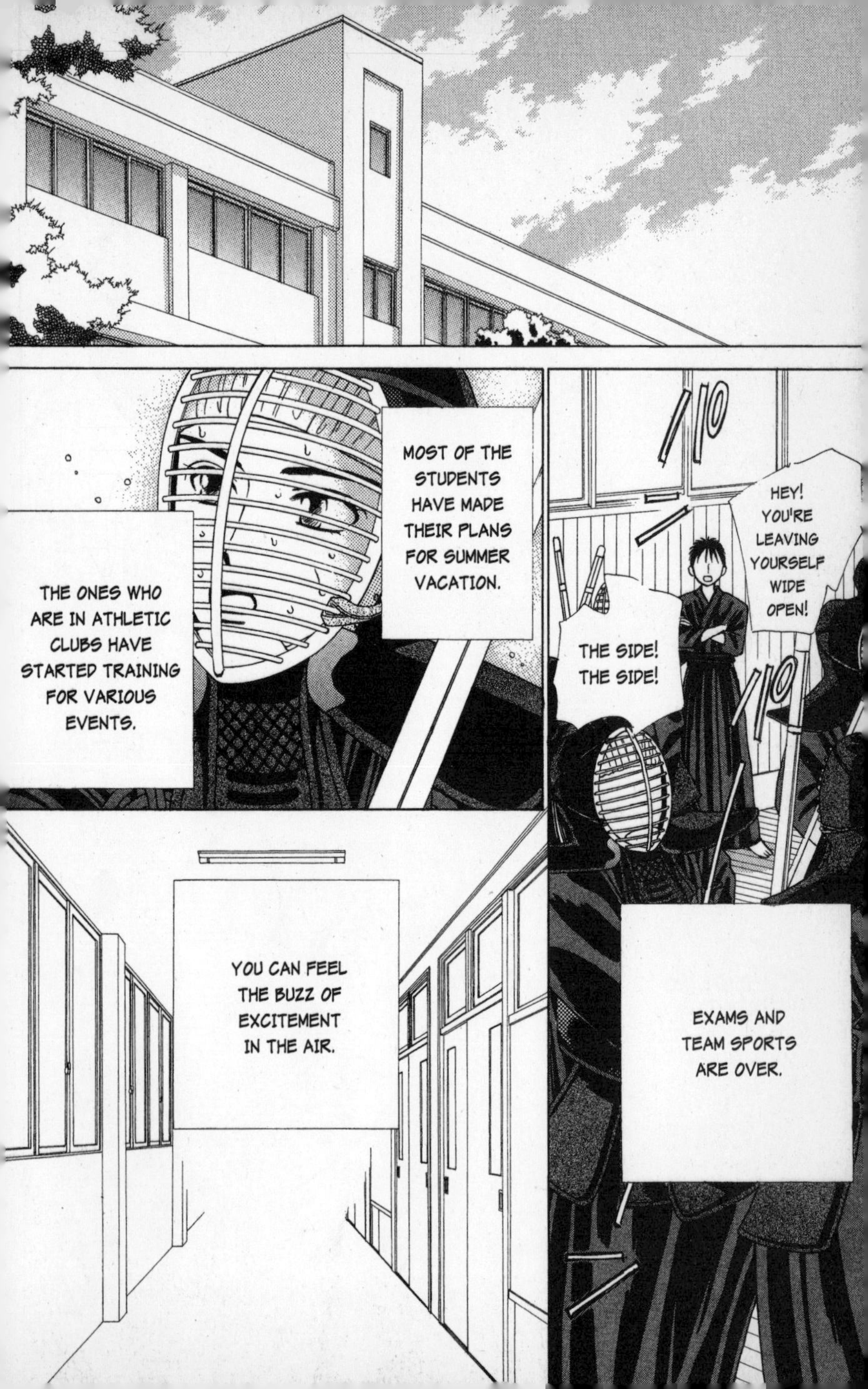
HEY! YOU'RE LEAVING YOURSELF WIDE OPEN!
THE SIDE! THE SIDE!
EXAMS AND TEAM SPORTS ARE OVER.
MOST OF THE STUDENTS HAVE MADE THEIR PLANS FOR SUMMER VACATION.
THE ONES WHO ARE IN ATHLETIC CLUBS HAVE STARTED TRAINING FOR VARIOUS EVENTS.
YOU CAN FEEL THE BUZZ OF EXCITEMENT IN THE AIR.

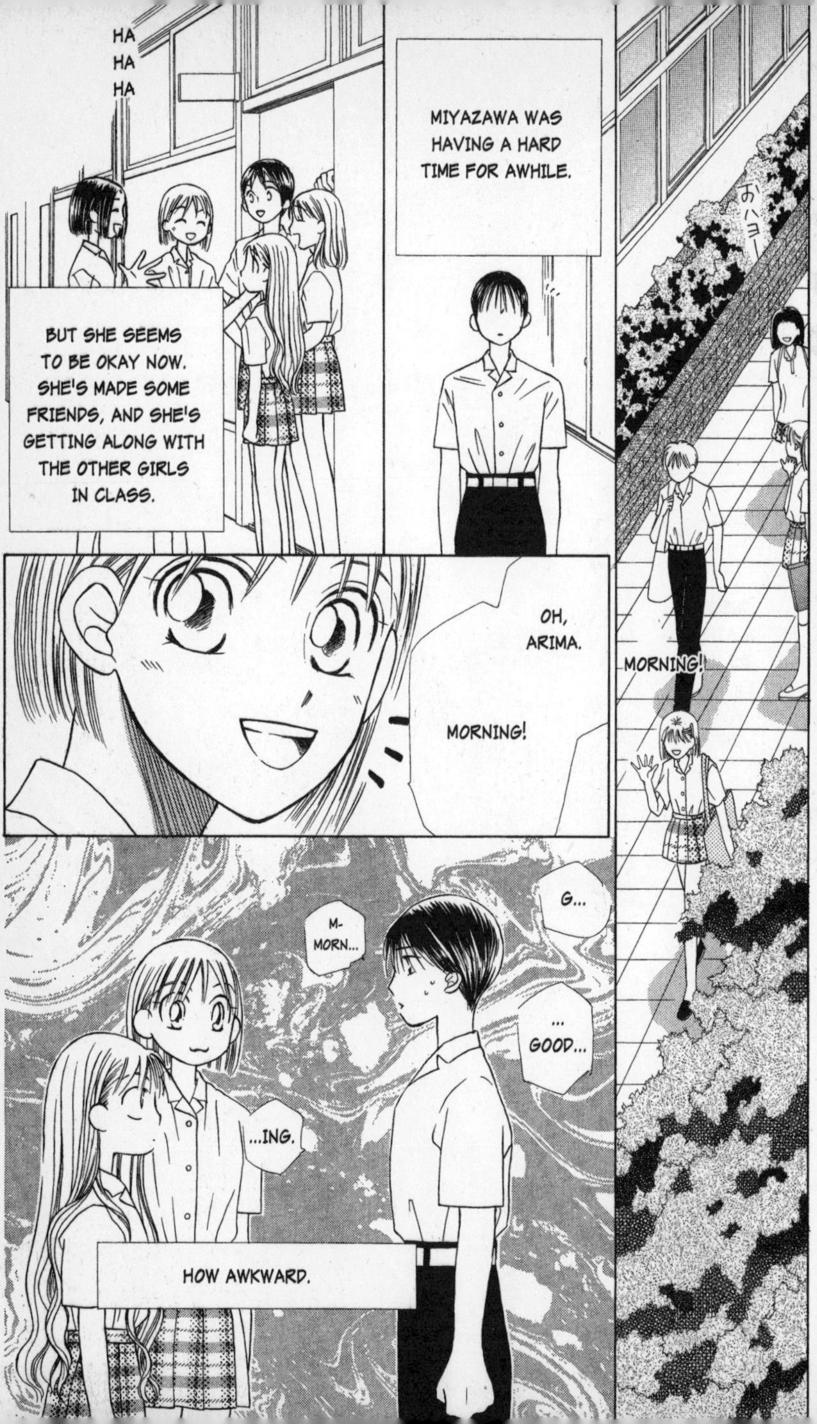
おハヨー
MORNING!
MIYAZAWA WAS HAVING A HARD TIME FOR AWHILE.
HA HA HA
BUT SHE SEEMS TO BE OKAY NOW. SHE'S MADE SOME FRIENDS, AND SHE'S GETTING ALONG WITH THE OTHER GIRLS IN CLASS.
OH, ARIMA.
MORNING!
G...
M-MORN...
...GOOD...
...ING.
HOW AWKWARD.

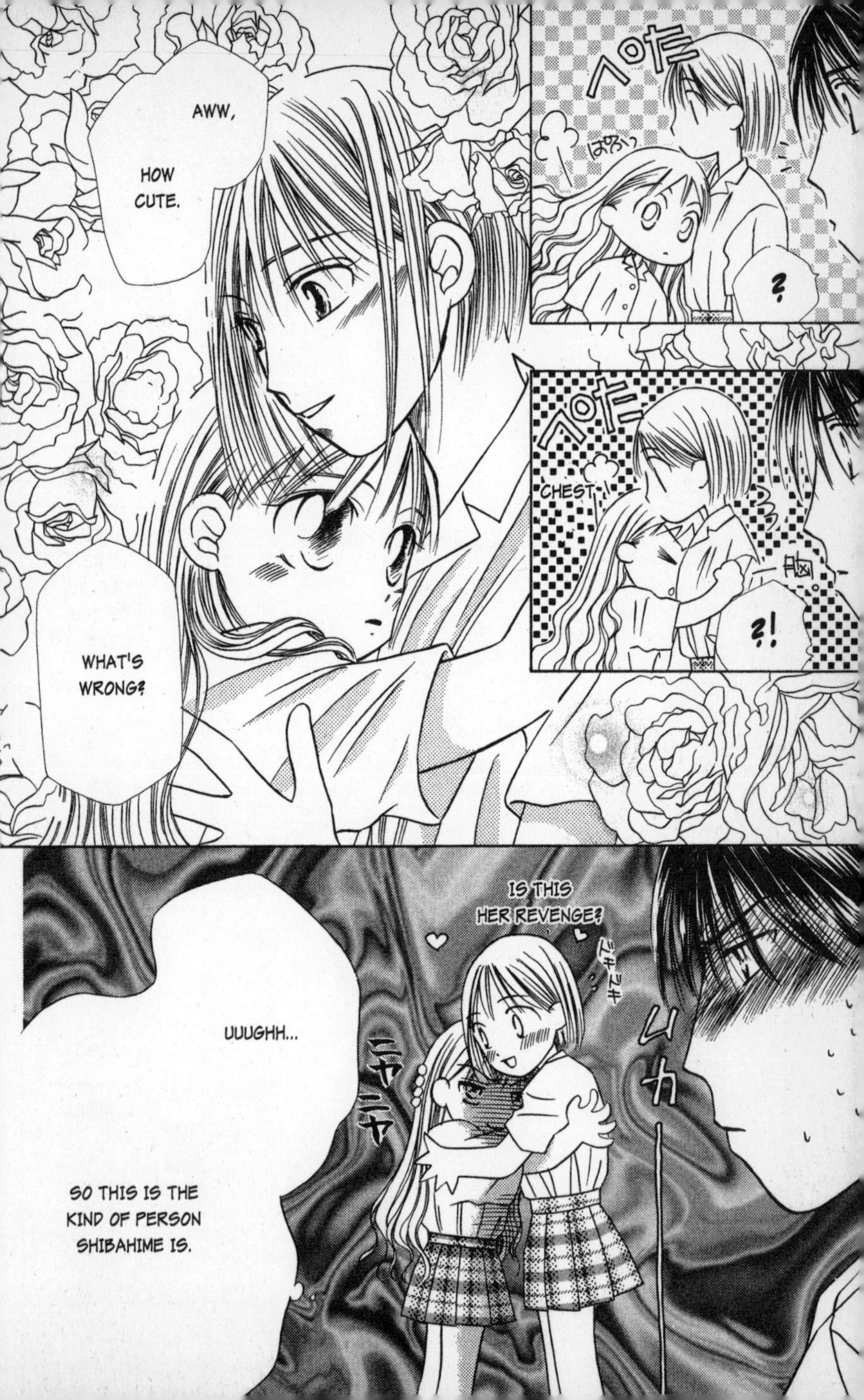
?
CHEST
胸
?!
AWW,
HOW CUTE.
WHAT'S WRONG?
IS THIS HER REVENGE?
ドキドキ
ムカ
ニヤニヤ
UUUGHH...
SO THIS IS THE KIND OF PERSON SHIBAHIME IS.

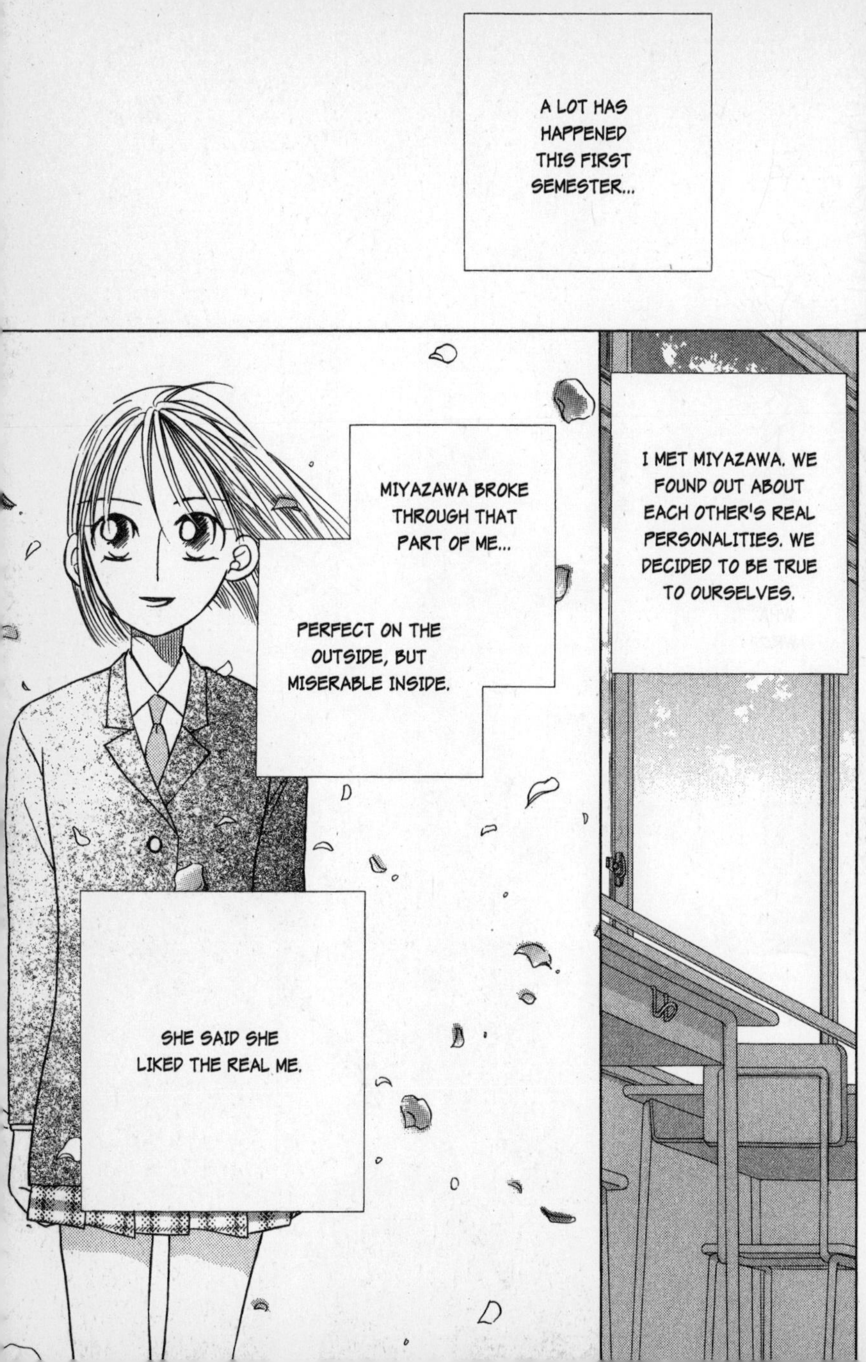
A LOT HAS HAPPENED THIS FIRST SEMESTER...
I MET MIYAZAWA. WE FOUND OUT ABOUT EACH OTHER'S REAL PERSONALITIES. WE DECIDED TO BE TRUE TO OURSELVES.
MIYAZAWA BROKE THROUGH THAT PART OF ME...
PERFECT ON THE OUTSIDE, BUT MISERABLE INSIDE.
SHE SAID SHE LIKED THE REAL ME.

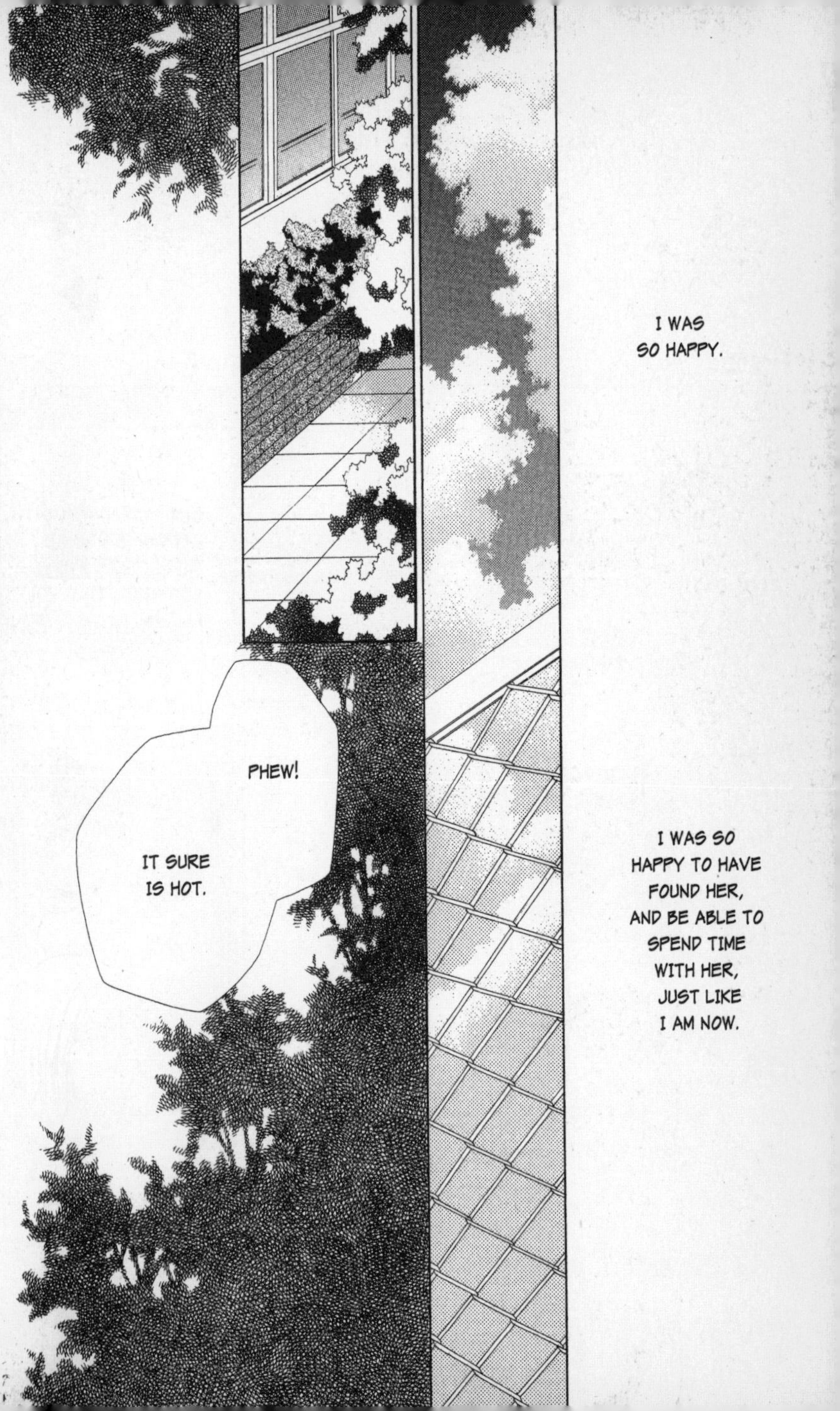
I WAS SO HAPPY.
I WAS SO HAPPY TO HAVE FOUND HER, AND BE ABLE TO SPEND TIME WITH HER, JUST LIKE I AM NOW.
PHEW!
IT SURE IS HOT.

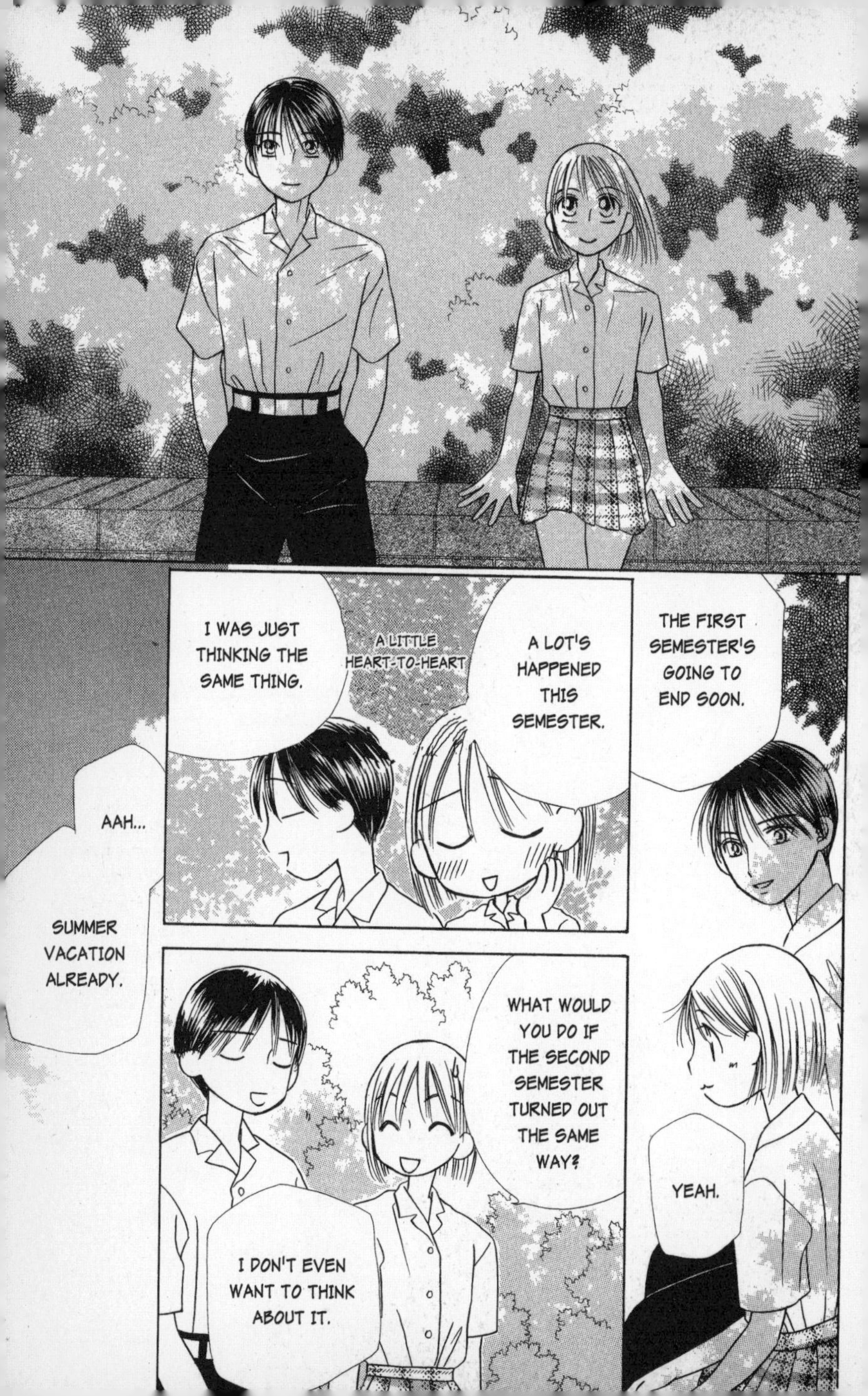
THE FIRST SEMESTER'S GOING TO END SOON.
A LOT'S HAPPENED THIS SEMESTER.
A LITTLE HEART-TO-HEART
I WAS JUST THINKING THE SAME THING.
AAH...
SUMMER VACATION ALREADY.
YEAH.
WHAT WOULD YOU DO IF THE SECOND SEMESTER TURNED OUT THE SAME WAY?
I DON'T EVEN WANT TO THINK ABOUT IT.

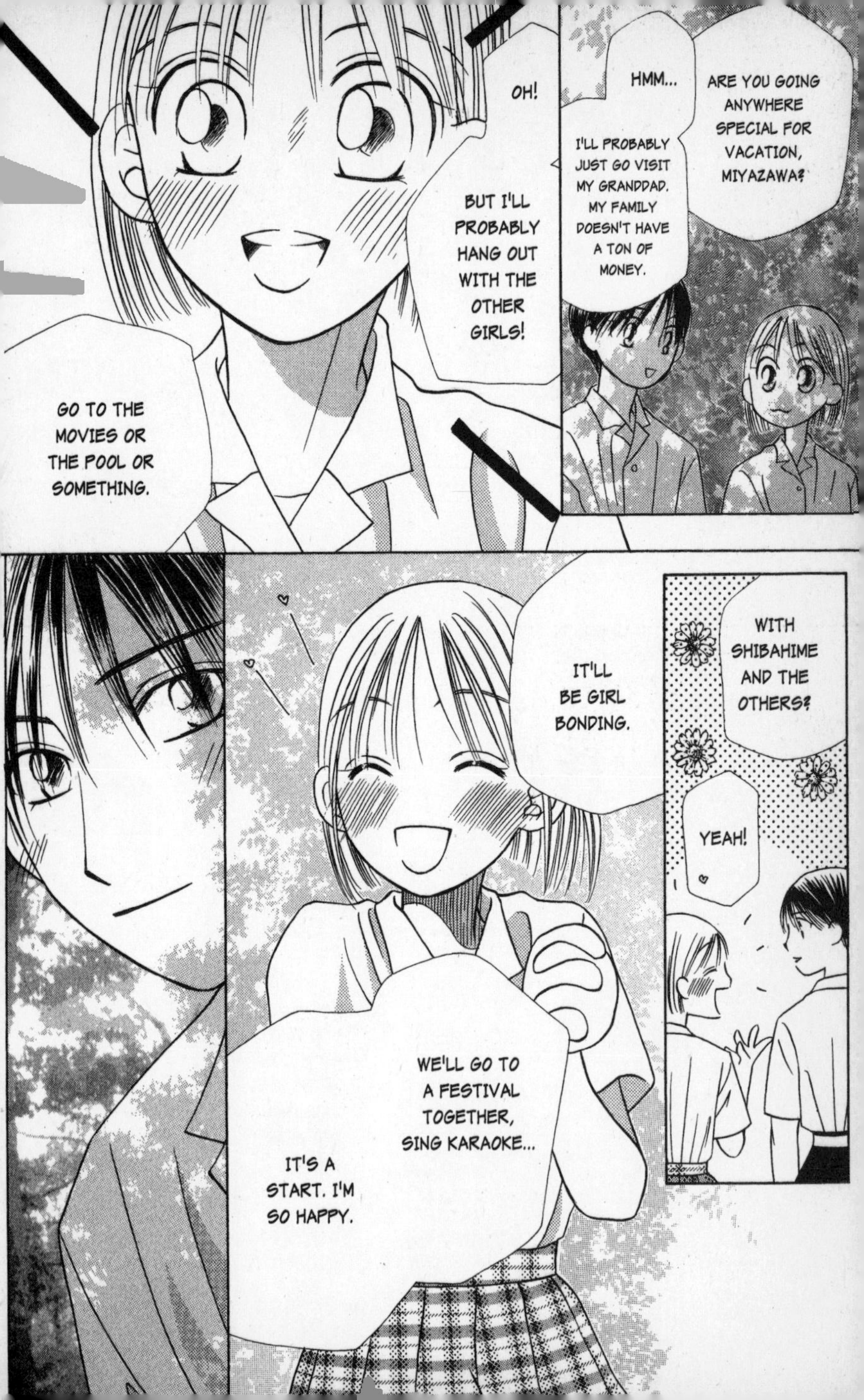
ARE YOU GOING ANYWHERE SPECIAL FOR VACATION, MIYAZAWA?
HMM...
I'LL PROBABLY JUST GO VISIT MY GRANDDAD. MY FAMILY DOESN'T HAVE A TON OF MONEY.
OH!
BUT I'LL PROBABLY HANG OUT WITH THE OTHER GIRLS!
GO TO THE MOVIES OR THE POOL OR SOMETHING.
WITH SHIBAHIME AND THE OTHERS?
YEAH!
IT'LL BE GIRL BONDING.
WE'LL GO TO A FESTIVAL TOGETHER, SING KARAOKE...
IT'S A START. I'M SO HAPPY.

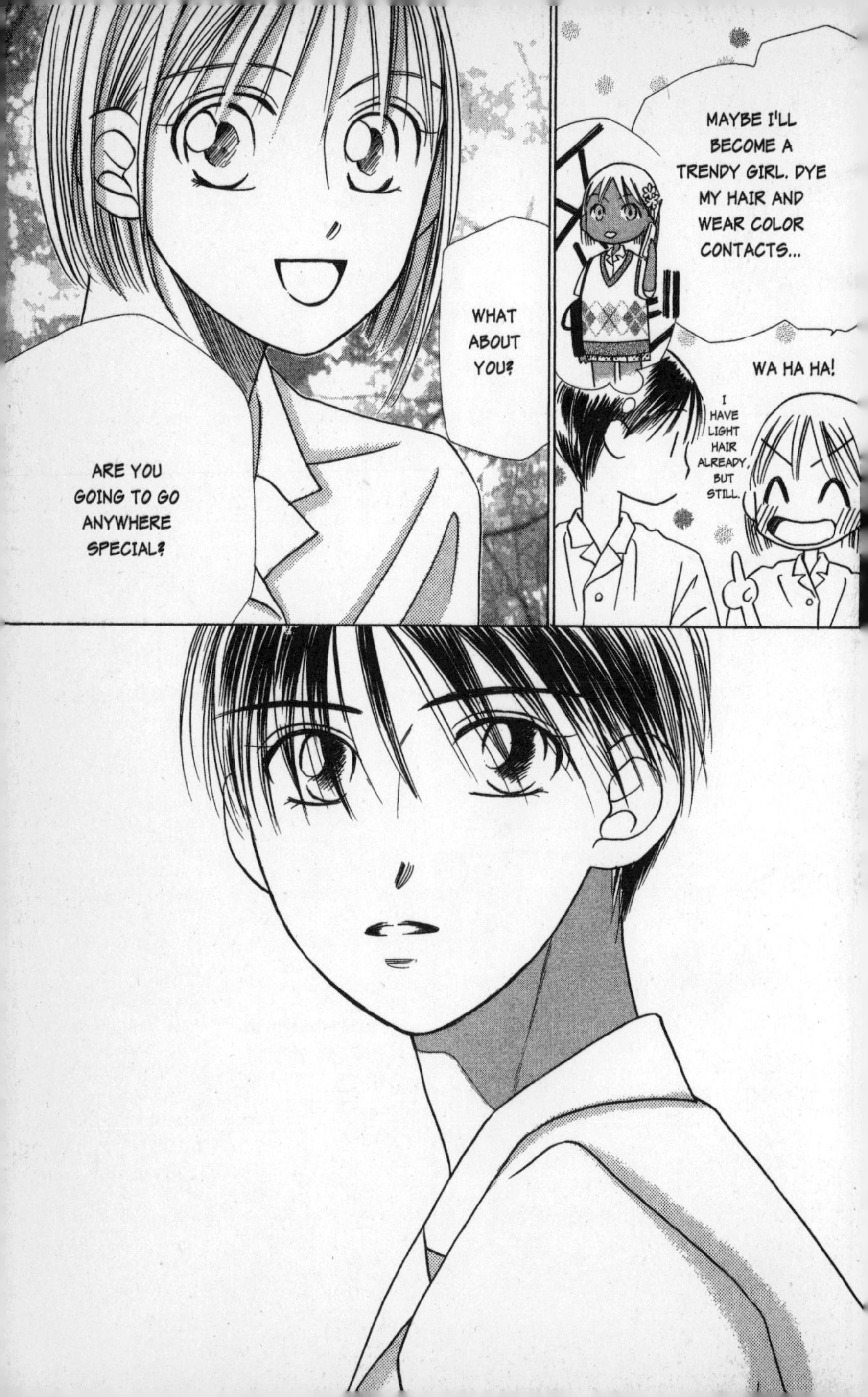
MAYBE I'LL BECOME A TRENDY GIRL. DYE MY HAIR AND WEAR COLOR CONTACTS...
WA HA HA!
I HAVE LIGHT HAIR ALREADY, BUT STILL.
WHAT ABOUT YOU?
ARE YOU GOING TO GO ANYWHERE SPECIAL?

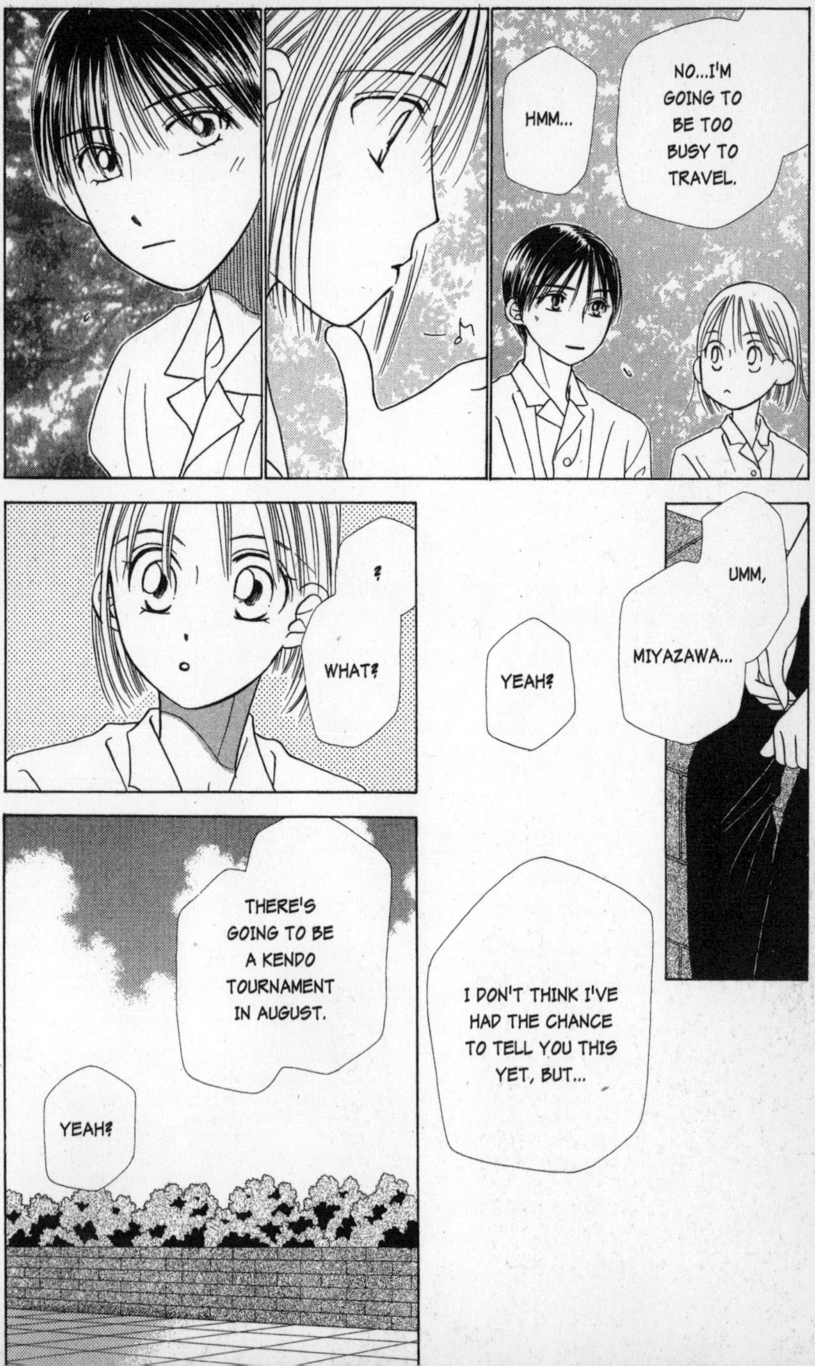
NO...I'M GOING TO BE TOO BUSY TO TRAVEL.
HMM...
UMM, MIYAZAWA...
YEAH?
?
WHAT?
I DON'T THINK I'VE HAD THE CHANCE TO TELL YOU THIS YET, BUT...
THERE'S GOING TO BE A KENDO TOURNAMENT IN AUGUST.
YEAH?

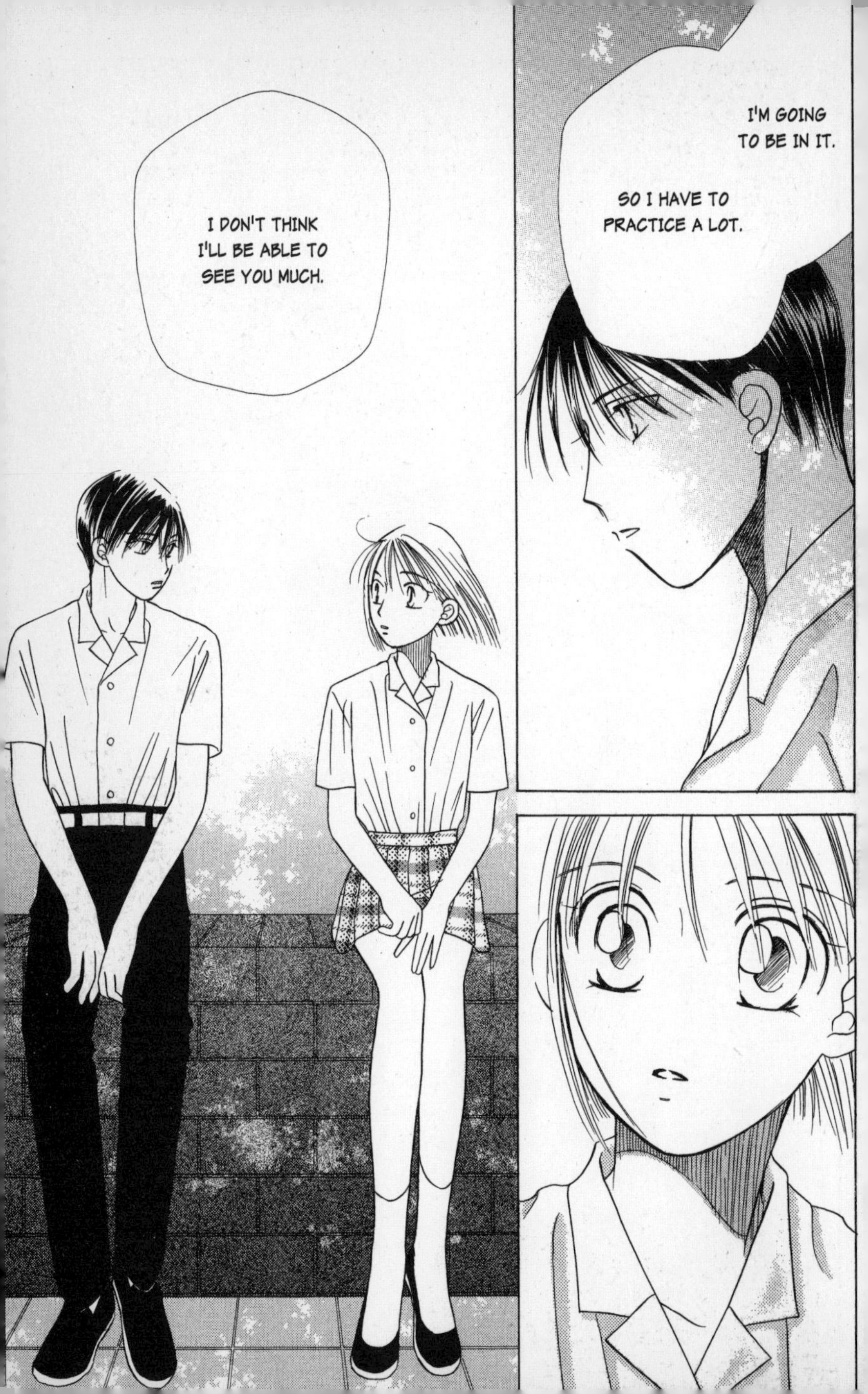
I'M GOING TO BE IN IT.
SO I HAVE TO PRACTICE A LOT.
I DON'T THINK I'LL BE ABLE TO SEE YOU MUCH.

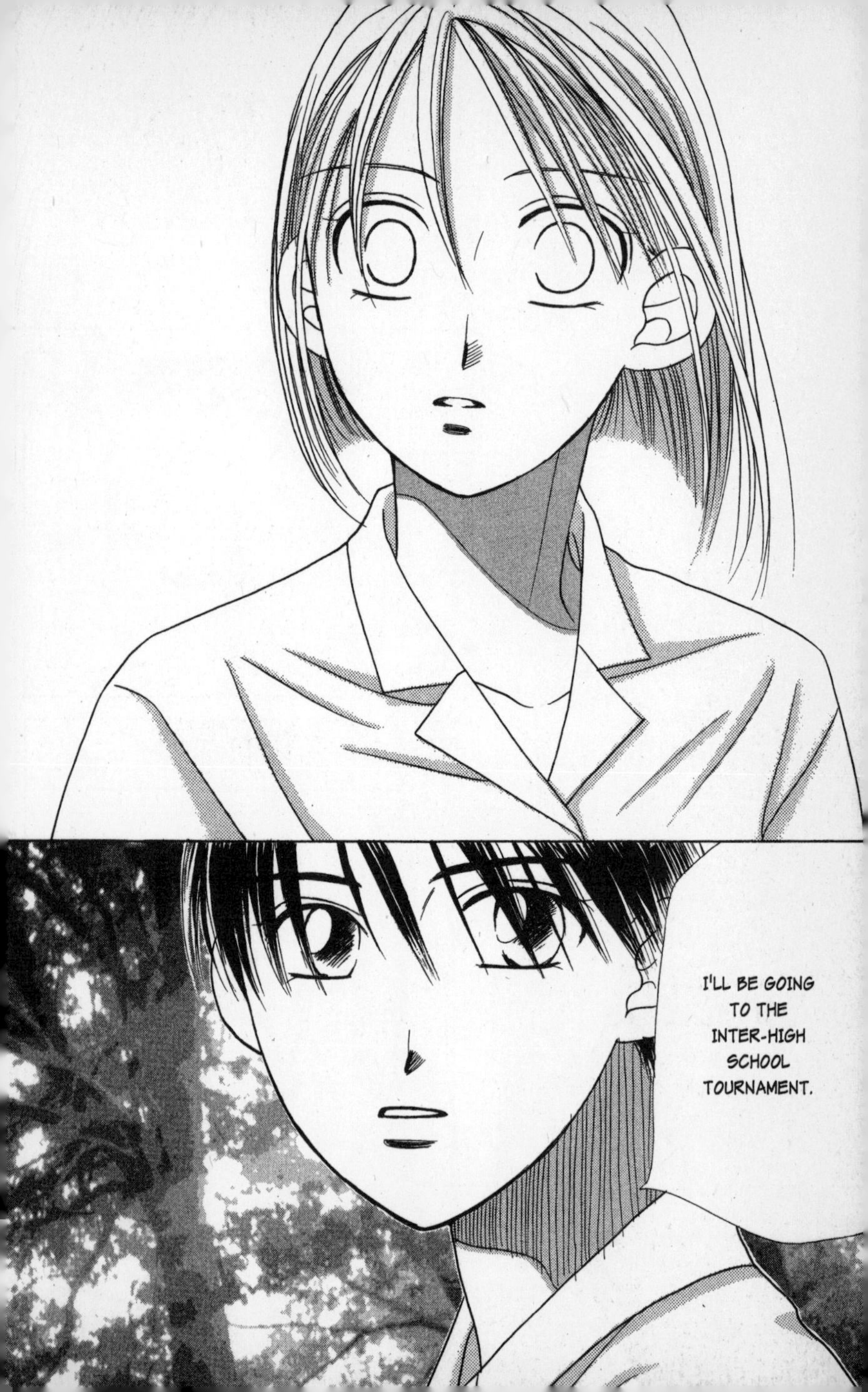
I'LL BE GOING TO THE INTER-HIGH SCHOOL TOURNAMENT.

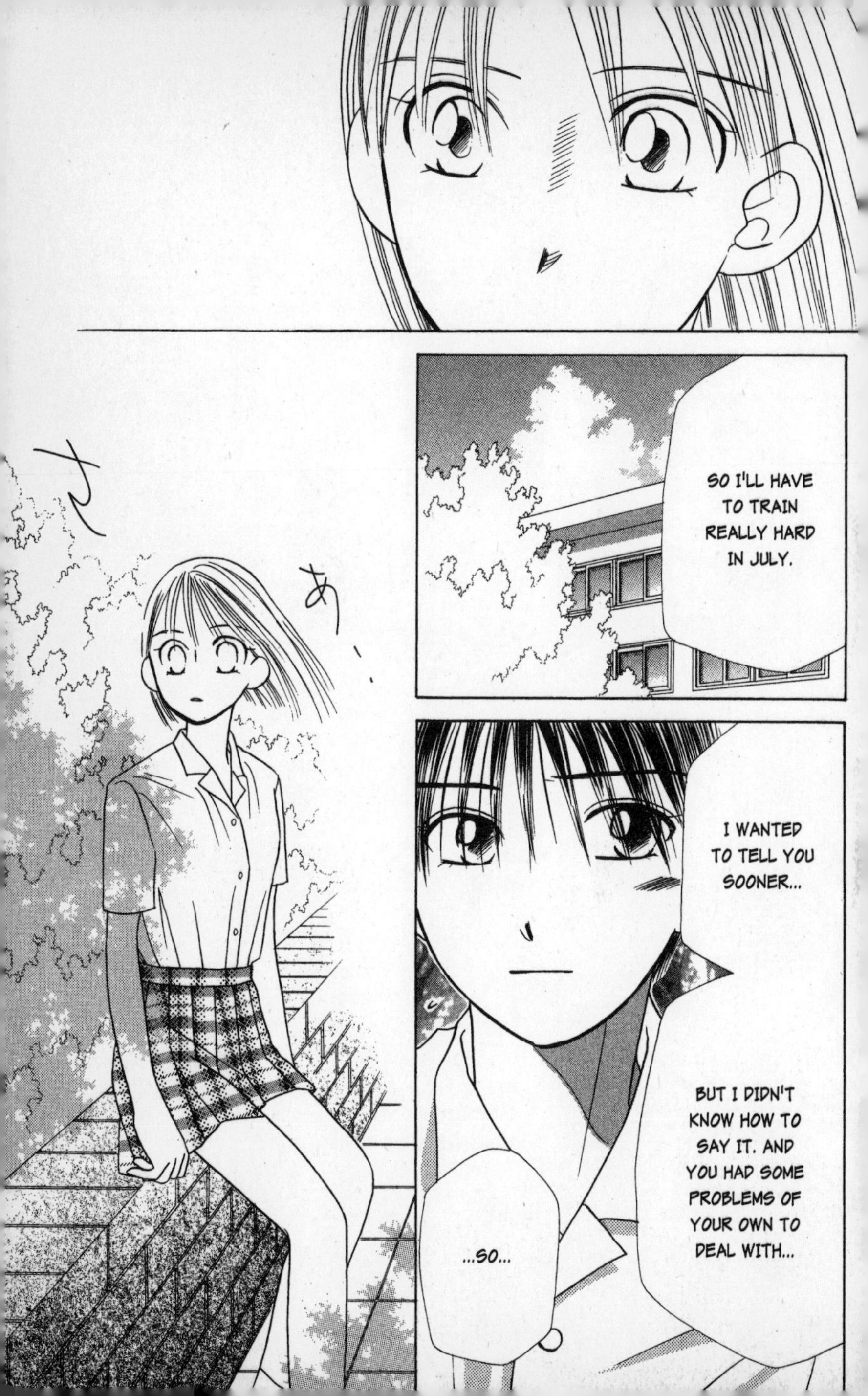
SO I'LL HAVE TO TRAIN REALLY HARD IN JULY.
I WANTED TO TELL YOU SOONER...
BUT I DIDN'T KNOW HOW TO SAY IT. AND YOU HAD SOME PROBLEMS OF YOUR OWN TO DEAL WITH...
...SO...
あ

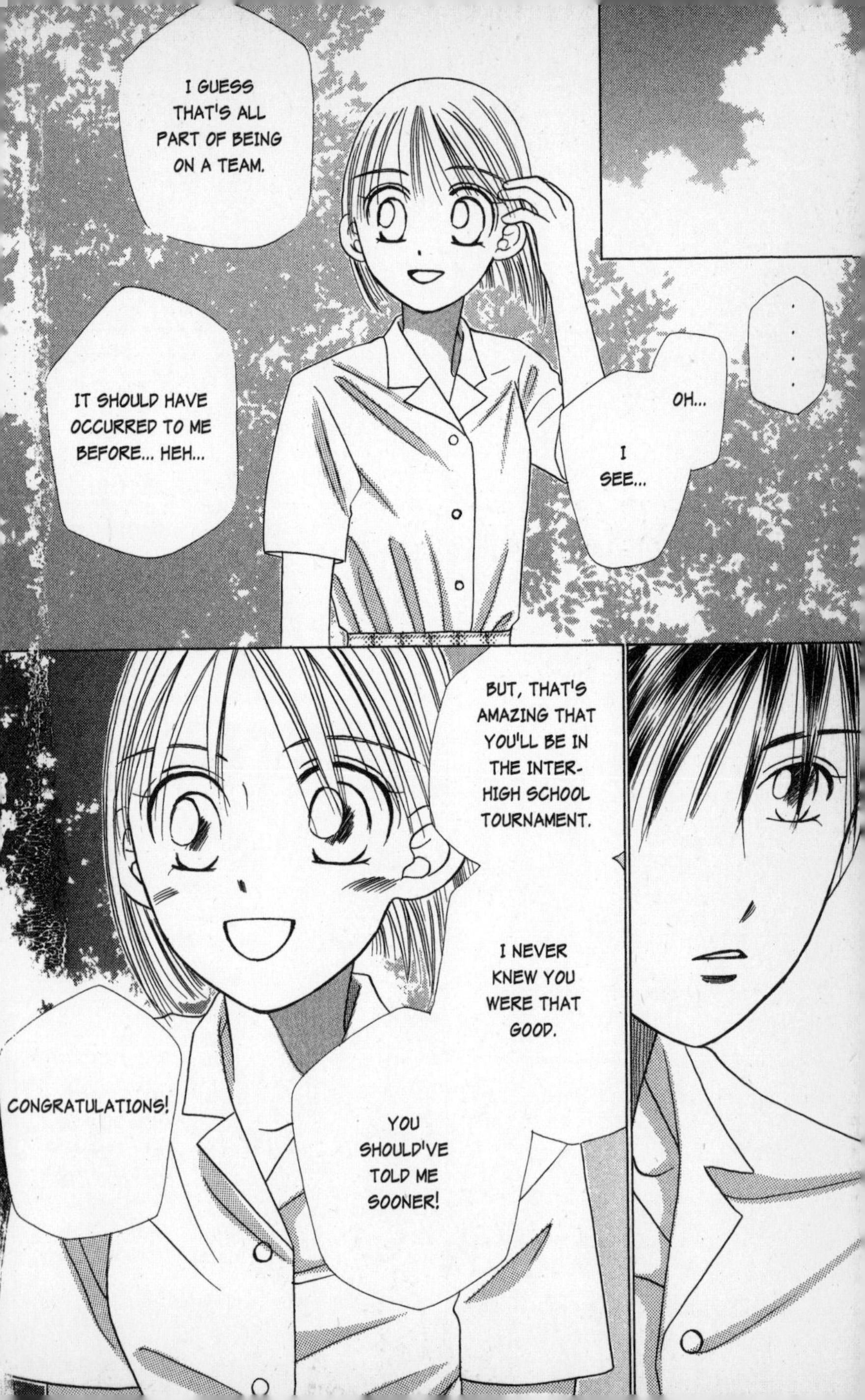
. . . .
OH... I SEE...
I GUESS THAT'S ALL PART OF BEING ON A TEAM.
IT SHOULD HAVE OCCURRED TO ME BEFORE... HEH...
BUT, THAT'S AMAZING THAT YOU'LL BE IN THE INTER-HIGH SCHOOL TOURNAMENT.
I NEVER KNEW YOU WERE THAT GOOD.
YOU SHOULD'VE TOLD ME SOONER!
CONGRATULATIONS!

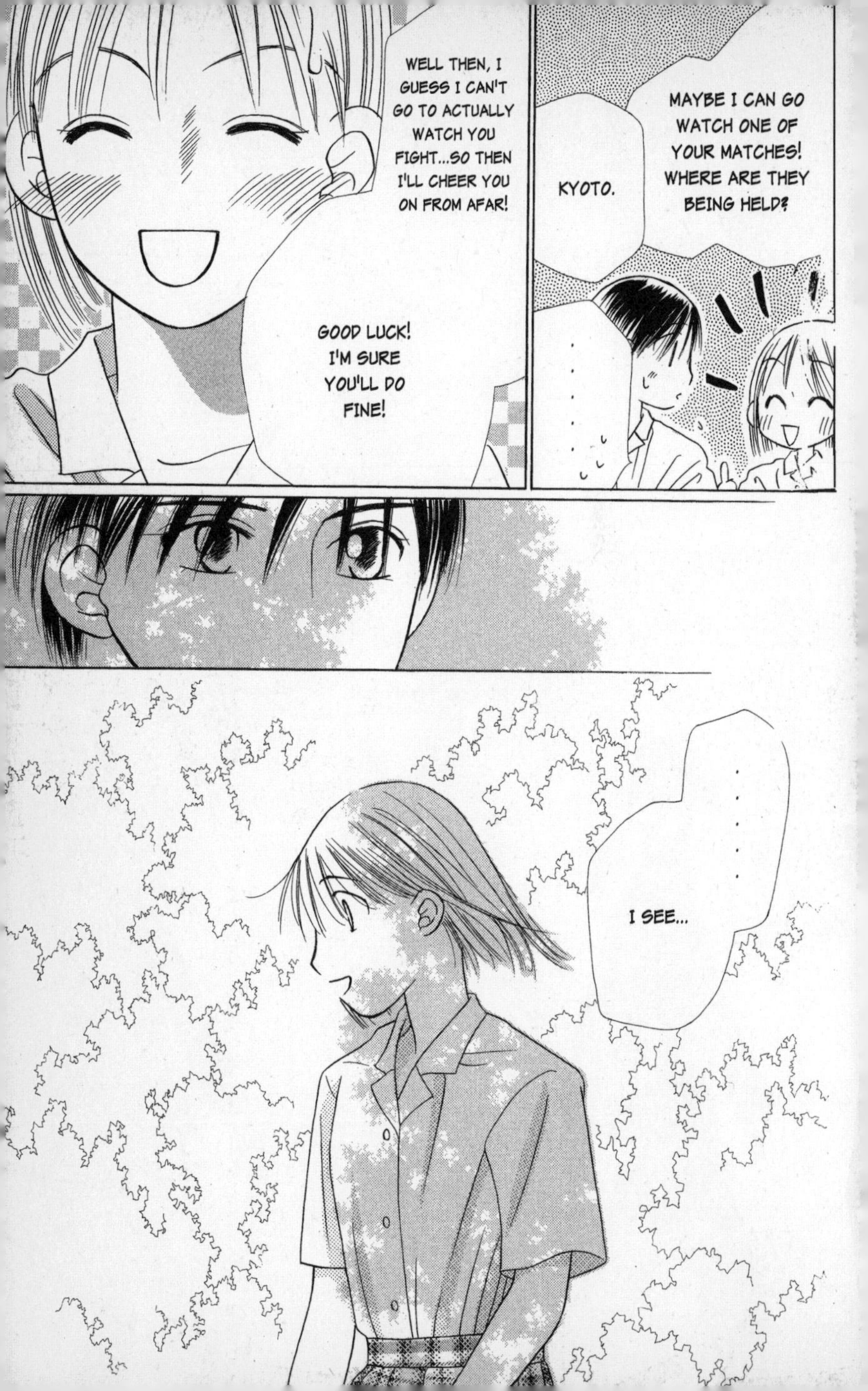
MAYBE I CAN GO WATCH ONE OF YOUR MATCHES! WHERE ARE THEY BEING HELD?
KYOTO.
WELL THEN, I GUESS I CAN'T GO TO ACTUALLY WATCH YOU FIGHT...SO THEN I'LL CHEER YOU ON FROM AFAR!
GOOD LUCK! I'M SURE YOU'LL DO FINE!
I SEE...

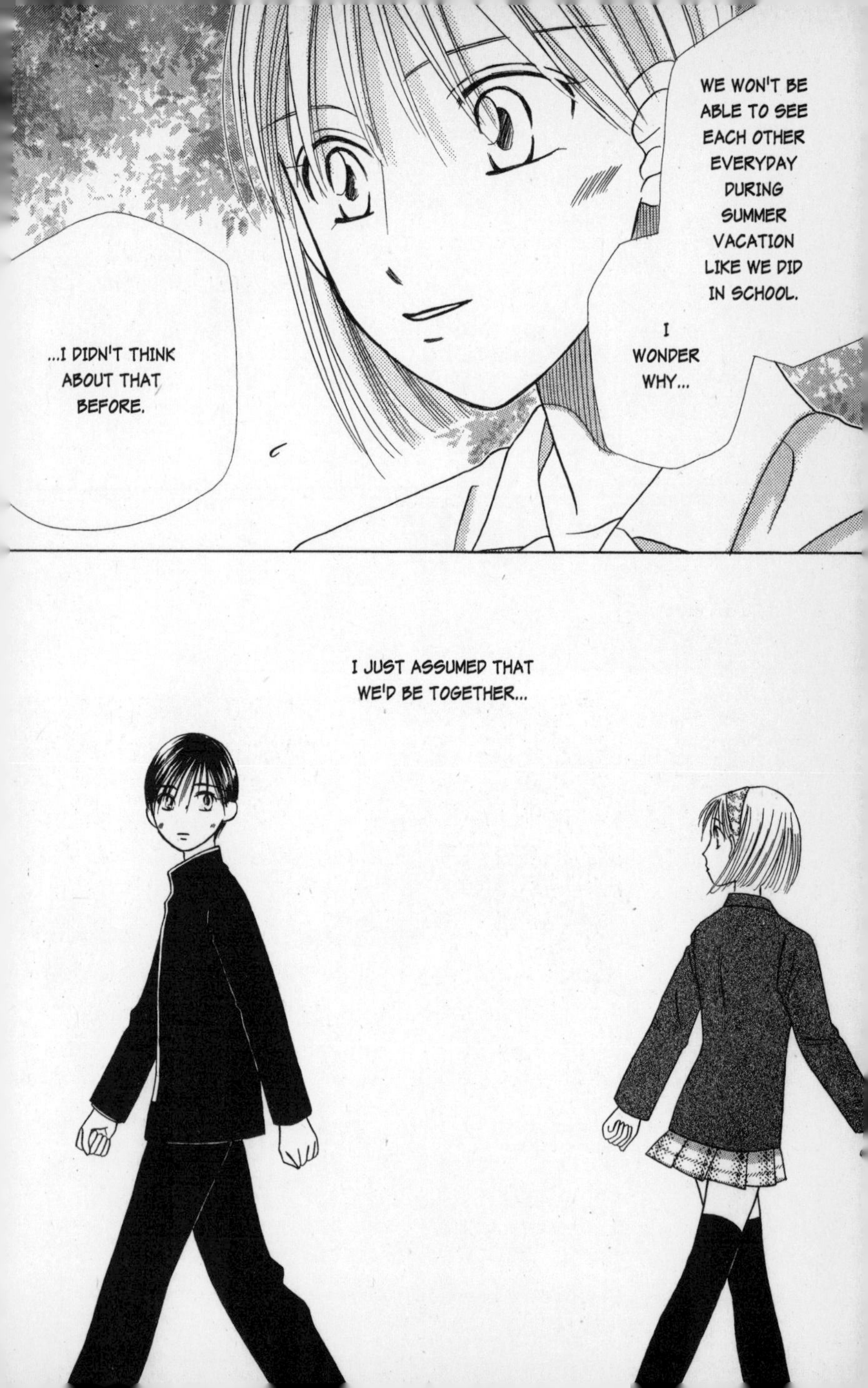
WE WON'T BE ABLE TO SEE EACH OTHER EVERYDAY DURING SUMMER VACATION LIKE WE DID IN SCHOOL.
I WONDER WHY...
...I DIDN'T THINK ABOUT THAT BEFORE.
I JUST ASSUMED THAT WE'D BE TOGETHER...

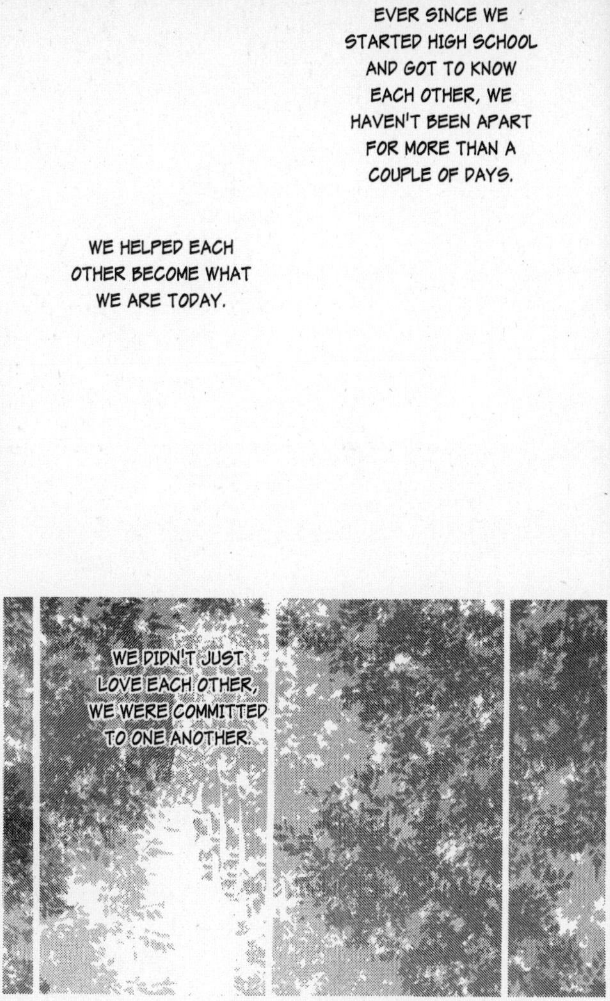
EVER SINCE WE STARTED HIGH SCHOOL AND GOT TO KNOW EACH OTHER, WE HAVEN'T BEEN APART FOR MORE THAN A COUPLE OF DAYS.
WE HELPED EACH OTHER BECOME WHAT WE ARE TODAY.
WE DIDN'T JUST LOVE EACH OTHER, WE WERE COMMITTED TO ONE ANOTHER.

4

I love white chocolate!

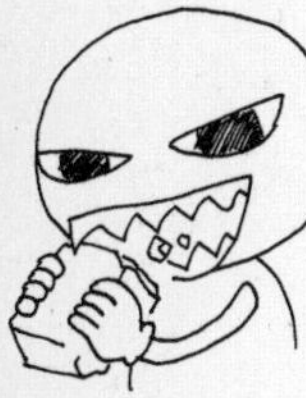

Hand-made white chocolate is the best! It's sooo good!

I'VE REALIZED FOR THE FIRST TIME...

...JUST HOW SPECIAL MIYAZAWA IS.

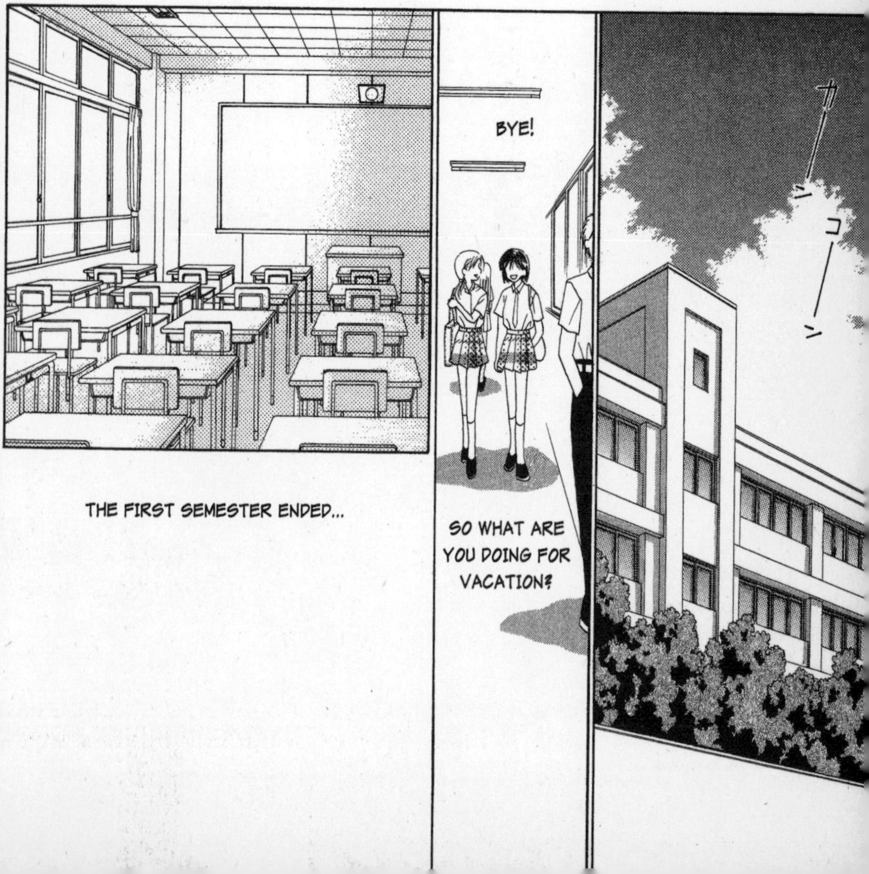
カーンコーン
BYE!
SO WHAT ARE YOU DOING FOR VACATION?
THE FIRST SEMESTER ENDED...

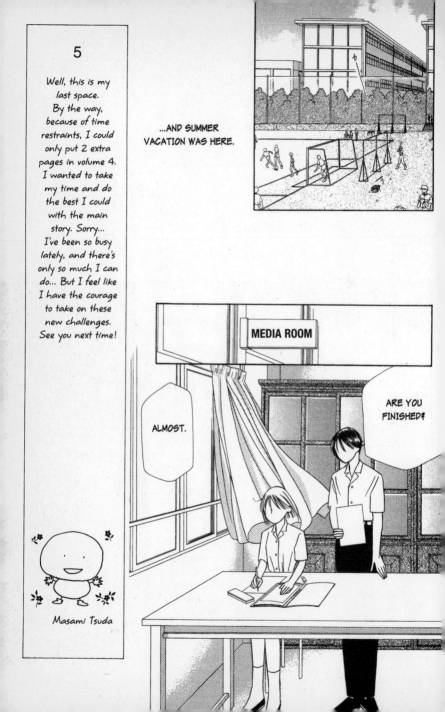

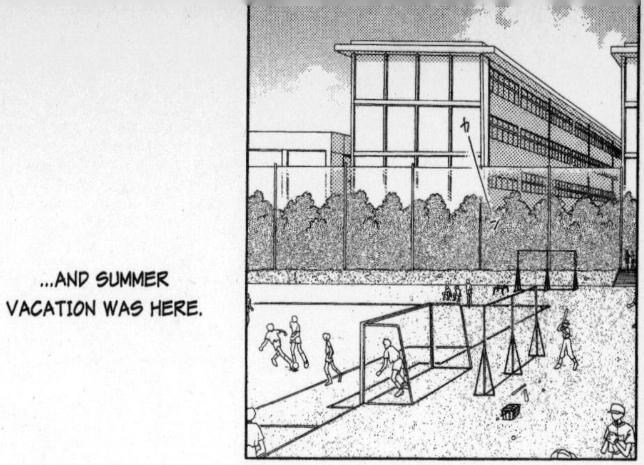
...AND SUMMER VACATION WAS HERE.

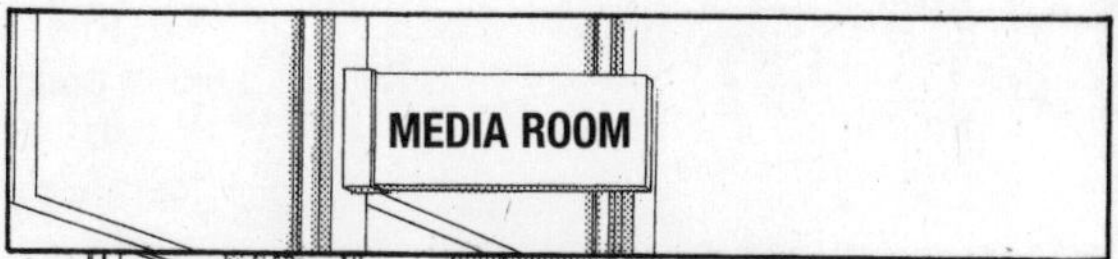
MEDIA ROOM

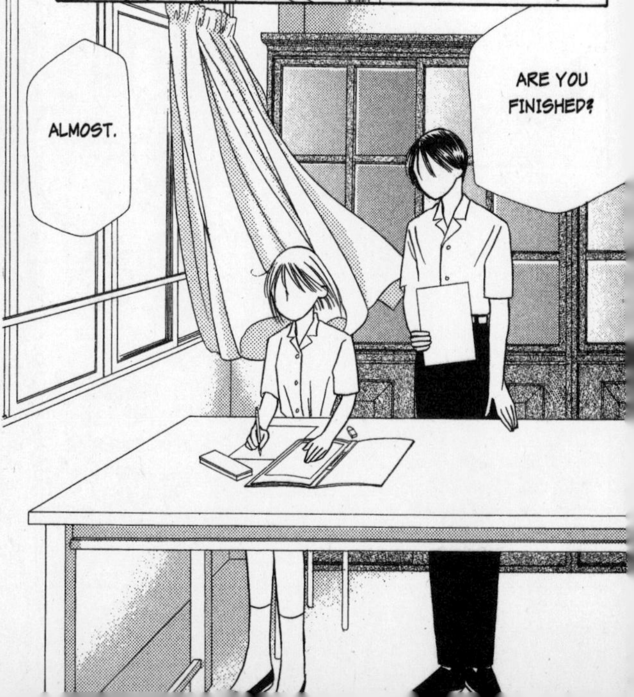
ARE YOU FINISHED?
ALMOST.

5

Well, this is my last space. By the way, because of time restraints, I could only put 2 extra pages in volume 4. I wanted to take my time and do the best I could with the main story. Sorry... I've been so busy lately, and there's only so much I can do... But I feel like I have the courage to take on these new challenges. See you next time!

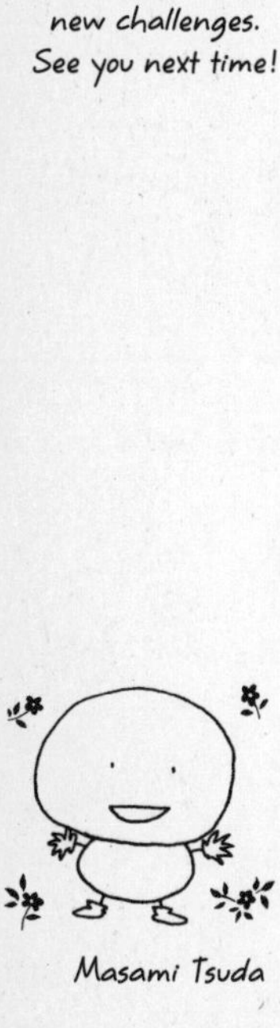

Masami Tsuda

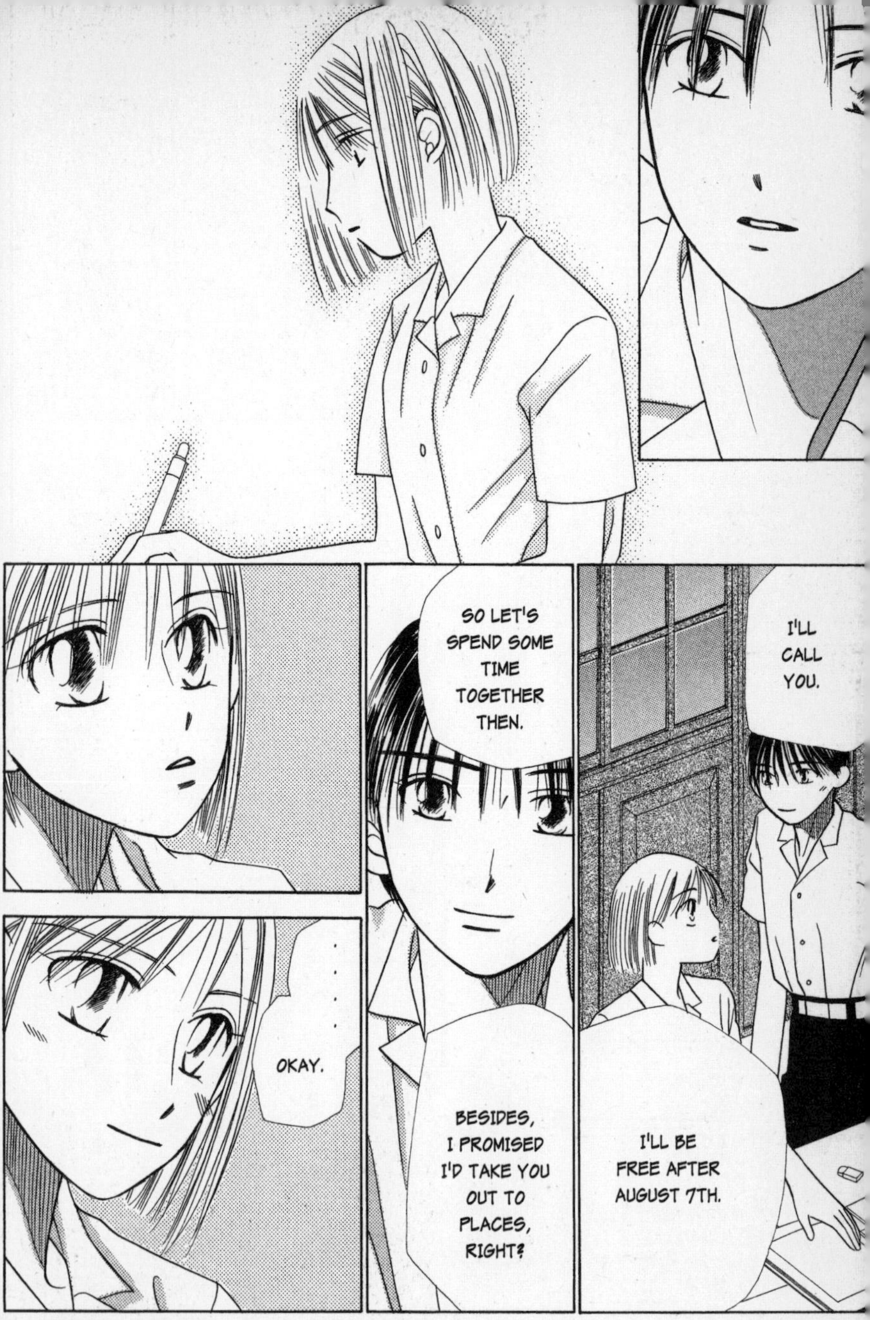
I'LL CALL YOU.
I'LL BE FREE AFTER AUGUST 7TH.
SO LET'S SPEND SOME TIME TOGETHER THEN.
BESIDES, I PROMISED I'D TAKE YOU OUT TO PLACES, RIGHT?
· · · ·
OKAY.

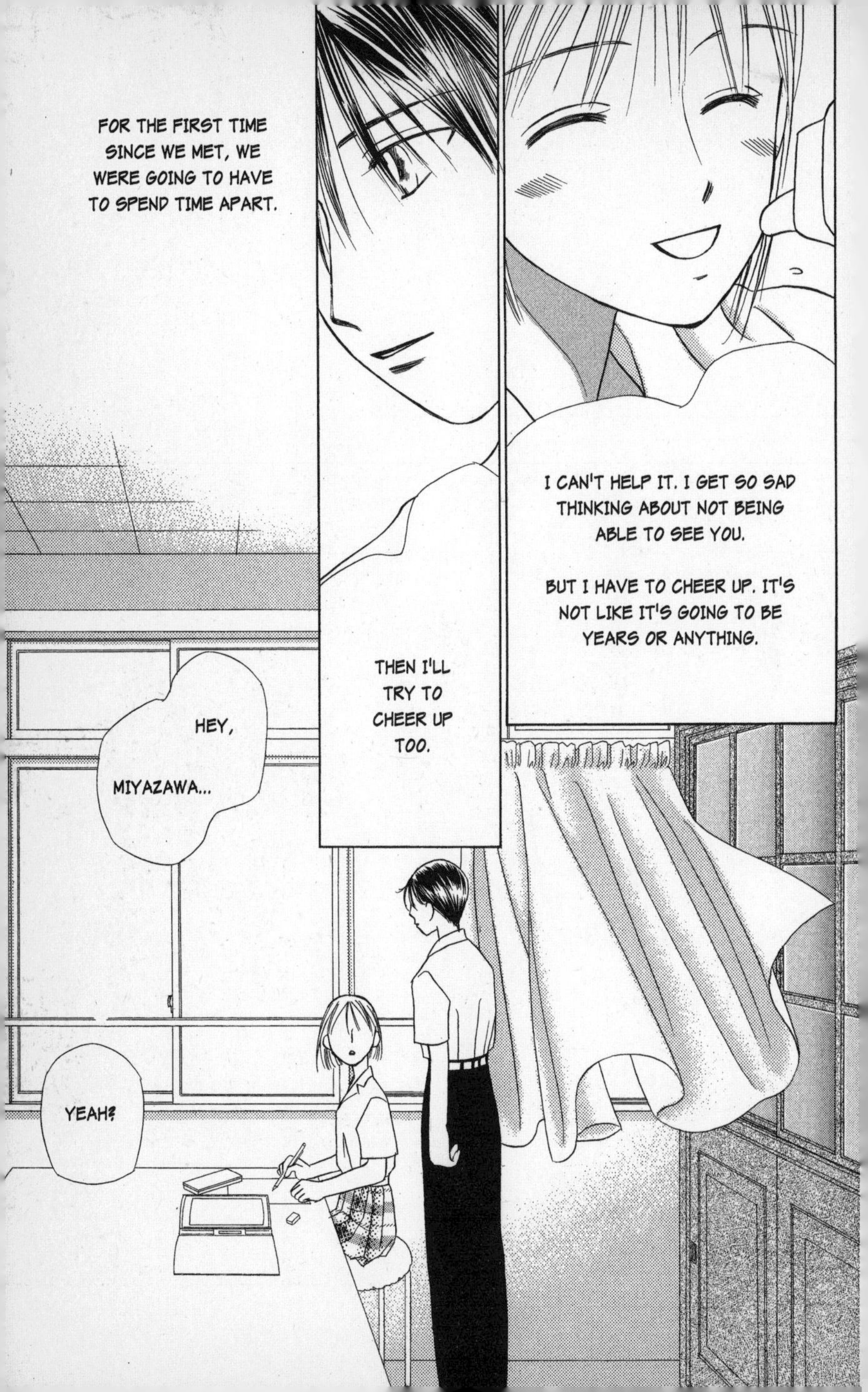
I CAN'T HELP IT. I GET SO SAD THINKING ABOUT NOT BEING ABLE TO SEE YOU.
BUT I HAVE TO CHEER UP. IT'S NOT LIKE IT'S GOING TO BE YEARS OR ANYTHING.
THEN I'LL TRY TO CHEER UP TOO.
FOR THE FIRST TIME SINCE WE MET, WE WERE GOING TO HAVE TO SPEND TIME APART.
HEY,
MIYAZAWA...
YEAH?

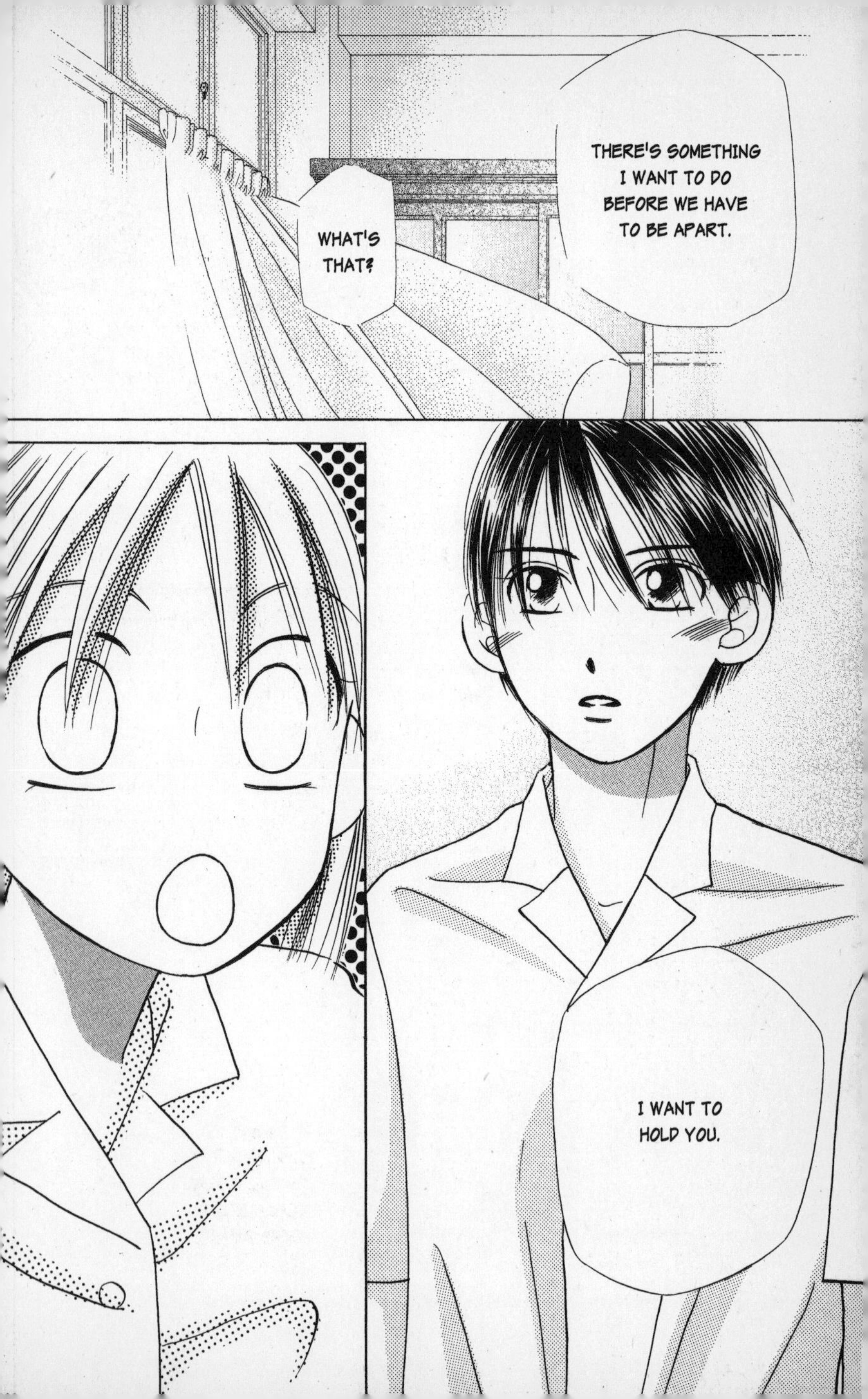
THERE'S SOMETHING I WANT TO DO BEFORE WE HAVE TO BE APART.
WHAT'S THAT?
I WANT TO HOLD YOU.

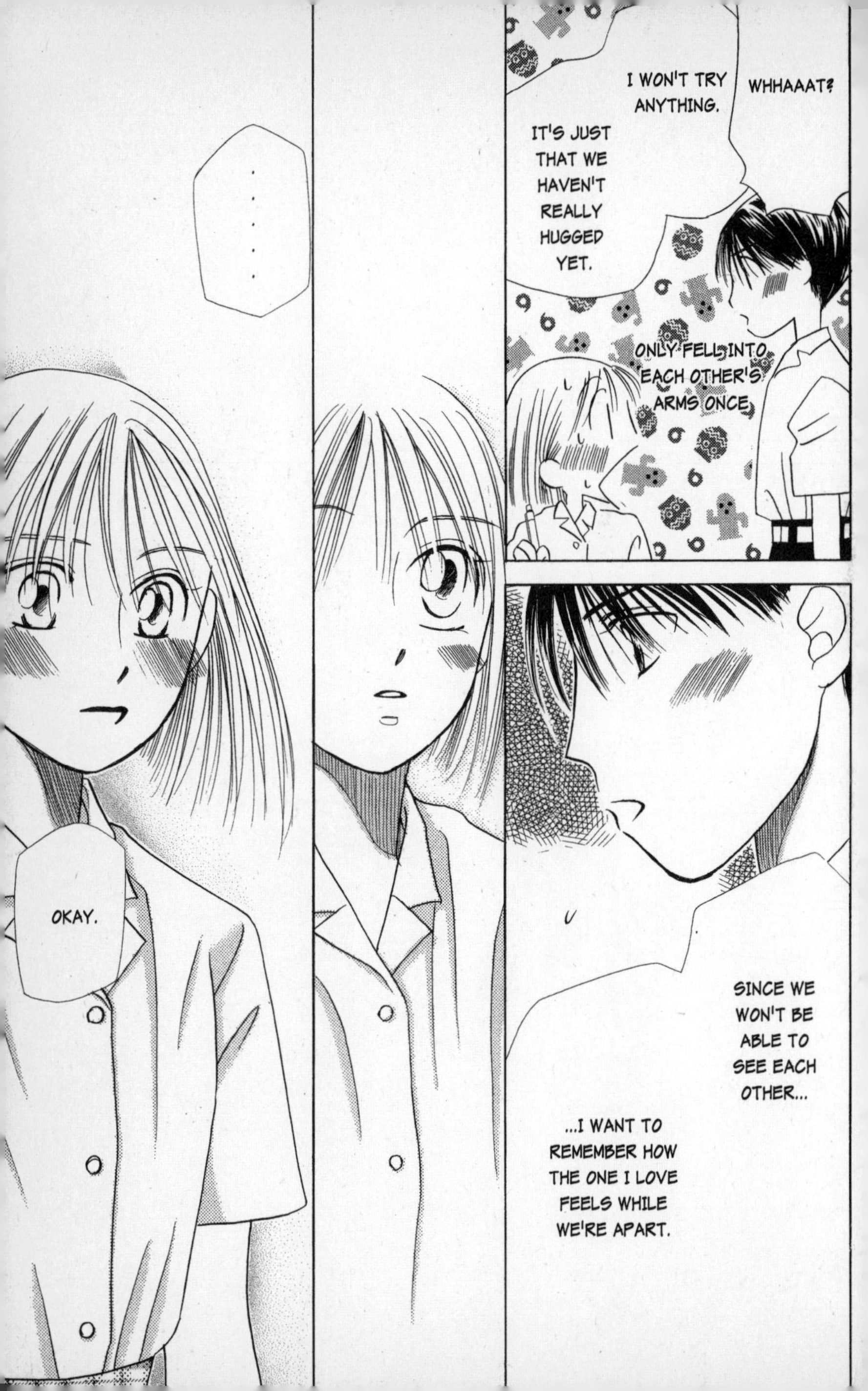
WHHAAAT?
I WON'T TRY ANYTHING.
IT'S JUST THAT WE HAVEN'T REALLY HUGGED YET.
ONLY FELL INTO EACH OTHER'S ARMS ONCE.
SINCE WE WON'T BE ABLE TO SEE EACH OTHER...
...I WANT TO REMEMBER HOW THE ONE I LOVE FEELS WHILE WE'RE APART.
....
OKAY.

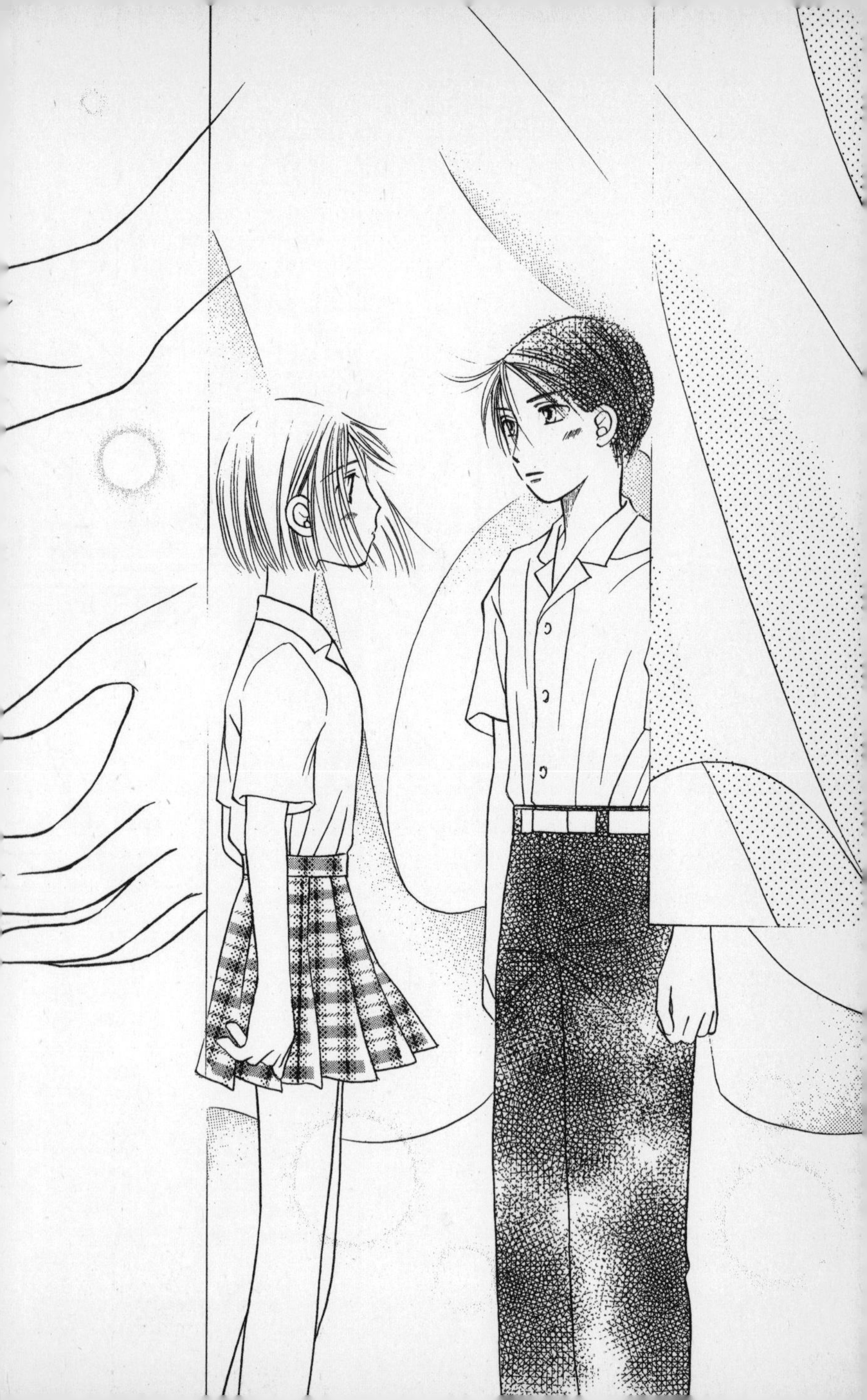

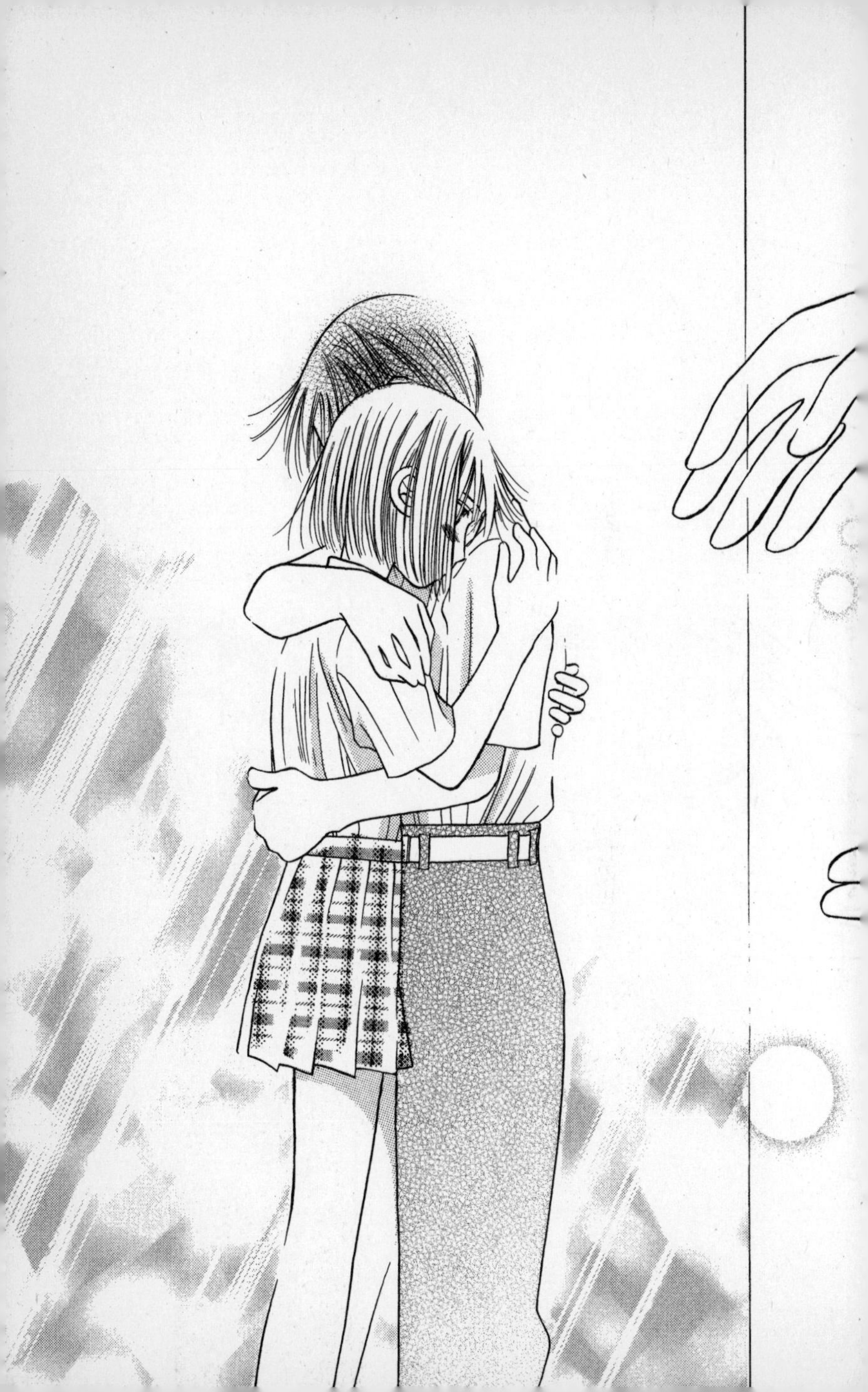

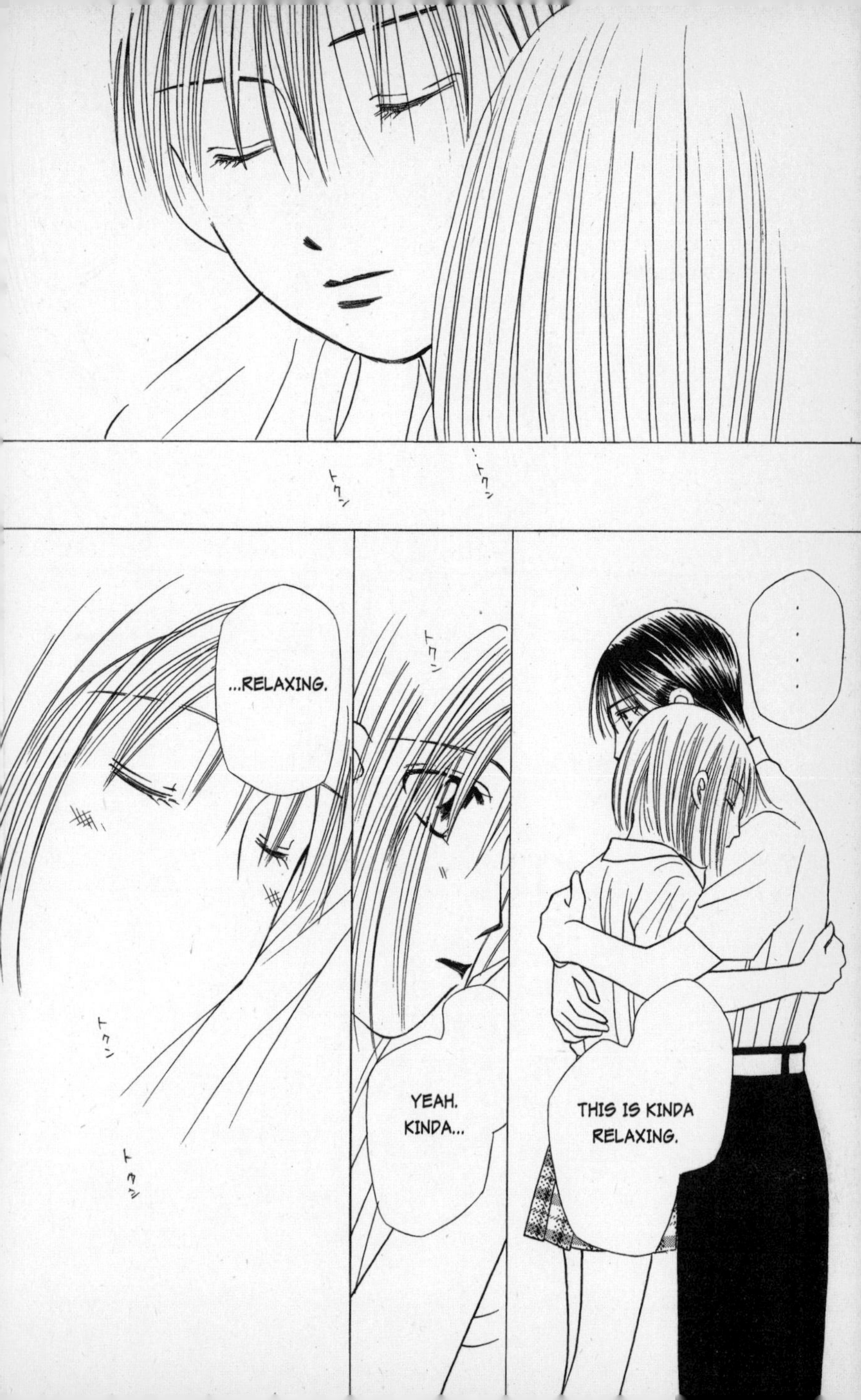
....
THIS IS KINDA RELAXING.
YEAH. KINDA...
...RELAXING.

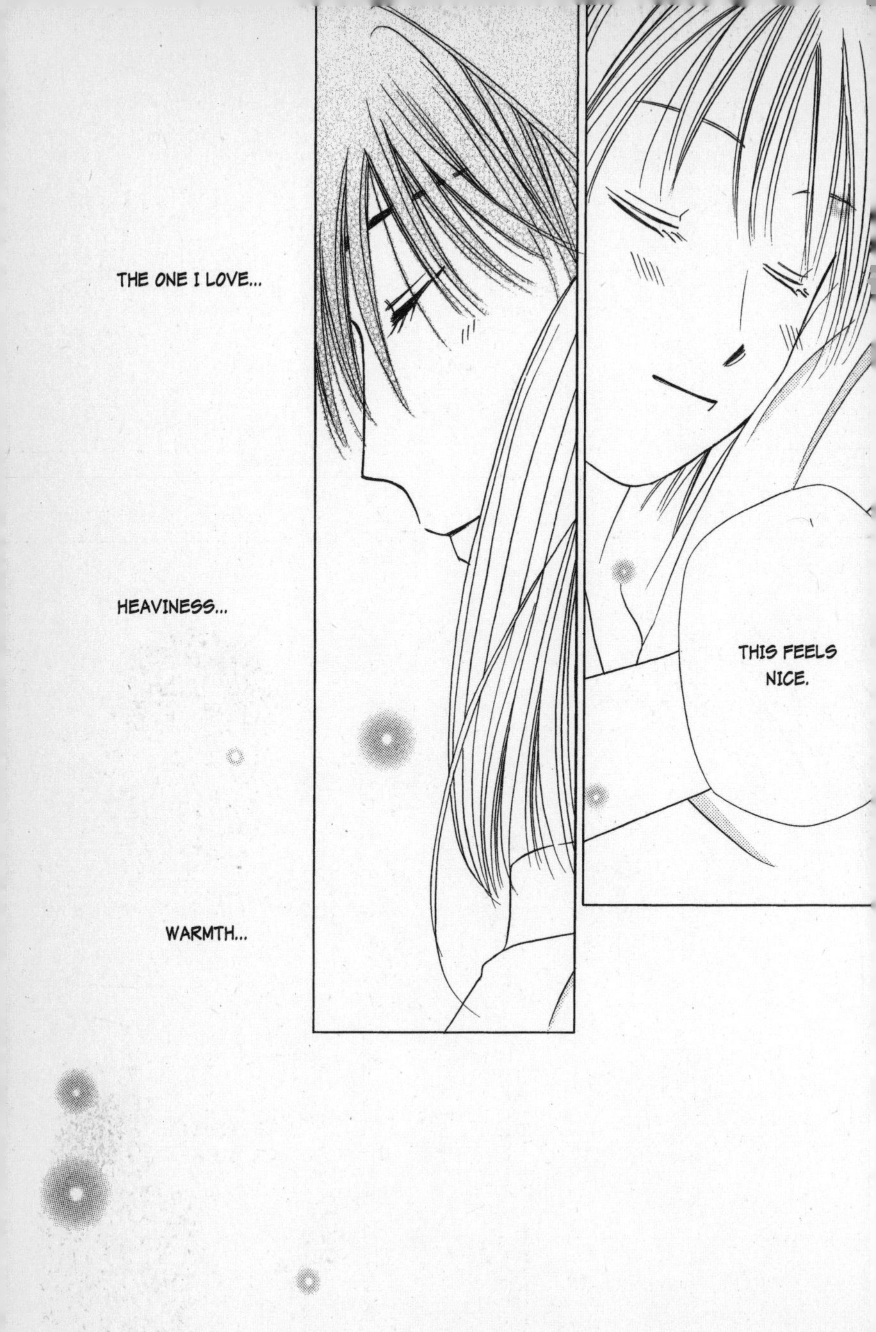
THIS FEELS NICE.
THE ONE I LOVE...
HEAVINESS...
WARMTH...

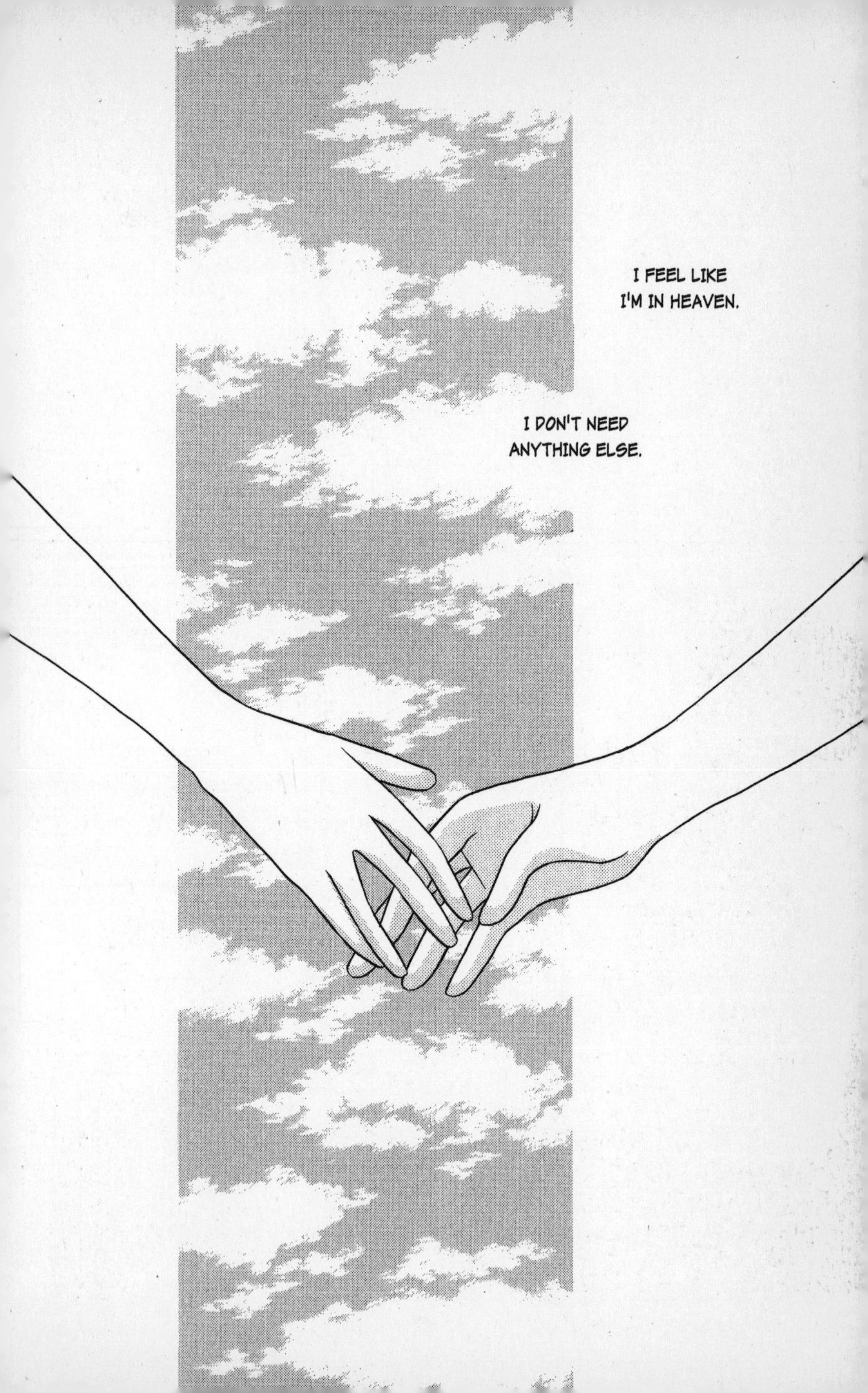
I FEEL LIKE
I'M IN HEAVEN.
I DON'T NEED
ANYTHING ELSE.

I NEVER KNEW
SUCH TRANQUILITY
EVEN EXISTED.

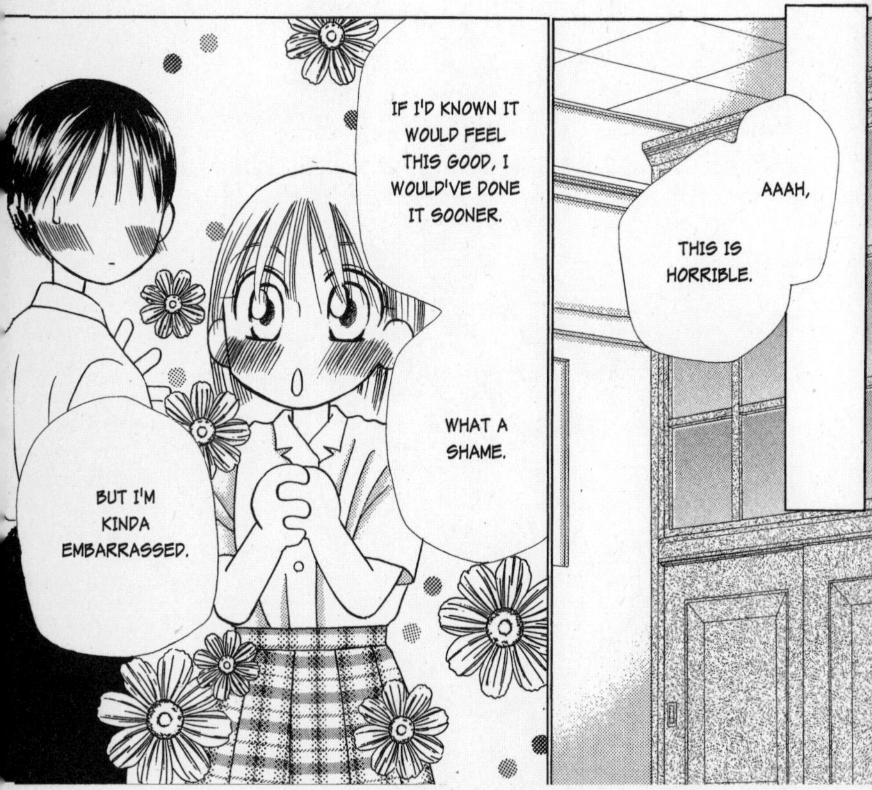
AAAH,
THIS IS HORRIBLE.
IF I'D KNOWN IT WOULD FEEL THIS GOOD, I WOULD'VE DONE IT SOONER.
WHAT A SHAME.
BUT I'M KINDA EMBARRASSED.

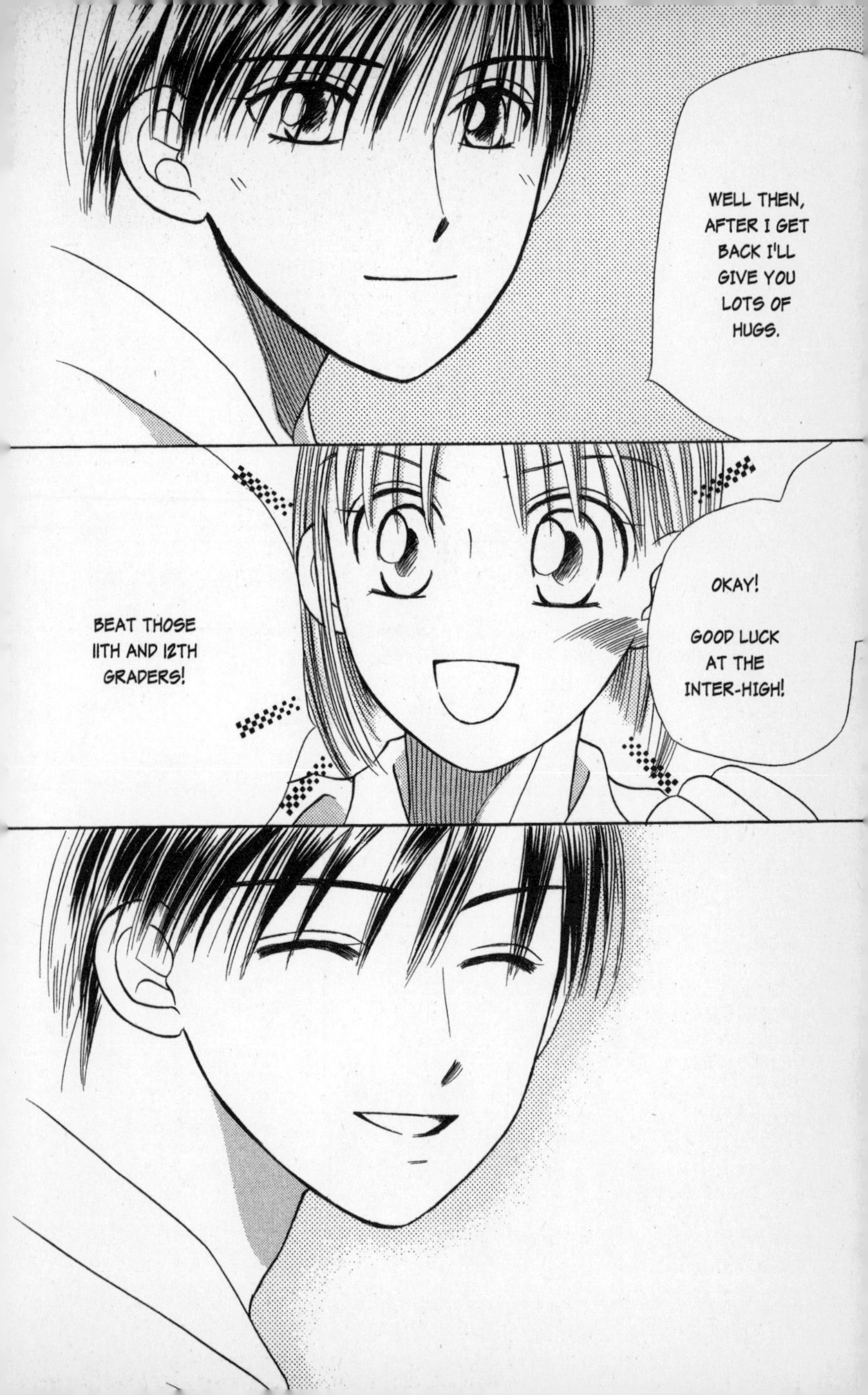
WELL THEN, AFTER I GET BACK I'LL GIVE YOU LOTS OF HUGS.
OKAY!
GOOD LUCK AT THE INTER-HIGH!
BEAT THOSE 11TH AND 12TH GRADERS!

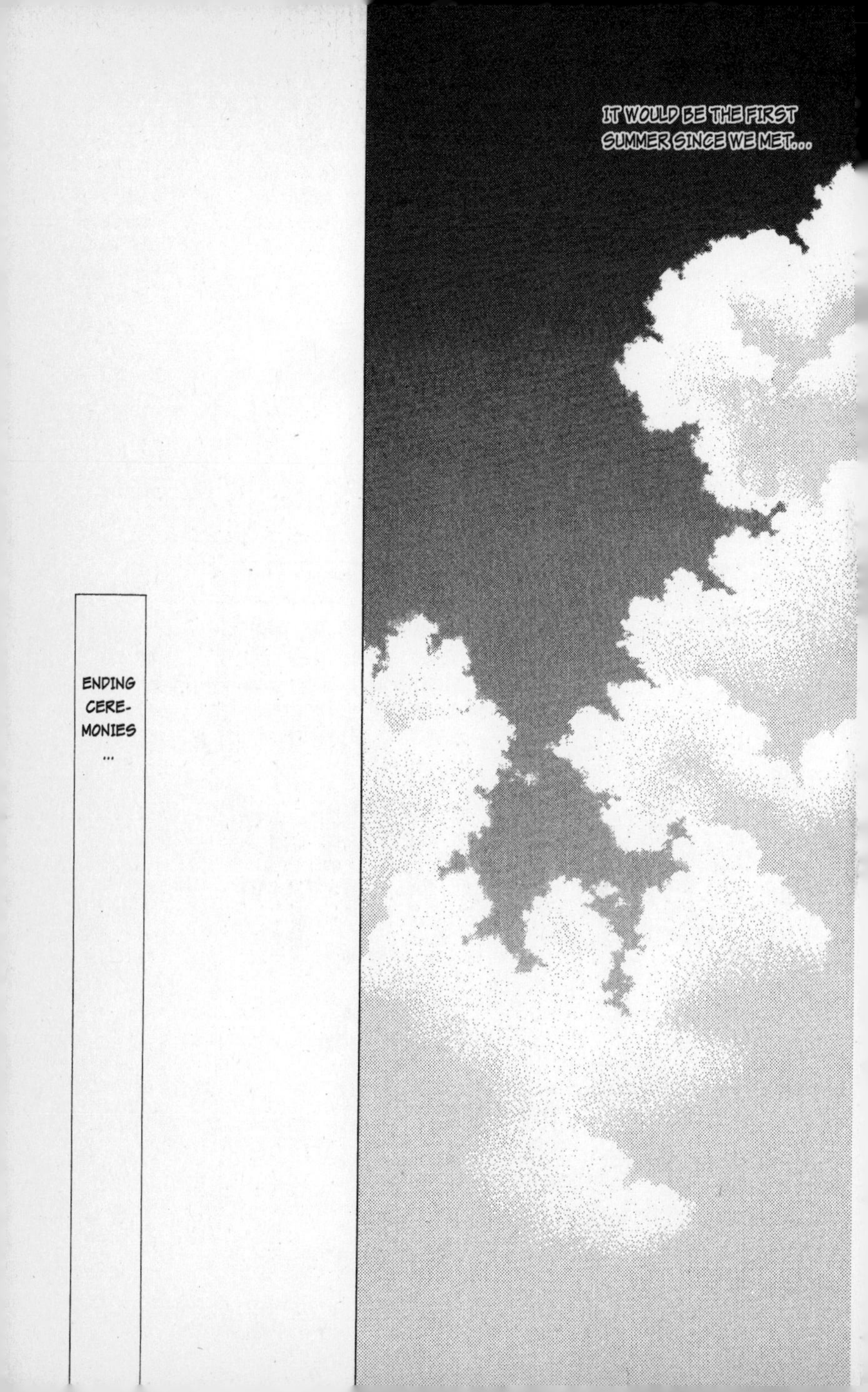
IT WOULD BE THE FIRST SUMMER SINCE WE MET...
ENDING CERE-MONIES ...

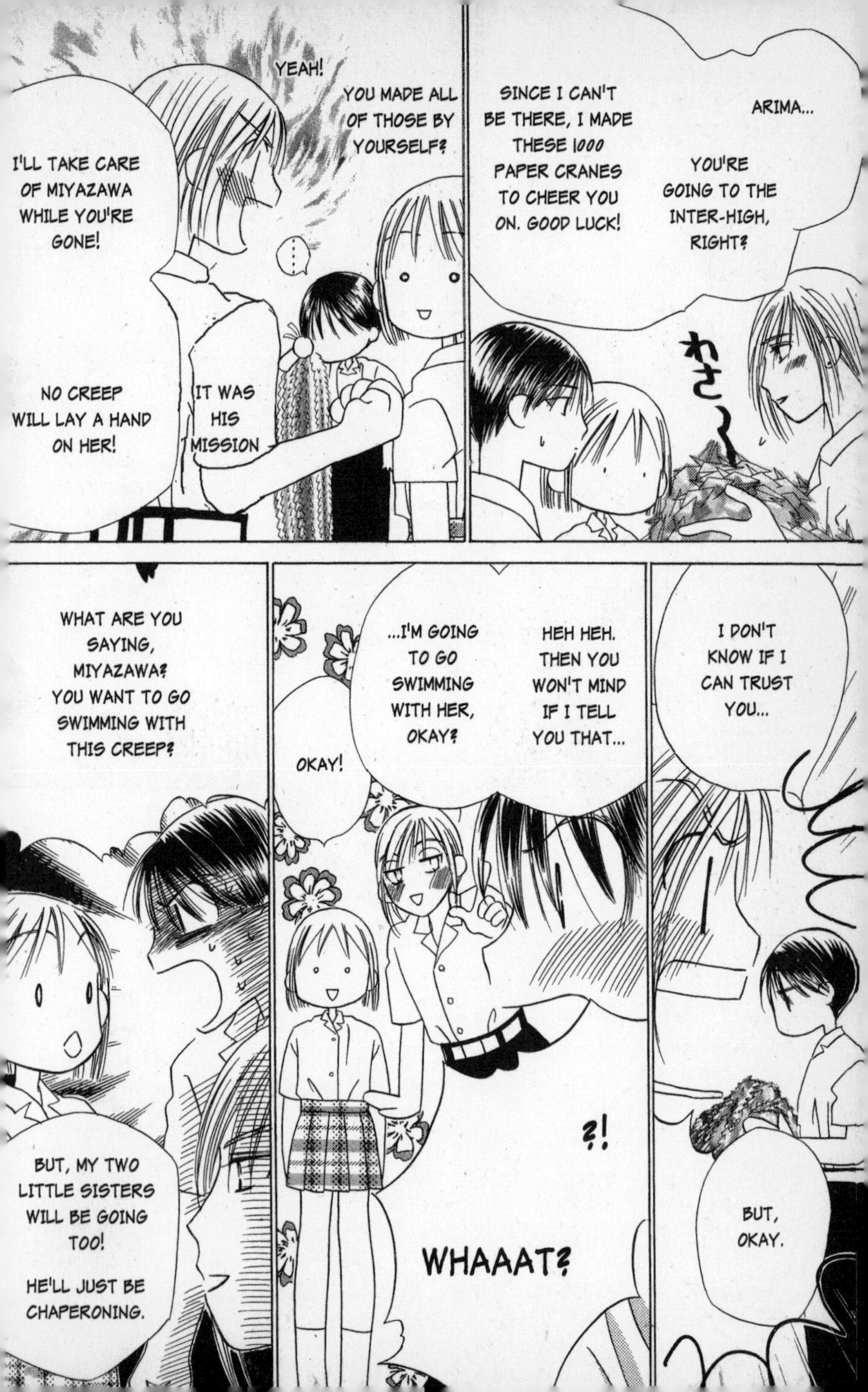
ARIMA...
YOU'RE GOING TO THE INTER-HIGH, RIGHT?
SINCE I CAN'T BE THERE, I MADE THESE 1000 PAPER CRANES TO CHEER YOU ON. GOOD LUCK!
わさ〜
YEAH!
YOU MADE ALL OF THOSE BY YOURSELF?
I'LL TAKE CARE OF MIYAZAWA WHILE YOU'RE GONE!
...
NO CREEP WILL LAY A HAND ON HER!
IT WAS HIS MISSION
I DON'T KNOW IF I CAN TRUST YOU...
BUT, OKAY.
HEH HEH. THEN YOU WON'T MIND IF I TELL YOU THAT...
...I'M GOING TO GO SWIMMING WITH HER, OKAY?
OKAY!
?!
WHAAAT?
WHAT ARE YOU SAYING, MIYAZAWA? YOU WANT TO GO SWIMMING WITH THIS CREEP?
BUT, MY TWO LITTLE SISTERS WILL BE GOING TOO!
HE'LL JUST BE CHAPERONING.

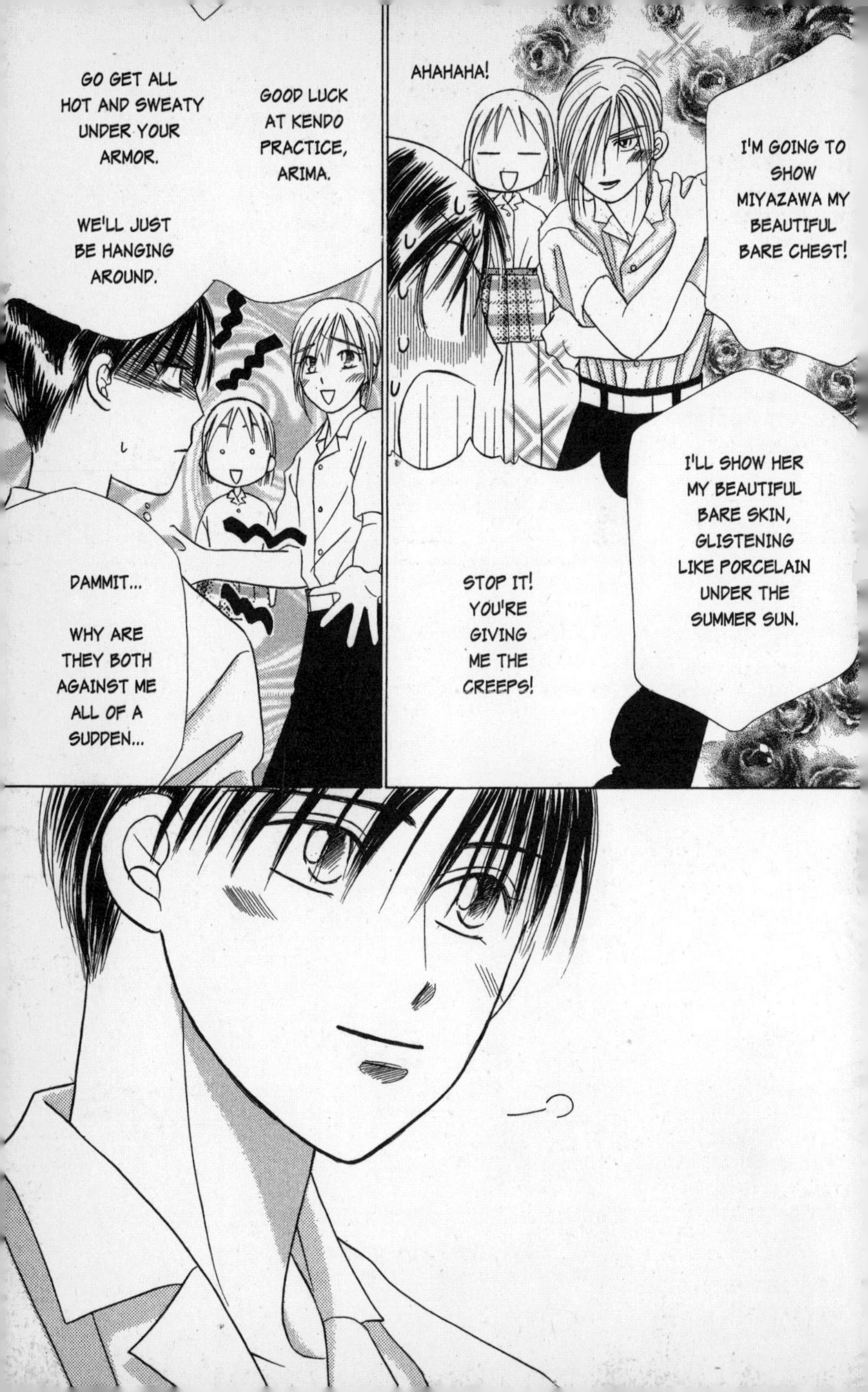
I'M GOING TO SHOW MIYAZAWA MY BEAUTIFUL BARE CHEST!
AHAHAHA!
I'LL SHOW HER MY BEAUTIFUL BARE SKIN, GLISTENING LIKE PORCELAIN UNDER THE SUMMER SUN.
STOP IT! YOU'RE GIVING ME THE CREEPS!
GOOD LUCK AT KENDO PRACTICE, ARIMA.
GO GET ALL HOT AND SWEATY UNDER YOUR ARMOR.
WE'LL JUST BE HANGING AROUND.
DAMMIT...
WHY ARE THEY BOTH AGAINST ME ALL OF A SUDDEN...

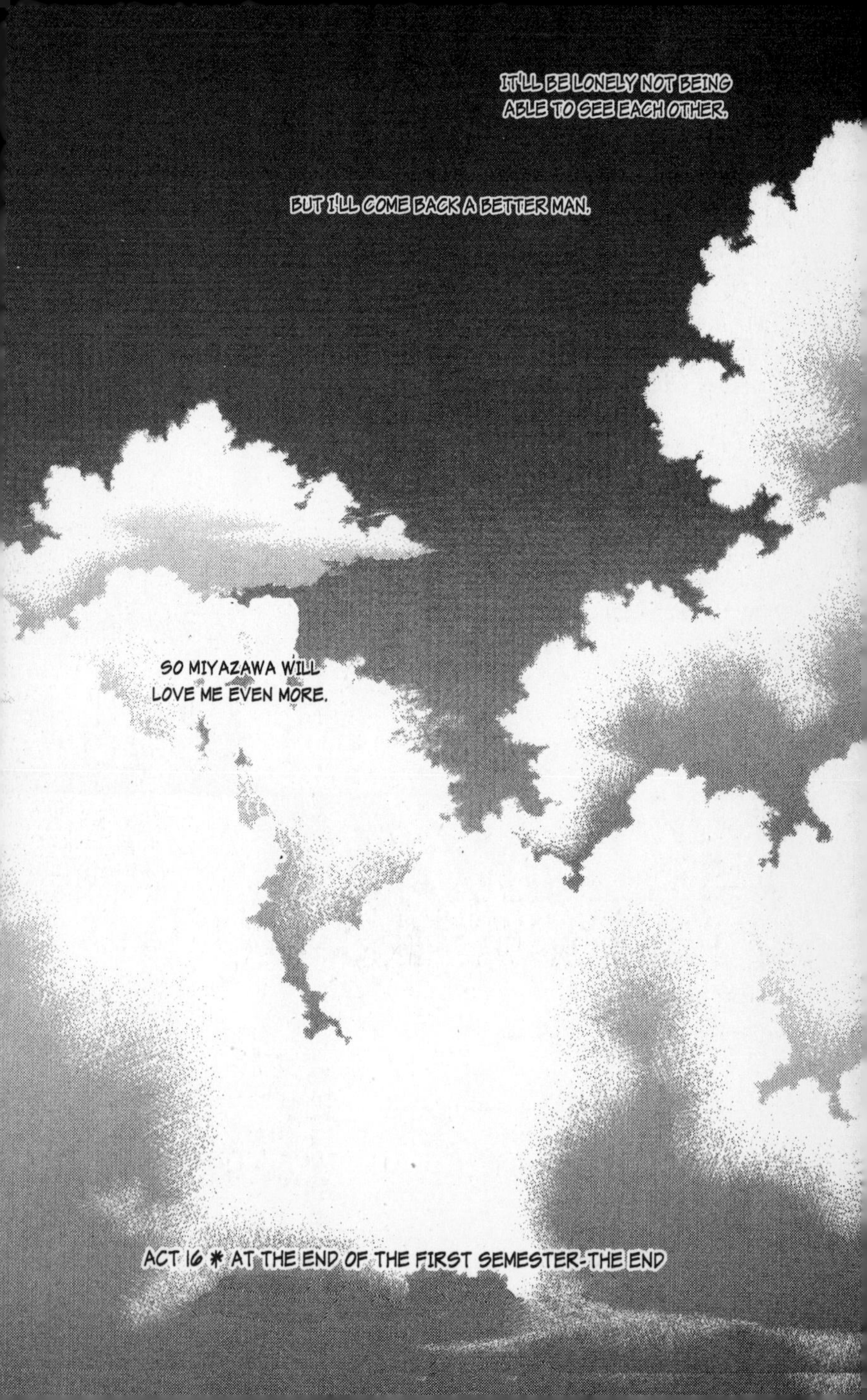
IT'LL BE LONELY NOT BEING ABLE TO SEE EACH OTHER.
BUT I'LL COME BACK A BETTER MAN.
SO MIYAZAWA WILL LOVE ME EVEN MORE.
ACT 16 * AT THE END OF THE FIRST SEMESTER-THE END

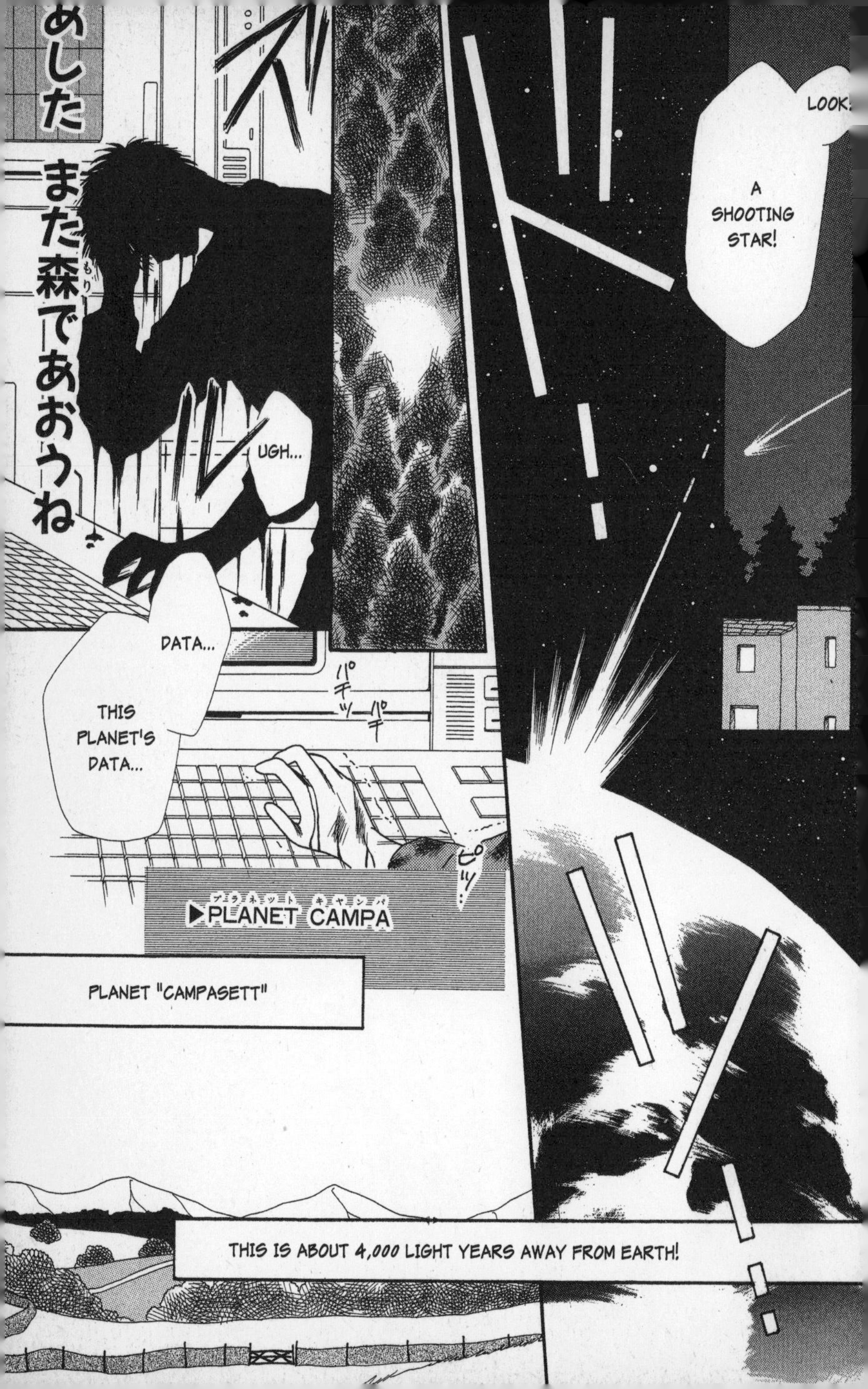
LOOK!
A SHOOTING STAR!
あした
また森であおうね
UGH...
DATA...
THIS PLANET'S DATA...
パチッ
パチ
ピッ
▶PLANET CAMPA
PLANET "CAMPASETT"
THIS IS ABOUT 4,000 LIGHT YEARS AWAY FROM EARTH!

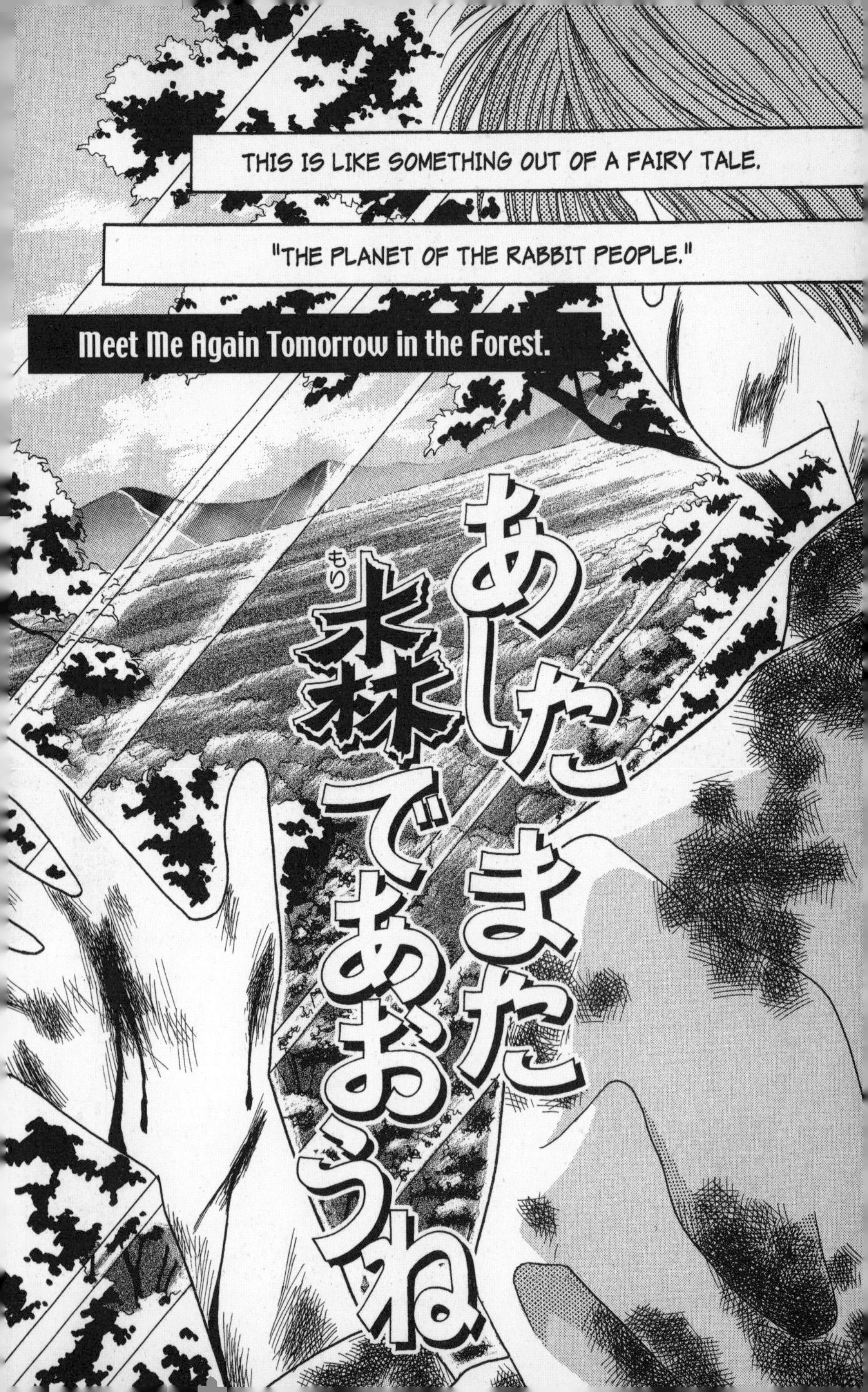
THIS IS LIKE SOMETHING OUT OF A FAIRY TALE.
"THE PLANET OF THE RABBIT PEOPLE."
Meet Me Again Tomorrow in the Forest.
あしたまた森(もり)であおうね

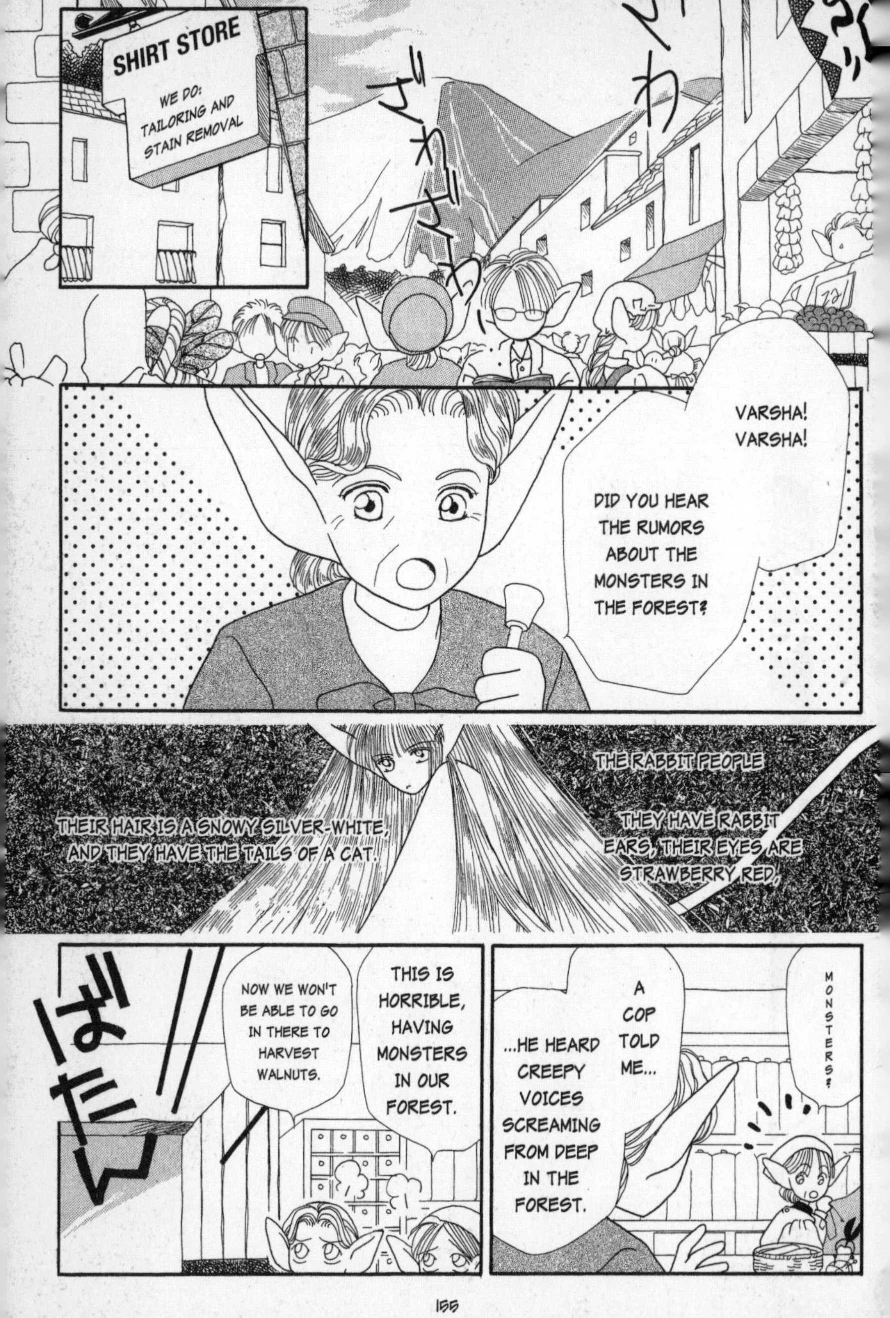
ざわ
ざわざわ
SHIRT STORE
WE DO: TAILORING AND STAIN REMOVAL
VARSHA! VARSHA!
DID YOU HEAR THE RUMORS ABOUT THE MONSTERS IN THE FOREST?
THE RABBIT PEOPLE
THEY HAVE RABBIT EARS, THEIR EYES ARE STRAWBERRY RED,
THEIR HAIR IS A SNOWY SILVER-WHITE, AND THEY HAVE THE TAILS OF A CAT.
MONSTERS?
A COP TOLD ME...
...HE HEARD CREEPY VOICES SCREAMING FROM DEEP IN THE FOREST.
THIS IS HORRIBLE, HAVING MONSTERS IN OUR FOREST.
NOW WE WON'T BE ABLE TO GO IN THERE TO HARVEST WALNUTS.
ばたん

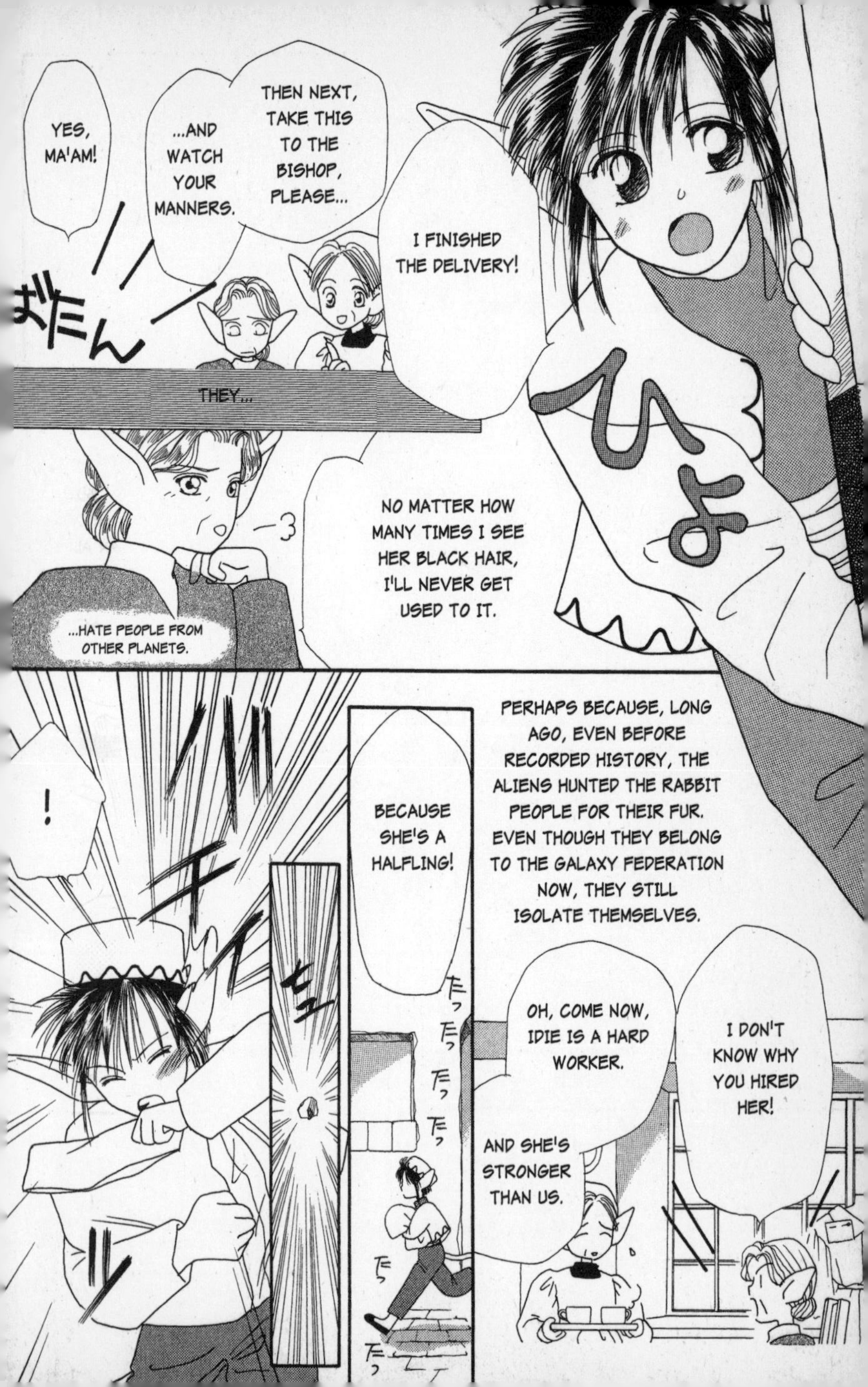
I FINISHED THE DELIVERY!
ひょ
THEN NEXT, TAKE THIS TO THE BISHOP, PLEASE...
...AND WATCH YOUR MANNERS.
YES, MA'AM!
ばたん
THEY...
NO MATTER HOW MANY TIMES I SEE HER BLACK HAIR, I'LL NEVER GET USED TO IT.
...HATE PEOPLE FROM OTHER PLANETS.
PERHAPS BECAUSE, LONG AGO, EVEN BEFORE RECORDED HISTORY, THE ALIENS HUNTED THE RABBIT PEOPLE FOR THEIR FUR. EVEN THOUGH THEY BELONG TO THE GALAXY FEDERATION NOW, THEY STILL ISOLATE THEMSELVES.
I DON'T KNOW WHY YOU HIRED HER!
OH, COME NOW, IDIE IS A HARD WORKER.
AND SHE'S STRONGER THAN US.
BECAUSE SHE'S A HALFLING!
!

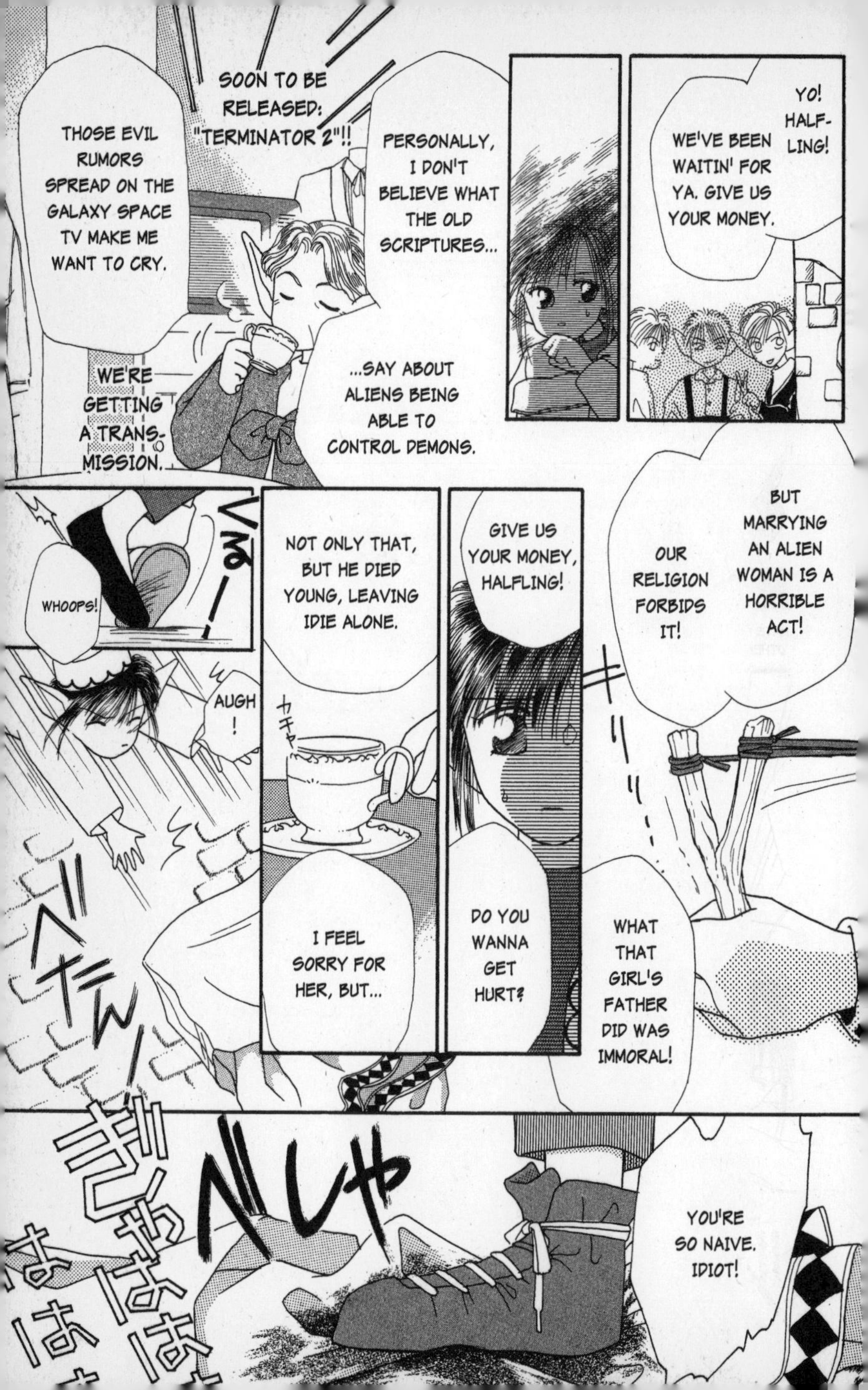
YO! HALF-LING!
WE'VE BEEN WAITIN' FOR YA. GIVE US YOUR MONEY.
PERSONALLY, I DON'T BELIEVE WHAT THE OLD SCRIPTURES...
...SAY ABOUT ALIENS BEING ABLE TO CONTROL DEMONS.
SOON TO BE RELEASED: "TERMINATOR 2"!!
THOSE EVIL RUMORS SPREAD ON THE GALAXY SPACE TV MAKE ME WANT TO CRY.
WE'RE GETTING A TRANS-MISSION.
BUT MARRYING AN ALIEN WOMAN IS A HORRIBLE ACT!
OUR RELIGION FORBIDS IT!
WHAT THAT GIRL'S FATHER DID WAS IMMORAL!
GIVE US YOUR MONEY, HALFLING!
DO YOU WANNA GET HURT?
NOT ONLY THAT, BUT HE DIED YOUNG, LEAVING IDIE ALONE.
I FEEL SORRY FOR HER, BUT...
WHOOPS!
AUGH!
YOU'RE SO NAIVE. IDIOT!
べしゃ

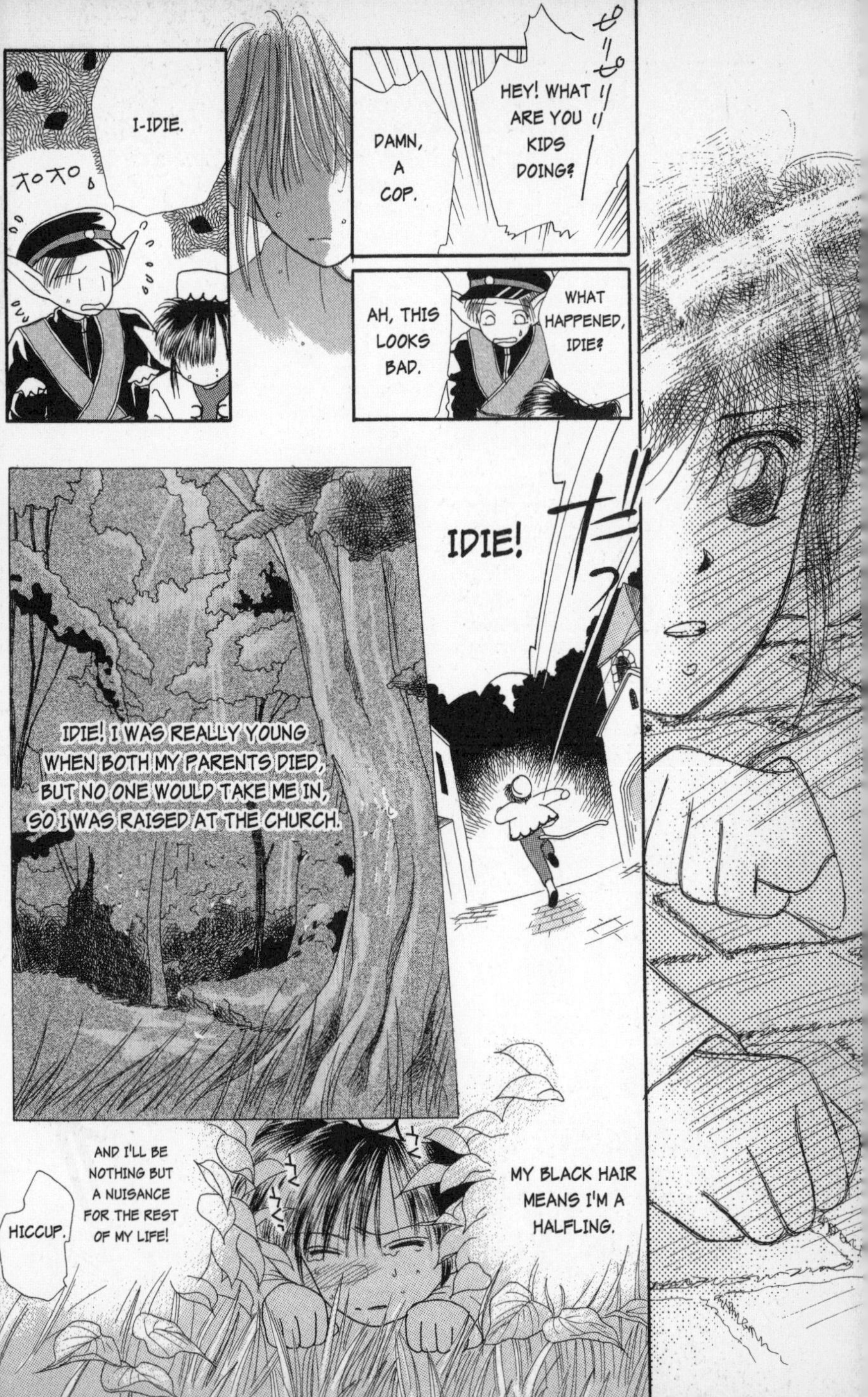
HEY! WHAT ARE YOU KIDS DOING?
DAMN, A COP.
WHAT HAPPENED, IDIE?
AH, THIS LOOKS BAD.
I-IDIE.
IDIE!
IDIE! I WAS REALLY YOUNG WHEN BOTH MY PARENTS DIED, BUT NO ONE WOULD TAKE ME IN, SO I WAS RAISED AT THE CHURCH.
MY BLACK HAIR MEANS I'M A HALFLING.
AND I'LL BE NOTHING BUT A NUISANCE FOR THE REST OF MY LIFE!
HICCUP.

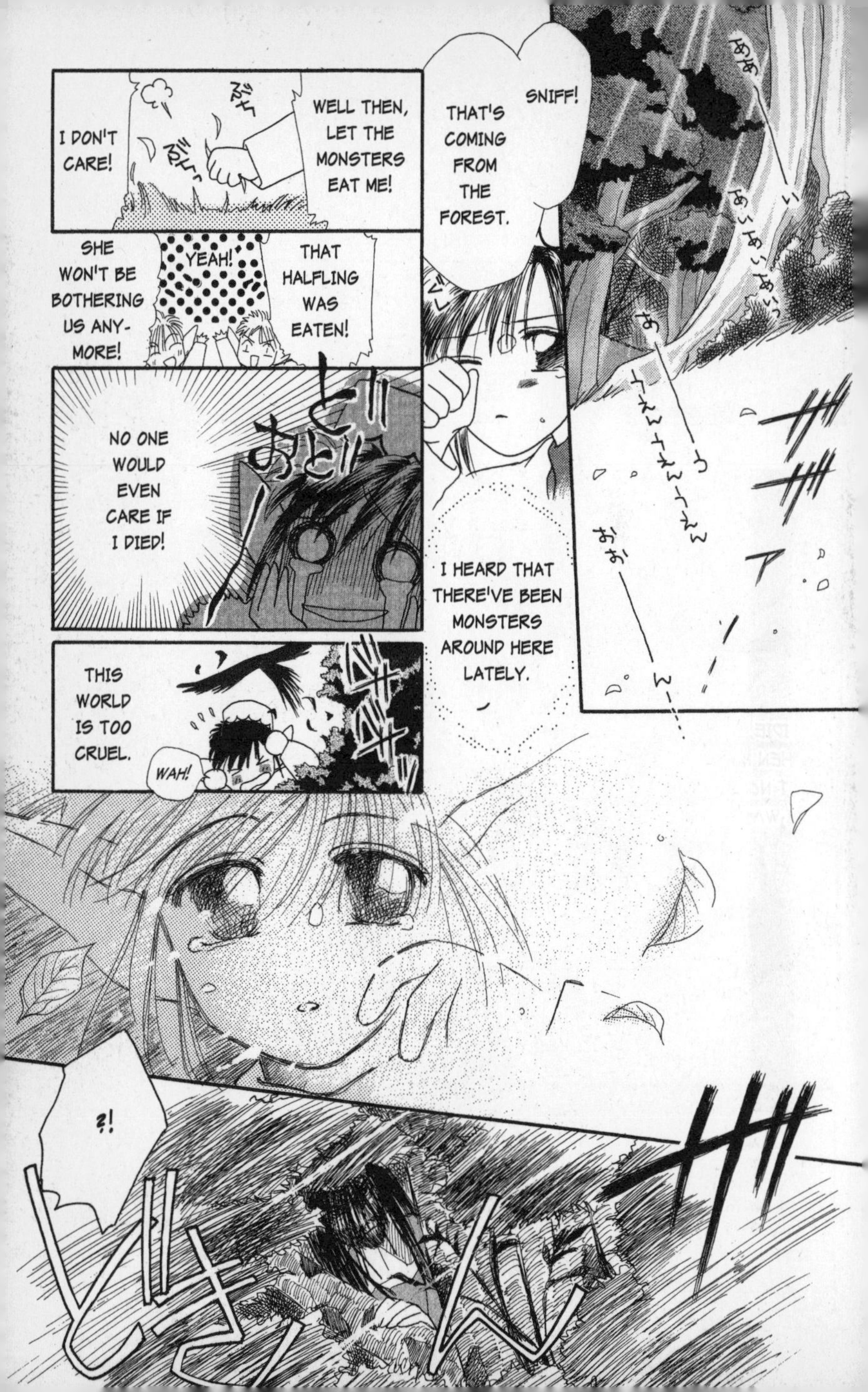

SNIFF!
THAT'S COMING FROM THE FOREST.
I HEARD THAT THERE'VE BEEN MONSTERS AROUND HERE LATELY.
WELL THEN, LET THE MONSTERS EAT ME!
I DON'T CARE!
THAT HALFLING WAS EATEN!
YEAH!
SHE WON'T BE BOTHERING US ANY-MORE!
NO ONE WOULD EVEN CARE IF I DIED!
THIS WORLD IS TOO CRUEL.
WAH!
?!

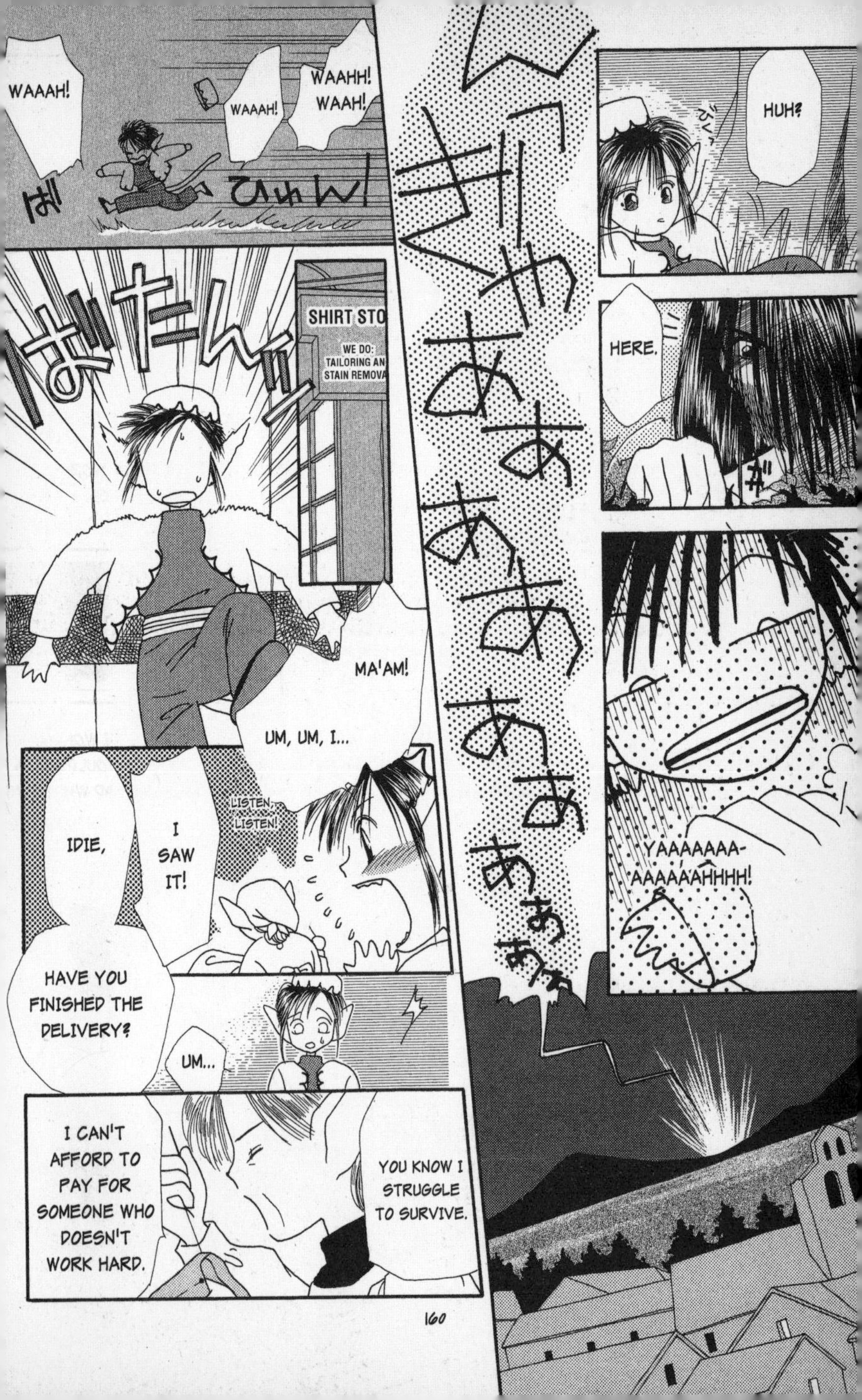
HUH?
びくっ
HERE.
ガ
YAAAAAAA-AAAAAAHHHH!
きゃあああああああああ
WAAHH! WAAH!
WAAAH!
WAAAH!
ひゅん!
ば!
ばたんっ
SHIRT STO
WE DO: TAILORING AN STAIN REMOVA
MA'AM!
UM, UM, I...
LISTEN, LISTEN!
I SAW IT!
IDIE,
HAVE YOU FINISHED THE DELIVERY?
UM...
YOU KNOW I STRUGGLE TO SURVIVE.
I CAN'T AFFORD TO PAY FOR SOMEONE WHO DOESN'T WORK HARD.

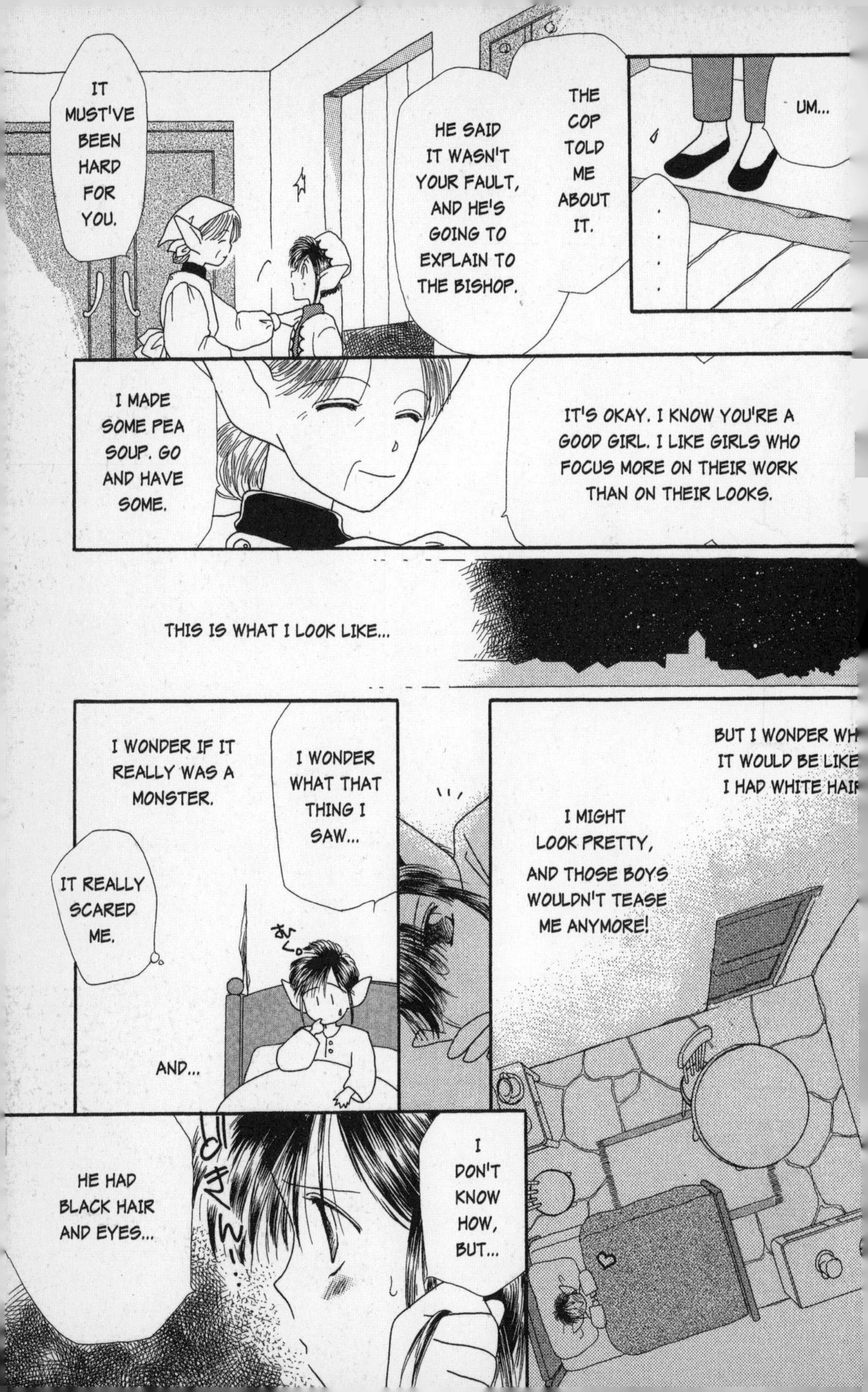
UM...
THE COP TOLD ME ABOUT IT.
HE SAID IT WASN'T YOUR FAULT, AND HE'S GOING TO EXPLAIN TO THE BISHOP.
IT MUST'VE BEEN HARD FOR YOU.
IT'S OKAY. I KNOW YOU'RE A GOOD GIRL. I LIKE GIRLS WHO FOCUS MORE ON THEIR WORK THAN ON THEIR LOOKS.
I MADE SOME PEA SOUP. GO AND HAVE SOME.
THIS IS WHAT I LOOK LIKE...
BUT I WONDER WH IT WOULD BE LIKE I HAD WHITE HAI
I MIGHT LOOK PRETTY, AND THOSE BOYS WOULDN'T TEASE ME ANYMORE!
I WONDER WHAT THAT THING I SAW...
I WONDER IF IT REALLY WAS A MONSTER.
IT REALLY SCARED ME.
AND...
I DON'T KNOW HOW, BUT...
HE HAD BLACK HAIR AND EYES...

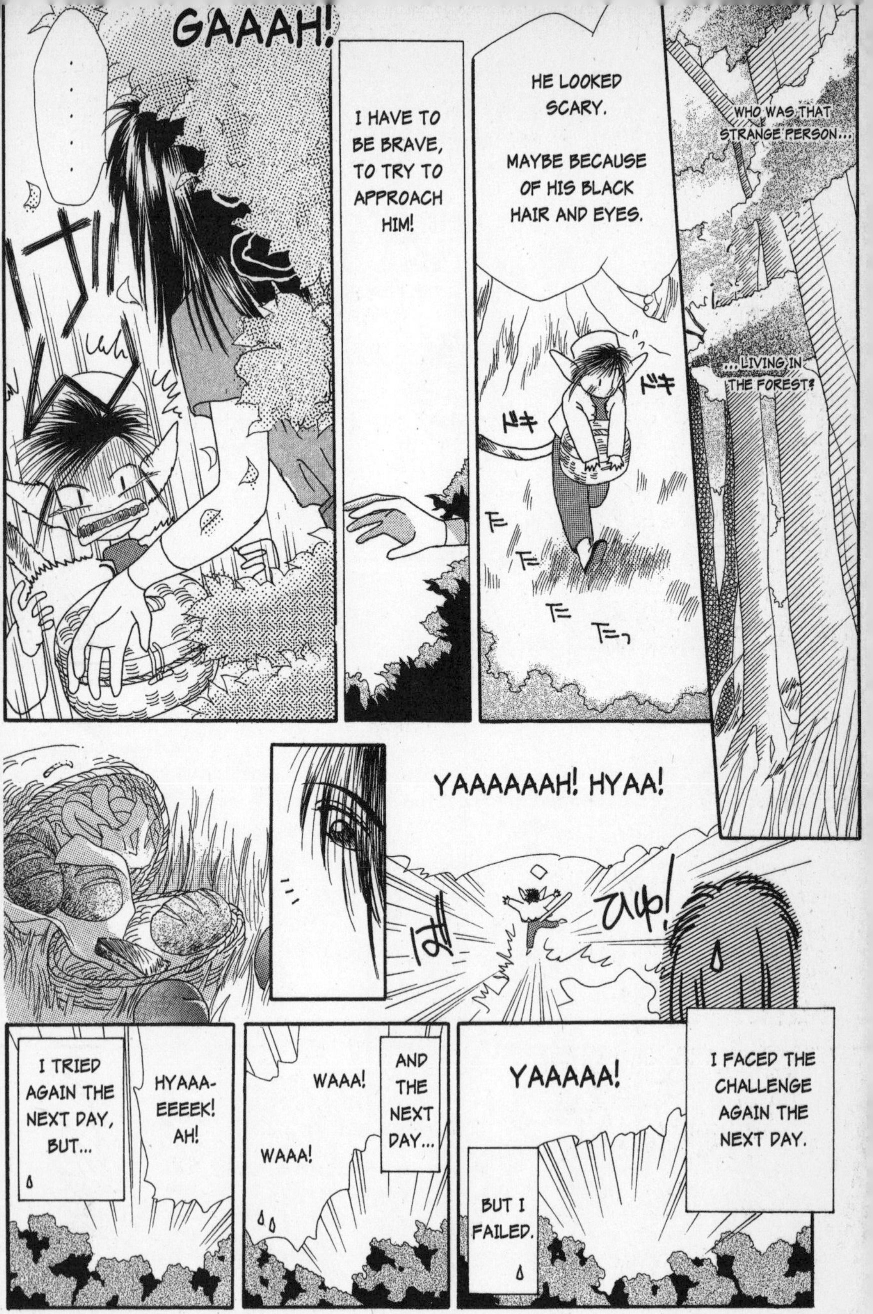
WHO WAS THAT STRANGE PERSON...
...LIVING IN THE FOREST?
HE LOOKED SCARY.
MAYBE BECAUSE OF HIS BLACK HAIR AND EYES.
ドキ
ドキ
I HAVE TO BE BRAVE, TO TRY TO APPROACH HIM!
GAAAH!
...
YAAAAAAH! HYAA!
ひゅ!
I FACED THE CHALLENGE AGAIN THE NEXT DAY.
YAAAAA!
BUT I FAILED.
AND THE NEXT DAY...
WAAA!
WAAA!
HYAAA-EEEEK! AH!
I TRIED AGAIN THE NEXT DAY, BUT...

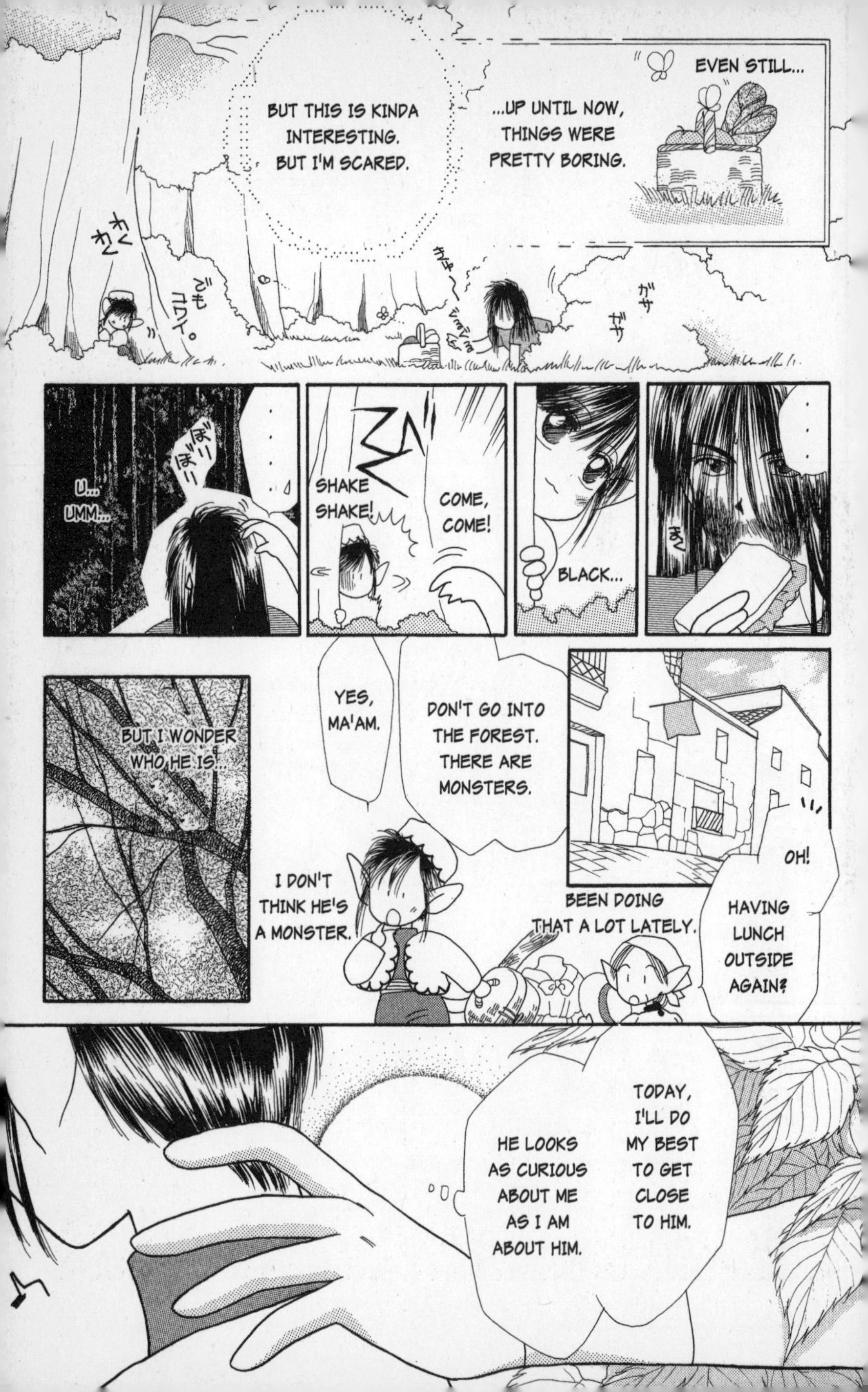
EVEN STILL...
...UP UNTIL NOW, THINGS WERE PRETTY BORING.
BUT THIS IS KINDA INTERESTING. BUT I'M SCARED.
ガサ ガサ
わく わく
でも コワイ。
...
BLACK...
SHAKE SHAKE!
COME, COME!
...
ぽり ぽり
U... UMM...
OH!
HAVING LUNCH OUTSIDE AGAIN?
BEEN DOING THAT A LOT LATELY.
DON'T GO INTO THE FOREST. THERE ARE MONSTERS.
YES, MA'AM.
I DON'T THINK HE'S A MONSTER.
BUT I WONDER WHO HE IS...
TODAY, I'LL DO MY BEST TO GET CLOSE TO HIM.
HE LOOKS AS CURIOUS ABOUT ME AS I AM ABOUT HIM.

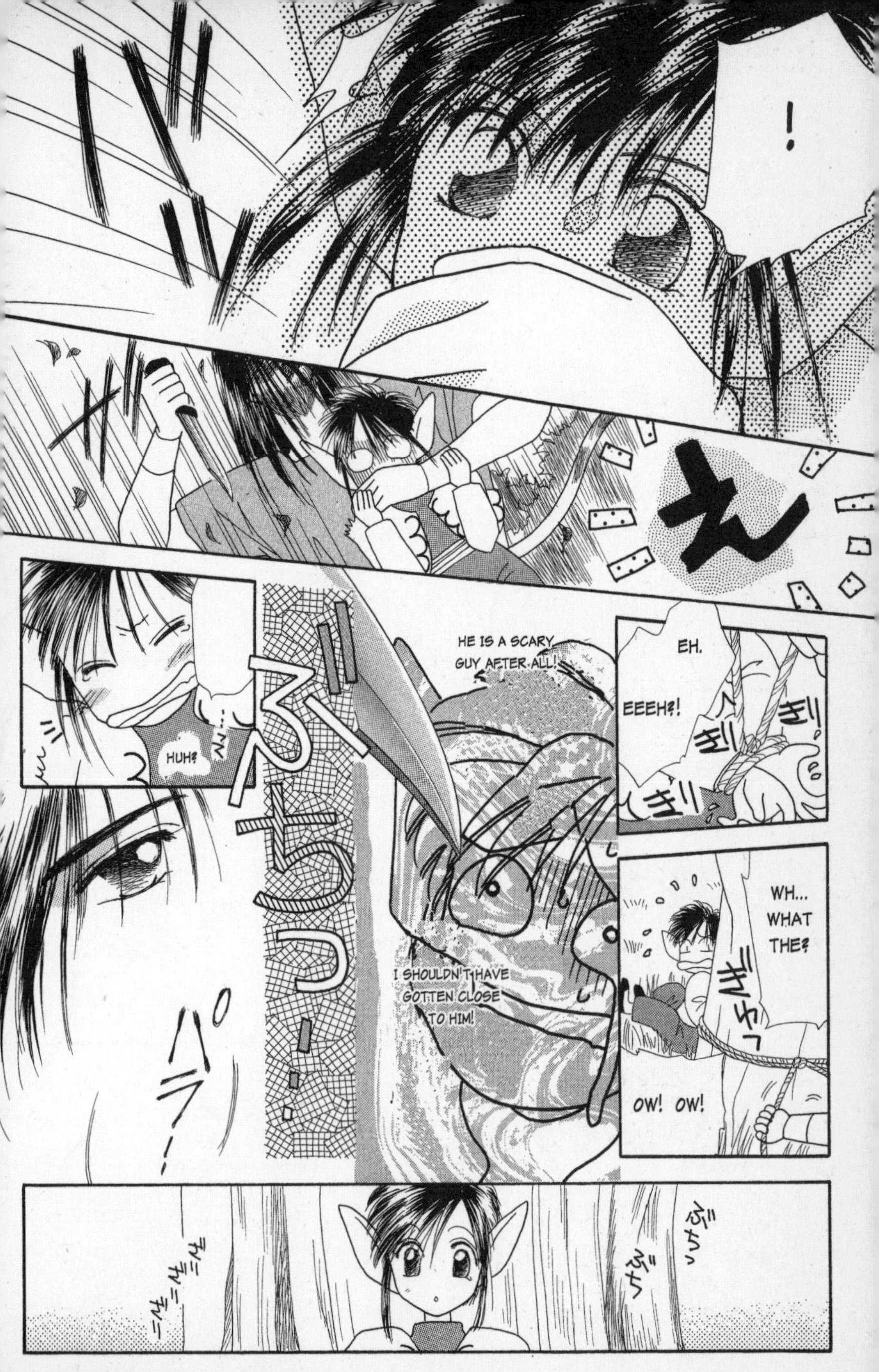
!
ん
EH.
EEEH?!
WH... WHAT THE?
OW! OW!
HE IS A SCARY GUY AFTER ALL!
I SHOULDN'T HAVE GOTTEN CLOSE TO HIM!
HUH?

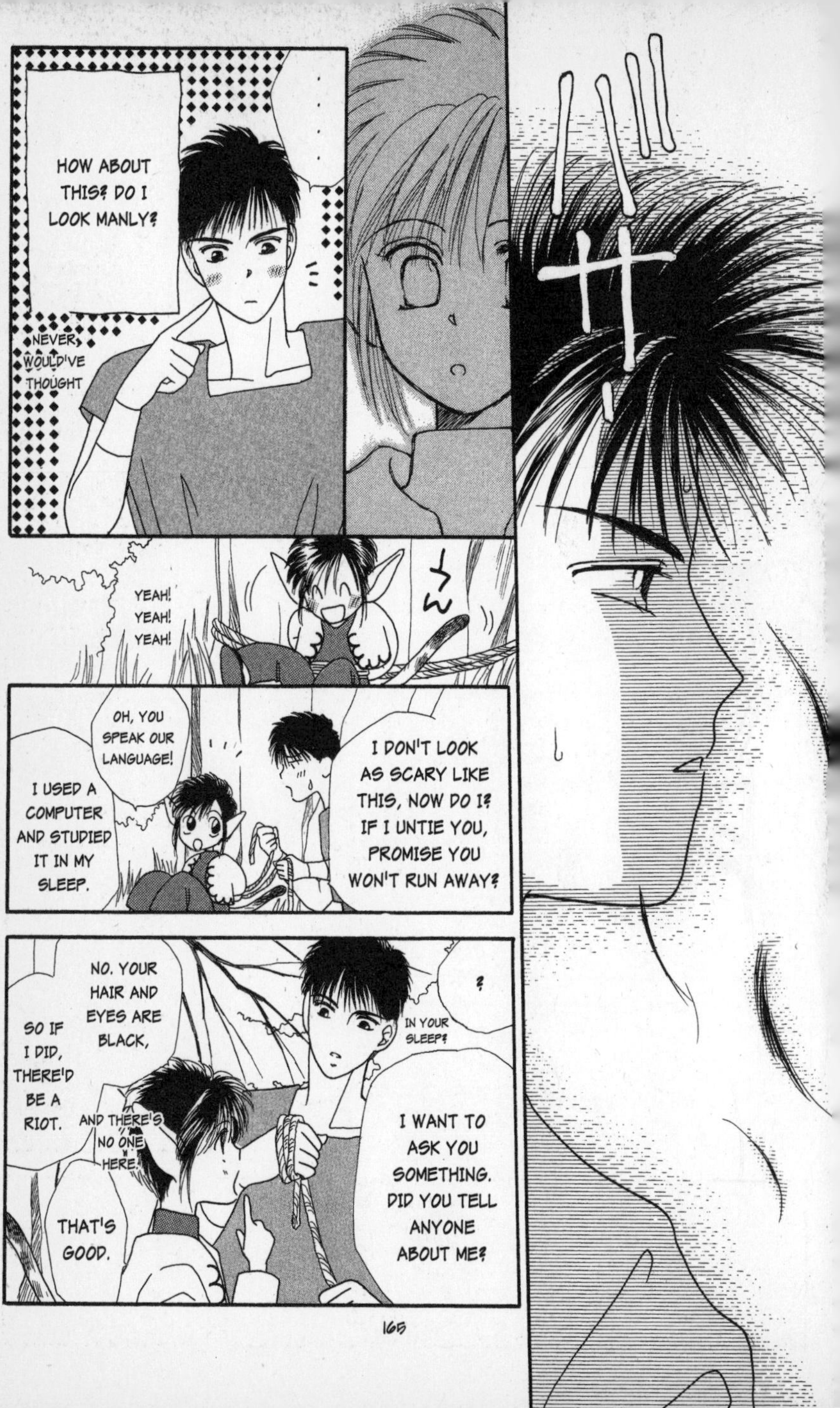
HOW ABOUT THIS? DO I LOOK MANLY?
NEVER WOULD'VE THOUGHT
YEAH! YEAH! YEAH!
I DON'T LOOK AS SCARY LIKE THIS, NOW DO I? IF I UNTIE YOU, PROMISE YOU WON'T RUN AWAY?
OH, YOU SPEAK OUR LANGUAGE!
I USED A COMPUTER AND STUDIED IT IN MY SLEEP.
?
IN YOUR SLEEP?
I WANT TO ASK YOU SOMETHING. DID YOU TELL ANYONE ABOUT ME?
NO. YOUR HAIR AND EYES ARE BLACK,
SO IF I DID, THERE'D BE A RIOT.
AND THERE'S NO ONE HERE.
THAT'S GOOD.

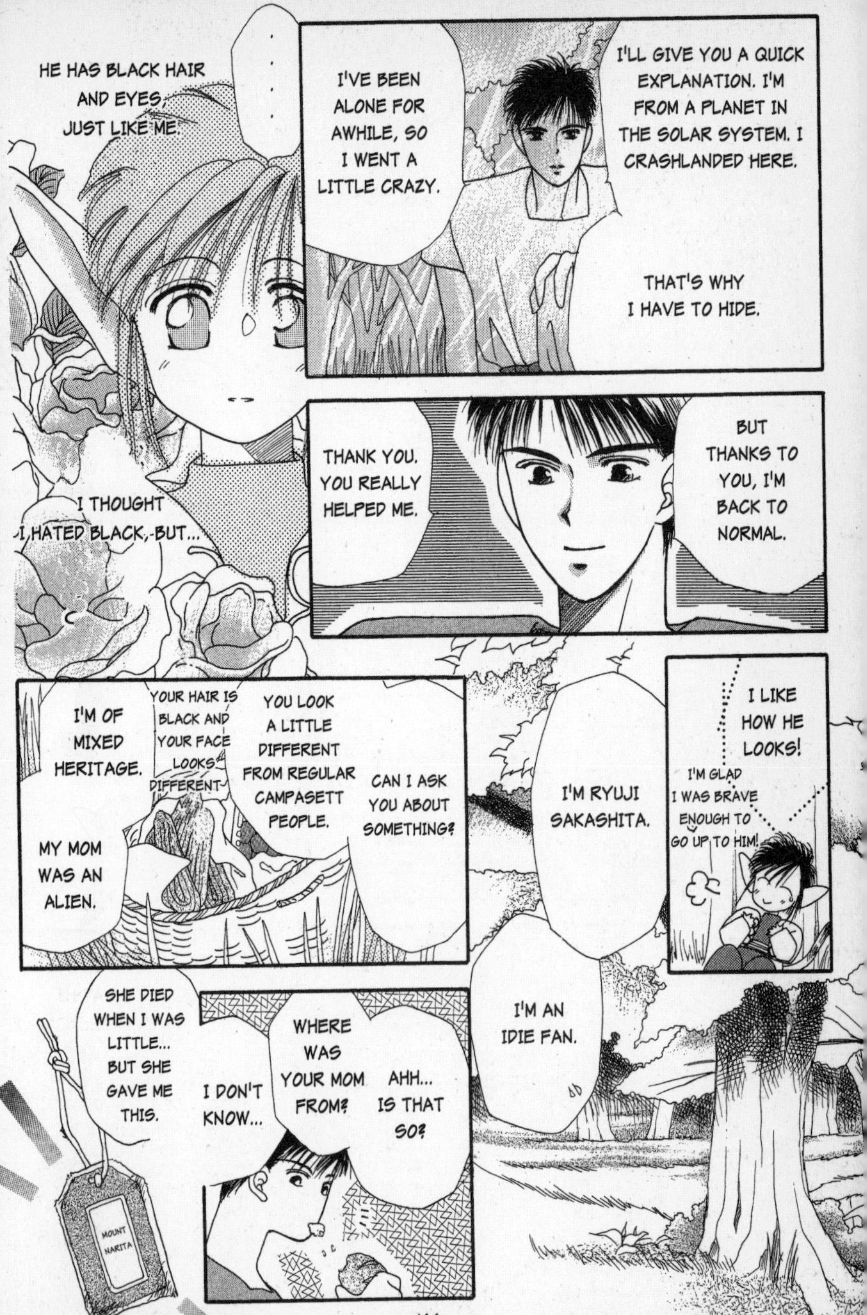
I'LL GIVE YOU A QUICK EXPLANATION. I'M FROM A PLANET IN THE SOLAR SYSTEM. I CRASHLANDED HERE.
I'VE BEEN ALONE FOR AWHILE, SO I WENT A LITTLE CRAZY.
THAT'S WHY I HAVE TO HIDE.
BUT THANKS TO YOU, I'M BACK TO NORMAL.
THANK YOU. YOU REALLY HELPED ME.
...
HE HAS BLACK HAIR AND EYES, JUST LIKE ME.
I THOUGHT I HATED BLACK, BUT...
I LIKE HOW HE LOOKS!
I'M GLAD I WAS BRAVE ENOUGH TO GO UP TO HIM!
I'M RYUJI SAKASHITA.
CAN I ASK YOU ABOUT SOMETHING?
YOU LOOK A LITTLE DIFFERENT FROM REGULAR CAMPASETT PEOPLE.
YOUR HAIR IS BLACK AND YOUR FACE LOOKS DIFFERENT
I'M OF MIXED HERITAGE.
MY MOM WAS AN ALIEN.
I'M AN IDIE FAN.
AHH... IS THAT SO?
WHERE WAS YOUR MOM FROM?
I DON'T KNOW...
SHE DIED WHEN I WAS LITTLE... BUT SHE GAVE ME THIS.
MOUNT NARITA

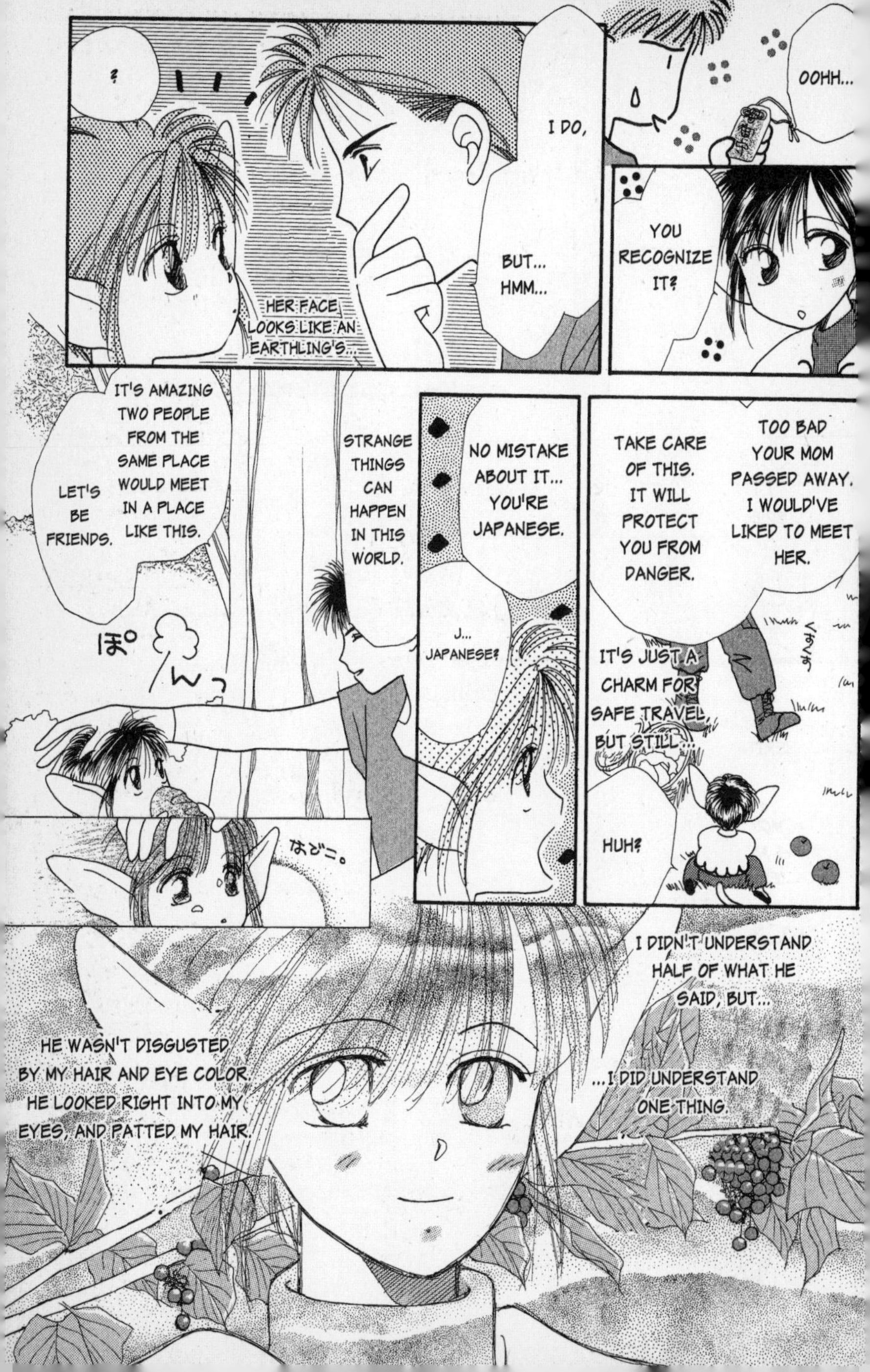
OOHH...
YOU RECOGNIZE IT?
?
I DO,
BUT... HMM...
HER FACE LOOKS LIKE AN EARTHLING'S...
TOO BAD YOUR MOM PASSED AWAY. I WOULD'VE LIKED TO MEET HER.
TAKE CARE OF THIS. IT WILL PROTECT YOU FROM DANGER.
IT'S JUST A CHARM FOR SAFE TRAVEL, BUT STILL...
HUH?
NO MISTAKE ABOUT IT... YOU'RE JAPANESE.
J... JAPANESE?
STRANGE THINGS CAN HAPPEN IN THIS WORLD.
IT'S AMAZING TWO PEOPLE FROM THE SAME PLACE WOULD MEET IN A PLACE LIKE THIS.
LET'S BE FRIENDS.
ぽんっ
なでこ。
I DIDN'T UNDERSTAND HALF OF WHAT HE SAID, BUT...
...I DID UNDERSTAND ONE THING.
HE WASN'T DISGUSTED BY MY HAIR AND EYE COLOR. HE LOOKED RIGHT INTO MY EYES, AND PATTED MY HAIR.

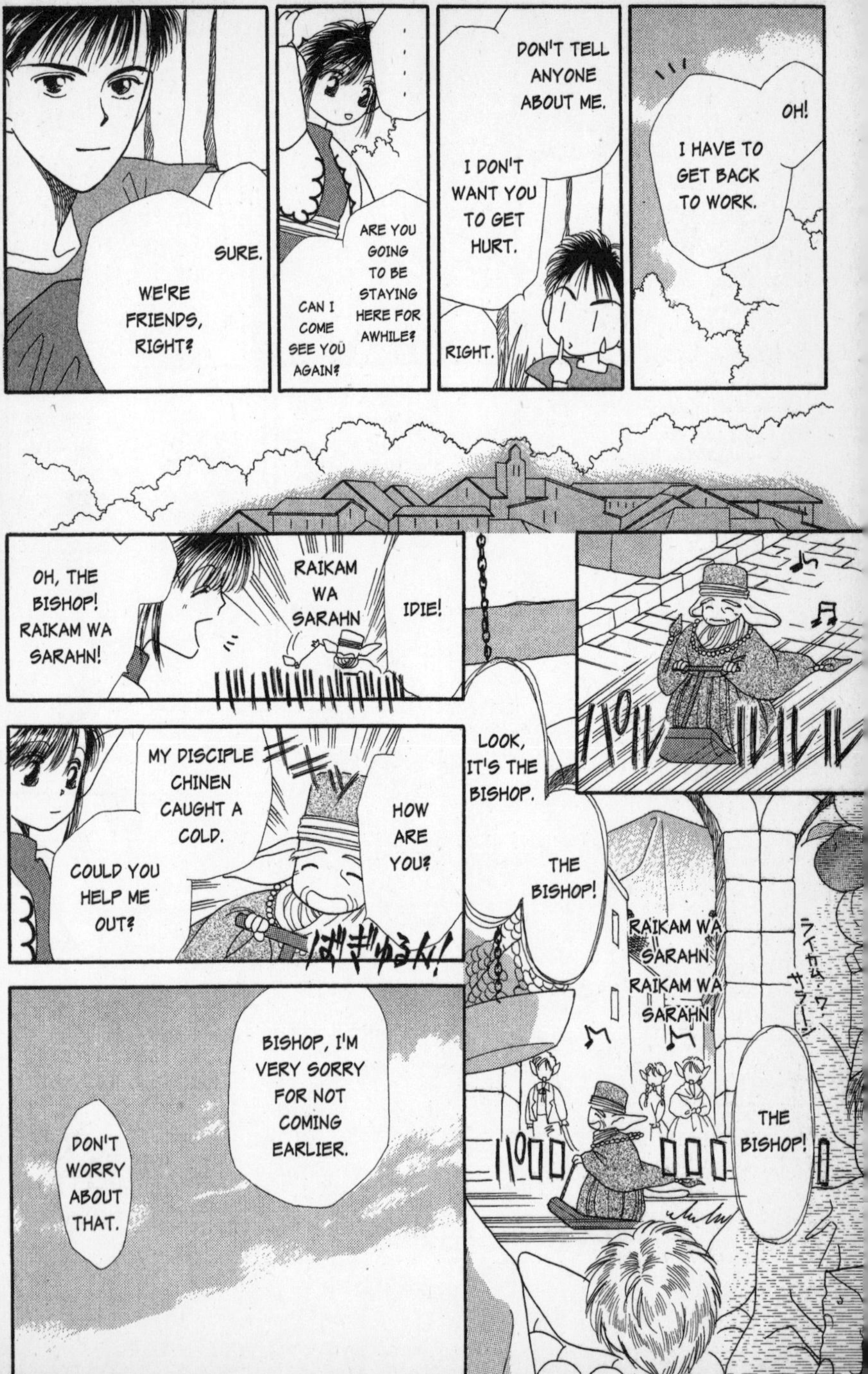
OH!
I HAVE TO GET BACK TO WORK.
DON'T TELL ANYONE ABOUT ME.
I DON'T WANT YOU TO GET HURT.
RIGHT.
...
ARE YOU GOING TO BE STAYING HERE FOR AWHILE?
CAN I COME SEE YOU AGAIN?
SURE.
WE'RE FRIENDS, RIGHT?
IDIE!
RAIKAM WA SARAHN
OH, THE BISHOP! RAIKAM WA SARAHN!
LOOK, IT'S THE BISHOP.
ライカム・ワ サラーン
THE BISHOP!
RAIKAM WA SARAHN RAIKAM WA SARAHN
THE BISHOP!
HOW ARE YOU?
ばぎゅるん!
MY DISCIPLE CHINEN CAUGHT A COLD.
COULD YOU HELP ME OUT?
BISHOP, I'M VERY SORRY FOR NOT COMING EARLIER.
DON'T WORRY ABOUT THAT.

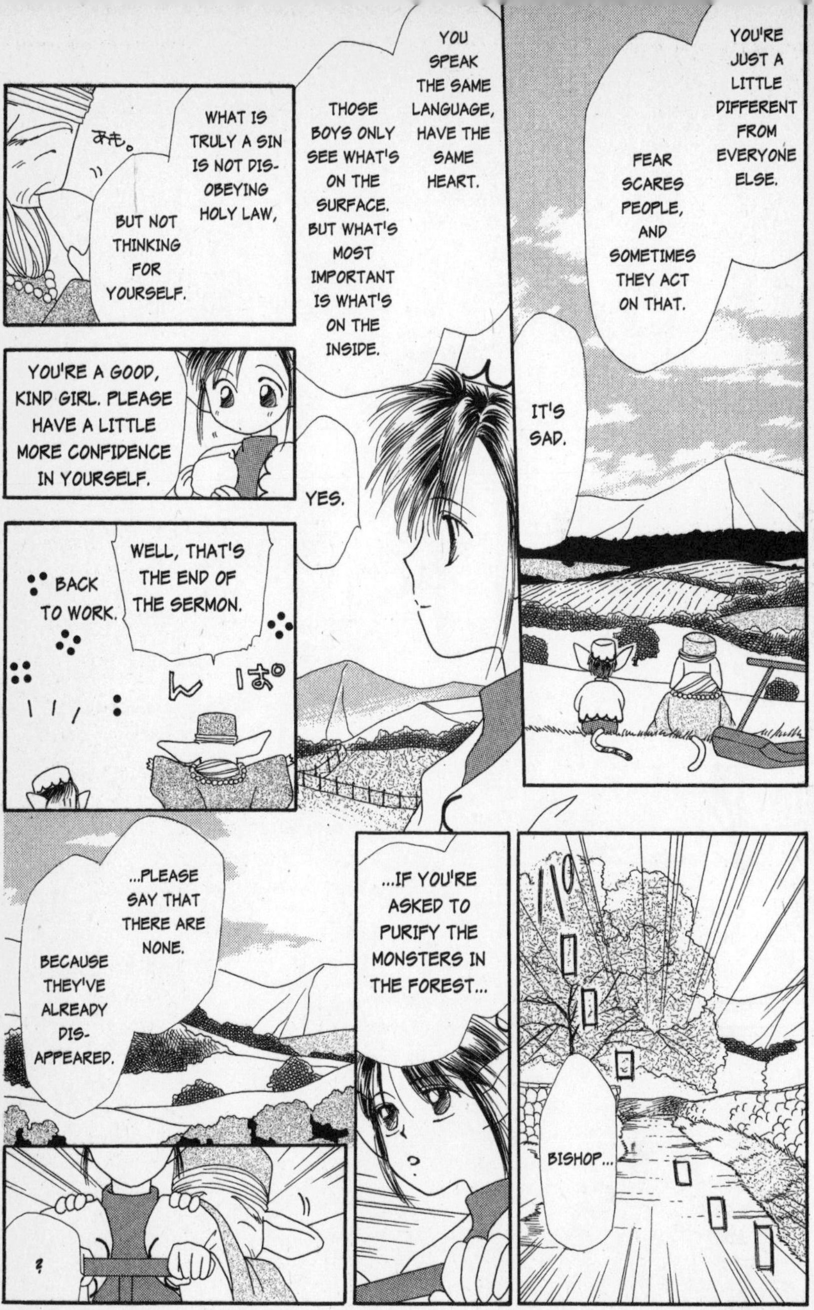
YOU'RE JUST A LITTLE DIFFERENT FROM EVERYONE ELSE.
FEAR SCARES PEOPLE, AND SOMETIMES THEY ACT ON THAT.
IT'S SAD.
YOU SPEAK THE SAME LANGUAGE, HAVE THE SAME HEART.
THOSE BOYS ONLY SEE WHAT'S ON THE SURFACE. BUT WHAT'S MOST IMPORTANT IS WHAT'S ON THE INSIDE.
YES.
WHAT IS TRULY A SIN IS NOT DIS-OBEYING HOLY LAW,
BUT NOT THINKING FOR YOURSELF.
YOU'RE A GOOD, KIND GIRL. PLEASE HAVE A LITTLE MORE CONFIDENCE IN YOURSELF.
WELL, THAT'S THE END OF THE SERMON.
BACK TO WORK.
BISHOP...
...IF YOU'RE ASKED TO PURIFY THE MONSTERS IN THE FOREST...
...PLEASE SAY THAT THERE ARE NONE.
BECAUSE THEY'VE ALREADY DIS-APPEARED.

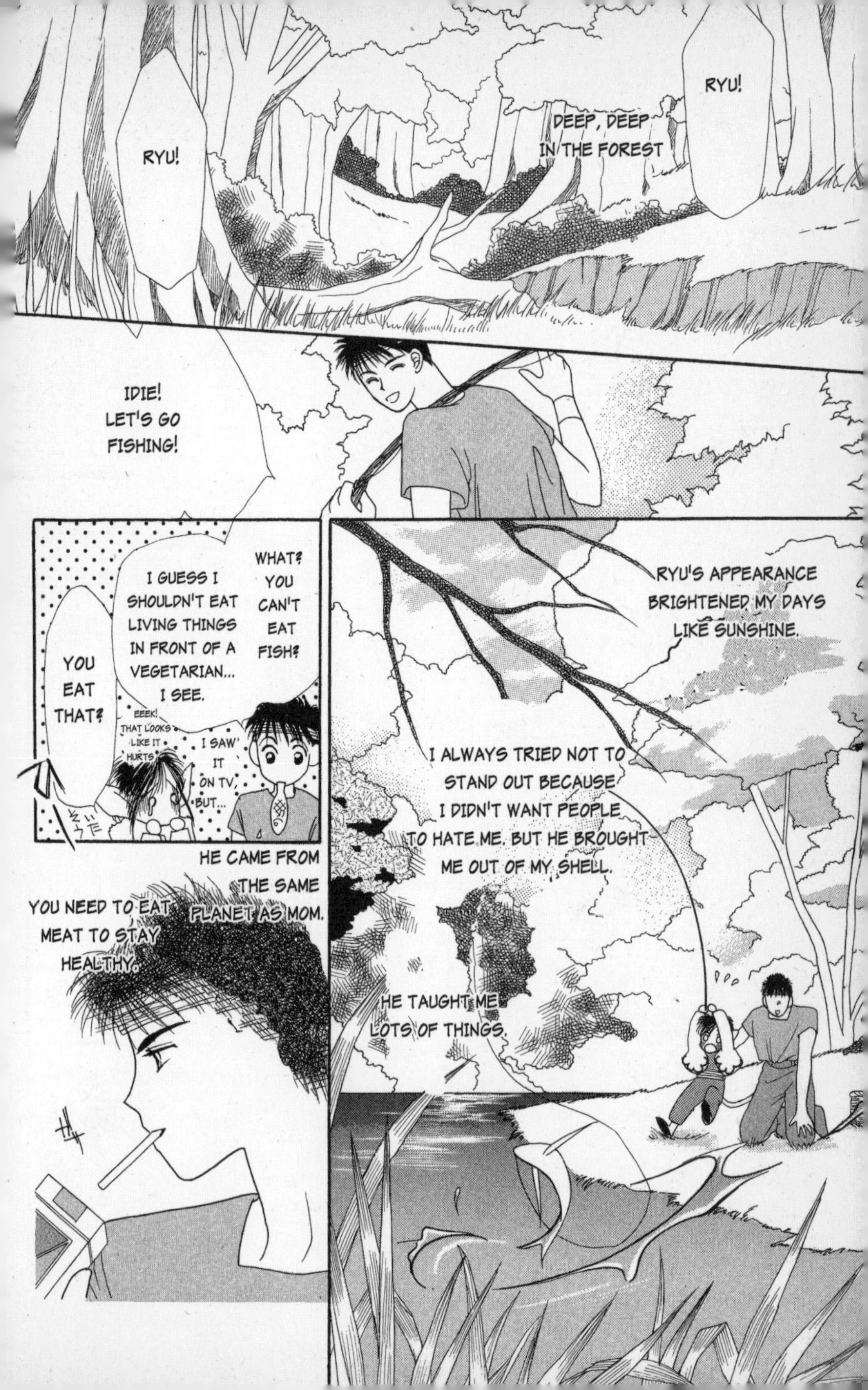
RYU!
DEEP, DEEP IN THE FOREST
RYU!
IDIE! LET'S GO FISHING!
RYU'S APPEARANCE BRIGHTENED MY DAYS LIKE SUNSHINE.
I ALWAYS TRIED NOT TO STAND OUT BECAUSE I DIDN'T WANT PEOPLE TO HATE ME. BUT HE BROUGHT ME OUT OF MY SHELL.
HE TAUGHT ME LOTS OF THINGS.
WHAT? YOU CAN'T EAT FISH?
I GUESS I SHOULDN'T EAT LIVING THINGS IN FRONT OF A VEGETARIAN... I SEE.
I SAW IT ON TV, BUT...
EEEK! THAT LOOKS LIKE IT HURTS
YOU EAT THAT?
HE CAME FROM THE SAME PLANET AS MOM.
YOU NEED TO EAT MEAT TO STAY HEALTHY.

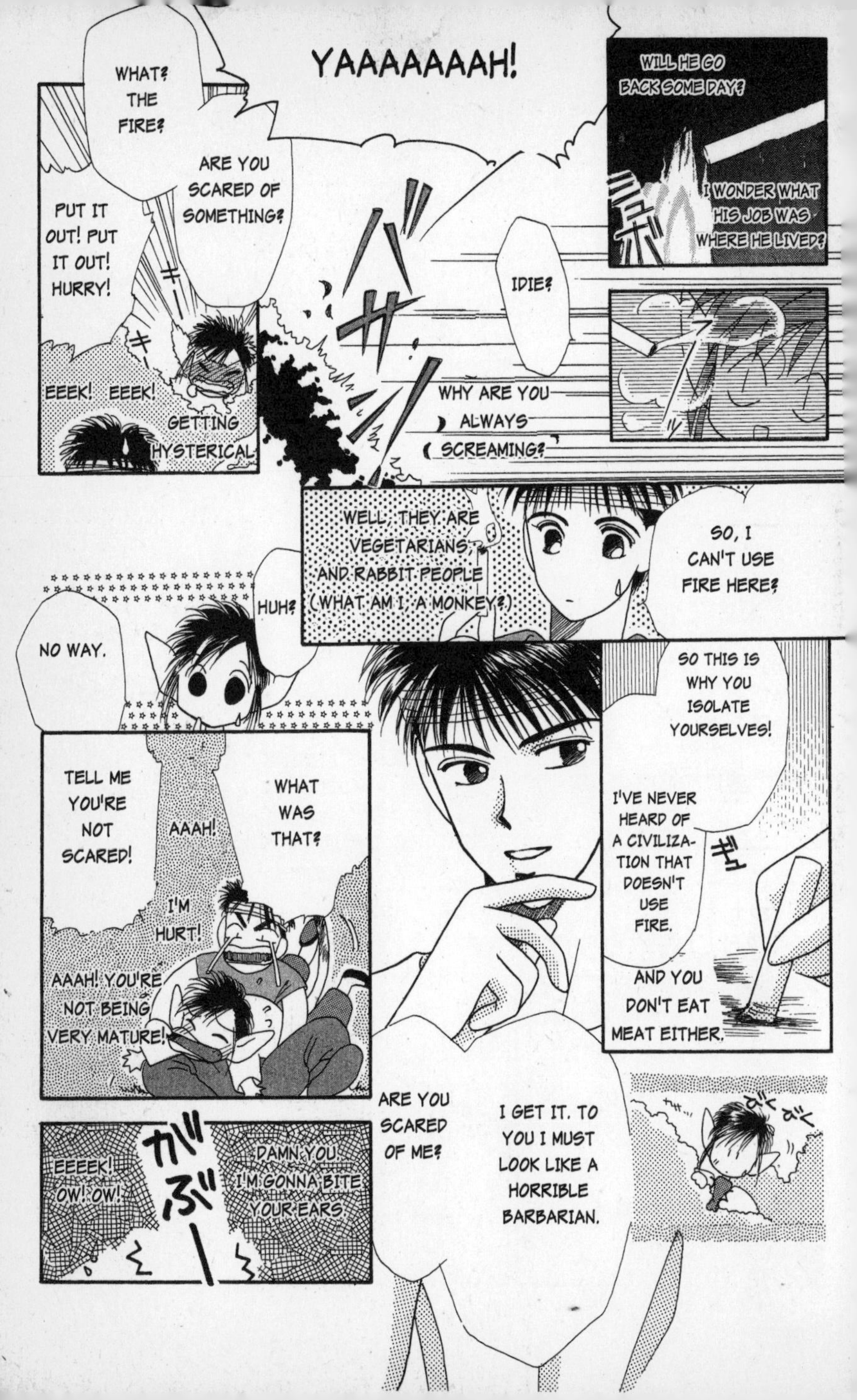

WILL HE GO BACK SOME DAY?
I WONDER WHAT HIS JOB WAS WHERE HE LIVED?
YAAAAAAAH!
IDIE?
WHY ARE YOU ALWAYS SCREAMING?
WHAT? THE FIRE?
ARE YOU SCARED OF SOMETHING?
PUT IT OUT! PUT IT OUT! HURRY!
EEEK! EEEK!
GETTING HYSTERICAL
SO, I CAN'T USE FIRE HERE?
WELL, THEY ARE VEGETARIANS, AND RABBIT PEOPLE (WHAT AM I, A MONKEY?)
HUH?
NO WAY.
SO THIS IS WHY YOU ISOLATE YOURSELVES!
I'VE NEVER HEARD OF A CIVILIZATION THAT DOESN'T USE FIRE.
AND YOU DON'T EAT MEAT EITHER.
WHAT WAS THAT?
AAAH!
TELL ME YOU'RE NOT SCARED!
I'M HURT!
AAAH! YOU'RE NOT BEING VERY MATURE!
I GET IT. TO YOU I MUST LOOK LIKE A HORRIBLE BARBARIAN.
ARE YOU SCARED OF ME?
DAMN YOU. I'M GONNA BITE YOUR EARS.
EEEEK! OW! OW!

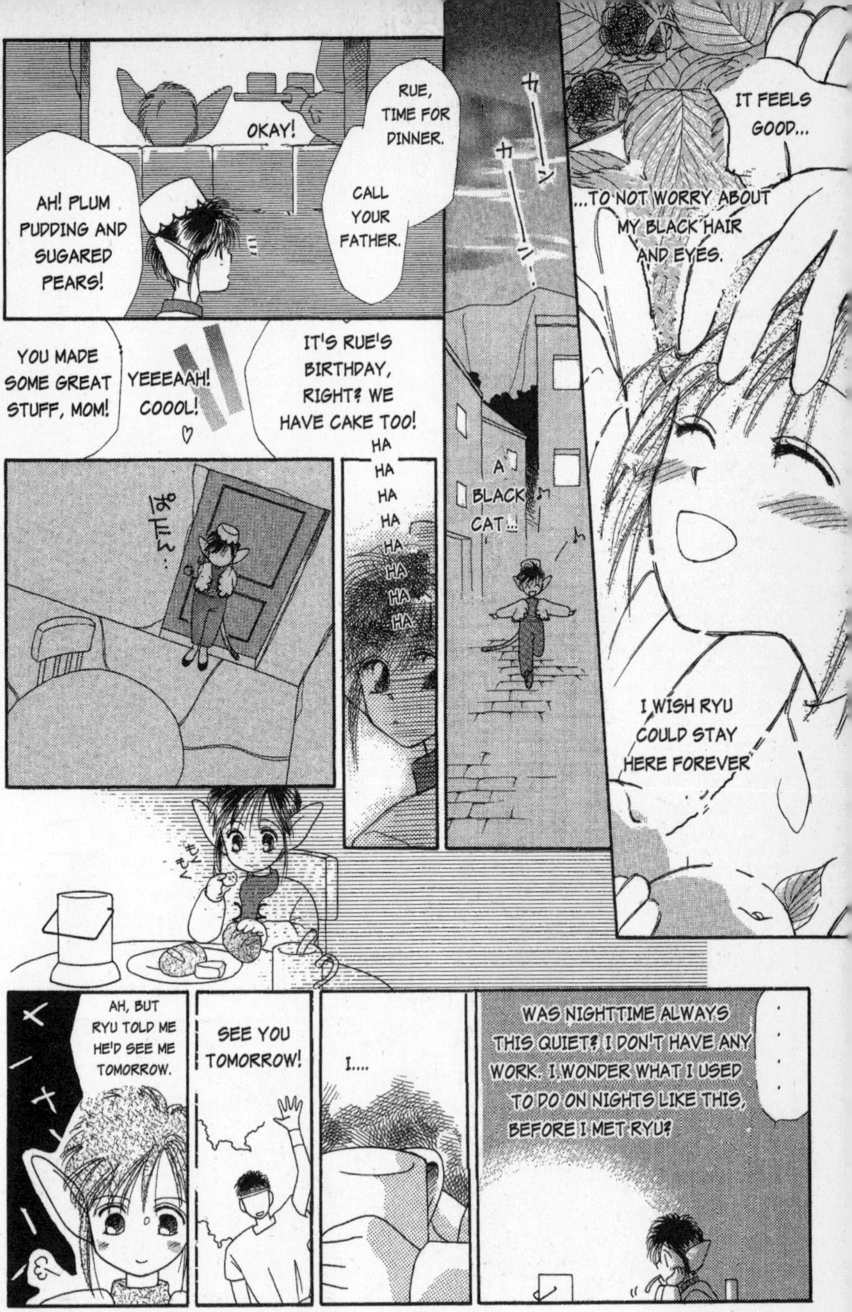
IT FEELS GOOD...
...TO NOT WORRY ABOUT MY BLACK HAIR AND EYES.
I WISH RYU COULD STAY HERE FOREVER
A BLACK CAT...
RUE, TIME FOR DINNER.
CALL YOUR FATHER.
OKAY!
AH! PLUM PUDDING AND SUGARED PEARS!
IT'S RUE'S BIRTHDAY, RIGHT? WE HAVE CAKE TOO!
YEEEAAH! COOOL!
YOU MADE SOME GREAT STUFF, MOM!
HA HA HA HA HA HA HA HA
WAS NIGHTTIME ALWAYS THIS QUIET? I DON'T HAVE ANY WORK. I WONDER WHAT I USED TO DO ON NIGHTS LIKE THIS, BEFORE I MET RYU?
...
I....
SEE YOU TOMORROW!
AH, BUT RYU TOLD ME HE'D SEE ME TOMORROW.

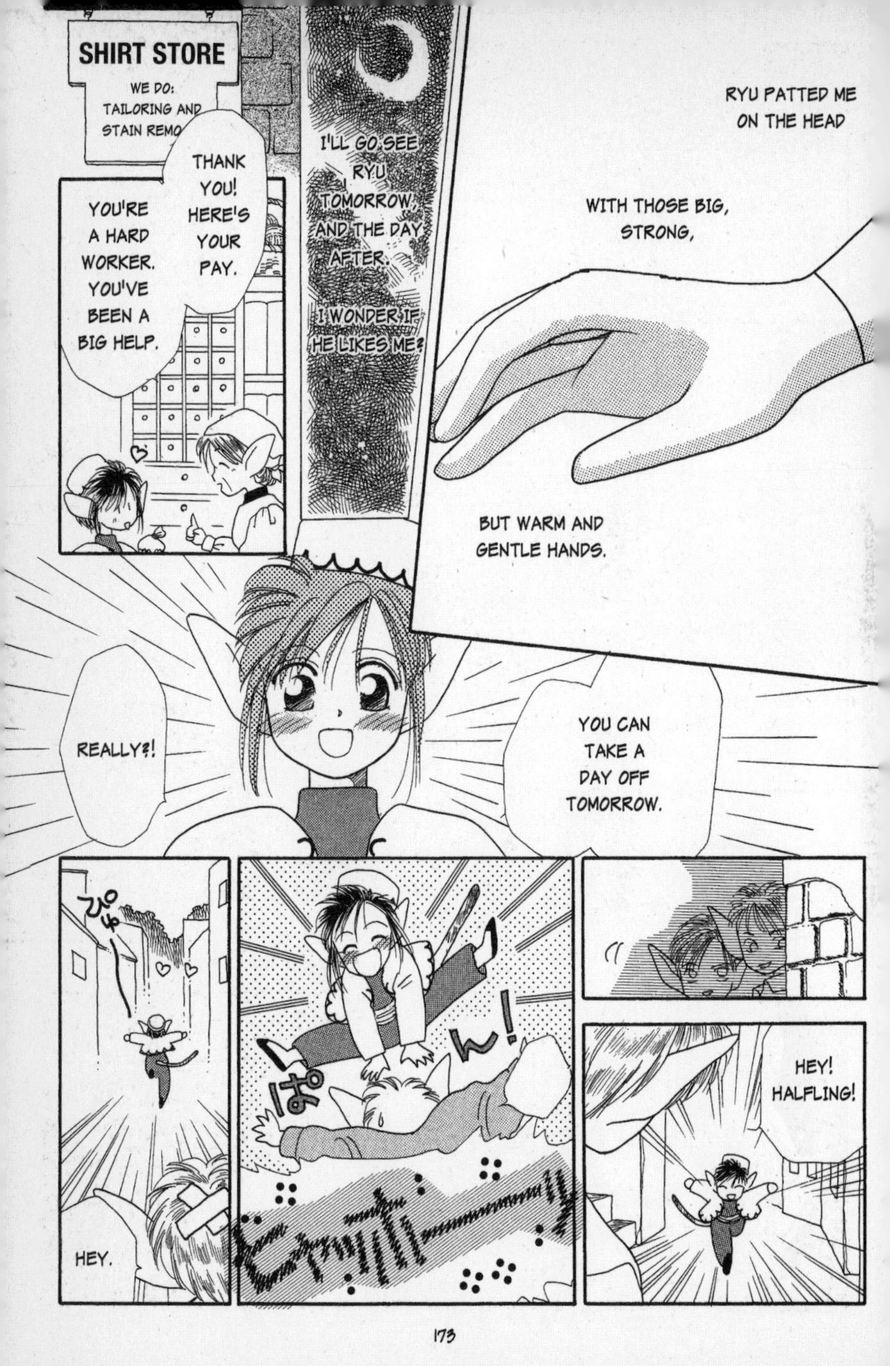
RYU PATTED ME ON THE HEAD
WITH THOSE BIG, STRONG,
BUT WARM AND GENTLE HANDS.
I'LL GO SEE RYU TOMORROW, AND THE DAY AFTER.
I WONDER IF HE LIKES ME?
SHIRT STORE
WE DO: TAILORING AND STAIN REMO
THANK YOU! HERE'S YOUR PAY.
YOU'RE A HARD WORKER. YOU'VE BEEN A BIG HELP.
YOU CAN TAKE A DAY OFF TOMORROW.
REALLY?!
HEY! HALFLING!
ぱん!
ぴゅー
HEY.

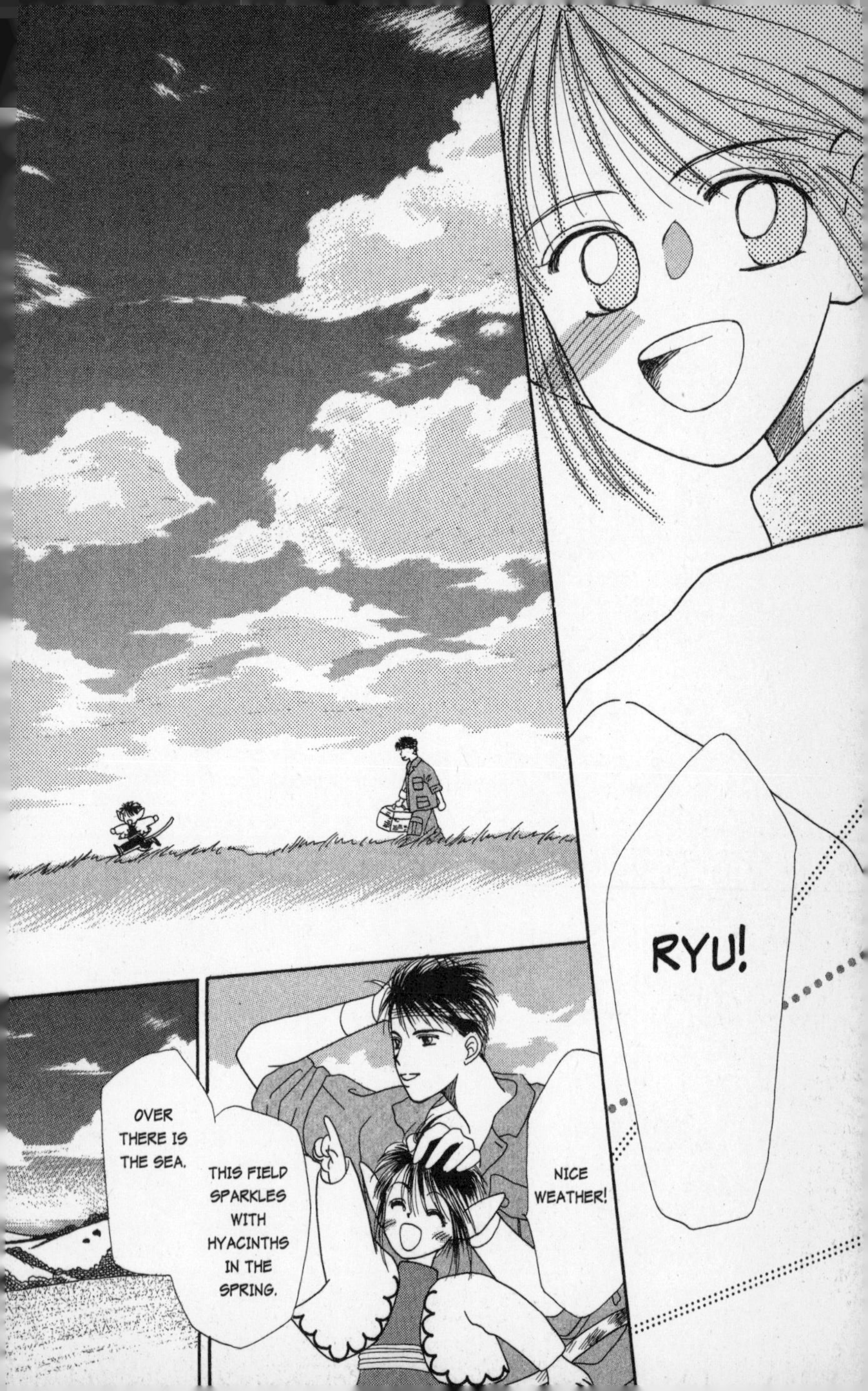
RYU!
NICE WEATHER!
OVER THERE IS THE SEA.
THIS FIELD SPARKLES WITH HYACINTHS IN THE SPRING.

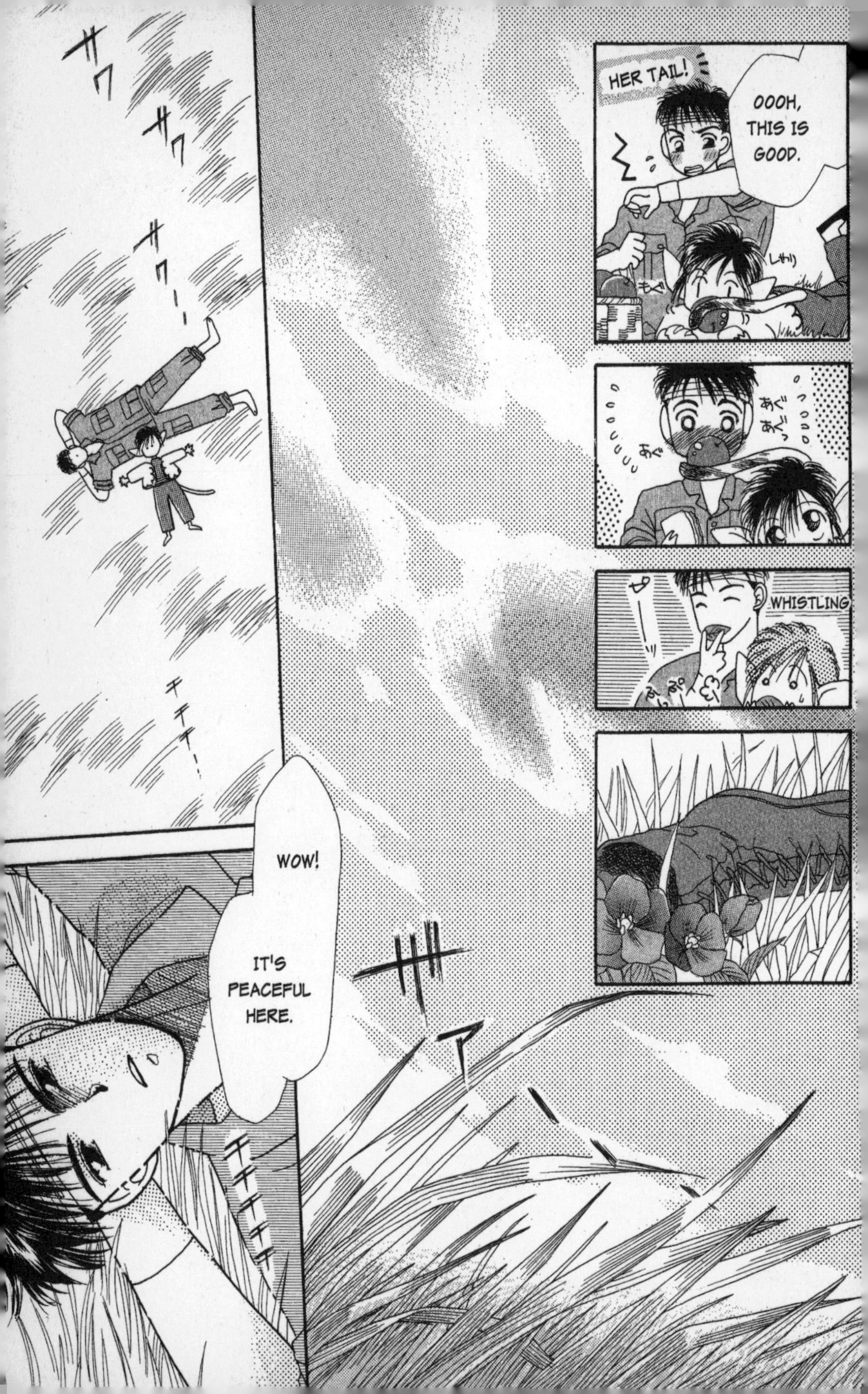
OOOH, THIS IS GOOD.
HER TAIL!
もぐ
あぐ
あぐ
あぐ
WHISTLING
ザワ
ザワ
ザワーー
チチチ‥
WOW!
IT'S PEACEFUL HERE.
チチチチチ
ザァーーー

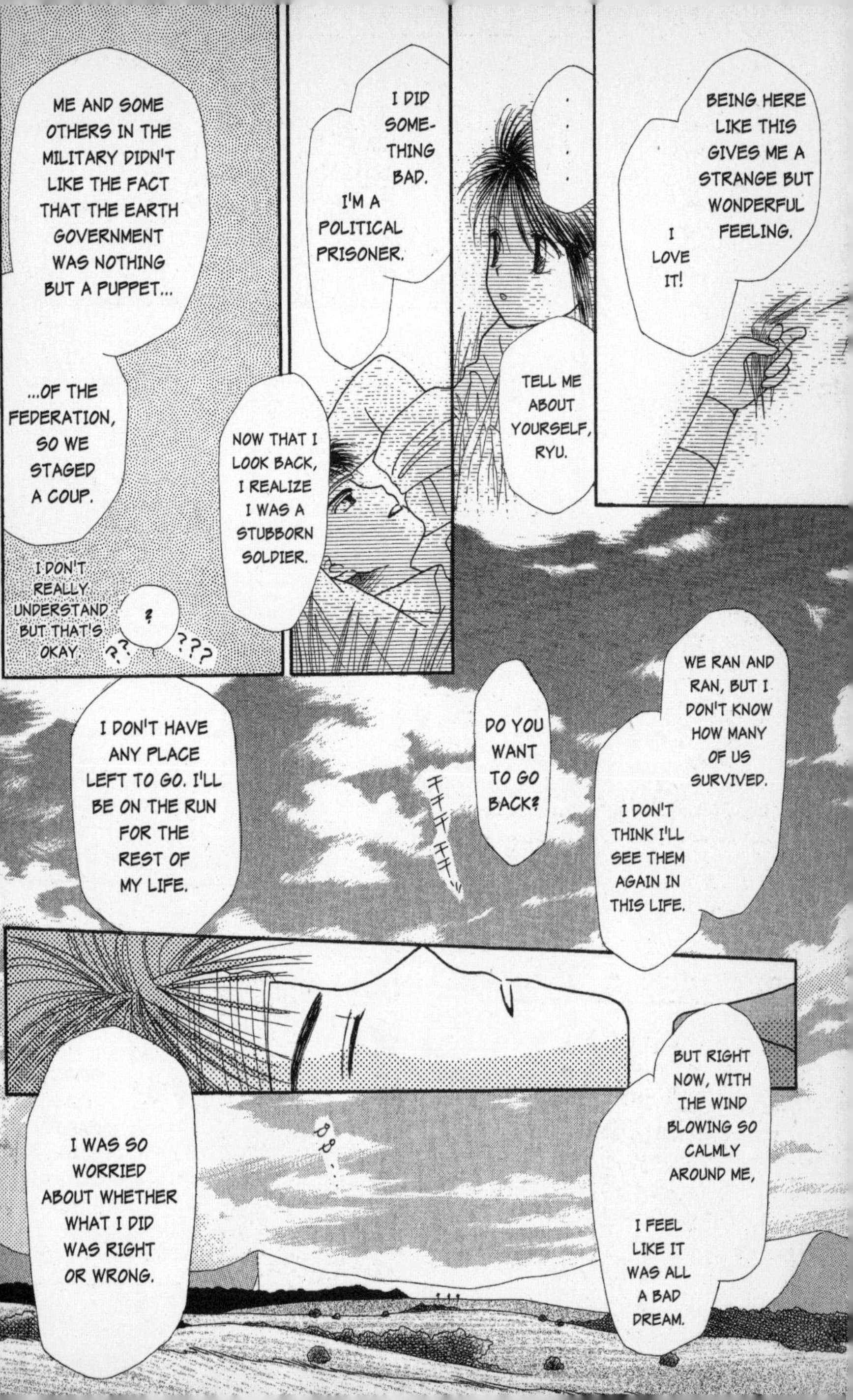
BEING HERE LIKE THIS GIVES ME A STRANGE BUT WONDERFUL FEELING.
I LOVE IT!
...
TELL ME ABOUT YOURSELF, RYU.
I DID SOME-THING BAD.
I'M A POLITICAL PRISONER.
NOW THAT I LOOK BACK, I REALIZE I WAS A STUBBORN SOLDIER.
ME AND SOME OTHERS IN THE MILITARY DIDN'T LIKE THE FACT THAT THE EARTH GOVERNMENT WAS NOTHING BUT A PUPPET...
...OF THE FEDERATION, SO WE STAGED A COUP.
I DON'T REALLY UNDERSTAND BUT THAT'S OKAY.
?
??
???
WE RAN AND RAN, BUT I DON'T KNOW HOW MANY OF US SURVIVED.
I DON'T THINK I'LL SEE THEM AGAIN IN THIS LIFE.
DO YOU WANT TO GO BACK?
I DON'T HAVE ANY PLACE LEFT TO GO. I'LL BE ON THE RUN FOR THE REST OF MY LIFE.
BUT RIGHT NOW, WITH THE WIND BLOWING SO CALMLY AROUND ME,
I FEEL LIKE IT WAS ALL A BAD DREAM.
I WAS SO WORRIED ABOUT WHETHER WHAT I DID WAS RIGHT OR WRONG.

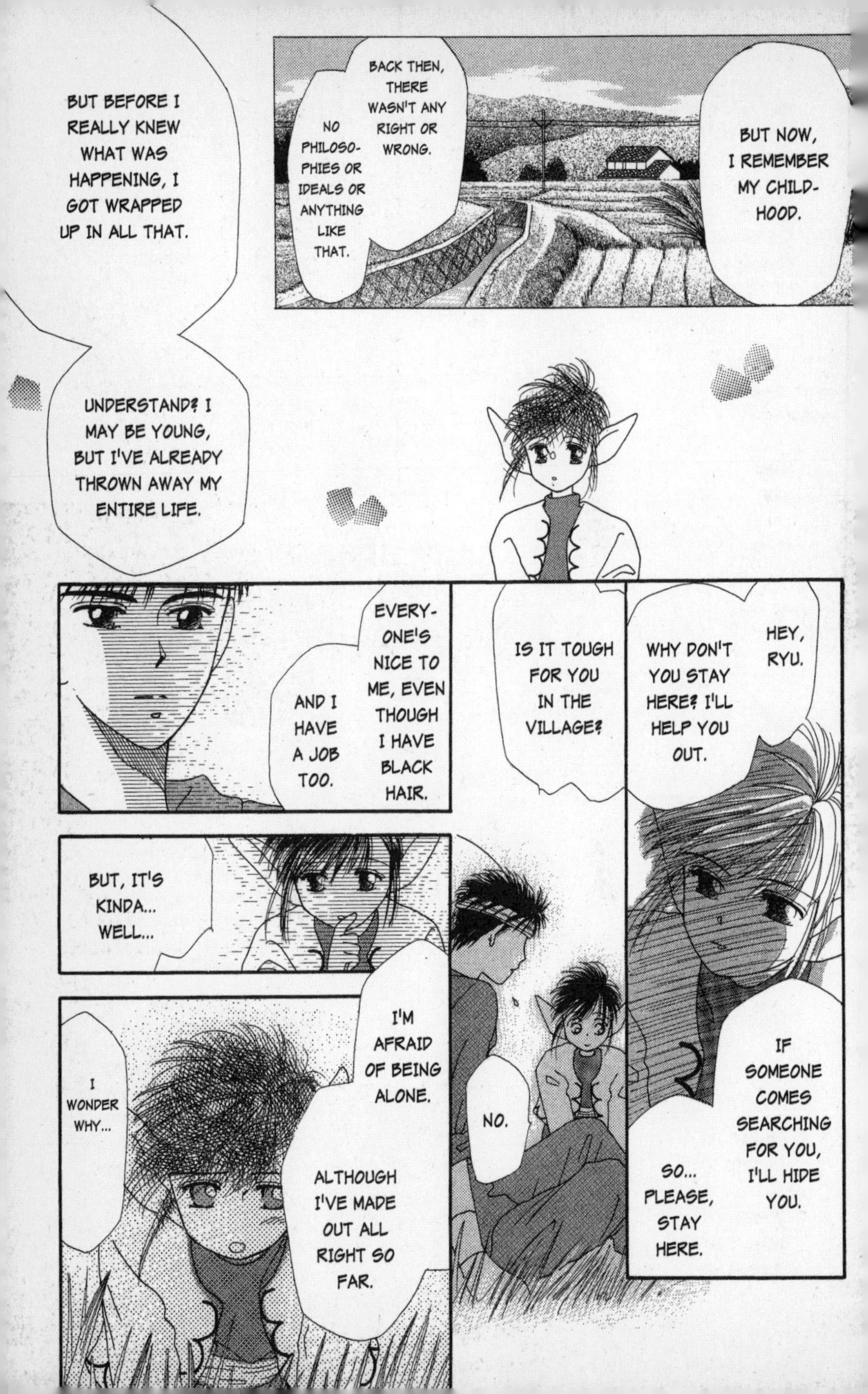
BUT NOW, I REMEMBER MY CHILD-HOOD.
BACK THEN, THERE WASN'T ANY RIGHT OR WRONG.
NO PHILOSO-PHIES OR IDEALS OR ANYTHING LIKE THAT.
BUT BEFORE I REALLY KNEW WHAT WAS HAPPENING, I GOT WRAPPED UP IN ALL THAT.
UNDERSTAND? I MAY BE YOUNG, BUT I'VE ALREADY THROWN AWAY MY ENTIRE LIFE.
HEY, RYU.
WHY DON'T YOU STAY HERE? I'LL HELP YOU OUT.
IF SOMEONE COMES SEARCHING FOR YOU, I'LL HIDE YOU.
SO... PLEASE, STAY HERE.
IS IT TOUGH FOR YOU IN THE VILLAGE?
NO.
EVERY-ONE'S NICE TO ME, EVEN THOUGH I HAVE BLACK HAIR.
AND I HAVE A JOB TOO.
BUT, IT'S KINDA... WELL...
I'M AFRAID OF BEING ALONE.
ALTHOUGH I'VE MADE OUT ALL RIGHT SO FAR.
I WONDER WHY...

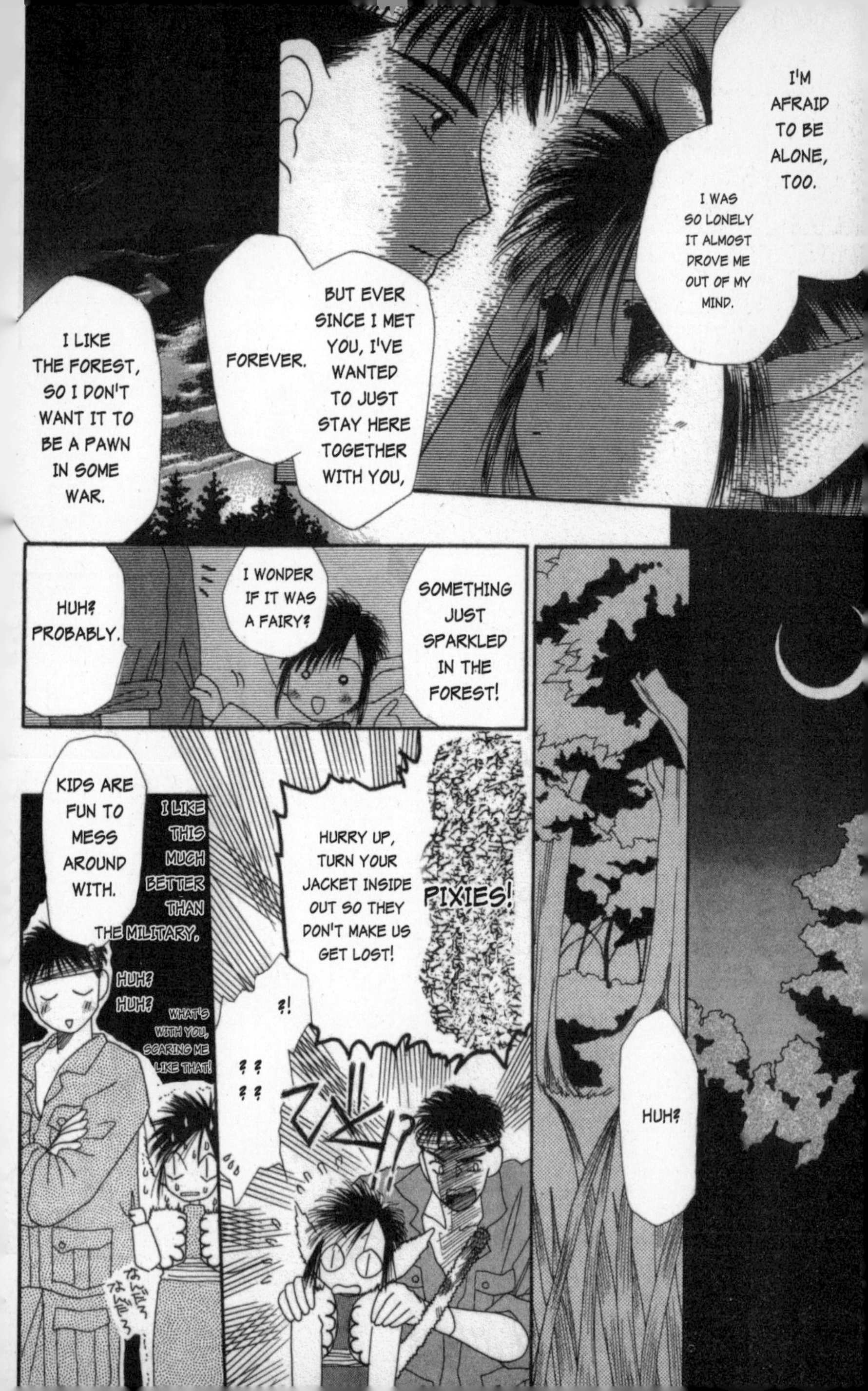
I'M AFRAID TO BE ALONE, TOO.
I WAS SO LONELY IT ALMOST DROVE ME OUT OF MY MIND.
BUT EVER SINCE I MET YOU, I'VE WANTED TO JUST STAY HERE TOGETHER WITH YOU,
FOREVER.
I LIKE THE FOREST, SO I DON'T WANT IT TO BE A PAWN IN SOME WAR.
HUH?
SOMETHING JUST SPARKLED IN THE FOREST!
I WONDER IF IT WAS A FAIRY?
HUH? PROBABLY.
PIXIES!
HURRY UP, TURN YOUR JACKET INSIDE OUT SO THEY DON'T MAKE US GET LOST!
?!
??
??
KIDS ARE FUN TO MESS AROUND WITH.
I LIKE THIS MUCH BETTER THAN THE MILITARY.
HUH? HUH?
WHAT'S WITH YOU, SCARING ME LIKE THAT!

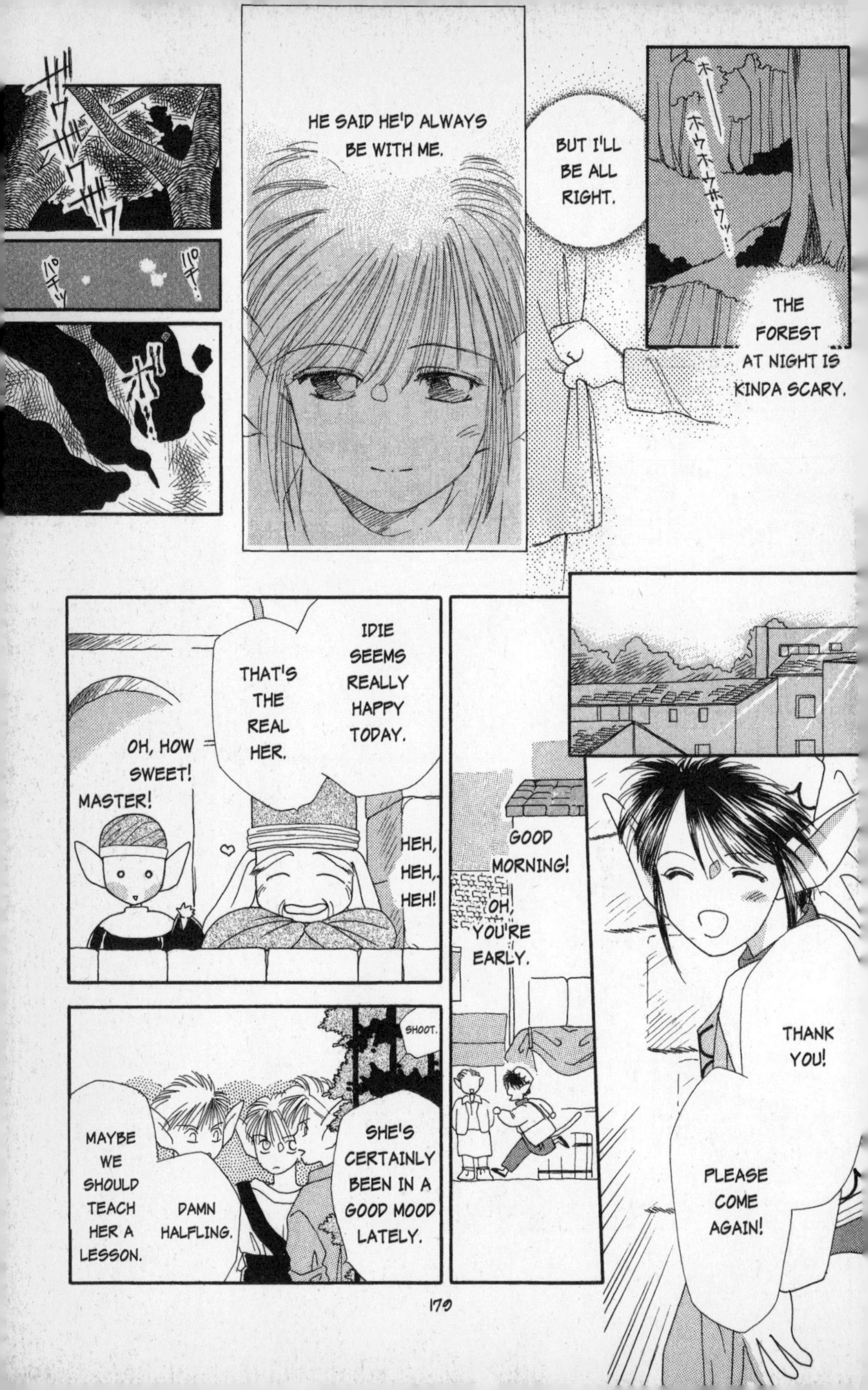
THE FOREST AT NIGHT IS KINDA SCARY.
BUT I'LL BE ALL RIGHT.
HE SAID HE'D ALWAYS BE WITH ME.
THANK YOU!
PLEASE COME AGAIN!
GOOD MORNING!
OH, YOU'RE EARLY.
IDIE SEEMS REALLY HAPPY TODAY.
THAT'S THE REAL HER.
HEH, HEH, HEH!
OH, HOW SWEET!
MASTER!
SHOOT.
SHE'S CERTAINLY BEEN IN A GOOD MOOD LATELY.
DAMN HALFLING.
MAYBE WE SHOULD TEACH HER A LESSON.

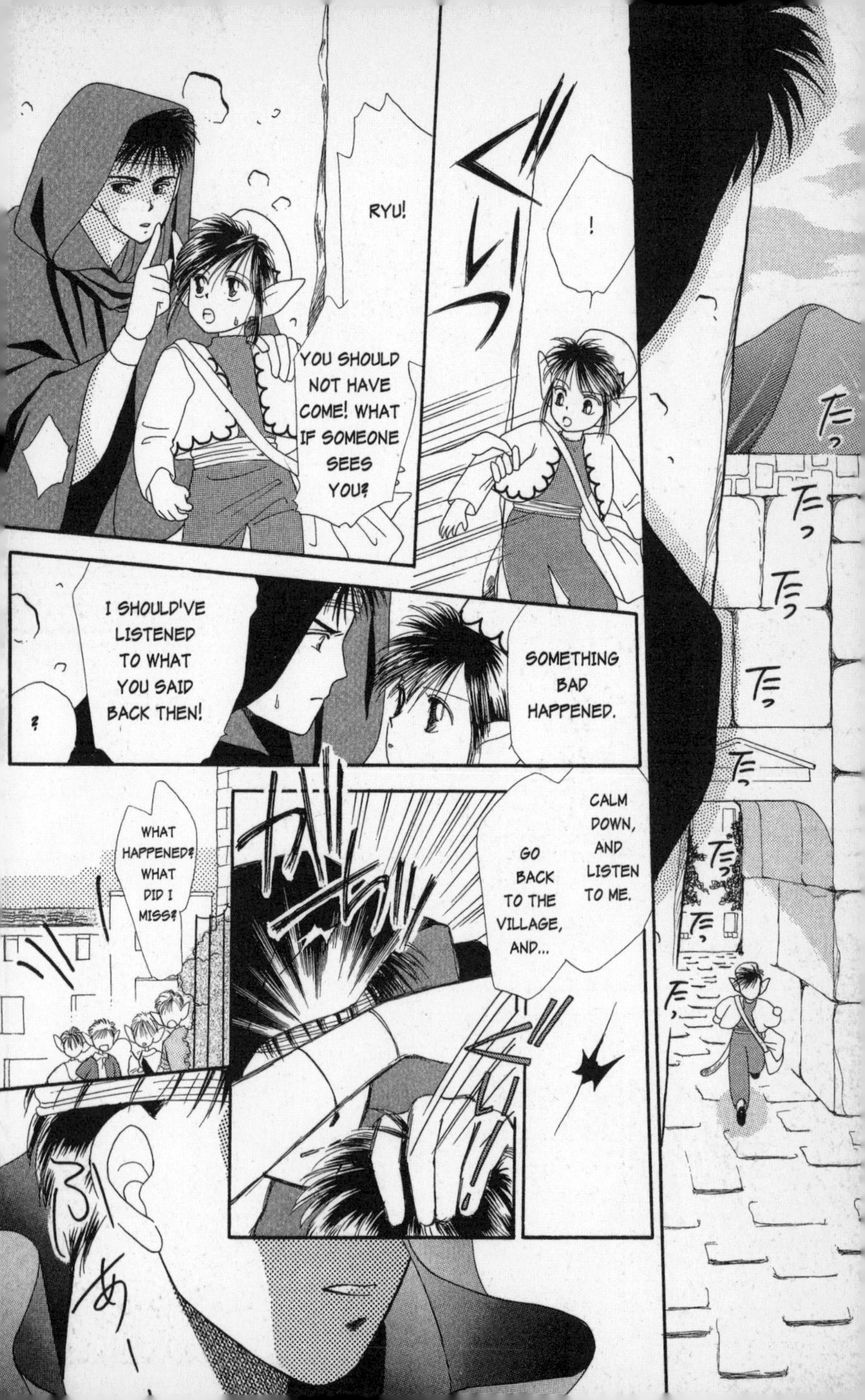
!
RYU!
YOU SHOULD NOT HAVE COME! WHAT IF SOMEONE SEES YOU?
SOMETHING BAD HAPPENED.
I SHOULD'VE LISTENED TO WHAT YOU SAID BACK THEN!
?
CALM DOWN, AND LISTEN TO ME.
GO BACK TO THE VILLAGE, AND...
WHAT HAPPENED? WHAT DID I MISS?

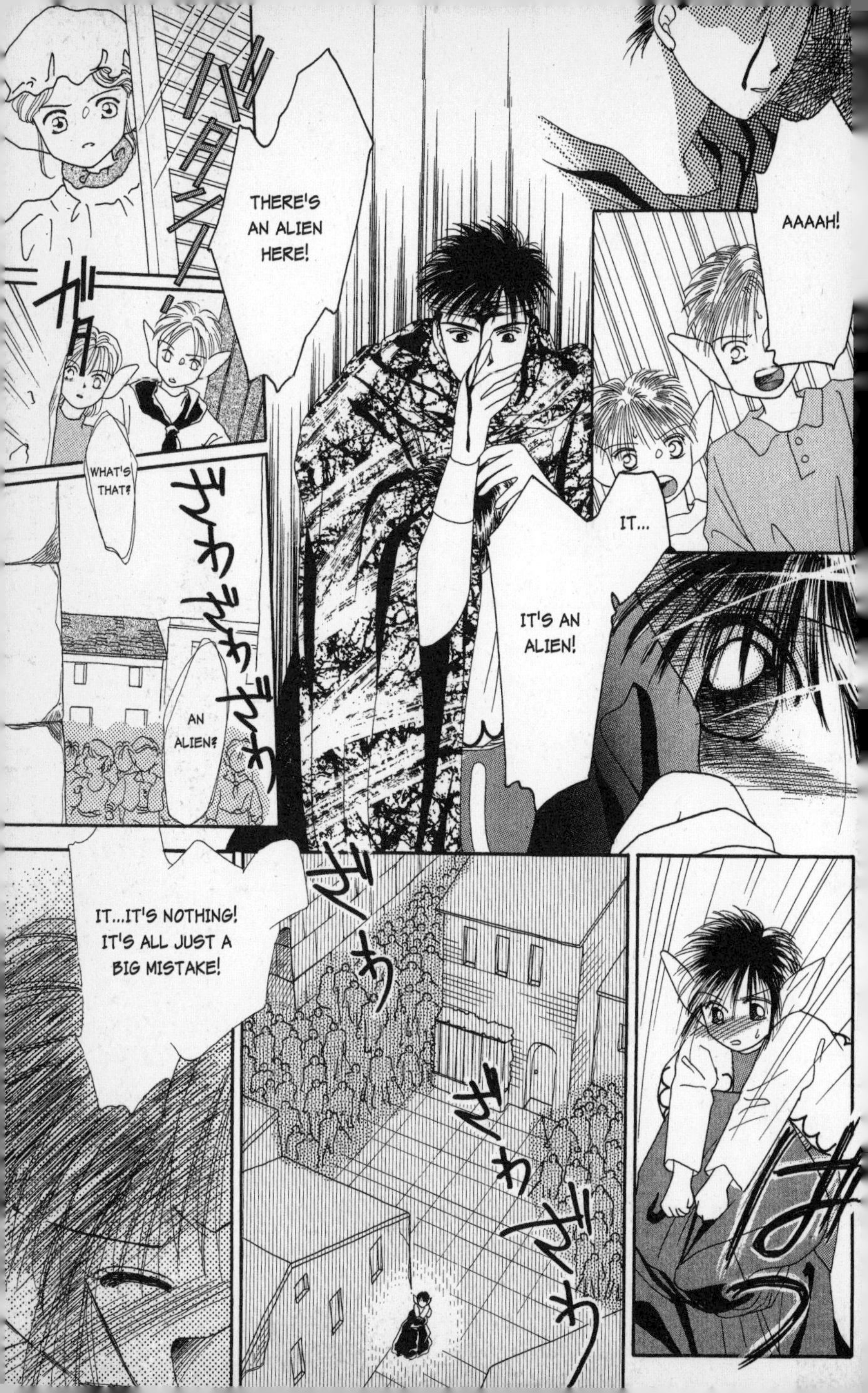
AAAAH!
IT...
IT'S AN ALIEN!
THERE'S AN ALIEN HERE!
WHAT'S THAT?
AN ALIEN?
IT...IT'S NOTHING! IT'S ALL JUST A BIG MISTAKE!

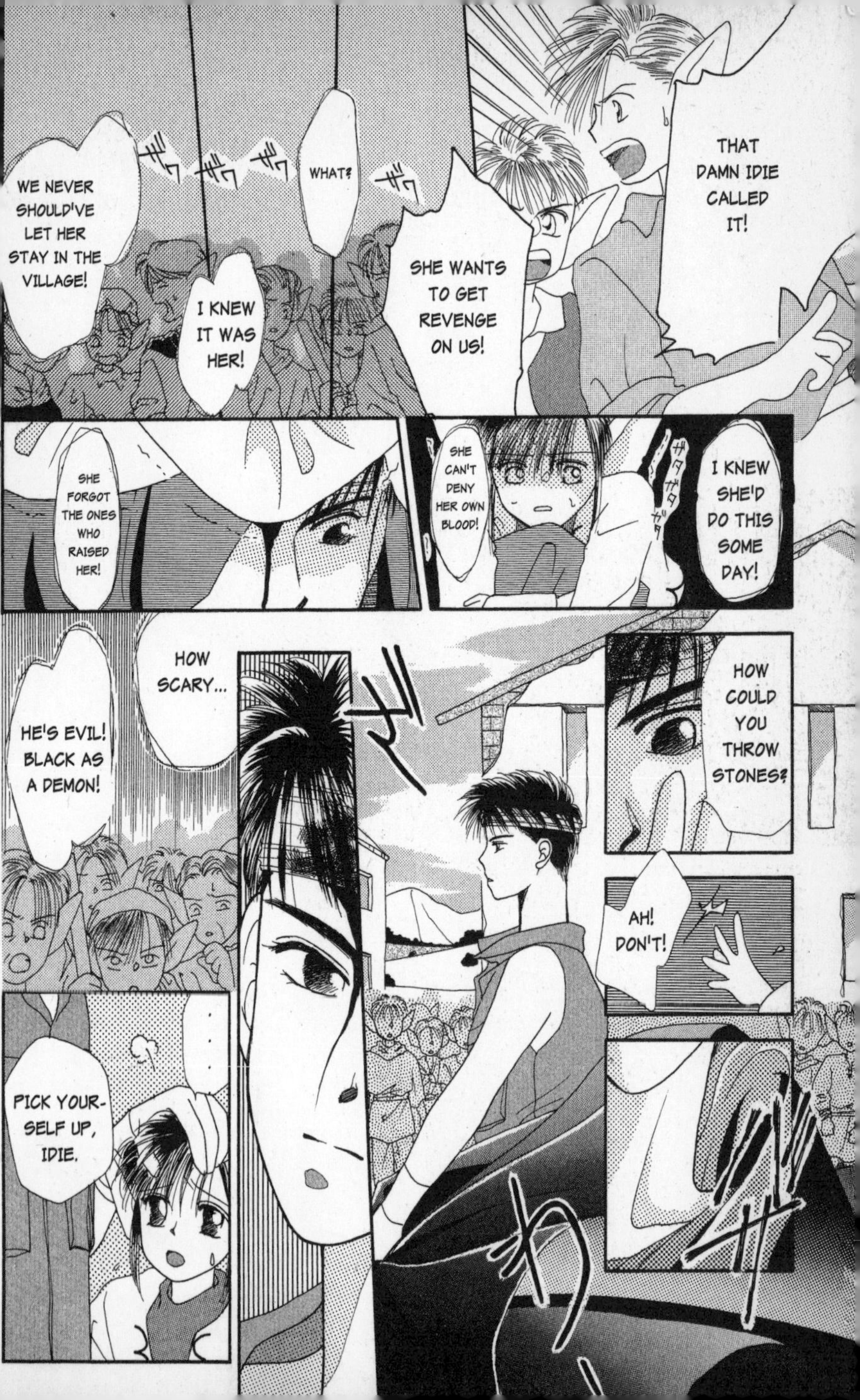
THAT DAMN IDIE CALLED IT!
SHE WANTS TO GET REVENGE ON US!
WHAT?
I KNEW IT WAS HER!
WE NEVER SHOULD'VE LET HER STAY IN THE VILLAGE!
I KNEW SHE'D DO THIS SOME DAY!
SHE CAN'T DENY HER OWN BLOOD!
SHE FORGOT THE ONES WHO RAISED HER!
HOW COULD YOU THROW STONES?
AH! DON'T!
HOW SCARY...
HE'S EVIL! BLACK AS A DEMON!
...
PICK YOURSELF UP, IDIE.

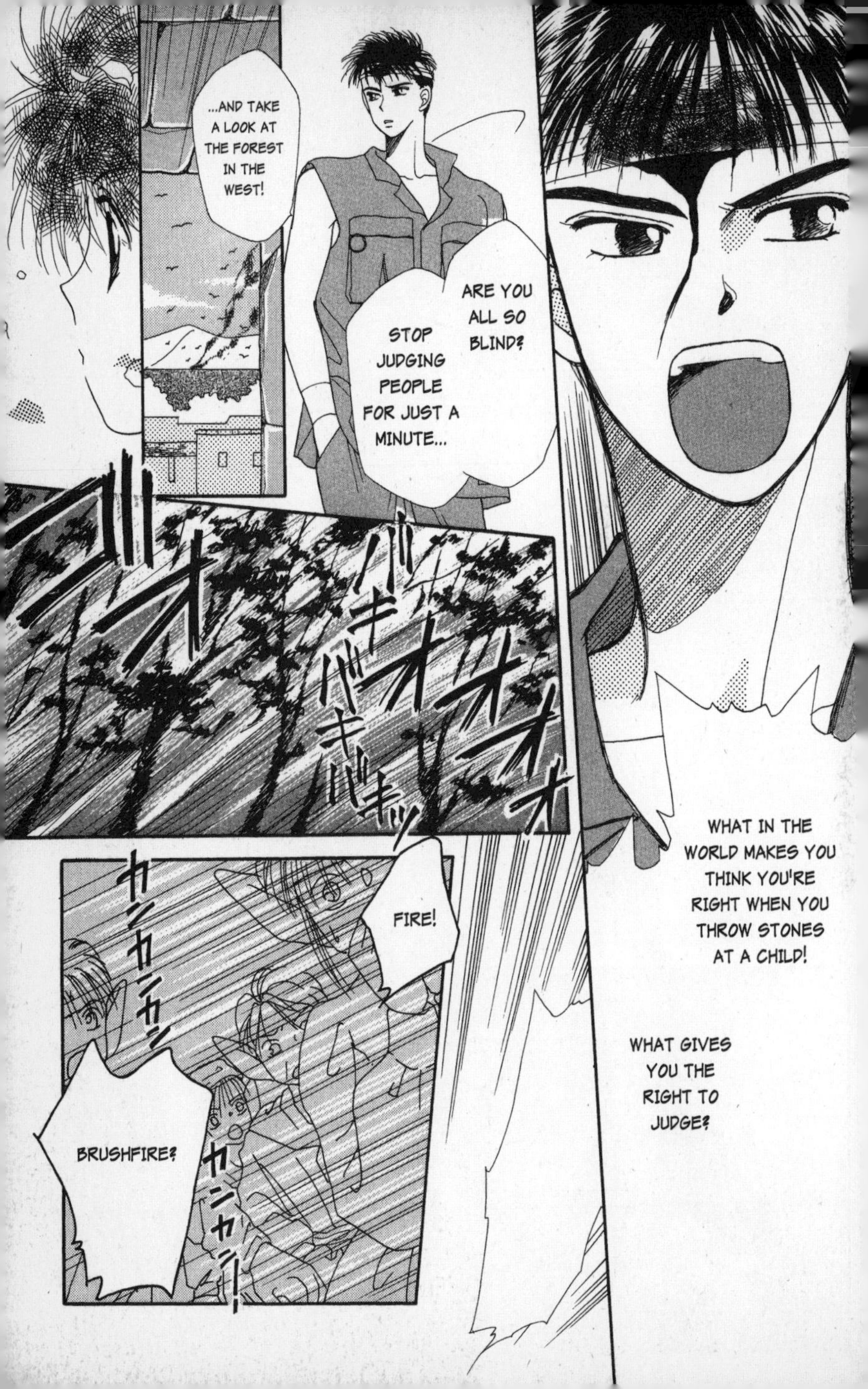

WHAT IN THE WORLD MAKES YOU THINK YOU'RE RIGHT WHEN YOU THROW STONES AT A CHILD!
WHAT GIVES YOU THE RIGHT TO JUDGE?
ARE YOU ALL SO BLIND?
STOP JUDGING PEOPLE FOR JUST A MINUTE...
...AND TAKE A LOOK AT THE FOREST IN THE WEST!
バキバキバキッ
ゴォオオオオ
FIRE!
カンカンカン
カンカン!
BRUSHFIRE?

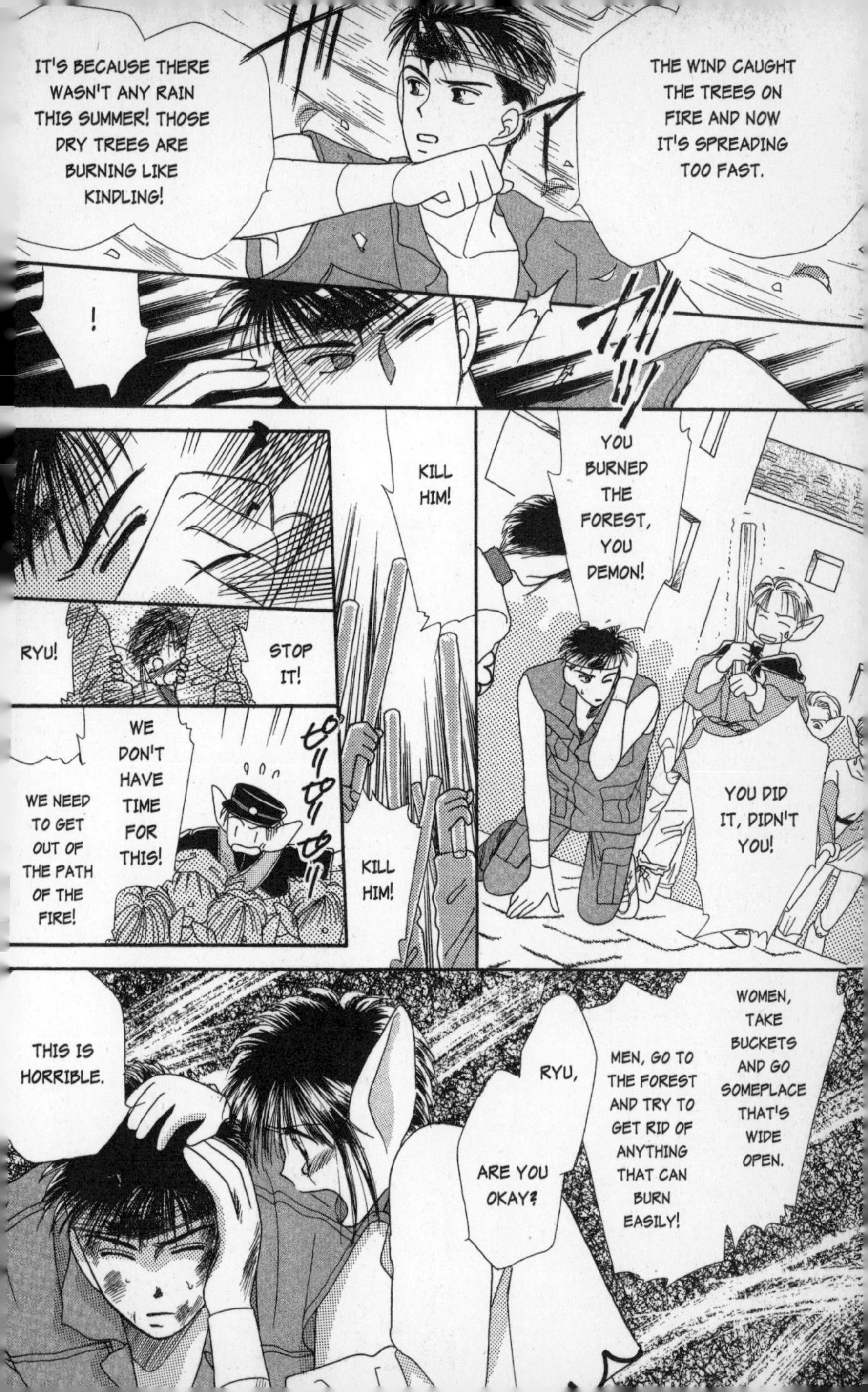
THE WIND CAUGHT THE TREES ON FIRE AND NOW IT'S SPREADING TOO FAST.
IT'S BECAUSE THERE WASN'T ANY RAIN THIS SUMMER! THOSE DRY TREES ARE BURNING LIKE KINDLING!
!
YOU BURNED THE FOREST, YOU DEMON!
YOU DID IT, DIDN'T YOU!
KILL HIM!
KILL HIM!
STOP IT!
RYU!
WE DON'T HAVE TIME FOR THIS!
WE NEED TO GET OUT OF THE PATH OF THE FIRE!
WOMEN, TAKE BUCKETS AND GO SOMEPLACE THAT'S WIDE OPEN.
MEN, GO TO THE FOREST AND TRY TO GET RID OF ANYTHING THAT CAN BURN EASILY!
RYU,
ARE YOU OKAY?
THIS IS HORRIBLE.

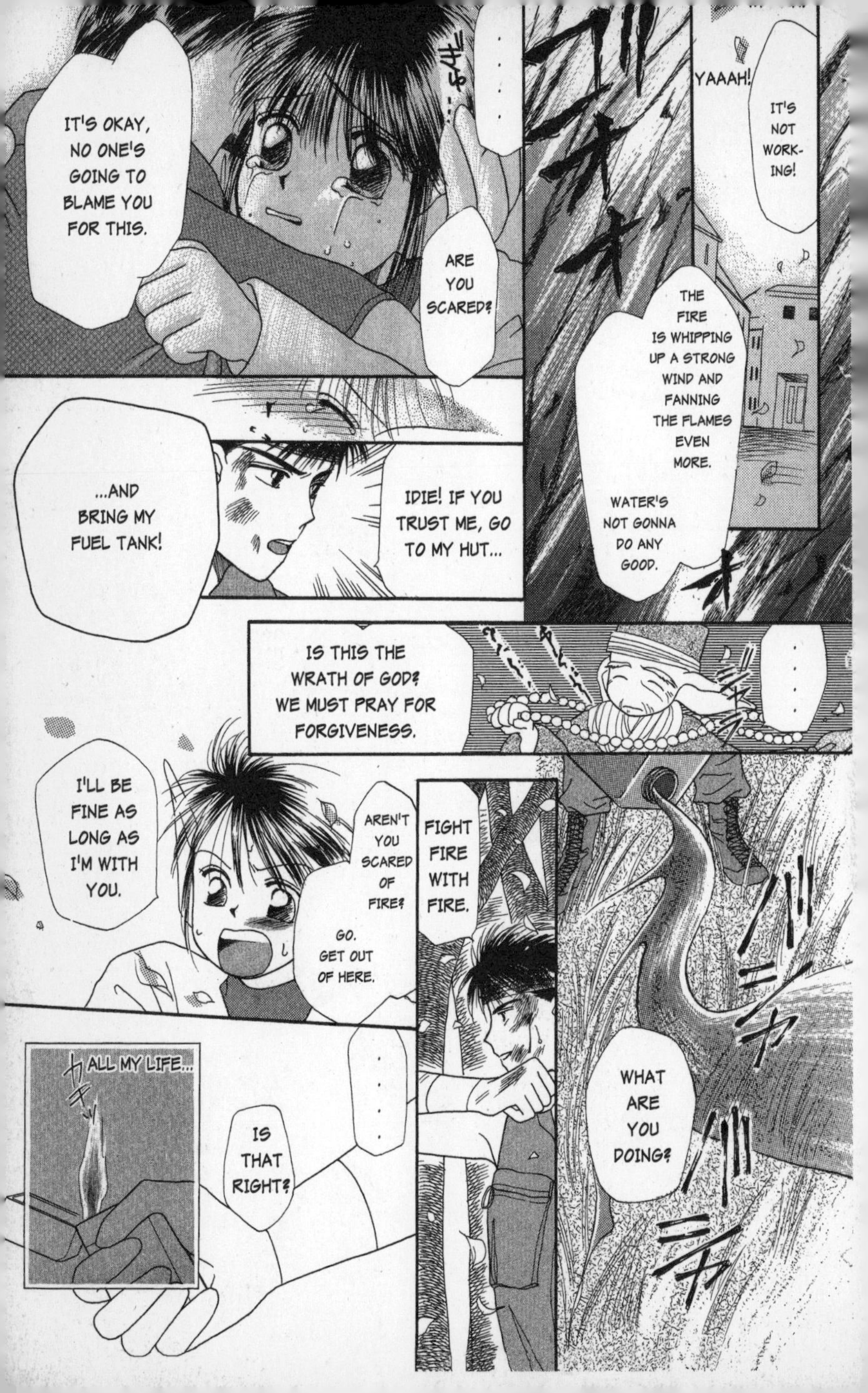
IT'S NOT WORKING!
YAAAH!
THE FIRE IS WHIPPING UP A STRONG WIND AND FANNING THE FLAMES EVEN MORE.
WATER'S NOT GONNA DO ANY GOOD.
. . .
ARE YOU SCARED?
IT'S OKAY, NO ONE'S GOING TO BLAME YOU FOR THIS.
IDIE! IF YOU TRUST ME, GO TO MY HUT...
...AND BRING MY FUEL TANK!
. . .
IS THIS THE WRATH OF GOD? WE MUST PRAY FOR FORGIVENESS.
WHAT ARE YOU DOING?
FIGHT FIRE WITH FIRE.
AREN'T YOU SCARED OF FIRE?
GO. GET OUT OF HERE.
I'LL BE FINE AS LONG AS I'M WITH YOU.
. . .
IS THAT RIGHT?
ALL MY LIFE...

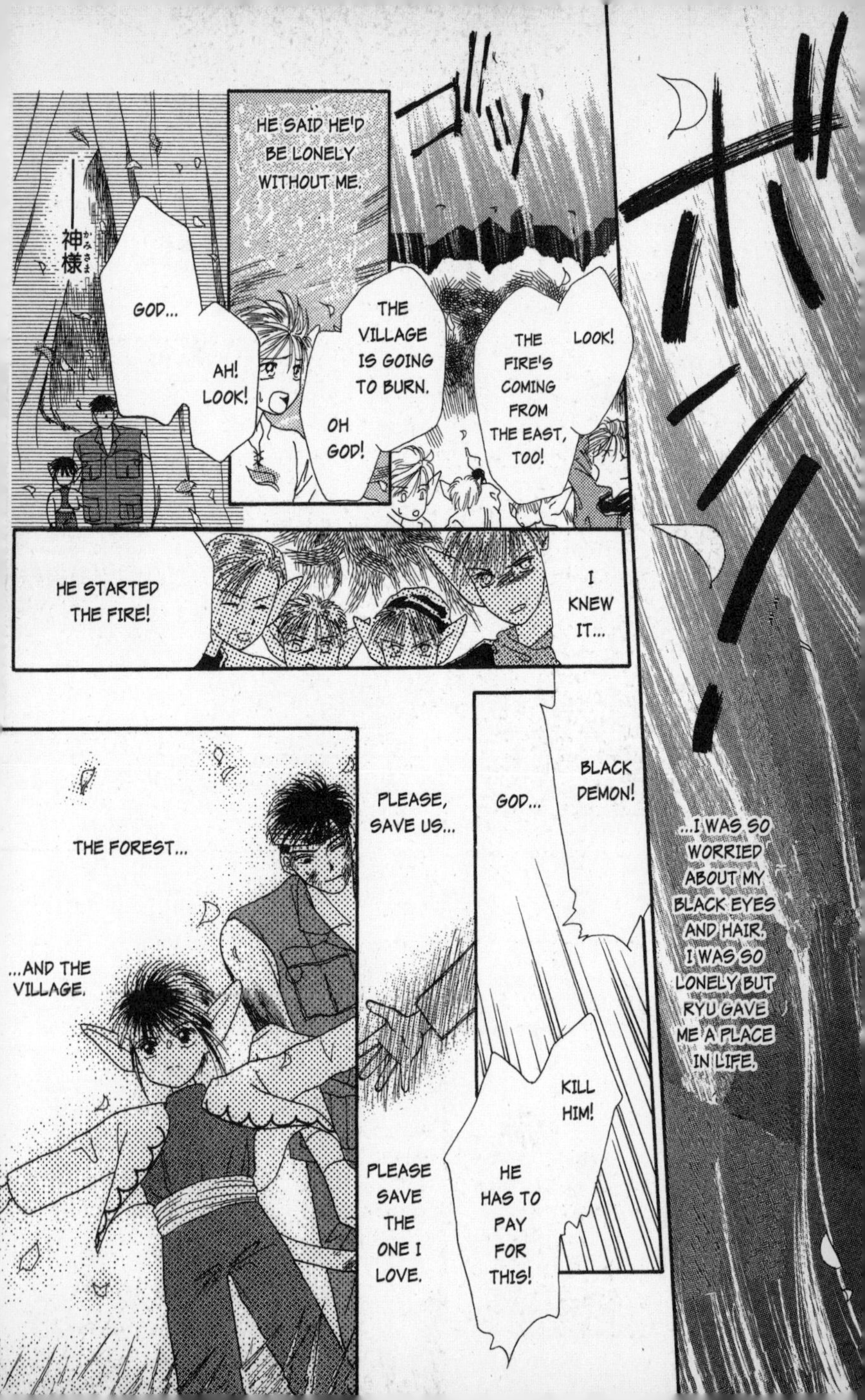
...I WAS SO WORRIED ABOUT MY BLACK EYES AND HAIR. I WAS SO LONELY BUT RYU GAVE ME A PLACE IN LIFE.
ゴッ
LOOK!
THE FIRE'S COMING FROM THE EAST, TOO!
HE SAID HE'D BE LONELY WITHOUT ME.
THE VILLAGE IS GOING TO BURN.
OH GOD!
AH! LOOK!
——神様
GOD...
I KNEW IT...
HE STARTED THE FIRE!
BLACK DEMON!
GOD...
KILL HIM!
HE HAS TO PAY FOR THIS!
PLEASE, SAVE US...
PLEASE SAVE THE ONE I LOVE.
THE FOREST...
...AND THE VILLAGE.

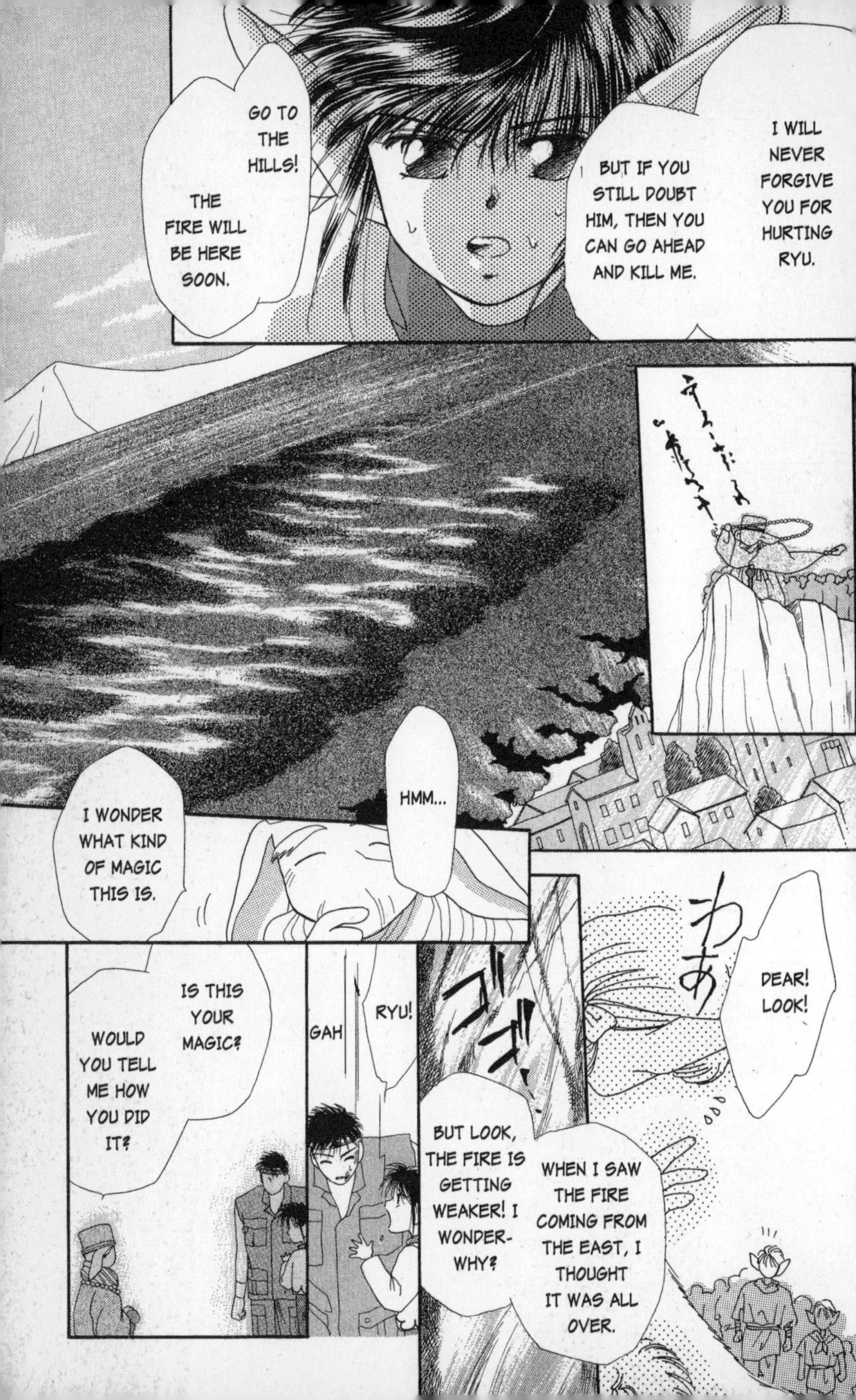
I WILL NEVER FORGIVE YOU FOR HURTING RYU.
BUT IF YOU STILL DOUBT HIM, THEN YOU CAN GO AHEAD AND KILL ME.
GO TO THE HILLS!
THE FIRE WILL BE HERE SOON.
HMM...
I WONDER WHAT KIND OF MAGIC THIS IS.
わあ
DEAR! LOOK!
WHEN I SAW THE FIRE COMING FROM THE EAST, I THOUGHT IT WAS ALL OVER.
BUT LOOK, THE FIRE IS GETTING WEAKER! I WONDER- WHY?
ゴゴ
RYU!
GAH
IS THIS YOUR MAGIC?
WOULD YOU TELL ME HOW YOU DID IT?

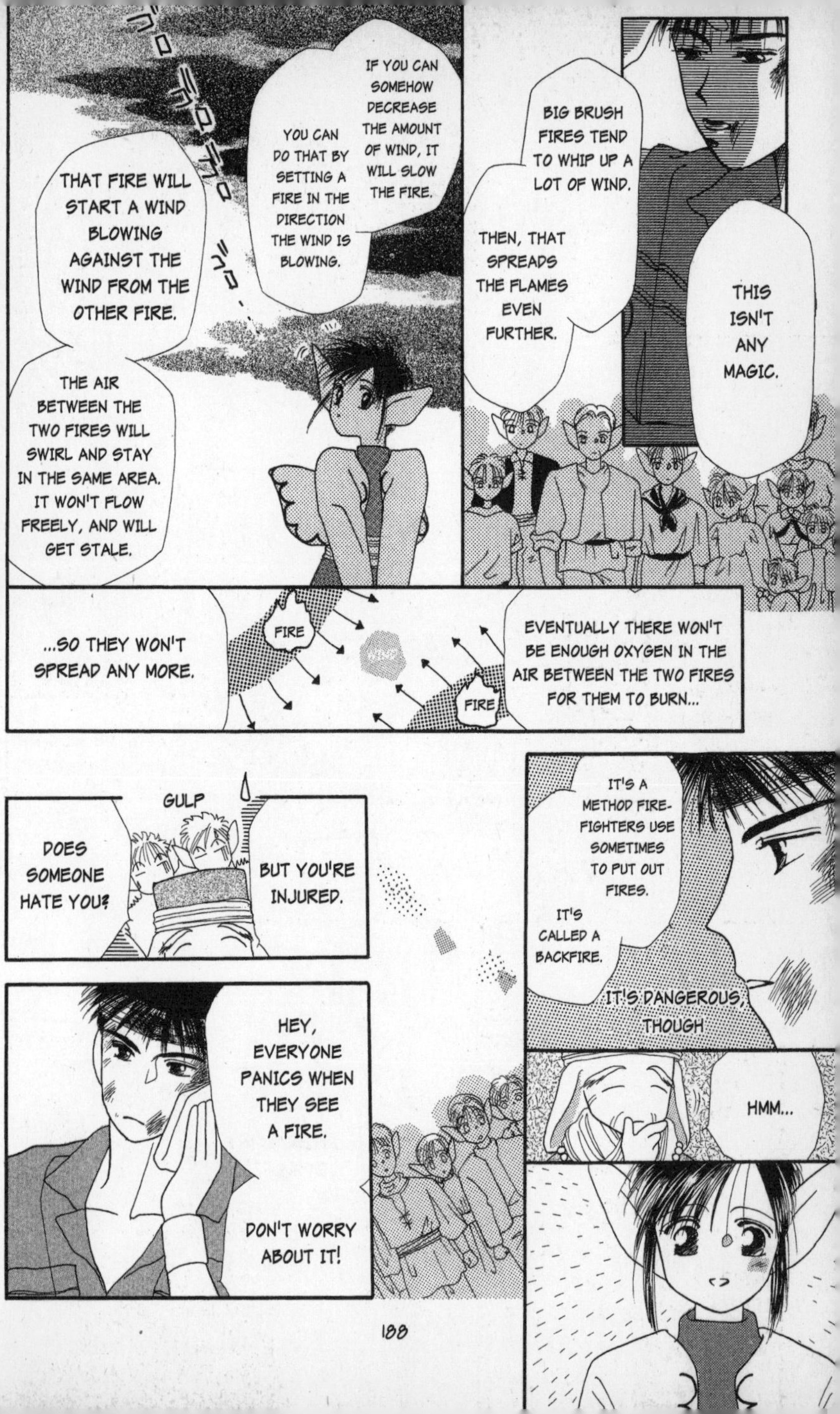
THIS ISN'T ANY MAGIC.
BIG BRUSH FIRES TEND TO WHIP UP A LOT OF WIND.
THEN, THAT SPREADS THE FLAMES EVEN FURTHER.
IF YOU CAN SOMEHOW DECREASE THE AMOUNT OF WIND, IT WILL SLOW THE FIRE.
YOU CAN DO THAT BY SETTING A FIRE IN THE DIRECTION THE WIND IS BLOWING.
THAT FIRE WILL START A WIND BLOWING AGAINST THE WIND FROM THE OTHER FIRE.
THE AIR BETWEEN THE TWO FIRES WILL SWIRL AND STAY IN THE SAME AREA. IT WON'T FLOW FREELY, AND WILL GET STALE.
EVENTUALLY THERE WON'T BE ENOUGH OXYGEN IN THE AIR BETWEEN THE TWO FIRES FOR THEM TO BURN...
FIRE
FIRE
...SO THEY WON'T SPREAD ANY MORE.
IT'S A METHOD FIRE-FIGHTERS USE SOMETIMES TO PUT OUT FIRES.
IT'S CALLED A BACKFIRE.
IT'S DANGEROUS, THOUGH
HMM...
BUT YOU'RE INJURED.
GULP
DOES SOMEONE HATE YOU?
HEY, EVERYONE PANICS WHEN THEY SEE A FIRE.
DON'T WORRY ABOUT IT!

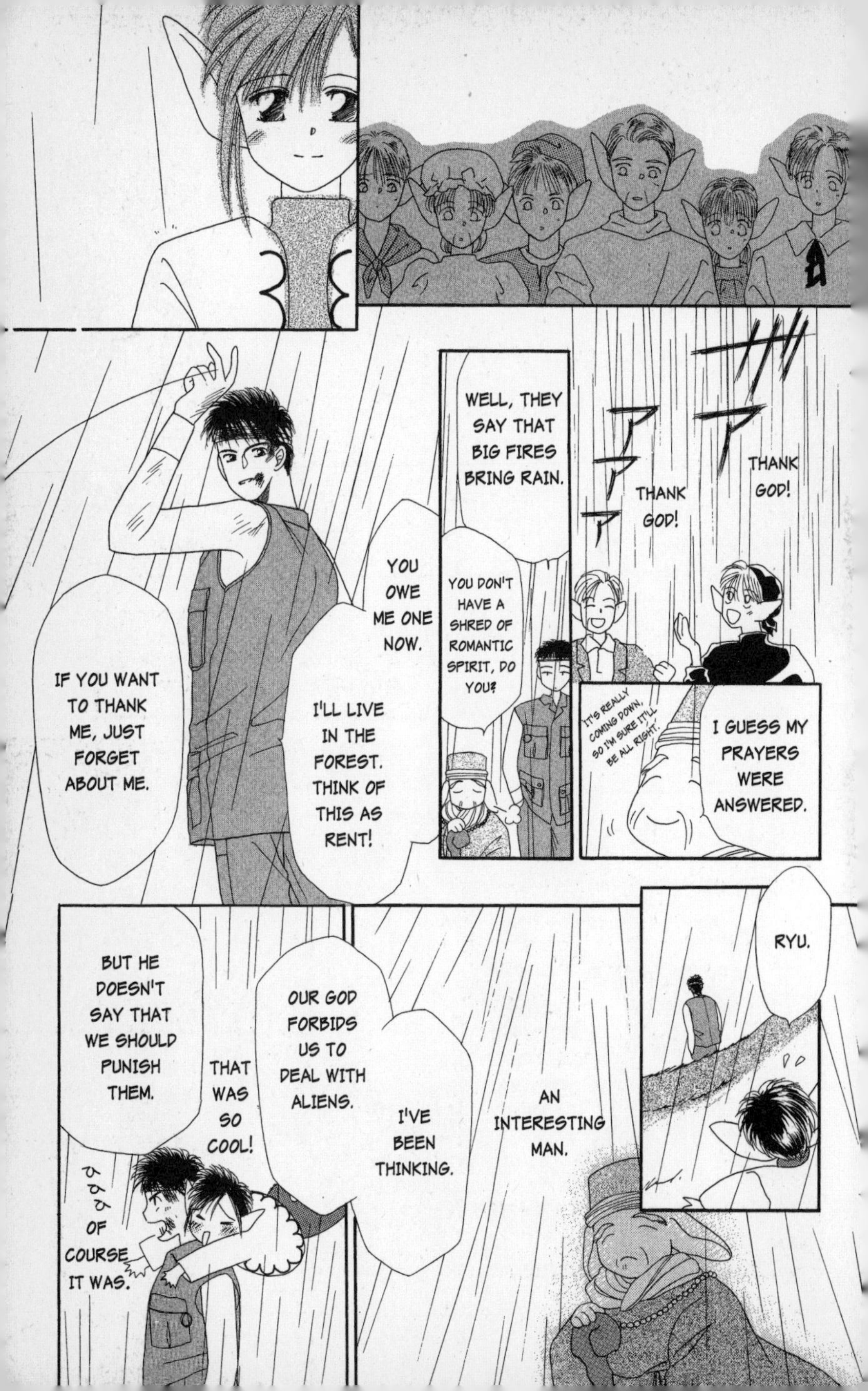
ザアアア
THANK GOD!
THANK GOD!
I GUESS MY PRAYERS WERE ANSWERED.
IT'S REALLY COMING DOWN, SO I'M SURE IT'LL BE ALL RIGHT.
WELL, THEY SAY THAT BIG FIRES BRING RAIN.
YOU DON'T HAVE A SHRED OF ROMANTIC SPIRIT, DO YOU?
YOU OWE ME ONE NOW.
I'LL LIVE IN THE FOREST. THINK OF THIS AS RENT!
IF YOU WANT TO THANK ME, JUST FORGET ABOUT ME.
RYU.
AN INTERESTING MAN.
I'VE BEEN THINKING.
OUR GOD FORBIDS US TO DEAL WITH ALIENS.
BUT HE DOESN'T SAY THAT WE SHOULD PUNISH THEM.
THAT WAS SO COOL!
OF COURSE IT WAS.

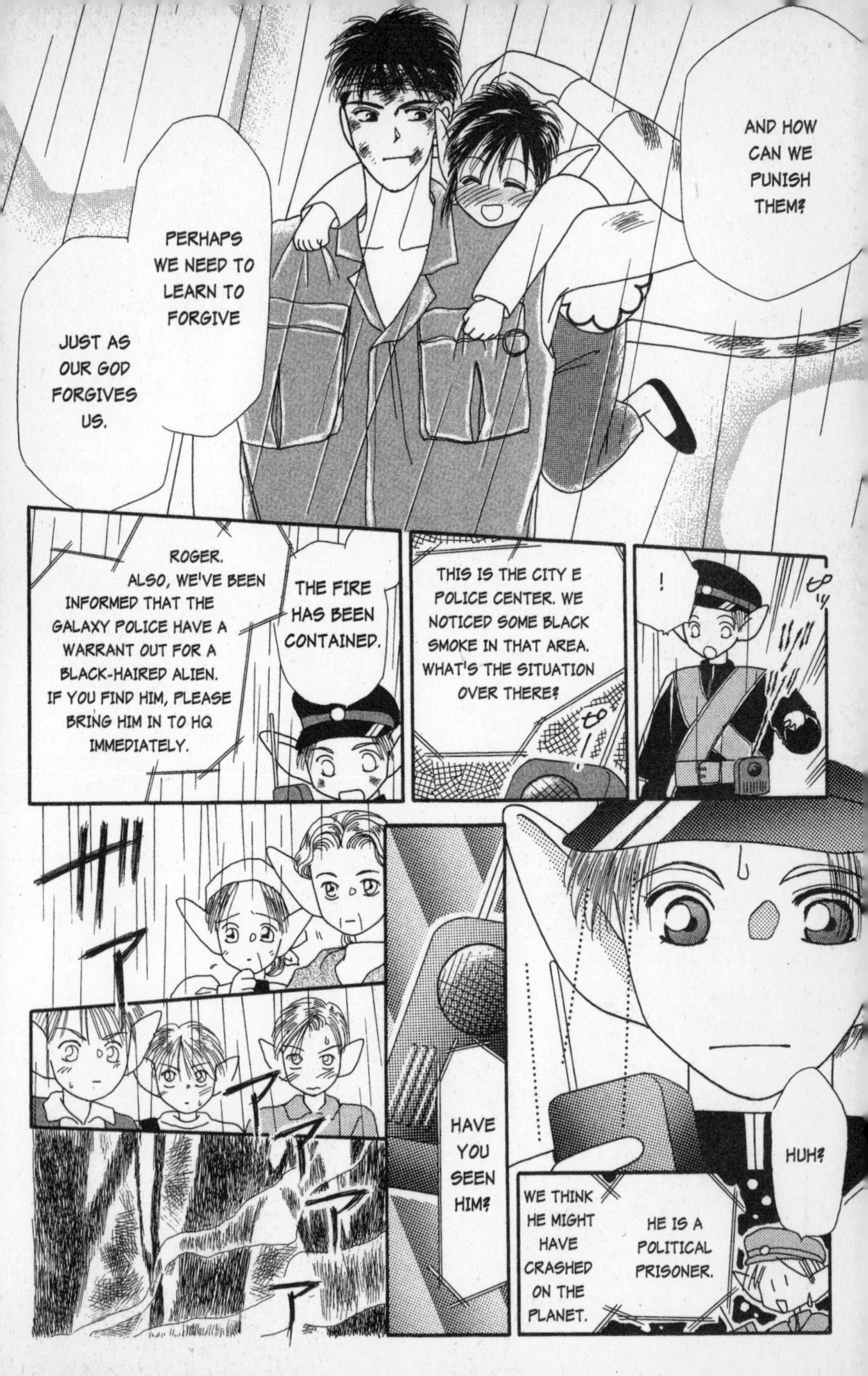
AND HOW CAN WE PUNISH THEM?
PERHAPS WE NEED TO LEARN TO FORGIVE
JUST AS OUR GOD FORGIVES US.
!
THIS IS THE CITY E POLICE CENTER. WE NOTICED SOME BLACK SMOKE IN THAT AREA. WHAT'S THE SITUATION OVER THERE?
THE FIRE HAS BEEN CONTAINED.
ROGER. ALSO, WE'VE BEEN INFORMED THAT THE GALAXY POLICE HAVE A WARRANT OUT FOR A BLACK-HAIRED ALIEN. IF YOU FIND HIM, PLEASE BRING HIM IN TO HQ IMMEDIATELY.
HUH?
HE IS A POLITICAL PRISONER.
WE THINK HE MIGHT HAVE CRASHED ON THE PLANET.
HAVE YOU SEEN HIM?

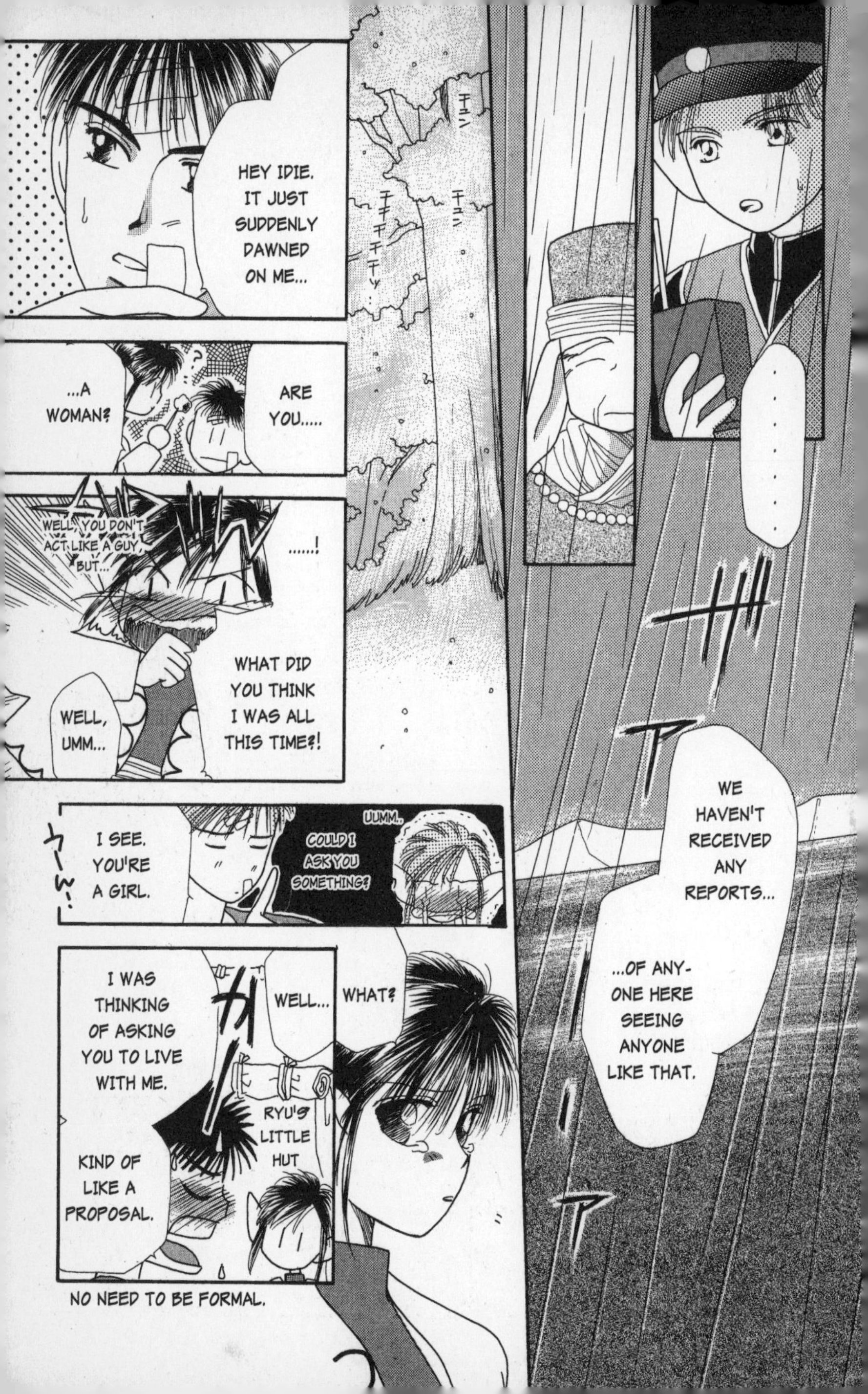

......
WE HAVEN'T RECEIVED ANY REPORTS...
...OF ANYONE HERE SEEING ANYONE LIKE THAT.
チュン
チュン
チチチチッ…
HEY IDIE. IT JUST SUDDENLY DAWNED ON ME...
ARE YOU.....
...A WOMAN?
......!
WELL, YOU DON'T ACT LIKE A GUY, BUT...
WHAT DID YOU THINK I WAS ALL THIS TIME?!
WELL, UMM...
UUMM.. COULD I ASK YOU SOMETHING?
I SEE. YOU'RE A GIRL.
WHAT?
WELL...
I WAS THINKING OF ASKING YOU TO LIVE WITH ME.
RYU'S LITTLE HUT
KIND OF LIKE A PROPOSAL.
NO NEED TO BE FORMAL.

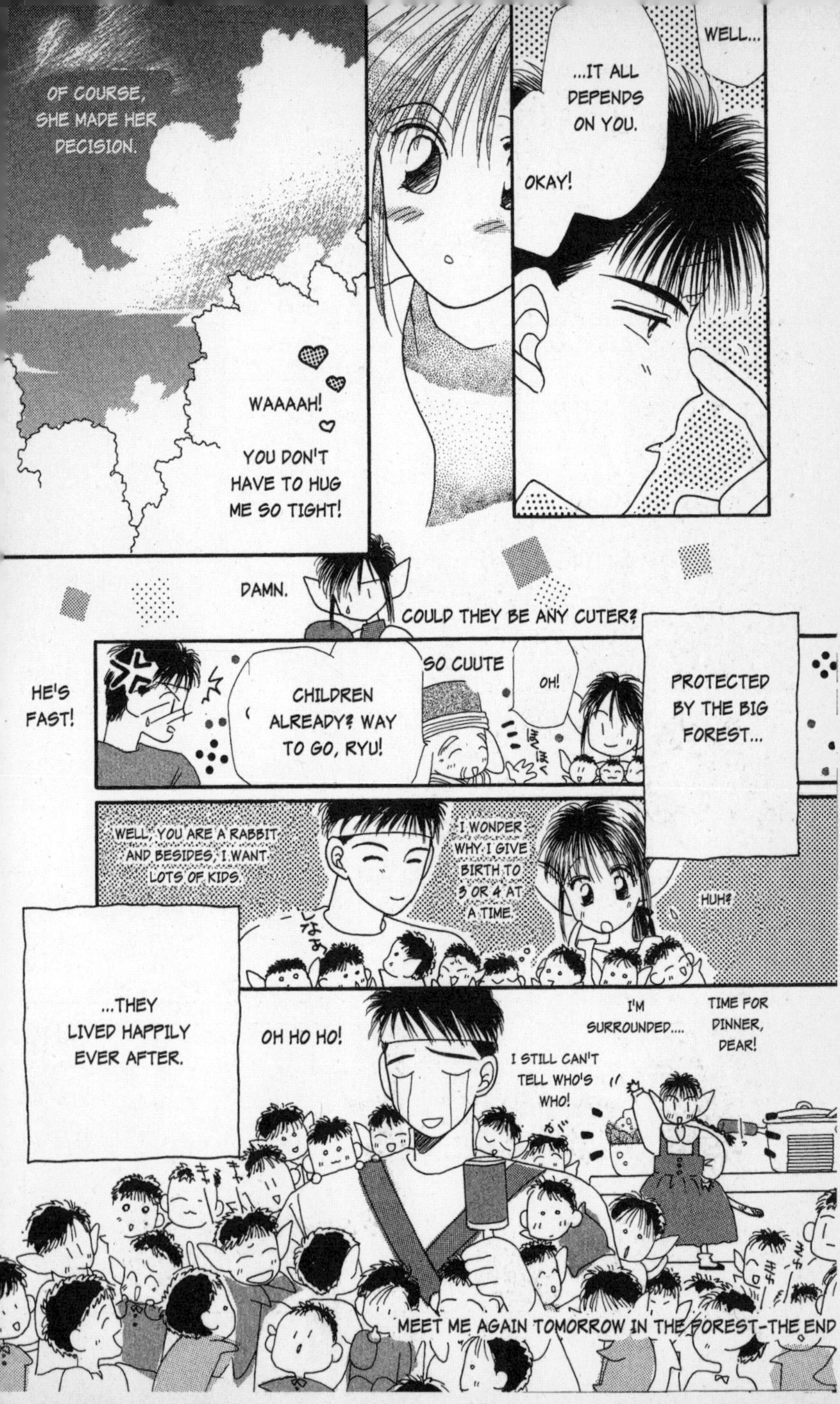
WELL...
...IT ALL DEPENDS ON YOU.
OKAY!
OF COURSE, SHE MADE HER DECISION.
WAAAAH!
YOU DON'T HAVE TO HUG ME SO TIGHT!
DAMN.
COULD THEY BE ANY CUTER?
PROTECTED BY THE BIG FOREST...
OH!
SO CUUTE
CHILDREN ALREADY? WAY TO GO, RYU!
HE'S FAST!
HUH?
I WONDER WHY I GIVE BIRTH TO 3 OR 4 AT A TIME.
WELL, YOU ARE A RABBIT AND BESIDES, I WANT LOTS OF KIDS.
TIME FOR DINNER, DEAR!
I'M SURROUNDED....
I STILL CAN'T TELL WHO'S WHO!
OH HO HO!
...THEY LIVED HAPPILY EVER AFTER.
MEET ME AGAIN TOMORROW IN THE FOREST–THE END

RELATIVES

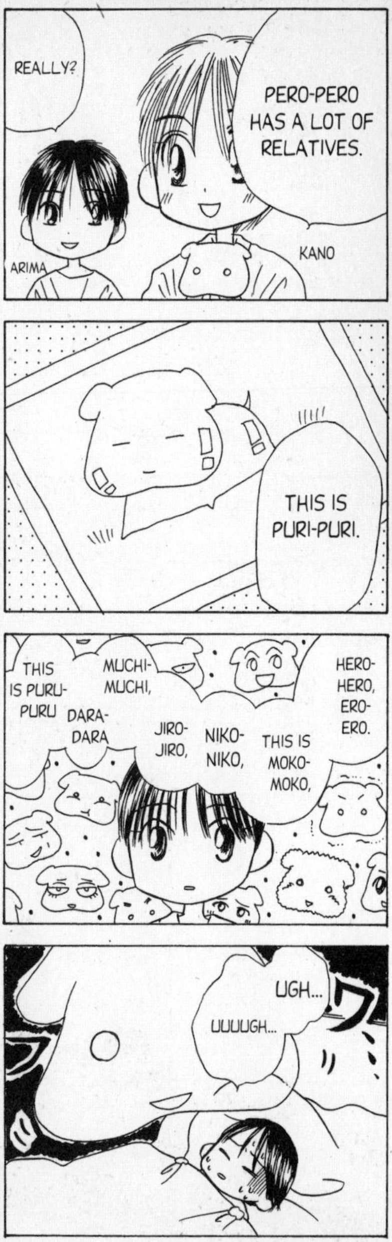
PERO-PERO HAS A LOT OF RELATIVES.
REALLY?
KANO
ARIMA
THIS IS PURI-PURI.
HERO-HERO, ERO-ERO.
THIS IS MOKO-MOKO,
NIKO-NIKO,
JIRO-JIRO,
MUCHI-MUCHI,
DARA-DARA
THIS IS PURU-PURU
UGH...
UUUUGH...

MALE BONDING

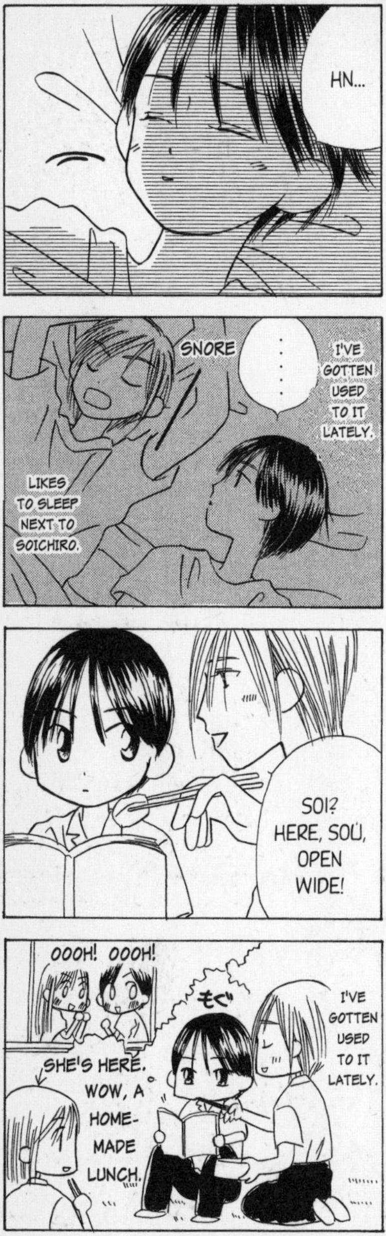
HN...
I'VE GOTTEN USED TO IT LATELY.
SNORE
LIKES TO SLEEP NEXT TO SOICHIRO.
SOI? HERE, SOU, OPEN WIDE!
I'VE GOTTEN USED TO IT LATELY.
もぐ
OOOH! OOOH!
SHE'S HERE.
WOW, A HOME-MADE LUNCH.

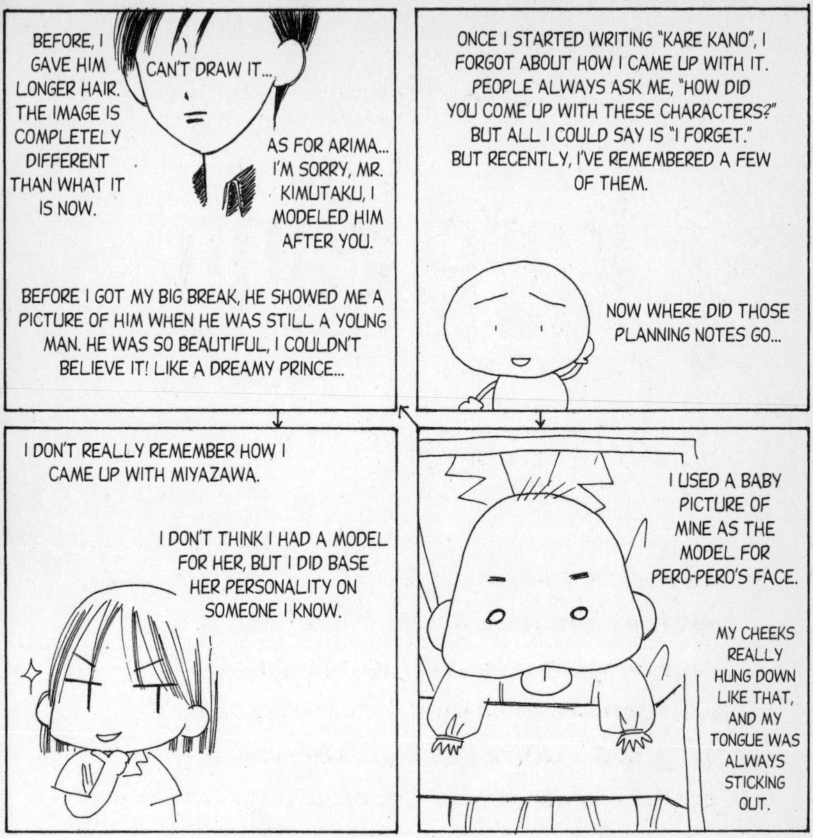
ONCE I STARTED WRITING "KARE KANO", I FORGOT ABOUT HOW I CAME UP WITH IT. PEOPLE ALWAYS ASK ME, "HOW DID YOU COME UP WITH THESE CHARACTERS?" BUT ALL I COULD SAY IS "I FORGET." BUT RECENTLY, I'VE REMEMBERED A FEW OF THEM.
NOW WHERE DID THOSE PLANNING NOTES GO...
I USED A BABY PICTURE OF MINE AS THE MODEL FOR PERO-PERO'S FACE.
MY CHEEKS REALLY HUNG DOWN LIKE THAT, AND MY TONGUE WAS ALWAYS STICKING OUT.
AS FOR ARIMA... I'M SORRY, MR. KIMUTAKU, I MODELED HIM AFTER YOU.
CAN'T DRAW IT...
BEFORE, I GAVE HIM LONGER HAIR. THE IMAGE IS COMPLETELY DIFFERENT THAN WHAT IT IS NOW.
BEFORE I GOT MY BIG BREAK, HE SHOWED ME A PICTURE OF HIM WHEN HE WAS STILL A YOUNG MAN. HE WAS SO BEAUTIFUL, I COULDN'T BELIEVE IT! LIKE A DREAMY PRINCE...
I DON'T REALLY REMEMBER HOW I CAME UP WITH MIYAZAWA.
I DON'T THINK I HAD A MODEL FOR HER, BUT I DID BASE HER PERSONALITY ON SOMEONE I KNOW.

SPECIAL THANKS TO:

Y. TANEOKA

N. SHIMIZU

M. SHIBATA

R. OGAWA

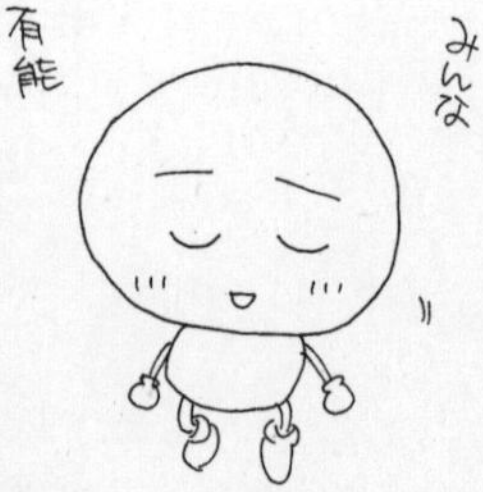
有能
みんな

THANKS, EVERYONE.

coming soon

kare kano

his and her circumstances

volume five

Yukino and Soichiro face their biggest crisis yet! It's summer vacation and like it or not, the young couple will have to spend it far away from each other. Yukino decides to hang out with her new girlfriends while Soichiro leaves town for a kendo tournament but no matter how busy their schedules are, all they really want is to be together. Will their fledgling love last or will their doubts come into play with so much distance between them?

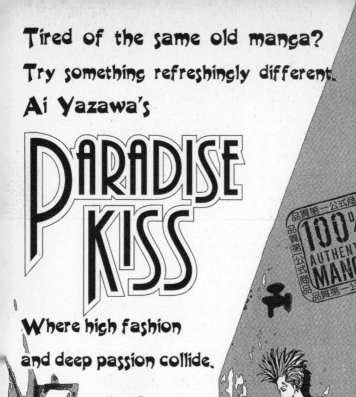

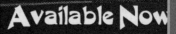

SANA'S STAGE

KODOCHA

Sana Kurata:
part student, part TV star
and always on center-stage!

Take one popular, young actress used to getting her way.
Add a handful of ruthless bullies, some humorous twists,
and a plastic toy hammer, and you've got the recipe for
one crazy story.

Graphic Novels
In Stores Now.

100%
AUTHENTIC
MANGA

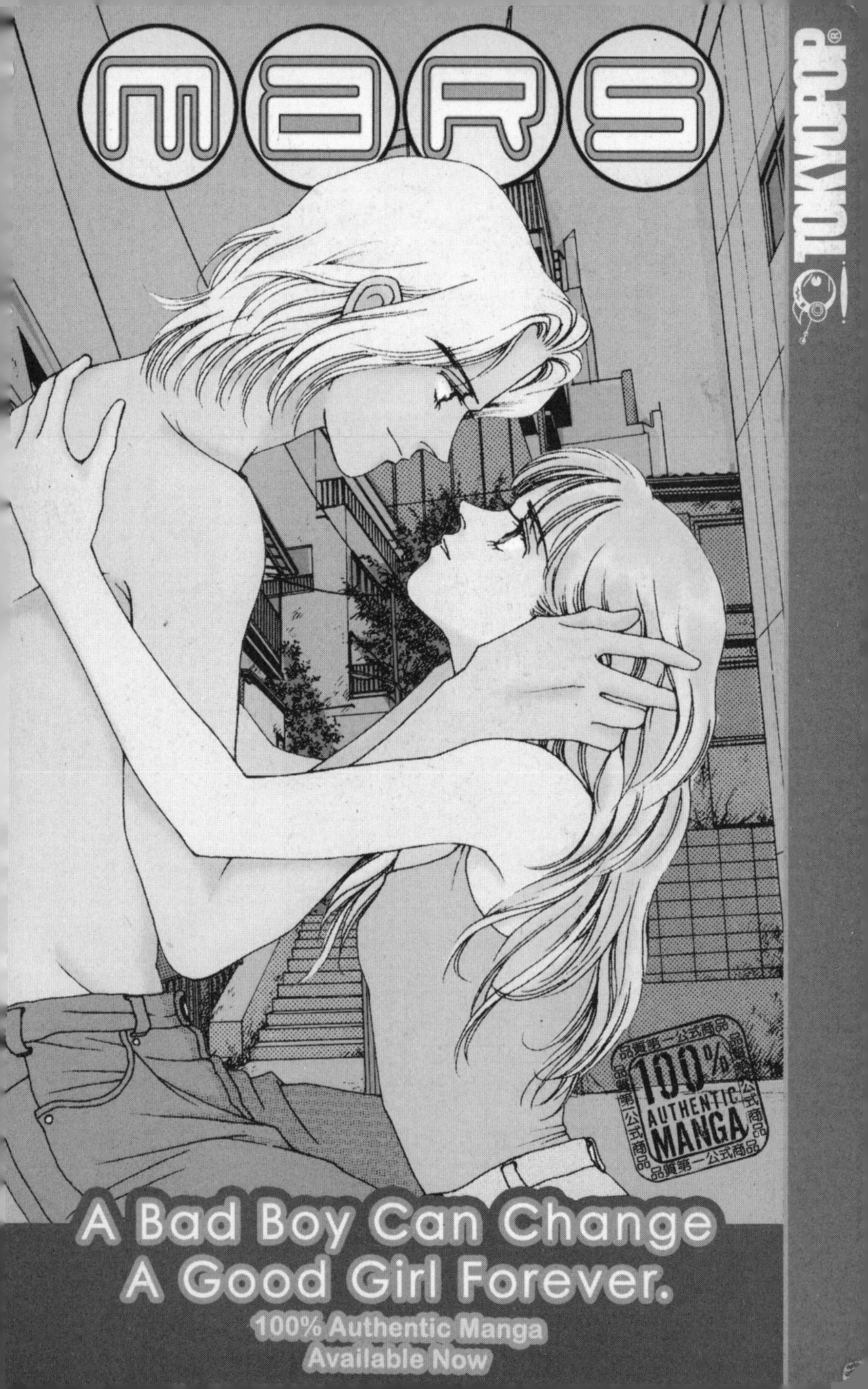
MARS
TOKYOPOP
品質第一公式商品
100%
AUTHENTIC
MANGA
A Bad Boy Can Change
A Good Girl Forever.
100% Authentic Manga
Available Now

kare kano

his and her circumstances

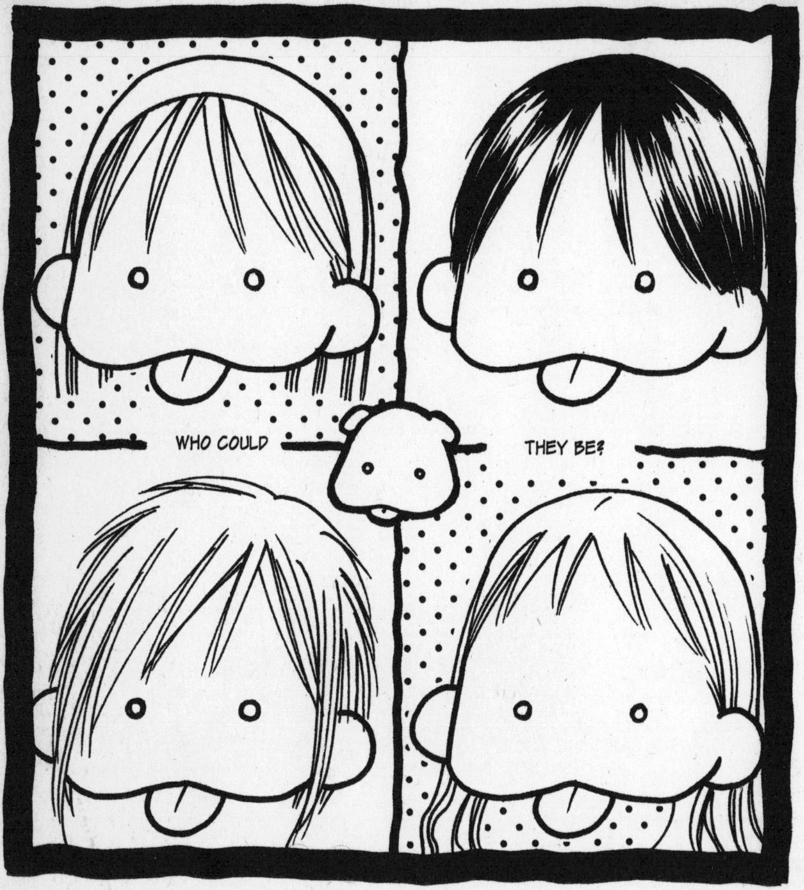
WHO COULD
THEY BE?

ALSO AVAILABLE FROM TOKYOPOP®

MANGA

.HACK//LEGEND OF THE TWILIGHT BRACELET (September 2003)
@LARGE (COMING SOON)
ANGELIC LAYER*
BABY BIRTH* (September 2003)
BATTLE ROYALE*
BRAIN POWERED*
BRIGADOON* (August 2003)
CARDCAPTOR SAKURA
CARDCAPTOR SAKURA: MASTER OF THE CLOW*
CHOBITS*
CHRONICLES OF THE CURSED SWORD
CLAMP SCHOOL DETECTIVES*
CLOVER
CONFIDENTIAL CONFESSIONS*
CORRECTOR YUI
COWBOY BEBOP*
COWBOY BEBOP: SHOOTING STAR*
DEMON DIARY
DIGIMON*
DRAGON HUNTER
DRAGON KNIGHTS*
DUKLYON: CLAMP SCHOOL DEFENDERS*
ERICA SAKURAZAWA*
FAKE*
FLCL* (September 2003)
FORBIDDEN DANCE* (August 2003)
GATE KEEPERS*
G GUNDAM*
GRAVITATION*
GTO*
GUNDAM WING
GUNDAM WING: BATTLEFIELD OF PACIFISTS
GUNDAM WING: ENDLESS WALTZ*
GUNDAM WING: THE LAST OUTPOST*
HAPPY MANIA*
HARLEM BEAT
I.N.V.U.
INITIAL D*
ISLAND
JING: KING OF BANDITS*
JULINE
KARE KANO*
KINDAICHI CASE FILES, THE*
KING OF HELL
KODOCHA: SANA'S STAGE*
LOVE HINA*
LUPIN III*
MAGIC KNIGHT RAYEARTH* (August 2003)
MAGIC KNIGHT RAYEARTH II* (COMING SOON)

MAN OF MANY FACES*
MARMALADE BOY*
MARS*
MIRACLE GIRLS
MIYUKI-CHAN IN WONDERLAND* (October 2003)
MONSTERS, INC.
PARADISE KISS*
PARASYTE
PEACH GIRL
PEACH GIRL: CHANGE OF HEART*
PET SHOP OF HORRORS*
PLANET LADDER*
PLANETES* (October 2003)
PRIEST
RAGNAROK
RAVE MASTER*
REALITY CHECK
REBIRTH
REBOUND*
RISING STARS OF MANGA
SABER MARIONETTE J*
SAILOR MOON
SAINT TAIL
SAMURAI DEEPER KYO*
SAMURAI GIRL: REAL BOUT HIGH SCHOOL*
SCRYED*
SHAOLIN SISTERS*
SHIRAHIME-SYO: SNOW GODDESS TALES* (Dec. 2003)
SHUTTERBOX (November 2003)
SORCERER HUNTERS
THE SKULL MAN*
THE VISION OF ESCAFLOWNE
TOKYO MEW MEW*
UNDER THE GLASS MOON
VAMPIRE GAME*
WILD ACT*
WISH*
WORLD OF HARTZ (COMING SOON)
X-DAY* (August 2003)
ZODIAC P.I. *

*INDICATES 100% AUTHENTIC MANGA (RIGHT-TO-LEFT FORMAT)

CINE-MANGA™

CARDCAPTORS
JACKIE CHAN ADVENTURES (COMING SOON)
JIMMY NEUTRON (September 2003)
KIM POSSIBLE
LIZZIE MCGUIRE
POWER RANGERS: NINJA STORM (August 2003)
SPONGEBOB SQUAREPANTS (September 2003)
SPY KIDS 2

NOVELS

KARMA CLUB (COMING SOON)
SAILOR MOON

TOKYOPOP KIDS

STRAY SHEEP (September 2003)

ART BOOKS

CARDCAPTOR SAKURA*
MAGIC KNIGHT RAYEARTH*

ANIME GUIDES

COWBOY BEBOP ANIME GUIDES
GUNDAM TECHNICAL MANUALS
SAILOR MOON SCOUT GUIDES

5-9-03

For more information visit www.TOKYOPOP.com